Essential Mathematics for Economics

Essential Mathematics for Economics covers mathematical topics that are essential for economic analysis in a concise but rigorous fashion. The book covers selected topics such as linear algebra, real analysis, convex analysis, constrained optimization, dynamic programming, and numerical analysis in a single volume. The book is entirely self-contained, and almost all propositions are proved.

Features
- Replete with exercises and illuminating examples
- Suitable as a primary text for an advanced undergraduate or postgraduate course on mathematics for economics
- Basic linear algebra and real analysis are the only prerequisites
- Supplementary materials such as Matlab® codes, teaching slides etc. are posted on the book website https://github.com/alexisakira/EME

Alexis Akira Toda was born in Montreal, Canada to a Japanese father and a French-Canadian mother and moved to Japan at the age of four. He received a B.A. in medicine from University of Tokyo in 2004 and then an M.A. in economics in 2008 while practicing anesthesia. He moved to the United States in 2008 and obtained a Ph.D. in economics from Yale University in 2013. After teaching mathematics for economics, mathematical economics, and finance at UC San Diego for eleven years, he moved to Emory University in 2024, where he is a professor of economics. He is the author of more than 40 research articles published in economics, mathematics, physics, and medical journals on a wide variety of topics including general equilibrium, macro-finance, consumption and savings, income and wealth distributions, asset price bubbles, power laws, dynamic programming, econometrics, and numerical methods, among others. He can be reached at https://alexisakira.github.io.

Essential Mathematics for Economics

Alexis Akira Toda
Emory University, USA

CRC Press
Taylor & Francis Group
Boca Raton London New York

CRC Press is an imprint of the
Taylor & Francis Group, an **informa** business

A CHAPMAN & HALL BOOK

Designed cover image: Alexis Akira Toda

First edition published 2025
by CRC Press
2385 NW Executive Center Drive, Suite 320, Boca Raton FL 33431

and by CRC Press
4 Park Square, Milton Park, Abingdon, Oxon, OX14 4RN

CRC Press is an imprint of Taylor & Francis Group, LLC

Library of Congress Cataloging-in-Publication Data
Names: Toda, Alexis Akira, author.
Title: Essential mathematics for economics / Alexis Akira Toda, Emory
University, USA.
Description: First edition. | Boca Raton : C&H/CRC Press, 2025. | Includes
bibliographical references and index.
Identifiers: LCCN 2024019785 (print) | LCCN 2024019786 (ebook) | ISBN
9781032680309 (hardback) | ISBN 9781032698946 (paperback) | ISBN
9781032698953 (ebook)
Subjects: LCSH: Economics, Mathematical. | Economics--Mathematical models.
Classification: LCC HB135 .T633 2025 (print) | LCC HB135 (ebook) | DDC
330.01/51--dc23/eng/20240603
LC record available at https://lccn.loc.gov/2024019785
LC ebook record available at https://lccn.loc.gov/2024019786

ISBN: 978-1-032-68030-9 (hbk)
ISBN: 978-1-032-69894-6 (pbk)
ISBN: 978-1-032-69895-3 (ebk)

DOI: 10.1201/9781032698953

Typeset in Latin Modern font
by KnowledgeWorks Global Ltd.

Publisher's note: This book has been prepared from camera-ready copy provided by the authors.

Contents

Preface

This is a textbook on mathematics used for economic analysis. The book evolved from my lecture notes for teaching this material to the first year economics PhD students at UC San Diego for about a decade.

There already exist many books on "mathematics for economics", so there must be some reason to add another. My goal is to present mathematical results that are essential for economic analysis concisely but rigorously. PhD students are busy. If they have not already studied most of the material in this book, they have to master it in a matter of a few weeks or months to keep up with other coursework and research. Reading existing textbooks in mathematics is not necessarily efficient for this purpose because they often include topics that are not so essential for economic applications. For instance, vector calculus is rarely used in economics (unlike in physics). On the other hand, general textbooks in mathematics often do not cover in sufficient depth some special topics that are highly relevant for economic applications. These topics include constrained optimization, nonnegative matrices, convex analysis, and dynamic programming. Although textbooks on "mathematics for economics" do cover some of these topics, the treatment is often not sufficiently rigorous, leaving students (at least those mathematically inclined) frustrated. For instance, I have not seen in textbooks a satisfactory proof of the Karush-Kuhn-Tucker theorem or a discussion of constrained qualifications in a general setting. Students who wish to learn these topics need to refer to monographs or research papers, which tend to be technical.

This book covers mathematical topics that are essential for economic analysis concisely but rigorously. By "concisely", I mean that I cover selected topics such as linear algebra, real analysis, convex analysis, constrained optimization, dynamic programming, and numerical analysis in a single volume. To keep the book at a manageable length, topics that are deemed not "essential" are omitted. For example, neither Riemann nor Lebesgue integration appear. This choice was made not because these topics are not important (they are) but because they are treated elsewhere (for example, Rudin (1976) and Folland (1999)), and remembering the basic rules of integration seems to be enough for solving economic problems. Similarly, I omit the theory of probability and stochastic processes. Whenever I use a Markov process, I only consider the finite-space case, which can be easily understood using matrices. Finally, by "rigorously", I mean that the book is (mostly) self-contained and almost all propositions are proved.

Given that the book covers many topics that are usually treated in multiple volumes, I put significant effort into making the book readable. Some of my efforts can be listed as follows. (i) To motivate the reader, I organized the chapters within each part by the economic problem one wishes to solve and not necessarily by mathematical topics. For instance, the chapters in the first part are geared toward solving a constrained optimization problem with linear constraints such as the utility maximization problem under a budget constraint. (ii) If a topic is introduced in chapter m and applied in chapter n, I tried to satisfy $m \leq n$ to be logically consistent but to minimize $n - m$ so that the reader has a fresh memory. (iii) I tried to strike an appropriate balance between obtaining the most interesting and useful results with the fewest number of pages and doing so at the highest level of generality. For instance, I tried to avoid general topology as much as possible and not to go much more abstract than metric spaces (for which the intuition from Euclidean spaces carry over), but many propositions are stated in a way that remains valid in general spaces. (iv) Results on linear algebra are scattered across a few chapters (1, 5, 6, 9). This is because linear algebra is already a collection of a variety of topics, and presenting them in one chapter (usually at the very beginning) is unappealing to readers interested in applications. (v) The book contains many figures (almost all of them drawn using TikZ) to help develop mathematical intuition. (vi) Examples, counterexamples, and straightforward propositions are often left as end-of-chapter problems with lots of hints, which makes the book concise and incentivizes students to work.

The prerequisites to this book are basic linear algebra and real analysis, for example at the level of Jänich (1994) or Axler (2024) for linear algebra and Rudin (1976) for real analysis. Every author of a "mathematics for economics" textbook would say basic linear algebra and real analysis are sufficient. That claim is usually false because some results such as the Karush-Kuhn-Tucker theorem are rarely proved rigorously. However, in this book, the claim that basic linear algebra and real analysis are sufficient is true, as I prove almost all results. Needless to say, certain "mathematical maturity" (for example, the ability to follow a logical argument or to come up with (counter)examples that (do not) satisfy the assumptions of a proposition) is essential, though I do not know how to teach this valuable skill.

As there are already many "mathematics for economics" textbooks, I discuss similarities and differences. In my opinion, the following three points make this book stand out:

(i) high degree of self-containedness,

(ii) emphasis on matrix analysis, and

(iii) modern treatment of dynamic programming.

I have already mentioned that (i) the book is mostly self-contained. Through my research in mathematical economics, I came to appreciate (ii) the importance of matrix analysis such as the spectral radius and nonnegative matrices, which is rarely covered in standard textbooks. I have had the privilege of contributing to (iii) the theory of dynamic programming, and this book covers some modern topics. The structure of this book is similar to Sundaram (1996) in that its main objective is the discussion of optimization techniques. Relative to Sundaram (1996), the present text is more self-contained, treats topics in linear algebra and nonlinear programming more systematically, and reflects the more recent developments in the theory of dynamic programming. Simon and Blume (1994) is less technical than the present text but contains many examples and problems, so it could be useful for undergraduate students. Furthermore, Simon and Blume (1994) cover differential equations but omit dynamic programming. Vohra (2005) is even more concise than the present text and covers some fixed point and lattice theory but does not cover linear algebra or dynamic programming, so it is complementary. None of these texts discuss numerical analysis, which is an important topic to have some knowledge for applied researchers.

I would like to express my sincere gratitude to those who have supported me over the past years. Takao Kumo taught me mathematics at the tutoring (cram) school SEG in Tokyo when I was in high school. His lectures on real analysis, differential equations, calculus of variations, and complex analysis inspired my curiosity. Ken'ichiro Tanaka, then my classmate, became an applied mathematician and a coauthor, from whom I learned numerical analysis. Yasuki Kobayashi and Hiroshi Yoshikawa at University of Tokyo ignited my interest in economics and supported me during the transition from medicine to economics. Truman Bewley and John Geanakoplos taught me general equilibrium theory at Yale, and together with Donald Brown and Larry Samuelson, supported me during the difficult time of transitioning from a student to an independent researcher. I learned dynamic programming from John Stachurski and the theory of nonnegative matrices through collaboration with Brendan Beare. Generations of PhD students at UCSD have suffered from my incomplete teaching material and corrected many typographical, grammatical, as well as a few mathematical errors. My children Minerva and Julius and my wife Junko have supported me and tolerated my absentmindedness.

Supplementary materials such as Matlab codes, teaching slides, and list of known typos and errors are posted at the book website `https://github.com/alexisakira/EME`.

List of Figures

List of Symbols

Notation	Meaning
$\forall x \ldots$	for all $x \ldots$
$\exists x \ldots$	there exists x such that $\ldots$
$x := \ldots$	x is defined as $\ldots$
$\emptyset$	empty set
$x \in A,\ A \ni x$	x is an element of the set A; A contains x
$A \subset B,\ B \supset A$	A is a subset of B; B includes A
$A \cap B$	intersection of sets A and B
$A \cup B$	union of sets A and B
$A \backslash B$	elements of A but not in B
$A^c := X \backslash A$	complement of A, if entire space X understood
$\mathbb{N}$	set of natural numbers $\{1, 2, \ldots\}$
$\mathbb{Z}$	set of integers $\{0, \pm 1, \pm 2, \ldots\}$
$\mathbb{Q}$	set of rational numbers
$\mathbb{R}$	set of real numbers
$\mathbb{C}$	set of complex numbers
$\bar{\mathbb{R}} = \mathbb{R} \cup \{\pm\infty\}$	set of extended real numbers
$\mathbb{R}^N$	set of vectors $x = (x_1, \ldots, x_N)$ with $x_n \in \mathbb{R}$
$\mathbb{R}^N_+$	set of $x = (x_1, \ldots, x_N)$ with $x_n \geq 0$ for all n
$\mathbb{R}^N_{++}$	set of $x = (x_1, \ldots, x_N)$ with $x_n > 0$ for all n
$x \leq y,\ y \geq x$	$x_n \leq y_n$ for all n; same as $y - x \in \mathbb{R}^N_+$
$x < y,\ y > x$	$x_n \leq y_n$ for all n and $x_n < y_n$ for some n; same as $y - x \in \mathbb{R}^N_+ \backslash \{0\}$
$x \ll y,\ y \gg x$	$x_n < y_n$ for all n; same as $y - x \in \mathbb{R}^N_{++}$
$\langle x, y \rangle$	inner product of x and y
$\|x\|$	norm of x
$\mathbb{R}^{M \times N}, \mathbb{C}^{M \times N}$	set of $M \times N$ real and complex matrices
$\mathbb{R}^{M \times N}_+, \mathbb{R}^{M \times N}_{++}$	set of $M \times N$ nonnegative and positive matrices
$A', A^\top$	transpose of matrix A
A^*	conjugate transpose of matrix A
A^{-1}	inverse of square matrix A
$\rho(A)$	spectral radius (largest absolute value of all eigenvalues) of square matrix A
$\mathrm{diag}[d_1, \ldots, d_N]$	diagonal matrix with diagonal entries $d_1, \ldots, d_N$

Notation	Meaning
δ_{mn}	Kronecker's delta, defined by $\delta_{mn} = 1$ if $m = n$ and $\delta_{mn} = 0$ if $m \neq n$
cl A	closure of A
int A	interior of A
co A	convex hull of A
$[a, b]$	closed interval $\{x : a \leq x \leq b\}$
(a, b)	open interval $\{x : a < x < b\}$
$(a, b], [a, b)$	half open intervals
$f : A \to B$	f is a function defined on A taking values in B
$g = \phi \circ f$	composition of ϕ and f, defined by $g(x) = \phi(f(x))$
dom f	effective domain of f, $\{x \in \mathbb{R}^N : f(x) < \infty\}$
epi f	epigraph of f, $\{(x, y) \in \mathbb{R}^N \times \mathbb{R} : y \geq f(x)\}$
$f \in bX$	function f is bounded on X
$f \in bcX$	function f is bounded and continuous on X
$f \in C(X)$	function f is continuous on X
$f \in C^r(X)$	function f is r times continuously differentiable on X
$f \leq g, g \geq f$	$f(x) \leq g(x)$ for all x
$Df(x)$	Jacobian (matrix of partial derivatives) of f at x
$D_x f(x, y)$	Jacobian of f with respect to x
$\nabla f(x)$	gradient (vector of partial derivatives) of f at x
$\nabla^2 f(x), D^2 f(x)$	Hessian (matrix of second derivatives) of f at x
$e = 2.71828\ldots$	Euler's number
$e^x, \exp(x)$	exponential of x
$\log x$	natural logarithm of x, defined as y with $e^y = x$

List of Important Theorems

Roadmap

A typical problem studied in economics is a constrained optimization problem. Consider the following example. There are N goods (commodities) indexed by $n = 1, \ldots, N$, which can be consumed in any nonnegative quantities. When an economic agent consumes $x_n \geq 0$ units of good n, where $n = 1, \ldots, N$, the agent derives utility

$$u(x_1, \ldots, x_N). \tag{0.1}$$

The price of one unit of good n is $p_n > 0$. If the agent consumes x_n units of good n, the expenditure on good n is $p_n x_n$, so the total expenditure is $p_1 x_1 + \cdots + p_N x_N$, which cannot exceed the disposable income of the agent denoted by $w > 0$. Therefore the objective of the agent is to maximize the utility (0.1) subject to the budget and nonnegativity constraints

$$p_1 x_1 + \cdots + p_N x_N \leq w, \tag{0.2a}$$

$$x_n \geq 0 \quad \text{for all } n. \tag{0.2b}$$

This problem is called a *utility maximization problem*, which is one of the most basic constrained optimization problems studied in economics.

We can ask many questions regarding the utility maximization problem or constrained optimization problems in general, such as:

(i) How do we define a solution?

(ii) Does a solution exist?

(iii) What are necessary or sufficient conditions that characterize the solution?

(iv) Is the solution unique?

(v) How do we compute the solution?

(vi) How does the solution change if we change the parameters p_n or w?

DOI: 10.1201/9781032698953-0

Part I introduces fundamental results in optimization. In Chapter 1, we (i) define what we mean by a solution and (ii) prove its existence. The main result of this chapter is the extreme value theorem (Theorem 1.11), which guarantees that continuous functions achieve minima and maxima on closed and bounded sets (bounded sets that include their boundaries, like the set defined by the constraints (0.2)). To get to this important result, we cannot avoid discussing the topological properties of the Euclidean space, so the material is somewhat technical.

In the next three chapters, we study (iii) conditions that characterize the solution. To make the book readable, instead of starting from the most general setting, we gradually increase the level of generality. In Chapter 2, we study the optimization of a function with only one variable. We discuss the first-order necessary condition and the second-order sufficient condition. In Chapter 3, we study the optimization of a function with multiple variables and focus on the case when constraints do not bind. At this point, we only discuss the first-order necessary condition because the second-order sufficient condition requires substantial knowledge of symmetric matrices. Chapter 4 is an introduction to constrained optimization problems with multiple variables. The main result of this chapter is the Karush-Kuhn-Tucker (KKT) theorem with linear constraints (Theorem 4.3). Because a rigorous proof of the KKT theorem is quite technical, the discussion in Chapter 4 is mostly based on geometric intuition and the complete proof is deferred to subsequent chapters.

Part II introduces miscellaneous tools in matrix analysis and nonlinear analysis that are required to study problems with multiple variables. Chapter 5 introduces vector spaces and matrices and discusses necessary and sufficient conditions for solving a system of linear equations. Chapter 6 introduces the notion of eigenvalues and eigenvectors of matrices and explains how these objects can be used to simplify matrices. Using these results, we provide (iii) second-order sufficient condition for the unconstrained optimization of a function with multiple variables. We also prove the Gelfand spectral radius formula (Theorem 6.15), which characterizes the behavior of the matrix power A^k as $k \to \infty$ and has many applications.

In Chapter 7, we depart from Euclidean spaces and introduce the more abstract notion of metric spaces, which are spaces on which we can define a distance. The main result in this chapter is the contraction mapping theorem (Theorem 7.3), which has many applications. However, the applications come much later, so it could be skipped until necessary. As an application of the contraction mapping theorem, in Chapter 8 we prove the implicit function theorem (Theorem 8.3), which allows us to (vi) study how a solution to an optimization problem depends on its parameters. This chapter also discusses the local stable manifold theorem (Theorem 8.9), which is useful for analyzing nonlinear dynamics.

Chapter 9 studies the properties of nonnegative matrices, which are real matrices with nonnegative entries. A typical example of such matrices is the transition probability matrix describing a Markov chain. We prove the important Perron-Frobenius theorem (Theorems 9.3, 9.7) by applying the contraction mapping theorem. I believe this proof is more concise and intuitive than existing proofs. Although nonnegative matrices play an important role in economic analysis, this book presents no applications other than stochastic matrices, so this chapter could be skipped.

Part III studies constrained optimization problems with full generality and rigor. Chapter 10 introduces the notion of convex sets and prove the important separating hyperplane theorem (Theorem 10.2). It also studies cones and dual cones, which play an important role in optimization. Chapter 11 introduces convex and quasi-convex functions and explains their importance for establishing (iii) sufficient conditions for optimality and (iv) uniqueness of a solution. Chapter 12 considers general nonlinear programming problems. We prove the Karush-Kuhn-Tucker theorem (Theorem 12.4), discuss various constraint qualifications, and introduce the duality principle for convex programming problems. Furthermore, by introducing second-order sufficient conditions, we prove the parametric continuity and differentiability of the solution and the envelope theorem, which answer (vi) how the solution changes with parameters.

Part IV studies dynamic programming problems, which are optimization problems under a sequential structure such as the passage of time. Chapter 13 provides many examples and formulates a dynamic program in an abstract setting. Chapter 14 studies infinite-horizon dynamic programs under additive and Markov assumptions using the contraction approach and discusses some techniques to numerically solve dynamic programs. Chapter 15 briefly presents the classical optimal control theory, which complements the more modern dynamic programming theory.

Appendix A provides an introduction to numerical analysis, which can be used to (v) compute solutions.

Table 0.1 summarizes the mutual dependence among chapters.

TABLE 0.1: Chapter dependence.

Part	Chapter	Prerequisites
I	2	1
	3	1, 2
	4	1–3
II	5	3
	6	1–3, 5
	7	1, 6
	8	1–3, 5–7
	9	5–7
III	10	1
	11	1–3, 6, 10
	12	1–6, 10, 11
IV	13	1
	14	1, 7, 11–13
	15	1–3, 11–14

I

Introduction to Optimization

CHAPTER 1

Existence of Solutions

1.1 INTRODUCTION

Suppose we would like to solve the problem

$$\text{minimize} \qquad f(x)$$
$$\text{subject to} \qquad x \in C, \qquad\qquad (1.1)$$

where C is some set (called the *constraint set*) and f is a real-valued function defined on C. To fix ideas, suppose C is a subset of the real line $\mathbb{R} = (-\infty, \infty)$. We say that a point $\bar{x} \in C$ is a *solution* to the minimization problem (1.1) if $f(\bar{x}) \leq f(x)$ for all $x \in C$. We also call $\bar{x}$ the *minimizer* or simply the *minimum*. In that case we write

$$f(\bar{x}) = \min_{x \in C} f(x)$$

and call $f(\bar{x})$ the *minimum value* or simply the *minimum* of the problem (1.1). (We use "minimum" in two different ways but the meaning should be clear from the context.) We also write

$$\bar{x} \in \arg\min_{x \in C} f(x),$$

where "arg min" refers to the set of minimizers (argument of the minimum).

For developing the theory of optimization, we mostly focus on minimization problems because maximization problems can be turned into minimization problems. For example, consider the maximization problem

$$\text{maximize} \qquad g(x)$$
$$\text{subject to} \qquad x \in C. \qquad\qquad (1.2)$$

Then $\bar{x}$ is a solution (or maximizer/maximum) if $g(\bar{x}) \geq g(x)$ for all $x \in C$. This condition is equivalent to $-g(\bar{x}) \leq -g(x)$ for all $x \in C$, so $\bar{x}$ is a solution to the minimization problem (1.1) with $f = -g$. We use the symbols "max" and "arg max" analogously.

DOI: 10.1201/9781032698953-1

Obviously, not all minimization problems of the form (1.1) have a solution. Figure 1.1 presents several examples. In the top-left diagram, the constraint set is the entire real line $(-\infty, \infty)$ (which is unbounded) and the function value $f(x)$ approaches a constant as x tends to plus or minus infinity, like $f(x) = 1/(1 + x^2)$. In this example, we have $f(x) > 0$ for all x, $f(x) \to 0$ as $x \to \pm\infty$, but the value 0 is never achieved, so there is no minimum. In the top right diagram, the constraint set has a "hole", like $C = [-1, 0) \cup (0, 1]$. The function $f(x) = x^2$ has a unique minimum over the entire real line at $x = 0$ but $0 \notin C$, so f has no minimum over C. In the bottom-left diagram, the graph of the function f has "gaps", for example, $f(x) = x^2$ for $x < 0$ and $f(x) = (x^2 + 1)/2$ for $x \geq 0$. Although $f(x)$ approaches 0 as $x \uparrow 0$, the value 0 is never achieved. In the bottom-right diagram, the function does achieve a minimum. Note that the function is continuous and the constraint set C is bounded and has no holes.

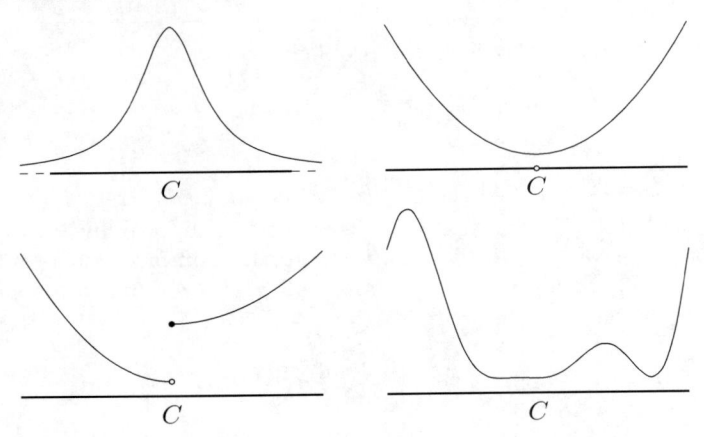

FIGURE 1.1: Minimum may not exist.

The goal of this chapter is to provide a simple sufficient condition for the existence of a solution to a minimization problem. The essence is that f will achieve a minimum on C if f is continuous and C is a bounded set that includes its boundary (has no holes). For now, these terms are vague but we will be more precise as we proceed.

1.2   THE REAL NUMBER SYSTEM

The set of natural numbers is denoted by $\mathbb{N} = \{1, 2, \ldots\}$. The set of integers is denoted by $\mathbb{Z} = \{0, \pm 1, \pm 2, \ldots\}$. The set of rational numbers is denoted by $\mathbb{Q} = \{m/n : m \in \mathbb{Z}, n \in \mathbb{N}\}$. The set of real numbers is denoted by $\mathbb{R}$. We leave the construction of $\mathbb{R}$ to standard textbooks of real analysis, for instance Rudin (1976, Chapter 1).

We introduce some notation and terminology used throughout the book. The *absolute value* of $x \in \mathbb{R}$ is denoted by

$$|x| = \begin{cases} x & \text{if } x \geq 0, \\ -x & \text{if } x < 0. \end{cases}$$

Let $A \subset \mathbb{R}$ be a set. A is *bounded above* if there exists $b \in \mathbb{R}$ such that $x \leq b$ for all $x \in A$, in which case b is called an upper bound. Similarly, A is *bounded below* if there exists $b \in \mathbb{R}$ such that $x \geq b$ for all $x \in A$, in which case b is called a lower bound. A is *bounded* if there exists $b \geq 0$ such that $|x| \leq b$ for all $x \in A$.

It is often convenient to consider the set of *extended real numbers* that includes plus or minus infinity, denoted by $\pm\infty$. The rules of algebra are

$$x \pm \infty = \pm\infty \text{ if } x \in \mathbb{R},$$
$$\infty + \infty = \infty,$$
$$x \times (\pm\infty) = \pm\infty \text{ if } x > 0,$$
$$x \times (\pm\infty) = \mp\infty \text{ if } x < 0,$$
$$x/(\pm\infty) = 0 \text{ if } x \in \mathbb{R}.$$

Note that $\infty - \infty$ and ∞/∞ are undefined. However, it is convenient to define $0 \times \infty = 0$, and we shall adopt this convention. The set of extended real numbers is denoted by $\bar{\mathbb{R}} = \mathbb{R} \cup \{\pm\infty\} = [-\infty, \infty]$.

If $x \leq a$ for all $x \in A$ and $a \in A$, we call a the *maximum* of A. The minimum is defined analogously. Obviously, maxima and minima may not exist even if A is bounded; for instance, consider the set

$$A = (-1, 1) = \{x \in \mathbb{R} : -1 < x < 1\}.$$

The defining property of the real number system is the following *least-upper-bound property*: if A is bounded above, there exists a least upper bound. More precisely, suppose $\emptyset \neq A \subset \mathbb{R}$ is bounded above and let B be the set of upper bounds of A (which is nonempty by definition). Then $\alpha = \min B$ exists. The least upper bound α is called the *supremum* of A and is denoted by $\alpha = \sup A$. A symmetric argument shows that if A is bounded below, then a greatest lower bound exists, which is called the *infimum* of A and is denoted by $\inf A$. If A is not bounded above (below), we define $\sup A = \infty$ ($\inf A = -\infty$). By convention, we define $\sup \emptyset = -\infty$ and $\inf \emptyset = \infty$. It is easy to show that $A \subset B$ implies $\sup A \leq \sup B$ and $\inf A \geq \inf B$.

1.3 CONVERGENCE OF SEQUENCES

In the discussion of Figure 1.1, we used the expression "approaches" without being precise. We now formalize the concept of convergence. Let $\{x_k\}_{k=1}^{\infty}$ be a real sequence, which can be thought of as a function from $\mathbb{N}$ to $\mathbb{R}$. We say that $\{x_k\}_{k=1}^{\infty}$ *converges* to $x \in \mathbb{R}$ if

$$(\forall \epsilon > 0)(\exists K > 0)(\forall k \geq K) \quad |x_k - x| < \epsilon, \tag{1.3}$$

that is, for any small error tolerance $\epsilon > 0$, we can find a large enough number K such that the distance between x_k and x can be made smaller than the error tolerance ϵ, provided that the index satisfies $k \geq K$. When $\{x_k\}_{k=1}^{\infty}$ converges to x, we write $\lim_{k \to \infty} x_k = x$ or $x_k \to x$ $(k \to \infty)$ and call x the *limit*. Sometimes we are sloppy and write $\lim x_k = x$ or $x_k \to x$. A sequence $\{x_k\}_{k=1}^{\infty}$ is *convergent* if it converges to some point.

We say that $\{x_k\}_{k=1}^{\infty} \subset \mathbb{R}$ *converges to infinity* if

$$(\forall \epsilon > 0)(\exists K > 0)(\forall k \geq K) \quad x_k > \epsilon. \tag{1.4}$$

We denote convergence by $\lim_{k \to \infty} x_k = \infty$, $x_k \to \infty$, etc. Convergence to $-\infty$ is defined analogously.

We say that $\{x_k\}_{k=1}^{\infty} \subset \mathbb{R}$ is *increasing* (*decreasing*) if $x_1 \leq x_2 \leq \cdots$ $(x_1 \geq x_2 \geq \cdots)$, that is, $x_k \leq x_{k+1}$ $(x_k \geq x_{k+1})$ for all k. A sequence that is either increasing or decreasing is simply called *monotone*.

An important property of monotone sequences is that they are always convergent if we allow $\pm\infty$ as the limit.

Proposition 1.1. *If* $\{x_k\}_{k=1}^{\infty} \subset \bar{\mathbb{R}}$ *is monotone, it is convergent.*

Proof. Without loss of generality, assume $\{x_k\}$ is increasing. Let $x = \sup\{x_k : k \in \mathbb{N}\}$. Let us show $x_k \to x$.

By the definition of the supremum, we have $x_k \leq x$ for all k. If $x = -\infty$, then $-\infty \leq x_k \leq x = -\infty$, so $x_k = -\infty$ for all k and convergence is trivial. Therefore, assume $x > -\infty$ and take any $\mathbb{R} \ni x' < x$. By the definition of the supremum, there exists $K \in \mathbb{N}$ such that $x_K > x'$. Since $\{x_k\}$ is increasing, we have $x_k > x'$ for all $k \geq K$.

If $x < \infty$, for any $\epsilon > 0$, take $x' = x - \epsilon$. Then $x - \epsilon < x_k \leq x$ for all $k \geq K$, so in particular $|x_k - x| < \epsilon$. By the definition of convergence, we have $x_k \to x$. If $x = \infty$, for any $\epsilon > 0$, take $x' = \epsilon$. Then $x_k > \epsilon$ for all $k \geq K$, so by definition $x_k \to \infty$. $\qquad\square$

Let $\{x_k\}_{k=1}^{\infty} \subset \bar{\mathbb{R}}$ be any sequence. Define

$$\alpha_k = \sup\{x_k, x_{k+1}, \ldots\} = \sup_{l \geq k} x_l.$$

Since the set $\{x_l : l \geq k\}$ is decreasing with k, clearly $\{\alpha_k\}_{k=1}^{\infty}$ is a decreasing sequence in $\bar{\mathbb{R}}$. Therefore by Proposition 1.1 the limit

$$\alpha := \lim_{k \to \infty} \alpha_k = \lim_{k \to \infty} \sup_{l \geq k} x_l$$

exists, which is called the *limit superior* of $\{x_k\}$ and is denoted by

$$\alpha = \limsup_{k \to \infty} x_k.$$

Similarly, we define the *limit inferior* of $\{x_k\}$ by

$$\beta = \liminf_{k \to \infty} x_k := \lim_{k \to \infty} \inf_{l \geq k} x_l.$$

1.4 THE SPACE $\mathbb{R}^N$

We are often interested in functions of several variables. Let $\mathbb{R}^N$ denote the set of N-tuples of real numbers $x = (x_1, \ldots, x_N) = (x_n)$. For $x, y \in \mathbb{R}^N$, define the sum entrywise by $x + y = (x_n + y_n)$. For $\alpha \in \mathbb{R}$ and $x \in \mathbb{R}^N$, define the scalar multiplication entrywise by $\alpha x = (\alpha x_n)$. In general, we call a set X a (real) *vector space* if the sum $x + y$ and the scalar product αx are defined and belong to X for all $x, y \in X$ and $\alpha \in \mathbb{R}$. Elements of a vector space are called *vectors*.

If X is a vector space and $f : X \to \mathbb{R}$, we say that f is *linear* if f preserves addition and scalar multiplication, i.e.,

$$f(\alpha x + \beta y) = \alpha f(x) + \beta f(y) \tag{1.5}$$

for all $x, y \in X$ and $\alpha, \beta \in \mathbb{R}$. An obvious example of a linear function $f : \mathbb{R}^N \to \mathbb{R}$ is

$$f(x) = a_1 x_1 + \cdots + a_N x_N = \sum_{n=1}^{N} a_n x_n,$$

where $a_1, \ldots, a_N \in \mathbb{R}$. In fact, we can show that all linear functions are of this form.

Proposition 1.2. *The function $f : \mathbb{R}^N \to \mathbb{R}$ is linear if and only if $f(x) = a_1 x_1 + \cdots + a_N x_N$ for some $a_1, \ldots, a_N \in \mathbb{R}$.*

Proof. Sufficiency is obvious so we prove necessity. Let e_n be the n-th unit vector, i.e., the vector whose n-th entry is 1 and all other entries are 0. By the definition of $\mathbb{R}^N$, we have

$$x = (x_1, \ldots, x_N) = x_1 e_1 + \cdots + x_N e_N.$$

If f is linear, then (1.5) holds, so

$$f(x) = x_1 f(e_1) + \cdots + x_N f(e_N).$$

Therefore, $f(x)$ has the desired form by setting $a_n = f(e_n)$. □

The expression of the form $a_1 x_1 + \cdots + a_N x_N$ appears so often that it deserves a special name and notation. Let $x = (x_1, \ldots, x_N)$ and $y = (y_1, \ldots, y_N)$ be two vectors in $\mathbb{R}^N$. Then

$$\langle x, y \rangle := x_1 y_1 + \cdots + x_N y_N = \sum_{n=1}^{N} x_n y_n$$

is called the *inner product* (also *vector product*) of x and y. Other common notations for the inner product are (x, y), $x \cdot y$, and $\langle x \mid y \rangle$, etc. Fixing x, the inner product $\langle x, y \rangle$ is linear in y, so we have

$$\langle x, \alpha_1 y_1 + \alpha_2 y_2 \rangle = \alpha_1 \langle x, y_1 \rangle + \alpha_2 \langle x, y_2 \rangle.$$

The same holds for x as well, fixing y. So the inner product is a *bilinear* function of x and y.

To do analysis, it is convenient to have a notion of the size of a vector or the distance between two vectors. Motivated by the Pythagorean theorem in elementary geometry, the *(Euclidean) norm* of $x \in \mathbb{R}^N$ is defined by

$$\|x\| := \sqrt{\langle x, x \rangle} = \sqrt{x_1^2 + \cdots + x_N^2}. \tag{1.6}$$

The Euclidean norm is also called the ℓ^2 norm for a reason that will become clear later. More generally, for a real vector space X, a function $\|\cdot\| : X \to \mathbb{R}$ is called a *norm* if it satisfies the following properties:

(i) (Nonnegativity) $\|x\| \geq 0$ for all $x \in X$, with equality if and only if $x = 0$,

(ii) (Positive homogeneity) $\|\alpha x\| = |\alpha|\, \|x\|$ for all $\alpha \in \mathbb{R}$ and $x \in X$,

(iii) (Triangle inequality) $\|x + y\| \leq \|x\| + \|y\|$ for all $x, y \in X$.

A vector space X equipped with a norm $\|\cdot\|$ is called a *normed space*.

The last inequality is called the *triangle inequality* because it says that the side of a triangle is shorter than the sum of the other two sides (Figure 1.2). The nonnegativity and positive homogeneity of the Euclidean norm (1.6) are trivial. The proof of the triangle inequality is in Problem 1.2.

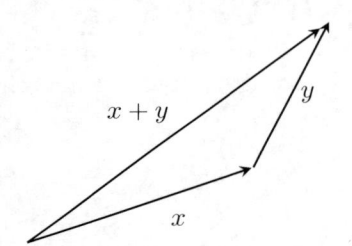

FIGURE 1.2: Triangle inequality.

There are many norms on $\mathbb{R}^N$. Some examples are

(ℓ^1 norm)	$\displaystyle \|x\|_1 := \sum_{n=1}^{N} |x_n|,$	(1.7a)
(ℓ^∞ or sup norm)	$\displaystyle \|x\|_\infty := \max_n |x_n|,$	(1.7b)
(ℓ^p norm for $p \geq 1$)	$\displaystyle \|x\|_p := \left(\sum_{n=1}^{N} |x_n|^p \right)^{1/p}.$	(1.7c)

By far these three are the most commonly used norms. The proofs that $\|\cdot\|_1$ and $\|\cdot\|_\infty$ are norms are straightforward (Problem 1.3). The proof that $\|\cdot\|_p$ is a norm uses the Minkowski inequality, proved in Chapter 11. Note that if $N = 1$ (so $\mathbb{R}^N = \mathbb{R}$), then the ℓ^p and ℓ^∞ norms all agree and equal the absolute value: $\|x\|_p = |x|$ for $x \in \mathbb{R}$.

At this point, the choice of the norm $\|\cdot\|$ to do analysis seems arbitrary. However, a remarkable property of finite-dimensional spaces is that it does not matter which norm we use as far as we are concerned with inequalities.

Theorem 1.3 (Equivalence of norms in $\mathbb{R}^N$). *Let $\|\cdot\|_1$, $\|\cdot\|_2$ be two norms on $\mathbb{R}^N$. Then there exist constants $0 < c \leq C$ such that*

$$c \|x\|_1 \leq \|x\|_2 \leq C \|x\|_1 \tag{1.8}$$

for all $x \in \mathbb{R}^N$.

In general, two norms $\|\cdot\|_1$ and $\|\cdot\|_2$ are said to be *equivalent* if (1.8) holds. Problem 1.11 proves Theorem 1.3 with lots of hints. Here let us show the equivalence of the Euclidean (ℓ^2) and sup (ℓ^∞) norms directly. Clearly

$$\|x\|_2 = \sqrt{\sum_{n=1}^N x_n^2} \geq |x_n|$$

for any n, so taking the maximum over n, we get $\|x\|_2 \geq \|x\|_\infty$. Furthermore, since by definition $|x_n| \leq \|x\|_\infty$ for all n, we get

$$\|x\|_2 = \sqrt{\sum_{n=1}^N x_n^2} \leq \sqrt{N \|x\|_\infty^2} = \sqrt{N} \|x\|_\infty .$$

Therefore $\|x\|_\infty \leq \|x\|_2 \leq \sqrt{N} \|x\|_\infty$, so we can take $c = 1$ and $C = \sqrt{N}$ in (1.8). An analogous argument shows $\|x\|_\infty \leq \|x\|_1 \leq N \|x\|_\infty$, so the ℓ^1 and ℓ^∞ norms are also equivalent.

Theorem 1.3 allows us to define bounded sets and convergence of sequences in $\mathbb{R}^N$ unambiguously. We say that $A \subset \mathbb{R}^N$ is *bounded* if there exists $b \geq 0$ such that $\|x\| \leq b$ for all $x \in A$. We say that a sequence $\{x_k\}_{k=1}^\infty \subset \mathbb{R}^N$ *converges* to $x \in \mathbb{R}^N$ if

$$(\forall \epsilon > 0)(\exists K > 0)(\forall k \geq K) \quad \|x_k - x\| < \epsilon, \tag{1.9}$$

Note that by Theorem 1.3, in (1.9) it does not matter which norm we use, and the definition of convergence (1.9) for $\mathbb{R}^1$ is consistent with (1.3) for $\mathbb{R}$.

A word of caution: Theorem 1.3 is proved in Problem 1.11 using the extreme value theorem (Theorem 1.11), which we have not stated yet. To avoid tautology, in the subsequent discussion the norm $\|\cdot\|$ should be understood as either the ℓ^1 norm $\|\cdot\|_1$, the ℓ^2 norm $\|\cdot\|_2$, or the sup norm $\|\cdot\|_\infty$ (which we already know are equivalent).

1.5   TOPOLOGY OF $\mathbb{R}^N$

In the top right diagram of Figure 1.1, we saw that a well-behaved function may not achieve a minimum on a set if it has holes. In this section, we define nice sets on which to do analysis.

Let $x \in \mathbb{R}^N$ and $\epsilon > 0$. The set

$$B_\epsilon(x) := \{y \in \mathbb{R}^N : \|y - x\| < \epsilon\} \qquad (1.10)$$

is called the *ball* with center x and radius ϵ, or simply the ϵ-ball about x. Figure 1.3 shows 1-balls (unit balls) about $x = 0$ for the ℓ^1, ℓ^2, and ℓ^∞ norms for the case $N = 2$. Note that the expression "ball" is consistent with common usage for the ℓ^2 norm, but for the ℓ^1 norm the ball is diamond-shaped and for the ℓ^∞ norm it is a cube.

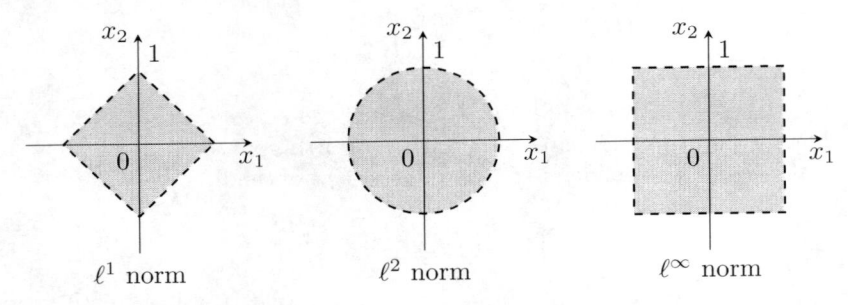

$$\ell^1 \text{ norm} \qquad \ell^2 \text{ norm} \qquad \ell^\infty \text{ norm}$$

FIGURE 1.3: 1-balls for ℓ^1, ℓ^2, and ℓ^∞ norms.

In general, let X be a normed space and $A \subset X$. We say that x is an *interior point* of A if there exists $\epsilon > 0$ such that $B_\epsilon(x) \subset A$, that is, we can draw a ball with center x and radius ϵ that is entirely included in A. If every $x \in A$ is an interior point of A, we say that A is an *open set*. Intuitively, an open set is a set that does not include its boundary. For instance, in Figure 1.4a, for any $x \in A$, by taking sufficiently small $\epsilon > 0$, we have $B_\epsilon(x) \subset A$. Therefore A is open. On the other hand, in Figure 1.4b, if $x \in A$ is on the boundary of A, then for any $\epsilon > 0$, part of $B_\epsilon(x)$ lies outside of A, so A is not open. We often use the symbols U and V to denote an open set because the French word for "open" is *ouvert* but the letter O is confusing due to the resemblance to 0. By definition, the empty set $\emptyset$ and the entire space X are open.

For $A \subset X$, let $A^c := X \backslash A = \{x \in X : x \notin A\}$ denote its *complement*. We say that A is a *closed set* if A^c is open. Intuitively, a closed set is a set that includes its boundary. We often use the symbol F to denote a closed set because the French word for "closed" is *fermé*. By definition, both $\emptyset, X$ are closed.

There are many examples of sets that are open, closed, or neither. The interval $(a, b) = \{x \in \mathbb{R} : a < x < b\}$ is open. The interval $[a, b] = \{x \in \mathbb{R} : a \leq x \leq b\}$ is closed. The interval $(a, b] = \{x \in \mathbb{R} : a < x \leq b\}$ is neither open nor closed. The ϵ-ball (1.10) is open. To see this, let $y \in B_\epsilon(x)$. By definition, $\|y - x\| < \epsilon$. Define $\delta := \epsilon - \|y - x\| > 0$. If $z \in B_\delta(y)$, then by the triangle inequality,

$$\|z - x\| \leq \|z - y\| + \|y - x\| < \delta + \|y - x\| = \epsilon,$$

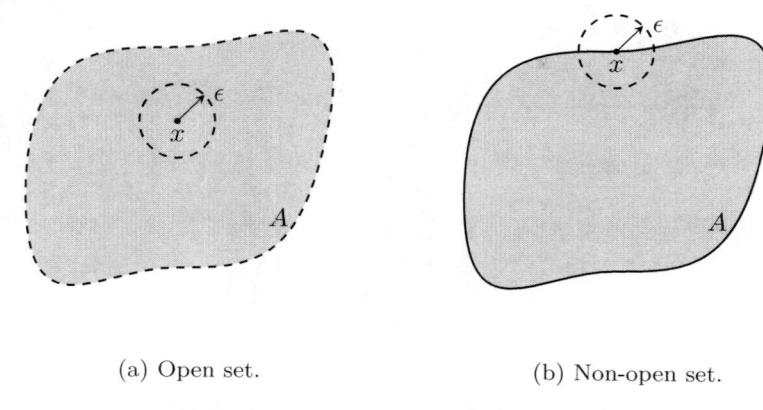

(a) Open set.   (b) Non-open set.

FIGURE 1.4: Open and non-open sets.

so $z \in B_\epsilon(x)$. Therefore $B_\delta(y) \subset B_\epsilon(x)$, so $B_\epsilon(x)$ is open.

The following proposition and corollary allow us to construct many open and closed sets.

Proposition 1.4. *(i) Any union of open sets is open: if I is any set and for each $i \in I$ the set U_i is open, so is $\bigcup_{i \in I} U_i$. (ii) Any finite intersection of open sets is open: if for each $j = 1, \ldots, J$ the set U_j is open, so is $\bigcap_{j=1}^{J} U_j$.*

Proof. (i) Suppose that U_i is open for each $i \in I$ and let $U = \bigcup_{i \in I} U_i$. If $x \in U$, then $x \in U_i$ for some i. Since U_i is open, we can take some $\epsilon > 0$ such that $B_\epsilon(x) \subset U_i \subset U$, so U is open.

(ii) Suppose that U_j is open for each $j = 1, \ldots, J$ and let $U = \bigcap_{j=1}^{J} U_j$. If $x \in U$, then in particular $x \in U_j$. Therefore we can take $\epsilon_j > 0$ such that $B_{\epsilon_j}(x) \subset U_j$. Let $\epsilon = \min_j \epsilon_j$. Then $B_\epsilon(x) \subset B_{\epsilon_j}(x) \subset U_j$ for all j, so $B_\epsilon(x) \subset \bigcap_{j=1}^{J} U_j = U$. Therefore U is open. □

Corollary 1.5. *(i) Any intersection of closed sets is closed: if I is any set and for each $i \in I$ the set F_i is closed, so is $\bigcap_{i \in I} F_i$. (ii) Any finite union of closed sets is closed: if for each $j = 1, \ldots, J$ the set F_j is closed, so is $\bigcup_{j=1}^{J} F_j$.*

Proof. Let $U_i = F_i^c$ and apply $\left(\bigcap_{i \in I} F_i \right)^c = \bigcup_{i \in I} F_i^c$ etc. □

Let $A \subset X$ be any set and let $(U_i)_{i \in I}$ be the collection of all open sets with $U_i \subset A$. There is at least one such U_i, namely the empty set $\emptyset$. By Proposition 1.4, $U := \bigcup_{i \in I} U_i$ is open, and it is clearly the largest open set included in A. This U is called the *interior* of A and is denoted by int A. Obviously, int $A = A$ if A is open.

Similarly, let $(F_i)_{i \in I}$ be the collection of all closed sets with $A \subset F_i$. There is at least one such F_i, namely the entire space X. By Corollary 1.5,

$F := \bigcap_{i \in I} F_i$ is closed, and it is clearly the smallest closed set including A. This F is called the *closure* of A and is denoted by $\mathrm{cl}\, A$. Obviously, $\mathrm{cl}\, A = A$ if A is closed.

By definition, we have $\mathrm{int}\, A \subset A \subset \mathrm{cl}\, A$. The set $\mathrm{cl}\, A \setminus \mathrm{int}\, A$ is called the *boundary* of A and is denoted by ∂A. The set $(\mathrm{cl}\, A)^c$ is called the *exterior* of A (Figure 1.5).

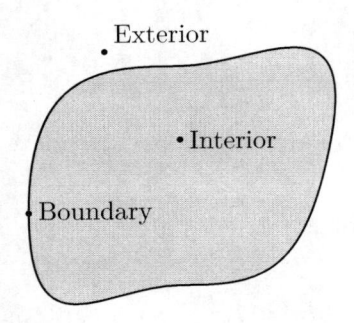

FIGURE 1.5: Interior, exterior, and boundary points.

A useful property is $\mathrm{cl}\, A = (\mathrm{int}\, A^c)^c$ and $\mathrm{int}\, A = (\mathrm{cl}\, A^c)^c$, which can be proved using the definition of interior, closure, and $\left(\bigcup_{i \in I} U_i\right)^c = \bigcap_{i \in I} U_i^c$ etc. (Problem 1.7). The following proposition characterizes the closure of a set using sequences.

Proposition 1.6. *Let $A \subset X$. Then $x \in \mathrm{cl}\, A$ if and only if there exists a sequence $\{x_k\}_{k=1}^{\infty} \subset A$ such that $x_k \to x$.*

Proof. Suppose $\{x_k\}_{k=1}^{\infty} \subset A$ such that $x_k \to x$. If $x \notin \mathrm{cl}\, A$, then $x \in (\mathrm{cl}\, A)^c$. Since this set is open, we can take $\epsilon > 0$ such that $B_\epsilon(x) \subset (\mathrm{cl}\, A)^c \subset A^c$. Since $x_k \to x$, we have $x_k \in A^c \iff x_k \notin A$ for large enough k, which is a contradiction. Therefore $x \in \mathrm{cl}\, A$.

Conversely, suppose $x \in \mathrm{cl}\, A$. We claim that for any $\epsilon > 0$, we have $B_\epsilon(x) \cap A \neq \emptyset$. To see this, suppose to the contrary that $B_\epsilon(x) \cap A = \emptyset$ for some $\epsilon > 0$. Then $B_\epsilon(x) \subset A^c$, so by definition $B_\epsilon(x) \subset \mathrm{int}\, A^c$. Therefore $x \in B_\epsilon(x) \cap \mathrm{cl}\, A = B_\epsilon(x) \cap (\mathrm{int}\, A^c)^c = \emptyset$, which is a contradiction. Now for each $k \in \mathbb{N}$, take $x_k \in B_{1/k}(x) \cap A$. Then clearly $\{x_k\}_{k=1}^{\infty} \subset A$ and $x_k \to x$. $\square$

An immediate corollary of Proposition 1.6 is that a set is closed if and only if sequences cannot escape the set.

Corollary 1.7. *Let $A \subset X$. Then A is closed if and only if $\{x_k\}_{k=1}^{\infty} \subset A$ and $x_k \to x$ imply $x \in A$.*

Corollary 1.7 shows that closed sets have no "holes". The set C in the top right diagram of Figure 1.1 has a hole and is not closed, which is one reason why the minimum of a function does not exist.

1.6   CONTINUOUS FUNCTIONS

The bottom left diagram of Figure 1.1 suggests that a minimization problem may not have a solution if the graph of the function has "gaps", even if the constraint set is nice (closed). Continuous functions have no gaps in their graphs, which avoids this problem.

Oftentimes, it is convenient to allow the function f to take values in the extended real numbers $\bar{\mathbb{R}} = \mathbb{R} \cup \{\pm\infty\} = [-\infty, \infty]$ instead of just $\mathbb{R} = (-\infty, \infty)$. For instance, instead of saying $\log x$ is defined for $x > 0$, it is convenient to define $\log 0 = -\infty$. We declare *open intervals* of $\bar{\mathbb{R}}$ to be the sets

$$\begin{cases} (a,b) = \{x \in \bar{\mathbb{R}} : a < x < b\} & \text{for } -\infty \leq a < b \leq \infty, \\ (a,\infty] = \{x \in \bar{\mathbb{R}} : a < x \leq \infty\} & \text{for } -\infty \leq a < \infty, \\ [-\infty,b) = \{x \in \bar{\mathbb{R}} : -\infty \leq x < b\} & \text{for } -\infty < b \leq \infty. \end{cases} \tag{1.11}$$

We say that the sequence $\{x_k\}_{k=1}^{\infty} \subset \bar{\mathbb{R}}$ converges to x if

$$(\forall \text{open interval } I \ni x)(\exists K > 0)(\forall k \geq K) \quad x_k \in I. \tag{1.12}$$

It is easy to see that this definition generalizes both (1.3) and (1.4).

Let X be a normed space and $A \subset X$. We say that the function $f : A \to [-\infty, \infty]$ is *continuous* at $x_0 \in A$ if

$$(\forall \text{open interval } I \ni f(x_0))(\exists \delta > 0)(\forall x \in A \cap B_\delta(x_0)) \quad f(x) \in I, \tag{1.13}$$

that is, if $x \in A$ is sufficiently close to x_0 in the sense that $\|x - x_0\| < \delta$, then the function value $f(x)$ is close to $f(x_0)$ in the sense that $f(x)$ is contained in a neighborhood of $f(x_0)$. (In general, if y is an interior point of the set B, we say that B is a *neighborhood* of y.) We say that f is continuous on A if it is continuous at every $x \in A$.

Just as we characterized closed sets using sequences in Corollary 1.7, we can characterize the continuity of functions using sequences.

Proposition 1.8. *$f : A \to [-\infty, \infty]$ is continuous at $x_0 \in A$ if and only if for any sequence $\{x_k\}_{k=1}^{\infty} \subset A$ with $x_k \to x_0$, we have $f(x_k) \to f(x_0)$.*

Proof. Suppose f is continuous at x_0 and take any sequence $\{x_k\}_{k=1}^{\infty} \subset A$ with $x_k \to x_0$. Take any open interval $I \ni f(x_0)$. Using (1.13), we can take $\delta > 0$ such that $f(x) \in I$ for all $x \in A \cap B_\delta(x_0)$. Since $x_k \to x_0$, we can take $K > 0$ such that $\|x_k - x_0\| < \delta$ for all $k \geq K$. Therefore $x_k \in A \cap B_\delta(x_0)$ for such k, so $f(x_k) \in I$. Hence by the definition (1.12), we have $f(x_k) \to f(x_0)$.

To show the converse, suppose that f is not continuous at x_0. Then (1.13) fails, so we can take an open interval $I \ni f(x_0)$ and $x_k \in A \cap B_{1/k}(x_0)$ such that $f(x_k) \notin I$ for all $k \in \mathbb{N}$. Then $\|x_k - x_0\| < 1/k$, so $x_k \to x_0$, but $f(x_k) \nrightarrow f(x_0)$. $\quad\square$

Sometimes, asking for the continuity of a function is too much. We thus introduce the concepts of upper and lower semicontinuity.

Let X be a normed space, $A \subset X$, and $f : A \to [-\infty, \infty]$. We say that f is *upper semicontinous (usc)* at $x_0 \in A$ if

$$(\forall y > f(x_0))(\exists \delta > 0)(\forall x \in A \cap B_\delta(x_0)) \quad f(x) < y. \tag{1.14}$$

We say that f is usc on A if it is usc at every $x \in A$. We say that f is *lower semicontinuous (lsc)* (at x) if $-f$ is usc (at x). Analogous to (1.14), f is lsc at $x_0 \in A$ if

$$(\forall y < f(x_0))(\exists \delta > 0)(\forall x \in A \cap B_\delta(x_0)) \quad f(x) > y. \tag{1.15}$$

Intuitively, upper (lower) semicontinuous functions are those that the function value can suddenly jump upward (downward); see Figure 1.6.

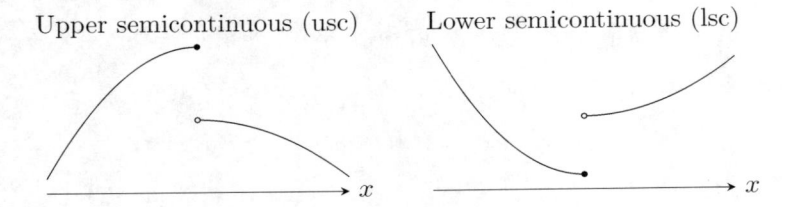

FIGURE 1.6: Semicontinuous functions.

We can also characterize semicontinuity using sequences.

Proposition 1.9. $f : A \to [-\infty, \infty]$ *is upper (lower) semicontinuous at* $x_0 \in A$ *if and only if for any sequence* $\{x_k\}_{k=1}^\infty \subset A$ *with* $x_k \to x_0$, *we have* $\limsup_{k \to \infty} f(x_k) \leq f(x_0)$ *($\liminf_{k \to \infty} f(x_k) \geq f(x_0)$).*

Proof. Problem 1.9. □

1.7 EXTREME VALUE THEOREM

Finally, we get to the main result of this chapter. The top left diagram of Figure 1.1 suggests that a continuous function f may not achieve a minimum on a constraint set C if C is unbounded. The top right diagram suggests that a minimum may not exist if C is not closed. The bottom left diagram suggests that a minimum may not exist if f jumps up, or is not lower semicontinuous. These observations suggest that f may achieve a minimum on C if f is lower semicontinuous and C is nonempty, closed, and bounded. This statement is indeed true. This section proves this *extreme value theorem*.

To this end, we introduce another concept. We say that a set $S \subset X$ is *sequentially compact* if every sequence in S has a convergent subsequence converging to a point in S, that is, if $\{x_k\}_{k=1}^\infty \subset S$, we can take $x \in S$ and indices $k_1 < k_2 < \cdots$ such that $x_{k_l} \to x \in S$ as $l \to \infty$.

Theorem 1.10 (Bolzano-Weierstrass theorem). *A set* $S \subset \mathbb{R}^N$ *is sequentially compact if and only if it is closed and bounded.*

Proof. **Sequentially compact** $\implies$ **closed and bounded.** Let S be sequentially compact. To show that S is closed, take any convergent sequence $\{x_k\} \subset S$ with $\lim x_k = x$. Since S is sequentially compact, we can take a subsequence $\{x_{k_l}\}$ such that $x_{k_l} \to y$ for some $y \in S$. Then

$$\|x - y\| \le \|x - x_{k_l}\| + \|x_{k_l} - y\| \to 0,$$

so $x = y \in S$. Therefore by Proposition 1.6, S is closed. To show that S is bounded, suppose that it is not. Then for any k we can find $x_k \in S$ such that $\|x_k\| > k$. Then for any x we have

$$\|x_k - x\| \ge \|x_k\| - \|x\| \ge k - \|x\| \to \infty$$

as $k \to \infty$, so any subsequence of $\{x_k\}$ cannot converge to x. Therefore S is not sequentially compact, which is a contradiction. Therefore S is bounded.

    Closed and bounded $\implies$ **sequentially compact.** Let S be closed and bounded. Since by Proposition 1.6 the limit of a convergent sequence in a closed set cannot escape that set, it suffices to show that any sequence of S has a convergent subsequence.

    We show the claim by induction on the dimension N. For $N = 1$, let $\{x_k\}_{k=1}^{\infty} \subset S \subset [-b, b]$, where $b > 0$. Define $\alpha_l = \sup_{k \ge l} x_k$. Since $x_k \in [-b, b]$, it follows that $\alpha_l \in [-b, b]$. By Proposition 1.1, we have $\alpha_l \to \alpha \in [-b, b]$. For each l, choose $k_l \ge l$ such that $|x_{k_l} - \alpha_l| < 1/l$, which is possible by the definition of α_l. Then

$$|x_{k_l} - \alpha| \le |x_{k_l} - \alpha_l| + |\alpha_l - \alpha| < \frac{1}{l} + |\alpha_l - \alpha| \to 0$$

as $l \to \infty$, so $x_{k_l} \to \alpha$. Therefore $\{x_k\}_{k=1}^{\infty}$ has a convergent subsequence $\{x_{k_l}\}_{l=1}^{\infty}$.

    Suppose that the claim is true up to dimension $N - 1$. Let $\{x_k\}_{k=1}^{\infty} \subset S \subset [-b, b]^N$. Write $x_k = (x_{1k}, \dots, x_{Nk})$. Since $\{x_{1k}\}_{k=1}^{\infty} \subset [-b, b]$, it has a convergent subsequence $\{x_{1k}'\}$. By the induction hypothesis, the sequence of $(N-1)$-vectors $\{(x_{2k}', \dots, x_{Nk}')\} \subset [-b, b]^{N-1}$ has a convergent subsequence $\{(x_{2k}'', \dots, x_{Nk}'')\}$. Since $\{x_{1k}''\}$ is a subsequence of $\{x_{1k}'\}$, it is also convergent. Therefore $\{x_k''\} = \{(x_{1k}'', \dots, x_{Nk}'')\} \subset [-b, b]^N$ also converges, so $\{x_k\}_{k=1}^{\infty}$ has a convergent subsequence. $\qquad\square$

    The main result of this chapter is the following extreme value theorem, which provides a simple sufficient condition for the existence of a solution to a minimization problem.

Theorem 1.11 (Extreme value theorem). *Let $\emptyset \neq S \subset \mathbb{R}^N$ be sequentially compact and $f : S \to [-\infty, \infty]$ be lower (upper) semicontinuous. Then f attains a minimum (maximum) over S.*

Proof. We show only for the case f is lsc. Let $m = \inf_{x \in S} f(x)$. Take a sequence $\{x_k\} \subset S$ such that $f(x_k) \to m$. Since S is sequentially compact, there is a subsequence such that $x_{k_l} \to x$ for some $x \in S$. Since f is lsc, we obtain

$$m \leq f(x) \leq \liminf_{l \to \infty} f(x_{k_l}) = m,$$

so $f(x) = m$. □

By Theorem 1.10, $S \subset \mathbb{R}^N$ is sequentially compact if and only if it is closed and bounded. Therefore Theorem 1.11 implies that any lower semicontinuous function defined on a nonempty, closed, and bounded subset of $\mathbb{R}^N$ attains a minimum.

1.A   TOPOLOGICAL SPACE

In §1.5, we studied the topological properties of the Euclidean space $\mathbb{R}^N$. However, $\mathbb{R}^N$ is special in the sense that it is a finite-dimensional vector space with a norm. To expand the applicability, we study the topological properties of more general spaces.

Let X be a nonempty set and $\mathcal{P}(X) = 2^X := \{A : A \subset X\}$ be its power set (the family of all subsets). We say that the collection of subsets $\mathcal{T} \subset \mathcal{P}(X)$ is a *topology* on X if the following conditions hold.

(i) $\emptyset, X \in \mathcal{T}$.

(ii) $\mathcal{T}$ is closed under arbitrary unions: if $\{U_i\}_{i \in I} \subset \mathcal{T}$, then $\bigcup_{i \in I} U_i \in \mathcal{T}$.

(iii) $\mathcal{T}$ is closed under finite intersections: if $\{U_j\}_{j=1}^{J} \subset \mathcal{T}$, then $\bigcap_{j=1}^{J} U_j \in \mathcal{T}$.

We say $(X, \mathcal{T})$ is a *topological space* if $\mathcal{T}$ is a topology on X. If the topology $\mathcal{T}$ is clear from the context, we just say X is a topological space. A set $U \in \mathcal{T}$ is called an *open set*. We say that $F \subset X$ is a *closed set* if $U := X \backslash F$ is open. By definition, $\emptyset$ and X are both open and closed. In $\mathbb{R}^N$, we proved properties (i)–(iii) (Proposition 1.4) for open sets; in general spaces, these are defining properties.

Example 1.1 (Normed space). Let $(X, \|\cdot\|)$ be a normed space. Declare $U \subset X$ to be open if, for any $x \in U$, there exists $\epsilon > 0$ such that

$$B_\epsilon(x) := \{y \in X : \|y - x\| < \epsilon\} \subset U.$$

Let $\mathcal{T}$ be the collection of all open sets. Then $(X, \mathcal{T})$ is a topological space.

Example 1.2 (Relative topology). Let $(X, \mathcal{T})$ be a topological space and $A \subset X$. Define $\mathcal{T}_A := \{U \cap A : U \in \mathcal{T}\}$. Then $(A, \mathcal{T}_A)$ is a topological space. The topology $\mathcal{T}_A$ is called the *relative topology* on A induced by $\mathcal{T}$.

If $\mathcal{T}_1 \subset \mathcal{T}_2$ are topologies on X, we say that $\mathcal{T}_1$ is *weaker* than $\mathcal{T}_2$.

Example 1.3 (Topology generated by a family). Let X be a nonempty set and $\mathcal{E} \subset \mathcal{P}(X)$ be a family of subsets of X. There exists a weakest topology including $\mathcal{E}$, denoted by $\mathcal{T}(\mathcal{E})$ and called the topology *generated* by $\mathcal{E}$. It is easy to show that $\mathcal{T}(\mathcal{E})$ consists of arbitrary unions of finite intersections of sets in $\mathcal{E}$.

Example 1.4 (Extended real number). Let $\bar{\mathbb{R}} = \mathbb{R} \cup \{\pm\infty\} = [-\infty, \infty]$ be the set of extended real numbers and let $\mathcal{E}$ be the family of open intervals defined by (1.11). Then $(\bar{\mathbb{R}}, \mathcal{T}(\mathcal{E}))$ is a topological space.

Let $(X, \mathcal{T})$ be a topological space and $A \subset X$. If $x \in A$ and there exists an open set U such that $x \in U \subset A$, we say that x is an *interior point* of A and that A is a *neighborhood* of x.

Topological spaces are suitable for studying continuous functions. Let X, Y be topological spaces and $f : X \to Y$. We say that f is *continuous* at $x_0 \in X$ if for every open neighborhood V of $f(x_0)$, there exists an open neighborhood U of x_0 such that $f(U) \subset V$. An equivalent statement is that for every open $V \ni f(x_0)$, the *inverse image*

$$f^{-1}(V) := \{x \in X : f(x) \in V\}$$

is a neighborhood of x_0. This definition clearly generalizes the ϵ-δ definition in (1.13).

Upper and lower semicontinuity can be defined in an obvious way. We say that $f : X \to [-\infty, \infty]$ is *upper semicontinuous (usc)* at $x_0 \in X$ if, for every $y > f(x_0)$, the set $f^{-1}([-\infty, y))$ is a neighborhood of x_0. Similarly, f is *lower semicontinuous (lsc)* if for every $y < f(x_0)$, the set $f^{-1}((y, \infty])$ is a neighborhood of x_0. Clearly, f is continuous if it is both usc and lsc. These notions generalize those in (1.14) and (1.15). When f is continuous (usc, lsc) at every point $x_0 \in X$, we say f is continuous (usc, lsc). The following proposition provides an alternative characterization of continuous functions.

Proposition 1.12. *Let X, Y be topological spaces and $f : X \to Y$. Then f is continuous if and only if for any open $V \subset Y$, the inverse image $f^{-1}(V)$ is open in X.*

Proof. Suppose $f^{-1}(V)$ is open for any open $V \subset Y$. Take any $x \in X$ and any open $V \subset Y$ such that $f(x) \in V$. Then $U := f^{-1}(V)$ is open and contains x, so f is continuous at x. Since $x \in X$ is arbitrary, f is continuous.

Conversely, suppose f is continuous. For any open $V \subset Y$, let $U := f^{-1}(V)$ and $x \in U$. Then $f(x) \in V$, so there exists an open neighborhood U_x of x such that $f(U_x) \subset V$, or equivalently $U_x \subset f^{-1}(V)$. Therefore

$$f^{-1}(V) = U \subset \bigcup_{x \in U} U_x \subset f^{-1}(V),$$

so $f^{-1}(V) = U = \bigcup_{x \in U} U_x$ is open. $\qquad\square$

A similar characterization holds for usc and lsc functions (Problem 1.14).

Here we started from two topological spaces X, Y and asked if a function $f : X \to Y$ is continuous, but we can also go the other way round. If Y is a topological space and $\{f_i\}_{i \in I}$ is a family of functions from X to Y, we could consider the weakest topology on X that makes all f_i's continuous. By Proposition 1.12, this topology is generated by the sets of the form $f_i^{-1}(V_i)$, where V_i is open in Y, and is called the *weak topology* generated by $\{f_i\}_{i \in I}$.

Example 1.5 (Product topology). For each $i \in I$, let $(X_i, \mathcal{T}_i)$ be a topological space. Let $X = \prod_{i \in I} X_i$ be the Cartesian product. Define the projection $\pi_i : X \to X_i$ by $\pi_i(x) = x_i$, where $x = (x_i)$. The topology on X generated by $\{\pi_i\}_{i \in I}$ is called the *product topology*. Clearly, the product topology is generated by the sets of the form $\prod_{i \in I} U_i$, where $U_i \subset X_i$ is open and $U_i = X_i$ except one i. (Such sets are called *cylinders*.)

When we consider the Cartesian product of topological spaces, we always endow it with the product topology.

The extreme value theorem (Theorem 1.11) states that a continuous function defined on a sequentially compact subset achieves minima and maxima. To extend this result to general topological spaces, we introduce another concept called *compactness*. We say that a collection of sets $(U_i)_{i \in I}$ *covers* A if $A \subset \bigcup_{i \in I} U_i$. A cover $(U_i)_{i \in I}$ is called an *open cover* if each U_i is open, and it is called a *finite cover* if I is a finite set.

We say that a topological space X is *compact* if every open cover has a finite subcover, that is, if $X = \bigcup_{i \in I} U_i$ and each U_i is open, then we can take a finite set $J \subset I$ such that $X = \bigcup_{j \in J} U_j$. We say $S \subset X$ is a compact set if it is compact in the relative topology, or equivalently, if $S \subset \bigcup_{i \in I} U_i$ and each U_i is open, then we can take a finite set $J \subset I$ such that $S \subset \bigcup_{j \in J} U_j$.

Noting that closed sets are the complement of open sets, we may provide an alternative formulation of compactness. We say that a family of sets $\{F_i\}_{i \in I}$ has the *finite intersection property* if $\bigcap_{j \in J} F_j \neq \emptyset$ for every finite $J \subset I$.

Proposition 1.13. *A topological space X is compact if and only if for any family of closed sets $\{F_i\}_{i \in I}$ with the finite intersection property, we have $\bigcap_{i \in I} F_i \neq \emptyset$.*

Proof. Let $U_i = X \backslash F_i = F_i^c$, which is open.

Suppose X is compact. If $\bigcap_{i \in I} F_i = \emptyset$, then $\bigcup_{i \in I} U_i = X$. By the definition of compactness, we can take a finite set $J \subset I$ such that $X = \bigcup_{j \in J} U_j$, so $\bigcap_{j \in J} F_j = \emptyset$. Therefore if $\{F_i\}_{i \in I}$ is a family of closed sets with the finite intersection property, then $\bigcap_{i \in I} F_i \neq \emptyset$.

Conversely, if X is not compact, we can take an open cover $\{U_i\}_{i \in I}$ without any finite subcover. Then $\bigcap_{i \in I} F_i = \emptyset$ but $\bigcap_{j \in J} F_j \neq \emptyset$ for every finite $J \subset I$. □

For normed spaces (or more generally metric spaces that are introduced in Chapter 7), we can show that compactness and sequential compactness are equivalent. (For a proof, see, for instance, Folland (1999, Theorem 0.25)).) For this reason, in the subsequent discussion we just say "compact sets" when referring to sequentially compact sets.

Compact sets are suitable for studying minima and maxima of continuous functions. In fact, we can generalize the extreme value theorem as follows.

Theorem 1.14 (Extreme value theorem for topological space). *Let X be a compact topological space and $f : X \to [-\infty, \infty]$ be lower (upper) semicontinuous. Then f attains a minimum (maximum) over X.*

Proof. We show only for the case f is lsc. Let $m = \inf_{x \in X} f(x)$. Suppose to the contrary that there is no x such that $f(x) = m$. For any $y > m$, define $U_y := f^{-1}((y, \infty])$, which is open because f is lsc. Since by assumption $m \notin f(X)$, we have $X = \bigcup_{y>m} U_y$. Since X is compact, we can take finitely many $y_1, \ldots, y_J > m$ such that $X = \bigcup_{j=1}^{J} U_{y_j}$. Then for any $x \in X$, we have $f(x) \geq \min_j y_j > m$, which contradicts the assumption $m = \inf_{x \in X} f(x)$. $\square$

PROBLEMS

1.1. Let $a, b \in \mathbb{R}^N$ and $\|\cdot\|$ denote the Euclidean norm (1.6). This problem asks you to prove the *Cauchy-Schwarz inequality* $\|a\| \|b\| \geq |\langle a, b \rangle|$. Note that this inequality is trivial if $a = 0$, so assume $a \neq 0$.

   (i) Let $a = (a_n)$, $b = (b_n)$, and define the function $f : \mathbb{R} \to \mathbb{R}$ by $f(x) = \sum_{n=1}^{N} (a_n x - b_n)^2$. By expanding terms, write $f(x) = px^2 + qx + r$ and obtain concrete expressions for p, q, r.

  (ii) Noting that $f(x) \geq 0$ for all x, prove the Cauchy-Schwarz inequality using the discriminant $D = q^2 - 4pr$.

1.2. Let $\|\cdot\|$ denote the Euclidean norm (1.6) in $\mathbb{R}^N$. Prove the triangle inequality $\|x + y\| \leq \|x\| + \|y\|$. (Hint: take the square of both sides and apply the Cauchy-Schwarz inequality.)

1.3. Prove that the ℓ^1 norm (1.7a) and the ℓ^∞ norm (1.7b) are indeed norms according to the definition.

1.4. Define the sequence $\{x_k\}_{k=0}^{\infty}$ by $x_0 = 2$ and

$$x_{k+1} = \frac{1}{2} x_k + \frac{1}{x_k}$$

for all $k \geq 0$.

   (i) Show that

$$x_{k+1} - \sqrt{2} = \frac{1}{2x_k} (x_k - \sqrt{2})^2.$$

  (ii) Show that $x_k > \sqrt{2}$ for all k.

(iii) Show that $x_{k+1} < x_k$ for all k.

(iv) Show that $\lim_{k \to \infty} x_k = \sqrt{2}$.

(v) Can you provide an estimate of the error $|x_k - \sqrt{2}|$?

1.5. Let $x_0 > 0$ be given, and define $\{x_k\}_{k=0}^{\infty}$ by $x_{k+1} = \beta x_k^{\alpha}$, where $\alpha \in (0, 1)$ and $\beta > 0$ are parameters. Prove that $\{x_k\}$ converges and explicitly compute its limit.

1.6. (i) Let A, B be any set. Prove that $\mathrm{int}(A \cap B) = \mathrm{int}\, A \cap \mathrm{int}\, B$ and $\mathrm{cl}(A \cup B) = \mathrm{cl}\, A \cup \mathrm{cl}\, B$.

(ii) Show through an example that $\mathrm{int}(A \cup B)$ need not equal $\mathrm{int}\, A \cup \mathrm{int}\, B$.

1.7. Prove $\mathrm{cl}\, A = (\mathrm{int}\, A^c)^c$ and $\mathrm{int}\, A = (\mathrm{cl}\, A^c)^c$.

1.8. Let F be closed and $x_0 \notin F$.

(i) Prove that $\epsilon := \inf_{x \in F} \|x - x_0\| > 0$.

(ii) Prove that $U := \bigcup_{x \in F} B(x, \epsilon/2)$ is open.

(iii) Let $V := B(x_0, \epsilon/2)$. Prove that $F \subset U$, $x_0 \in V$, and $U \cap V = \emptyset$.

1.9. Prove Proposition 1.9. (Hint: imitate the proof of Proposition 1.8.)

1.10. A sequence $\{x_k\}_{k=1}^{\infty} \subset \mathbb{R}^N$ is called *Cauchy* if

$$(\forall \epsilon > 0)(\exists K > 0)(\forall k, l \geq K) \quad \|x_k - x_l\| < \epsilon,$$

that is, the terms with sufficiently large indices are arbitrarily close to each other.

(i) Prove that a Cauchy sequence is bounded.

(ii) Prove that a sequence $\{x_k\}_{k=1}^{\infty} \subset \mathbb{R}^N$ is convergent if and only if it is Cauchy. (Hint: use Theorem 1.10. This property is called the *completeness* of $\mathbb{R}^N$.)

1.11. This problem asks you to prove Theorem 1.3.

(i) For any norm $\|\cdot\|$ on $\mathbb{R}^N$, define $f : \mathbb{R}^N \to \mathbb{R}$ by $f(x) = \|x\|$. Show that f is continuous, where we define the convergence of sequences using the sup norm $\|\cdot\|_{\infty}$. (Hint: express $x = (x_n)$ as $x = \sum_{n=1}^{N} x_n e_n$, where e_n is the n-th unit vector, and use the triangle inequality.)

(ii) Define the unit sphere $S = \{x \in \mathbb{R}^N : \|x\|_{\infty} = 1\}$. Show that S is nonempty, closed, and bounded.

(iii) Define $g : S \to \mathbb{R}$ by $g(x) = f(x)/\|x\|_{\infty}$. Show that g is continuous.

(iv) Show that there exist constants $0 < c \leq C$ such that

$$c \left\| x \right\|_\infty \leq \left\| x \right\| \leq C \left\| x \right\|_\infty$$

for all $x \in \mathbb{R}^N$.

(v) Prove Theorem 1.3.

1.12. Prove the *intermediate value theorem*: if $f : [a, b] \to \mathbb{R}$ is continuous and $f(a) \leq 0 \leq f(b)$, then there exists $c \in [a, b]$ such that $f(c) = 0$. (Hint: let $A = \{x \in [a, b] : f(x) \leq 0\}$ and consider $c = \sup A$.)

1.13. Let $f : (a, b) \to \mathbb{R}$ be increasing, so $a < x_1 \leq x_2 < b$ implies $f(x_1) \leq f(x_2)$.

(i) Show that for each $x \in (a, b)$, $g^\pm(x) := \lim_{h \downarrow 0} f(x \pm h)$ exists,[1] and that $g^-(x) \leq g^+(x)$ for all $x \in (a, b)$.

(ii) Show that f is continuous on (a, b) except at at most countably many points. (Hint: if $g^-(x) < g^+(x)$, then there is a rational number in between.)

1.14. Let X be a topological space and $f : X \to [-\infty, \infty]$. Show that f is upper (lower) semicontinuous if and only if for any $y \in \mathbb{R}$, the set $f^{-1}([-\infty, y))$ $(f^{-1}((y, \infty]))$ is open in X.

---

[1] We write $\lim_{h \downarrow 0} f(x + h) = y$ if $\lim_{k \to \infty} f(x + h_k) = y$ for all sequences $\{h_k\}_{k=1}^\infty$ with $h_k > 0$ and $h_k \to 0$.

CHAPTER 2

One-variable Optimization

2.1 INTRODUCTION

In Chapter 1, we showed by proving the extreme value theorem (Theorem 1.11) that the minimization problem

$$\begin{array}{ll}\text{minimize} & f(x) \\ \text{subject to} & x \in C, \end{array} \qquad (2.1)$$

has a solution $\bar{x}$ if $C \subset \mathbb{R}^N$ is nonempty, closed, and bounded, and f is lower semicontinuous on C. In practice, we are not only interested in proving the existence of a solution but also in its characterization.

The goal of this chapter is to derive necessary or sufficient conditions for $\bar{x}$ to be a solution to the minimization problem (2.1) when f is a one-variable function, i.e., $C \subset \mathbb{R}$. To this end, we introduce some terminology. We say that a point $x \in C$ is *feasible* in the optimization problem (2.1). We say that $\bar{x} \in C$ is a *(global) solution* to (2.1) or a *(global) minimum* of f on C if $f(\bar{x}) \le f(x)$ for all $x \in C$. We say that $\bar{x} \in C$ is a *local solution* or a *local minimum* if there exists a neighborhood $U \subset C$ of x such that $f(\bar{x}) \le f(x)$ for all $x \in U$. If this inequality is strict whenever $x \ne \bar{x}$, we say that $\bar{x}$ is a strict local solution. Global and local maxima are defined analogously. Clearly, a global solution is a local solution but the converse is generally not true. For instance, in Figure 2.1, the point m_1 is a (global) minimum; m_2 is a local (but not global) minimum; M is a local (but not global) maximum.

2.2 DIFFERENTIATION

A powerful tool for solving nonlinear optimization problems is *differentiation* (taking derivatives), which is basically approximating a nonlinear function by a linear one. Suppose we wish to approximate a function $f(x)$ by a linear

---

DOI: 10.1201/9781032698953-2

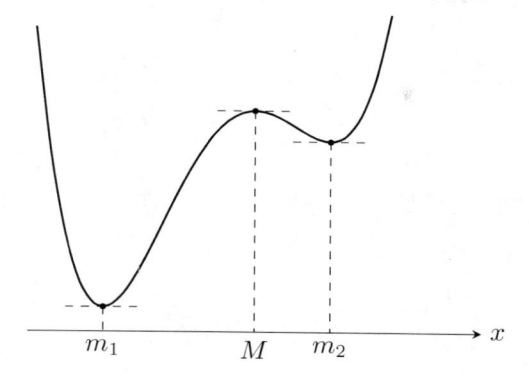

FIGURE 2.1: Global and local minima.

function around the point $x = a$, so

$$f(x) \approx p(x - a) + q \tag{2.2}$$

for some numbers p, q. The approximation (2.2) should be exact at $x = a$, so setting $x = a$ we must have $q = f(a)$. Subtracting q from both sides of (2.2) and dividing by $x - a$ (when $x \neq a$), we obtain

$$p \approx \frac{f(x) - f(a)}{x - a}. \tag{2.3}$$

Since the approximation (2.2) is for x close to a, it makes sense to define p by the limit of (2.3) as $x \to a$. The quantity

$$p = f'(a) := \lim_{x \to a} \frac{f(x) - f(a)}{x - a}, \tag{2.4}$$

if it exists, is called the *derivative* of f at $x = a$. Letting $x = a + h$ with $h \neq 0$, we can also write (2.4) as

$$f'(a) = \lim_{h \to 0} \frac{f(a + h) - f(a)}{h}.$$

In summary, we can rewrite (2.2) as

$$f(x) \approx f'(a)(x - a) + f(a). \tag{2.5}$$

Figure 2.2 clarifies the linear approximation (2.5).

Example 2.1. Let $f(x) = x$. Then

$$f'(a) = \lim_{h \to 0} \frac{(a + h) - a}{h} = \lim_{h \to 0} \frac{h}{h} = \lim_{h \to 0} 1 = 1.$$

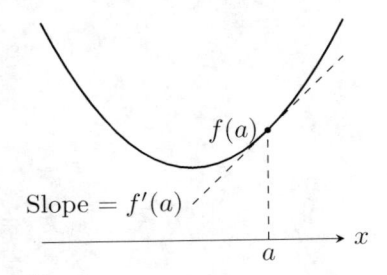

FIGURE 2.2: Derivative of a function.

Example 2.2. Let $f(x) = x^2$. Then

$$f'(a) = \lim_{h \to 0} \frac{(a+h)^2 - a^2}{h} = \lim_{h \to 0} \frac{2ah + h^2}{h} = \lim_{h \to 0} (2a + h) = 2a.$$

If the derivative of f exists at every point of an interval (a, b), then the function f is called *differentiable* on (a, b). The derivative of f at $x \in (a, b)$ is denoted by $f'(x)$. The derivative $f'(x)$ is itself another function. If f' is continuous, then f is called *continuously differentiable*, or simply a C^1 function. When we want to stress that f is C^1 on (a, b), we write $f \in C^1(a, b)$. If $f'(x)$ is again differentiable, then its derivative is denoted by $f''(x)$ and is called the second derivative of f. We can define $f'''(x)$, $f''''(x)$, etc. analogously. The r-th derivative of f is usually denoted by $f^{(r)}(x)$. If f is r times differentiable and $f^{(r)}(x)$ is continuous ("r times continuously differentiable"), then f is called a C^r function.

The following proposition shows that a function that is differentiable at a point is continuous at that point.

Proposition 2.1. *Let $f : (a, b) \to \mathbb{R}$ be differentiable at $c \in (a, b)$. Then f is continuous at c.*

Proof. Let $x \neq c$ and consider the identity

$$f(x) = \frac{f(x) - f(c)}{x - c}(x - c) + f(c).$$

Letting $x \to c$ and using the definition of the derivative, we obtain

$$\lim_{x \to c} f(x) = f'(c) \cdot 0 + f(c) = f(c). \qquad \square$$

Obviously, not every continuous function is differentiable, as we can see from $f(x) = |x|$ at $x = 0$.

2.3 NECESSARY CONDITION

Let us go back to the minimization problem (2.1). The following proposition shows why differentiation is a powerful tool for solving optimization problems.

Proposition 2.2 (Necessity of first-order condition). *Consider the minimization problem* (2.1). *If $\bar{x} \in \operatorname{int} C$ is a local solution and f is differentiable at $\bar{x}$, then $f'(\bar{x}) = 0$.*

Proof. Since $\bar{x}$ is an interior point of C, we have $x + h \in C$ for small enough $|h|$. Since $\bar{x}$ attains the minimum of f in a neighborhood of $\bar{x}$, we have

$$f(\bar{x} + h) \geq f(\bar{x})$$

for sufficiently small $|h|$. Subtracting $f(\bar{x})$ from both sides and dividing by $h > 0$, we obtain

$$\frac{f(\bar{x} + h) - f(\bar{x})}{h} \geq 0.$$

Letting $h \to 0$ and using the definition of the derivative, we get $f'(\bar{x}) \geq 0$. By considering the case $h < 0$, we can show $f'(\bar{x}) \leq 0$. Therefore $f'(\bar{x}) = 0$. $\square$

Proposition 2.2 says that to minimize a differentiable function (with no constraints), it is *necessary* that the derivative is zero. Thus if we know that a solution exists (say by applying the extreme value theorem) and lies in the interior of C, then we may find the candidates for the solution by solving the equation $f'(\bar{x}) = 0$. The condition $f'(\bar{x}) = 0$ in Proposition 2.2 is called the *first-order condition* for optimality. Figure 2.3 clarifies this condition.

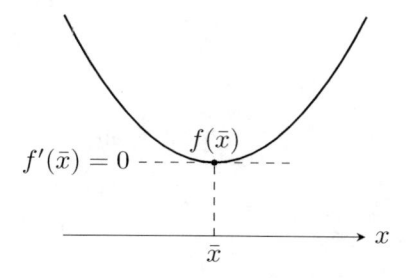

FIGURE 2.3: First-order condition is necessary.

Obviously, setting the derivative to zero is not sufficient for optimality in general, as the following example shows.

Example 2.3. Let $f(x) = x^3/3 - x$. Then

$$f'(x) = x^2 - 1 = (x - 1)(x + 1),$$

so $f'(x) = 0 \iff x = \pm 1$. But clearly $f(x) \to \pm\infty$ as $x \to \pm\infty$, so $x = \pm 1$ are neither the minimum nor the maximum of f (Figure 2.4).

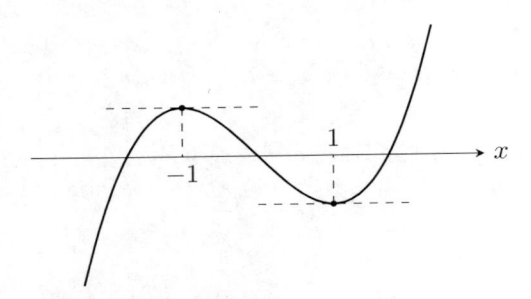

FIGURE 2.4: First-order condition is not sufficient.

2.4 MEAN VALUE AND TAYLOR'S THEOREM

Let f be a differentiable function. By definition, $f'(a)$ is the limit of $\frac{f(b)-f(a)}{b-a}$ —the slope between the points $(a, f(a))$ and $(b, f(b))$—as b approaches a. Is there an exact relationship between f' and arbitrary b? The mean value theorem gives an answer.

Proposition 2.3 (Mean value theorem). *Let f be continuous on $[a, b]$ and differentiable on (a, b). Then there exists $c \in (a, b)$ such that*

$$\frac{f(b) - f(a)}{b - a} = f'(c). \tag{2.6}$$

Proof. Let

$$\phi(x) := f(x) - f(a) - \frac{f(b) - f(a)}{b - a}(x - a).$$

Clearly $\phi(a) = \phi(b) = 0$. If $\phi \equiv 0$ on $[a, b]$, then

$$0 = \phi'(x) = f'(x) - \frac{f(b) - f(a)}{b - a}$$

on (a, b), so we can take any $c \in (a, b)$. Suppose there exists $x \in [a, b]$ such that $\phi(x) < 0$. Since ϕ is continuous, by the extreme value theorem (Theorem 1.11) it attains a minimum at some point $c \in [a, b]$. Since $\phi(a) = \phi(b) = 0$ and ϕ takes a negative value, it must be $c \in (a, b)$. By Proposition 2.2, we have

$$0 = \phi'(c) = f'(c) - \frac{f(b) - f(a)}{b - a} \iff \frac{f(b) - f(a)}{b - a} = f'(c).$$

The proof if ϕ takes a positive value is similar. □

Recall that differentiation is essentially a linear approximation; see (2.5). Changing the notation in the mean value theorem (2.6) such that $b = x$ and $c = \xi$, we obtain

$$f'(\xi) = \frac{f(x) - f(a)}{x - a} \iff f(x) = f(a) + f'(\xi)(x - a).$$

There is no reason to stop at a linear (first-order) approximation. If, for example, we continue to a quadratic (second-order) approximation, we can show that for each x, there exists a number ξ between a and x such that

$$f(x) = f(a) + f'(a)(x - a) + \frac{1}{2}f''(\xi)(x - a)^2. \tag{2.7}$$

More generally, by increasing the order of polynomial approximation, we obtain the following Taylor's theorem.

Proposition 2.4 (Taylor's theorem). *Let f be n times differentiable around $x = a$. Then for each x, there exists a number ξ between a and x such that*

$$f(x) = \sum_{k=0}^{n-1} \frac{f^{(k)}(a)}{k!}(x - a)^k + \frac{f^{(n)}(\xi)}{n!}(x - a)^n. \tag{2.8}$$

Proof. Problem 2.7. □

Obviously, the mean value theorem (2.6) is a special case of Taylor's theorem (2.8) for $n = 1$. Similarly, the quadratic approximation (2.7) is a special case of (2.8) for $n = 2$.

2.5 SUFFICIENT CONDITION

Proposition 2.2 tells us that if a function is differentiable, the derivative is zero at the optimum (maximum or minimum). Therefore, setting the derivative to zero (first-order condition) is a *necessary* condition for optimality. Is there a *sufficient* condition for optimality? The answer is yes: there is a special but large enough class of functions such that the first-order condition is also sufficient.

We say that a function f is *convex* if for any x_1, x_2 and $\alpha \in [0, 1]$ we have

$$f((1 - \alpha)x_1 + \alpha x_2) \leq (1 - \alpha)f(x_1) + \alpha f(x_2). \tag{2.9}$$

Graphically, a function is convex if the segment joining the points $(x_1, f(x_1))$ and $(x_2, f(x_2))$ lies above the graph of f (Figure 2.5). We say that f is *strictly convex* if the inequality (2.9) is strict for $\alpha \in (0, 1)$. We say that f is *concave* if $-f$ is convex.

As shown in Problems 2.10 and 2.11 (and more generally in Chapter 11), a twice continuously differentiable function f is convex if and only if the second derivative is nonnegative, so $f''(x) \geq 0$. The intuitive explanation is as follows. When $f''(x) \geq 0$, then $f'(x)$—the derivative or the slope of f—is increasing. Therefore if you imagine flying along the graph of f, you will be constantly turning upwards. Therefore the segment that joins arbitrary two points on the trajectory must lie above the actual trajectory.

The following proposition shows that setting the derivative to zero is sufficient for optimization when the objective function is convex or concave.

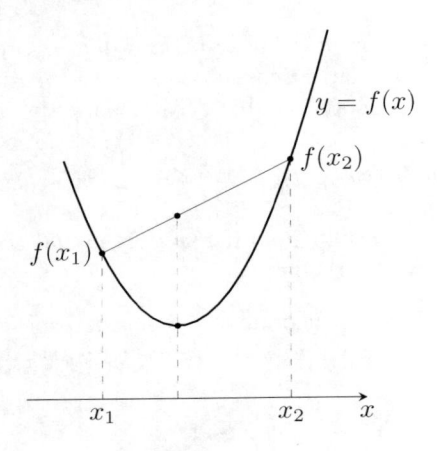

FIGURE 2.5: Convex function.

Proposition 2.5 (Sufficiency of first-order condition for convex functions). *Let f be twice differentiable and convex (concave). If $f'(\bar{x}) = 0$, then $\bar{x}$ is the minimum (maximum) of f.*

Proof. Suppose that f is convex, so $f''(x) \geq 0$. Applying Taylor's theorem (Proposition 2.4) for $a = \bar{x}$ and $n = 2$, for any x there exists ξ such that

$$f(x) = f(\bar{x}) + f'(\bar{x})(x - \bar{x}) + \frac{1}{2}f''(\xi)(x - \bar{x})^2.$$

Since by assumption $f'(\bar{x}) = 0$ and $f''(\xi) \geq 0$, we obtain $f(x) \geq f(\bar{x})$. Therefore $\bar{x}$ is the minimum of f. A similar argument holds when f is concave. $\square$

When the function is not convex, all we can hope is to characterize local solutions, as in the following proposition.

Proposition 2.6 (Characterization of local solutions). *Let $U \subset \mathbb{R}$ be open and $f : U \to \mathbb{R}$ be twice differentiable. Then the following statements are true.*

(i) If $\bar{x} \in U$ is a local minimum, then $f'(\bar{x}) = 0$ and $f''(\bar{x}) \geq 0$.

(ii) If $f'(\bar{x}) = 0$ and $f''(\bar{x}) > 0$, then $\bar{x}$ is a strict local minimum.

The proof is similar to Proposition 2.5 and is left as Problem 2.13. Similar statements hold for local maxima by flipping the sign of f.

2.6 OPTIMAL SAVINGS PROBLEM

To illustrate how to use Proposition 2.5, we provide an example with a step-by-step analysis.

Consider an agent who lives for two dates indexed by $t = 1, 2$. The agent is endowed with initial wealth $w > 0$, and at $t = 1$ the agent needs to decide how much to consume or save. The gross interest rate on savings is $R > 0$. Thus if the agent consumes c at $t = 1$, savings is $w - c$, and the wealth at $t = 2$ is $R(w - c)$. Suppose that the agent wishes to maximize the utility

$$U(c_1, c_2) = \frac{c_1^{1-\gamma}}{1 - \gamma} + \beta \frac{c_2^{1-\gamma}}{1 - \gamma}, \tag{2.10}$$

where $0 < \gamma \neq 1$ is a curvature parameter and $\beta > 0$ is the discount factor. Setting $c_1 = c$ and $c_2 = R(w - c)$ in (2.10), the objective function is

$$f(c) := \frac{c^{1-\gamma}}{1 - \gamma} + \beta \frac{(R(w - c))^{1-\gamma}}{1 - \gamma} = \frac{1}{1 - \gamma} \left(c^{1-\gamma} + \beta R^{1-\gamma}(w - c)^{1-\gamma} \right). \tag{2.11}$$

If $0 < \gamma < 1$, then f is positive and continuous on $[0, w]$. If $\gamma > 1$, then f is negative and continuous on $[0, w]$ if we allow the value $-\infty$. Hence by the extreme value theorem (Theorem 1.11), there exists a solution.[1]

For $c \in (0, w)$, the first and second derivatives are

$$f'(c) = c^{-\gamma} - \beta R^{1-\gamma}(w - c)^{-\gamma},$$
$$f''(c) = -\gamma(c^{-\gamma-1} + \beta R^{1-\gamma}(w - c)^{-\gamma-1}).$$

Since $f''(c) < 0$, by the remark after (2.9), f is concave. The first-order condition is

$$\begin{aligned} f'(c) = 0 &\iff c^{-\gamma} = \beta R^{1-\gamma}(w - c)^{-\gamma} \\ &\iff c = (\beta R^{1-\gamma})^{-1/\gamma}(w - c) \\ &\iff c = \frac{w}{1 + (\beta R^{1-\gamma})^{1/\gamma}}. \end{aligned}$$

By Proposition 2.5, this c is the optimal consumption.

PROBLEMS

2.1. Using the definition (2.4), compute the derivative of the following functions.

(i) $f(x) = x^3$.

(ii) $f(x) = x^4$.

(iii) $f(x) = x^n$, where $n \in \mathbb{N}$. (Hint: binomial theorem.)

(iv) $f(x) = 1/x$, where $x \neq 0$.

(v) $f(x) = \sqrt{x}$, where $x > 0$.

---

[1] As this argument shows, working with extended real numbers is convenient to avoid cases. In the usual sense, f in (2.11) is "undefined" at $c = 0, w$ if $\gamma > 1$.

2.2. Let f, g be differentiable and $\alpha \in \mathbb{R}$. Prove the following statements.

(i) $(f(x) + g(x))' = f'(x) + g'(x)$,

(ii) $(\alpha f(x))' = \alpha f'(x)$,

(iii) $(f(x)g(x))' = f'(x)g(x) + f(x)g'(x)$ (product rule).

(iv) $(f(x)/g(x))' = \frac{f'(x)g(x) - f(x)g'(x)}{g(x)^2}$ if $g(x) \neq 0$ (quotient rule).

(v) $(g(f(x)))' = g'(f(x))f'(x)$ (chain rule).

2.3. The exponential function is defined by

$$e^x = 1 + x + \frac{1}{2}x^2 + \frac{1}{6}x^3 + \cdots = \sum_{n=0}^{\infty} \frac{1}{n!}x^n,$$

where $e = 2.718281828\ldots$. It satisfies $e^{x+y} = e^x e^y$ and $(e^x)' = e^x$. The logarithmic function is the inverse function of the exponential, so $e^{\log x} = x$ and $\log e^x = x$. Using the chain rule, show that

(i) $(\log x)' = 1/x$,

(ii) $(x^\alpha)' = \alpha x^{\alpha - 1}$.

2.4. Define f by $f(x) = x^2 \sin(1/x)$ if $x \neq 0$ and $f(0) = 0$.

(i) Compute $f'(x)$ when $x \neq 0$.

(ii) Using the definition, compute $f'(0)$.

(iii) Show that f is differentiable but not continuously differentiable.

2.5. (i) Fill in the details of the proof of Proposition 2.2.

(ii) Show that Proposition 2.2 also holds for maximization.

2.6. (i) Let $f : (a, b) \to \mathbb{R}$ be differentiable and $f' > 0$. Show that f is strictly increasing, i.e., $x_1 < x_2$ implies $f(x_1) < f(x_2)$. (Hint: use the mean value theorem.)

(ii) Let $f : [a, b] \to \mathbb{R}$ be continuous and differentiable on (a, b). Let $\bar{x} \in [a, b]$ be a maximum of f, which exists by the extreme value theorem. If $f'(x) > 0$ for x sufficiently close to a, show that $\bar{x} \neq a$.

2.7. This problem asks you to prove Taylor's theorem. Let I be an open interval containing a and $f : I \to \mathbb{R}$. Suppose that f is n times differentiable and $f^{(k)}(x)$ is continuous on I for $k = 1, \ldots, n - 1$.

(i) Define the polynomial $P(x) = \sum_{k=0}^{n-1} \frac{f^{(k)}(a)}{k!}(x-a)^k$, let $M = \frac{f(b)-P(b)}{(b-a)^n}$, and

$$\phi(x) = f(x) - P(x) - M(x-a)^n.$$

Show that $\phi(a) = \phi'(a) = \cdots = \phi^{(n-1)}(a) = 0$ and $\phi^{(n)}(x) = f^{(n)}(x) - n!M$.

(ii) Prove Taylor's theorem.

2.8. For each of the following functions, determine whether it is convex, concave, or neither.

(i) $f(x) = 10x - x^2$,

(ii) $f(x) = x^4 + 6x^2 + 12x$,

(iii) $f(x) = 2x^3 - 3x^2$,

(iv) $f(x) = x^4 + x^2$,

(v) $f(x) = x^3 + x^4$,

(vi) $f(x) = e^x$,

(vii) $f(x) = \log x$ $(x > 0)$,

(viii) $f(x) = x \log x$ $(x > 0)$,

(ix) $f(x) = x^\alpha$, where $\alpha \neq 0$ and $x > 0$. (Hint: there are a few cases to consider.)

2.9. Suppose that you are running a firm that produces an output good using an input good. When the input is x, the output is Ax^α, where $A > 0$ and $\alpha \in (0, 1)$. Suppose that the unit price of the input is c and the unit price of the output is p. Compute the input level that maximizes the profit.

The following two problems ask you to show that a twice-differentiable function is convex if and only if the second derivative is nonnegative.

2.10. Let f be differentiable.

(i) Fix $x \neq y$ and let $g(t) = \frac{f((1-t)x+ty)-f(x)}{t}$, where $t > 0$. For $0 < s < t$, show that

$$g(s) \leq g(t) \iff f((1-s)x + sy) \leq \left(1 - \frac{s}{t}\right) f(x) + \frac{s}{t} f((1-t)x + ty).$$

(ii) Show that the function g is increasing if and only if f is convex.

(iii) Compute $g(1)$ and $\lim_{t \to 0} g(t)$.

(iv) Show that f is convex if and only if

$$f(y) - f(x) \geq f'(x)(y - x)$$

for all x, y.

2.11. Using Taylor's theorem and Problem 2.10, show that a twice continuously differentiable function f is convex if and only if $f''(x) \geq 0$ for all x.

2.12. Prove Proposition 2.5 assuming only that f is differentiable (but not necessarily twice differentiable). (Hint: Problem 2.10.)

2.13. Prove Proposition 2.6.

2.14. Let f be strictly convex. If f has a minimum, show that it is unique. (Hint: assume there are two minima x_1, x_2 and derive a contradiction by using the definition of convexity.)

2.15. Let $p, q > 0$ be numbers such that $1/p + 1/q = 1$.

(i) Fixing $b \geq 0$, define $f(x) = \frac{1}{p}x^p - bx + \frac{1}{q}b^q$ for $x \geq 0$. Show that f is convex.

(ii) For all $a, b \geq 0$, prove Young's inequality

$$\frac{1}{p}a^p + \frac{1}{q}b^q \geq ab.$$

(iii) Let $x, y \in \mathbb{R}^N$. Define $\|x\|_p = \left(\sum_{n=1}^N |x_n|^p\right)^{1/p}$. Prove Hölder's inequality

$$\|x\|_p \|y\|_q \geq \sum_{n=1}^N |x_n y_n|. \tag{2.12}$$

(Hint: set $a = |x_n| / \|x\|_p$, $b = |y_n| / \|y\|_q$ and use Young.)

(iv) Verify that if $p = q = 2$, then Hölder's inequality is equivalent to the Cauchy-Schwarz inequality.

CHAPTER 3

Multi-variable Unconstrained Optimization

3.1 INTRODUCTION

In Chapter 2, we derived necessary or sufficient conditions for the minimization problem

$$\text{minimize} \qquad f(x)$$
$$\text{subject to} \qquad x \in C \qquad \qquad (3.1)$$

to have a solution $\bar{x}$ when f was differentiable and $C \subset \mathbb{R}$. This chapter extends those results when $C \subset \mathbb{R}^N$ but the solution $\bar{x}$ is an interior point of the constraint set C.

Although the extensions are conceptually straightforward, we need to introduce the notion of matrices to make the notation manageable.

3.2 LINEAR MAPS AND MATRICES

Instead of a linear function $f : \mathbb{R}^N \to \mathbb{R}$, consider a *linear map* $f : \mathbb{R}^N \to \mathbb{R}^M$. This means that (i) for each $x \in \mathbb{R}^N$, the map f associates a vector $f(x) \in \mathbb{R}^M$, and (ii) f is linear (preserves addition and scalar multiplication): $f(\alpha x + \beta y) = \alpha f(x) + \beta f(y)$ for all $x, y \in \mathbb{R}^N$ and $\alpha, \beta \in \mathbb{R}$. Let $f_m(x)$ be the m-th entry of f, so $f(x) = (f_1(x), \ldots, f_M(x))$. Then clearly each $f_m(x)$ is a linear function of x, so by Proposition 1.2 we have

$$f_m(x) = a_{m1}x_1 + \cdots + a_{mN}x_N$$

for some numbers $a_{m1}, \ldots, a_{mN}$. Since this is true for any m, a linear map has a one-to-one correspondence with numbers (a_{mn}), where $1 \leq m \leq M$ and

DOI: 10.1201/9781032698953-3

$1 \leq n \leq N$. We write

$$
A = (a_{mn}) = \begin{bmatrix}
a_{11} & \cdots & a_{1n} & \cdots & a_{1N} \\
\vdots & \ddots & \vdots & \ddots & \vdots \\
a_{m1} & \cdots & a_{mn} & \cdots & a_{mN} \\
\vdots & \ddots & \vdots & \ddots & \vdots \\
a_{M1} & \cdots & a_{Mn} & \cdots & a_{MN}
\end{bmatrix}
$$

and call it a *matrix*. For an $M \times N$ matrix A and an N-vector x, we define the M-vector Ax by the vector whose m-th entry is

$$
a_{m1}x_1 + \cdots + a_{mN}x_N.
$$

So $f : \mathbb{R}^N \to \mathbb{R}^M$ defined by $f(x) = Ax$ is a linear map. By defining addition and scalar multiplication entrywise, the set of all $M \times N$ matrices can be identified as $\mathbb{R}^{MN}$, the MN-dimensional Euclidean space. The set of all $M \times N$ matrices is denoted by $\mathbb{R}^{M \times N}$. When a matrix A is $N \times N$, so the corresponding linear map $f(x) = Ax$ maps $\mathbb{R}^N$ to itself, we say that A is a *square matrix*. The null function $f : \mathbb{R}^M \to \mathbb{R}^N$ defined by $f(x) = 0$ for all x is clearly linear. The corresponding matrix A clearly has entries $a_{mn} = 0$ for all m, n. This matrix is called the *null matrix* or *zero matrix* and is denoted by $A = 0_{M,N}$. When the dimension of the zero matrix is clear from the context, we simply write $A = 0$. The identity map id : $\mathbb{R}^N \to \mathbb{R}^N$ defined by $\mathrm{id}(x) = x$ is clearly linear and has a corresponding matrix I. By simple calculation I is square and its diagonal (off-diagonal) entries are all 1 (0). This matrix is called the *identity matrix* and is denoted by I_N. When the dimension is clear from the context, we simply write $A = I$.

Now consider two linear maps $f : \mathbb{R}^N \to \mathbb{R}^M$ and $g : \mathbb{R}^M \to \mathbb{R}^L$. Since f, g are linear, we can find an $M \times N$ matrix $A = (a_{mn})$ and an $L \times M$ matrix $B = (b_{lm})$ such that $f(x) = Ax$ and $g(y) = By$. We can also consider the composition of these two maps, $h = g \circ f$ defined by $h(x) := g(f(x))$. It is easy to see that h is a linear map from $\mathbb{R}^N$ to $\mathbb{R}^L$, and therefore it can be written as $h(x) = Cx$ with an $L \times N$ matrix $C = (c_{ln})$. Using the definition $h(x) = g(f(x)) = B(Ax)$, it is easy to see (Problem 3.1) that

$$
c_{ln} = \sum_{m=1}^{M} b_{lm}a_{mn}. \tag{3.2}
$$

So it makes sense to define the multiplication of matrices $C = BA$ by (3.2). You can use all standard rules of algebra such as $B(A_1 + A_2) = BA_1 + BA_2$, $A(BC) = (AB)C$, etc. The proofs are immediate by carrying out the algebra or thinking about linear maps.

Recall that the inner product of vectors $x = (x_1, \ldots, x_N)$ and $y = (y_1, \ldots, y_N)$ is defined by

$$
\langle x, y \rangle = x_1 y_1 + \cdots + x_N y_N. \tag{3.3}
$$

Using the definition of matrix multiplication and the fact that 1×1 matrices can be identified as real numbers, (3.3) can be written as the product of a $1 \times N$ matrix and an $N \times 1$ matrix

$$\langle x, y \rangle = \begin{bmatrix} x_1 & \cdots & x_N \end{bmatrix} \begin{bmatrix} y_1 \\ \vdots \\ y_N \end{bmatrix}. \tag{3.4}$$

Clearly, an $N \times 1$ matrix can be identified as a vector in $\mathbb{R}^N$. When we do so, we call $y \in \mathbb{R}^N$ a *column vector*.

Let $x = (x_m) \in \mathbb{R}^M$, $y = (y_n) \in \mathbb{R}^N$, and $A = (a_{mn}) \in \mathbb{R}^{M \times N}$. Then by the definition of the inner product and matrix multiplication, we have

$$\langle x, Ay \rangle = \sum_{m=1}^{M} x_m \left(\sum_{n=1}^{N} a_{mn} y_n \right) = \sum_{m=1}^{M} \sum_{n=1}^{N} x_m a_{mn} y_n. \tag{3.5}$$

The right-hand side of (3.5) can also be interpreted as the inner product $\langle A'x, y \rangle$, where $A' := (a_{nm}) \in \mathbb{R}^{N \times M}$. This $N \times M$ matrix A' is called the *transpose* of A and is also denoted by $A^\top$. If we identify an N-vector as an $N \times 1$ matrix and a scalar as a 1×1 matrix, then (3.4) can be written as $\langle x, y \rangle = x'y$. The $1 \times N$ matrix

$$x' = \begin{bmatrix} x_1 & \cdots & x_N \end{bmatrix}$$

is sometimes called the *row vector*. If the matrix product AB is defined, then by definition

$$\langle (AB)'x, y \rangle = \langle x, ABy \rangle = \langle A'x, By \rangle = \langle B'A'x, y \rangle$$

for all vectors x, y, so $(AB)' = B'A'$. In general, when dealing with matrices, to simplify notation, it is important to use these algebraic rules and avoid entrywise calculations as much as possible.

3.3 DIFFERENTIATION

In Chapter 2, we defined the derivative of a one-variable function f by the limit

$$f'(x) = \lim_{h \to 0} \frac{f(x+h) - f(x)}{h}. \tag{3.6}$$

The definition (3.6) is inconvenient for generalizing to multi-variable functions because h would be a vector but the division by a vector is undefined. We thus seek a more general definition. Note that (3.6) implies that

$$f(x+h) - f(x) \approx f'(x)h$$

for small h, so the change in the function value $f(x + h) - f(x)$ when x is perturbed by a small deviation h is approximately a linear function $f'(x)h$ of h. More precisely, (3.6) is equivalent to

$$\lim_{|h| \to 0} \frac{|f(x + h) - f(x) - f'(x)h|}{|h|} = 0.$$

Motivated by these observations, we define differentiation of multi-variable functions as follows. Let $U \subset \mathbb{R}^N$ be open and $f : U \to \mathbb{R}^M$. Equip $\mathbb{R}^N$ and $\mathbb{R}^M$ with some norms, which we simply denote by $\|\cdot\|$ for simplicity. (For instance, $\mathbb{R}^N$ could be equipped with the ℓ^1 norm $\|\cdot\|_1$, whereas $\mathbb{R}^M$ could be equipped with the ℓ^2 norm $\|\cdot\|_2$. The choice of the norm does not matter by Theorem 1.3.) Then we say that f is *differentiable* at $x \in U$ if there exists an $M \times N$ matrix A such that

$$\lim_{\|h\| \to 0} \frac{\|f(x + h) - f(x) - Ah\|}{\|h\|} = 0. \tag{3.7}$$

It is easy to show by a similar argument as Proposition 2.1 that f is continuous if it is differentiable.

Suppose $f : U \to \mathbb{R}^M$ is differentiable at $x \in U$ and let A be as in (3.7). We can characterize the matrix $A = (a_{mn})$ as follows. First, let $h = te_n$, where $t \neq 0$ and e_n is the n-th unit vector of $\mathbb{R}^N$. By considering the sup norm on $\mathbb{R}^M$, for each $m = 1, \dots, M$ the definition of differentiability (3.7) implies that

$$a_{mn} = \frac{\partial f_m}{\partial x_n}(x) := \lim_{t \to 0} \frac{f_m(x_1, \dots, x_n + t, \dots, x_N) - f_m(x)}{t}, \tag{3.8}$$

that is, a_{mn} equals the derivative of f_m with respect to the single variable x_n when we treat other variables $x_1, \dots, x_{n-1}, x_{n+1}, \dots, x_N$ as constants. The quantity $\partial f_m / \partial x_n$ defined by the limit (3.8) is called the (m, n)-th *partial derivative* of f at x. The matrix of partial derivatives $(\partial f_m / \partial x_n)$ is called the *Jacobian* and is denoted by $Df(x)$.

We clarify some notions of the differentiability of multi-variable functions. Let $U \subset \mathbb{R}^N$ be open and $f : U \to \mathbb{R}^M$. By definition, f is differentiable at $x \in U$ if (3.7) holds with $A = Df(x)$. We say that f is *partially differentiable* at x if the limit (3.8) exists for all m, n. Clearly, if f is differentiable, it is partially differentiable, but the converse is generally not true (Problem 3.2). If f is partially differentiable and the partial derivatives are continuous, we say that f is *continuously differentiable* or C^1. If f is C^1, then it is differentiable (Problem 3.3).

3.4   CHAIN RULE

We extend the chain rule $(g(f(x)))' = g'(f(x))f'(x)$ of one-variable functions to multi-variable functions.

Proposition 3.1. *Let $U \subset \mathbb{R}^N$ and $V \subset \mathbb{R}^M$ be open. Let $f : U \to V$ be differentiable at $a \in U$ and $g : V \to \mathbb{R}^L$ be differentiable at $b := f(a) \in V$. Then $g \circ f : U \to \mathbb{R}^L$ defined by $(g \circ f)(x) = g(f(x))$ is differentiable at a and*

$$\underbrace{D(g \circ f)(a)}_{L \times N} = \underbrace{Dg(b)}_{L \times M} \underbrace{Df(a)}_{M \times N}. \tag{3.9}$$

Proof. Let $A = Df(a)$ be the Jacobian of f at a and define

$$\epsilon(h) := f(a + h) - f(a) - Ah$$

for $h \in \mathbb{R}^N$ close enough to 0. By the definition of differentiability (3.7), we have $\epsilon(h)/\|h\| \to 0$ as $h \to 0$. Similarly, if we define $B = Dg(b)$ and

$$\delta(k) := g(b + k) - g(b) - Bk$$

for $k \in \mathbb{R}^M$ close enough to 0, we have $\delta(k)/\|k\| \to 0$ as $k \to 0$.

Letting $k = f(a + h) - f(a)$, we obtain

$$\begin{aligned}
g(f(a + h)) - g(f(a)) &= g(b + k) - g(b) = Bk + \delta(k) \\
&= B(f(a + h) - f(a)) + \delta(f(a + h) - f(a)) \\
&= B(Ah + \epsilon(h)) + \delta(Ah + \epsilon(h)) \\
&= BAh + B\epsilon(h) + \delta(Ah + \epsilon(h)).
\end{aligned}$$

Since ϵ and δ are negligible compared with their arguments, we obtain

$$\frac{(g \circ f)(a + h) - (g \circ f)(b) - BAh}{\|h\|} \to 0$$

as $h \to 0$, so $g \circ f$ is differentiable at $x = a$ and

$$D(g \circ f)(a) = BA = Dg(b)Df(a). \qquad \square$$

To understand the chain rule (3.9), consider the following example. Let g be a real-valued function of two variables, say $g(x_1, x_2)$. Let f be a vector-valued function of one variable, say $f(t) = (f_1(t), f_2(t))$. Since

$$Dg = \begin{bmatrix} \frac{\partial g}{\partial x_1} & \frac{\partial g}{\partial x_2} \end{bmatrix} \quad \text{and} \quad Df = \begin{bmatrix} f_1'(t) \\ f_2'(t) \end{bmatrix},$$

it follows that

$$\frac{d}{dt} g(f_1(t), f_2(t)) = D(g \circ f) = DgDf$$

$$= \begin{bmatrix} \frac{\partial g}{\partial x_1} & \frac{\partial g}{\partial x_2} \end{bmatrix} \begin{bmatrix} f_1'(t) \\ f_2'(t) \end{bmatrix} = \frac{\partial g}{\partial x_1} f_1'(t) + \frac{\partial g}{\partial x_2} f_2'(t).$$

More generally, if f is an M-dimensional function of $x_1, \ldots, x_N$ and g is a real-valued function of $y_1, \ldots, y_M$, we have

$$\frac{\partial(g \circ f)}{\partial x_n} = \sum_{m=1}^{M} \frac{\partial g}{\partial y_m} \frac{\partial f_m}{\partial x_n}.$$

3.5   NECESSARY CONDITION

Let us go back to the minimization problem (3.1). In the one-variable case, the first-order condition was $f'(x) = 0$. We seek to generalize this condition for multi-variable optimization.

If $f : U \to \mathbb{R}$ is partially differentiable, its Jacobian

$$Df(x) = \begin{bmatrix} \frac{\partial f}{\partial x_1} & \cdots & \frac{\partial f}{\partial x_N} \end{bmatrix}$$

is a row vector. Its transpose (which is a column vector) is denoted by

$$\nabla f(x) := Df(x)^\top = \begin{bmatrix} \frac{\partial f}{\partial x_1} \\ \vdots \\ \frac{\partial f}{\partial x_N} \end{bmatrix}$$

and is called the *gradient*. (We read the symbol ∇ "nabla".)

The following proposition extends the first-order necessary condition for one-variable optimization in Proposition 2.2 to multi-variable optimization.

Proposition 3.2 (Necessity of first-order condition). *Consider the minimization problem* (3.1). *If $\bar{x} \in \operatorname{int} C$ is a local solution and f is differentiable at $\bar{x}$, then $\nabla f(\bar{x}) = 0$.*

Proof. Take any $v \in \mathbb{R}^N$ and define $\phi : \mathbb{R} \to \mathbb{R}^N$ by $\phi(t) = \bar{x} + vt$. Since $\bar{x}$ is an interior point of C, the function

$$g(t) := (f \circ \phi)(t) = f(\bar{x} + vt)$$

is well defined for t close enough to 0. Since $\bar{x}$ is a local solution to the minimization problem (3.1), clearly $t = 0$ is a local minimum of g. By Proposition 2.2, the chain rule, and the definition of the gradient, we obtain

$$0 = g'(0) = Df(\bar{x})v = \langle \nabla f(\bar{x}), v \rangle .$$

Since $v \in \mathbb{R}^N$ is arbitrary, we obtain $\nabla f(\bar{x}) = 0$.   □

PROBLEMS

3.1. Let $f : \mathbb{R}^N \to \mathbb{R}^M$ and $g : \mathbb{R}^M \to \mathbb{R}^L$ be linear and define $h = g \circ f$ to be their composition, which is linear. Let $A = (a_{mn})$, $B = (b_{lm})$, and $C = (c_{ln})$ be the matrix representations of f, g, h. Prove that

$$c_{ln} = \sum_{m=1}^{M} b_{lm} a_{mn}.$$

3.2. Define $f : \mathbb{R}^2 \to \mathbb{R}$ by

$$f(x_1, x_2) = \begin{cases} \frac{x_1^2 x_2}{x_1^4 + x_2^2}, & (x_1, x_2) \neq (0,0) \\ 0. & (x_1, x_2) = (0,0) \end{cases}$$

(i) Using the definition, compute the partial derivatives of f at $x = 0$.

(ii) Show that f is partially differentiable at any $x \in \mathbb{R}^2$.

(iii) Show that f is not differentiable at $x = 0$.

3.3. Let $f : \mathbb{R}^2 \to \mathbb{R}$ be a C^1 function (i.e., partially differentiable and the partial derivatives are continuous). Fix (a_1, a_2).

(i) Using the one-variable mean value theorem, show that there exist numbers $0 < \theta_1, \theta_2 < 1$ such that

$$f(a_1 + h_1, a_2 + h_2) - f(a_1, a_2)$$
$$= \frac{\partial f}{\partial x_1}(a_1 + \theta_1 h_1, a_2 + h_2)h_1 + \frac{\partial f}{\partial x_2}(a_1, a_2 + \theta_2 h_2)h_2.$$

(Hint: subtract and add $f(a_1, a_2 + h_2)$ from/to the left-hand side.)

(ii) Let
$$\epsilon(h) = f(a + h) - f(a) - \langle \nabla f(a), h \rangle,$$
where $a = (a_1, a_2)$ and $h = (h_1, h_2)$. Prove that $\epsilon(h)/\|h\| \to 0$ as $h \to 0$.

(iii) Prove that if $U \subset \mathbb{R}^N$ is open and $f : U \to \mathbb{R}$ is C^1, then it is differentiable.

3.4. Compute the partial derivatives and the gradient of the following functions.

(i) $f(x_1, x_2) = a_1 x_1 + a_2 x_2$, where a_1, a_2 are constants.

(ii) $f(x_1, x_2) = ax_1^2 + 2bx_1 x_2 + cx_2^2$, where a, b, c are constants.

(iii) $f(x_1, x_2) = x_1 x_2$.

(iv) $f(x_1, x_2) = x_1 \log x_2$, where $x_2 > 0$.

3.5. Compute the gradient of the following functions.

(i) $f(x) = \langle a, x \rangle$, where a, x are vectors of the same dimensions.

(ii) $f(x) = \langle x, Ax \rangle$, where A is a square matrix of the same dimension as the vector x.

3.6. Make the proof of Proposition 3.1 more rigorous.

3.7 (Least squares). Suppose that you would like to "explain" some quantity y (say the earnings of an individual) from other quantities $x = (x_1, \dots, x_N)$ (say a constant term, schooling, and job experience). You have a linear model

$$y = \beta_1 x_1 + \cdots + \beta_N x_N = x'\beta,$$

where $\beta = (\beta_1, \ldots, \beta_N)$ is the vector of coefficients. You have some data $\{(y_i, x_i)\}_{i=1}^{I}$, where $y_i \in \mathbb{R}$ and $x_i \in \mathbb{R}^N$ for each i. To determine the coefficient vector β, suppose you would like to minimize the sum of squared residuals

$$f(\beta) := \sum_{i=1}^{I}(y_i - x_i'\beta)^2.$$

(i) Define the vector $\mathbf{y} \in \mathbb{R}^I$ by $\mathbf{y} = (y_1, \ldots, y_I)$ and the matrix $\mathbf{X} \in \mathbb{R}^{I \times N}$ by $\mathbf{X} = (x_{in})$, where $x_i = (x_{i1}, \ldots, x_{iN})$. Show that

$$f(\beta) = \|\mathbf{y} - \mathbf{X}\beta\|^2,$$

where $\|\cdot\|$ denotes the ℓ^2 (Euclidean) norm.

(ii) Using the definition of the inner product and the transpose, show that

$$f(\beta) = \langle \mathbf{y}, \mathbf{y} \rangle - 2\langle \mathbf{X}'\mathbf{y}, \beta \rangle + \langle \beta, \mathbf{X}'\mathbf{X}\beta \rangle.$$

(iii) You would like to solve the problem

$$\min_{\beta \in \mathbb{R}^N} f(\beta).$$

Derive the first-order condition for optimality using only $\mathbf{y}$, $\mathbf{X}$, and β. (Avoid entrywise calculation!)

CHAPTER 4

Introduction to Constrained Optimization

4.1 INTRODUCTION

In Chapter 3, we derived a necessary condition for $\bar{x}$ to be a solution to the minimization problem

$$\begin{aligned}
\text{minimize} \quad & f(x) \\
\text{subject to} \quad & x \in C.
\end{aligned} \qquad (4.1)$$

The main result (Proposition 3.2) was that if $\bar{x}$ is an interior point of the constraint set C, the gradient of f must be zero: $\nabla f(\bar{x}) = 0$.

This necessary condition for characterizing the solution is unsatisfactory because, in many problems, the solution would not be an interior point of the constraint set. Consider, for example, the utility maximization problem discussed in Chapter 0:

$$\begin{aligned}
\text{maximize} \quad & u(x_1, \ldots, x_N) & (4.2\text{a}) \\
\text{subject to} \quad & p_1 x_1 + \cdots + p_N x_N \leq w, & (4.2\text{b}) \\
& (\forall n) x_n \geq 0. & (4.2\text{c})
\end{aligned}$$

Here u in (4.2a) denotes the utility function of the agent, $p_n > 0$ denotes the unit price of the good n, and $x_n \geq 0$ is the quantity of good n that the agent wishes to consume. The condition (4.2b) is the budget constraint. The constraint set is thus

$$C = \left\{ x \in \mathbb{R}_+^N : \langle p, x \rangle \leq w \right\},$$

where $\mathbb{R}_+^N = \left\{ x = (x_1, \ldots, x_N) \in \mathbb{R}^N : (\forall n) x_n \geq 0 \right\}$ denotes the nonnegative orthant of $\mathbb{R}^N$ and $p = (p_1, \ldots, p_N)$ denotes the price vector. In a typical situation where the agent likes all goods (i.e., the utility function u is strictly increasing in each argument), at the maximum $\bar{x}$ the agent will exhaust the budget, so $\langle p, \bar{x} \rangle = w$. To see this, if $\langle p, \bar{x} \rangle < w$, the agent can increase utility by increasing the consumption of some good slightly without violating the budget constraint, which contradicts optimality. Thus the solution $\bar{x}$ satisfies $\langle p, \bar{x} \rangle = w$, so $\bar{x}$ is on the boundary of the constraint set C.

In this chapter we derive necessary conditions for a solution to the optimization problem (4.1) when the constraint set C is given by linear inequalities as in (4.2b) and (4.2c). We make the discussion in this chapter intuitive at the expense of mathematical rigor. We shall obtain more general and rigorous results in Chapter 12.

4.2 ONE LINEAR CONSTRAINT

To build intuition, we start the discussion of constrained optimization from the simplest case, namely when there is a single linear constraint.

Consider the minimization problem with one linear constraint

$$
\begin{aligned}
&\text{minimize} &&f(x)\\
&\text{subject to} &&\langle a, x \rangle \le c,
\end{aligned}
$$

where $f : \mathbb{R}^N \to \mathbb{R}$ is differentiable, $a \in \mathbb{R}^N$ is a nonzero vector, and $c \in \mathbb{R}$ is a constant. Suppose a solution $\bar{x}$ exists. The goal is to derive a necessary condition for $\bar{x}$.

Define the constraint set by

$$ C = \left\{ x \in \mathbb{R}^N : \langle a, x \rangle \le c \right\}. $$

If $\langle a, \bar{x} \rangle < c$, so the constraint does not *bind* or is *inactive*, then $\bar{x}$ is an interior point of C and $\bar{x}$ is a local solution. Hence by Proposition 3.2 a necessary condition is $\nabla f(\bar{x}) = 0$. If $\langle a, \bar{x} \rangle = c$, so the constraint *binds* or is *active*, then the situation is more complicated. The boundary of C is the hyperplane $\langle a, x \rangle = c$. Figure 4.1 shows the constraint set C, the solution $\bar{x}$, and the vector a. Note that by assumption $\langle a, \bar{x} \rangle = c$. Hence if x is a boundary point of C, then $\langle a, x \rangle = c$, so $\langle a, x - \bar{x} \rangle = 0$. Therefore a is perpendicular to the boundary of C.

Consider moving toward the direction v from the solution $\bar{x}$. Since $\bar{x}$ is on the boundary, we have $\langle a, \bar{x} \rangle = c$. The point $x = \bar{x} + tv$ (where $t > 0$ is small) is feasible (belongs to the constraint set C) if and only if

$$ \langle a, \bar{x} + tv \rangle \le c = \langle a, \bar{x} \rangle \iff \langle a, v \rangle \le 0, \tag{4.3} $$

that is, the vectors a, v form an obtuse angle as in Figure 4.1. Since $\bar{x}$ is a solution, we have $f(\bar{x} + tv) \ge f(\bar{x})$ for small enough $t > 0$. Therefore applying the chain rule (Proposition 3.1), we obtain

$$ 0 \le \lim_{t \downarrow 0} \frac{f(\bar{x} + tv) - f(\bar{x})}{t} = \langle \nabla f(\bar{x}), v \rangle \iff \langle -\nabla f(\bar{x}), v \rangle \le 0. \tag{4.4} $$

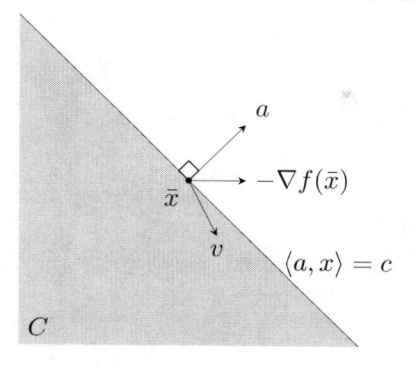

FIGURE 4.1: Gradient and feasible direction.

(The derivative in (4.4) is called the *directional derivative* or the *Gâteaux derivative* of f in the direction v.) The necessary condition (4.4) implies that the vectors $-\nabla f(\bar{x})$ and v form an obtuse angle. Therefore we obtain the following general principle for optimality:

> *If a and v form an obtuse angle, then so do $-\nabla f(\bar{x})$ and v.*   (4.5)

In Figure 4.1, the angle between $-\nabla f(\bar{x})$ and v is acute, so the principle (4.5) is violated.

The only case that $-\nabla f(\bar{x})$ and v form an obtuse angle whenever a and v do so is when $-\nabla f(\bar{x})$ and a point to the same direction, as in Figure 4.2. Therefore if $\bar{x}$ is a solution, there must be a number $\lambda \geq 0$ such that

$$-\nabla f(\bar{x}) = \lambda a \iff \nabla f(\bar{x}) + \lambda a = 0.$$

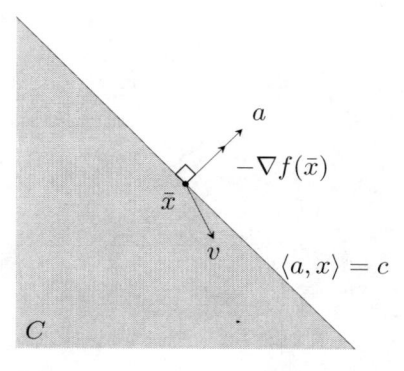

FIGURE 4.2: Necessary condition for optimality.

In the discussion above, we considered the cases in which the constraint binds (is active) or not, but the inactive case ($\nabla f(\bar{x}) = 0$) is a special case of the active case ($\nabla f(\bar{x})+\lambda a = 0$) by setting $\lambda = 0$. Therefore we can summarize the necessary condition for optimality as in the following proposition.

Proposition 4.1. *Consider the optimization problem*

$$\begin{array}{ll} \text{minimize} & f(x) \\ \text{subject to} & \langle a, x \rangle \leq c, \end{array}$$

where $f : \mathbb{R}^N \to \mathbb{R}$ *is differentiable,* $0 \neq a \in \mathbb{R}^N$, *and* $c \in \mathbb{R}$. *If* $\bar{x}$ *is a local solution, then there exists* $\lambda \geq 0$ *such that*

$$\nabla f(\bar{x}) + \lambda a = 0.$$

4.3   MULTIPLE LINEAR CONSTRAINTS

We next consider the optimization problem

$$\begin{array}{ll} \text{minimize} & f(x) \\ \text{subject to} & \langle a_1, x \rangle \leq c_1, \\ & \langle a_2, x \rangle \leq c_2, \end{array}$$

where f is differentiable, a_1, a_2 are nonzero vectors, and c_1, c_2 are constants. Let $\bar{x}$ be a solution and C be the constraint set

$$C = \{x : g_1(x) \leq 0, g_2(x) \leq 0\},$$

where $g_i(x) = \langle a_i, x \rangle - c_i$ for $i = 1, 2$. Functions of this form (linear plus a constant) are called *affine*. Assume that both constraints are active at the solution. Figure 4.3 shows the situation.

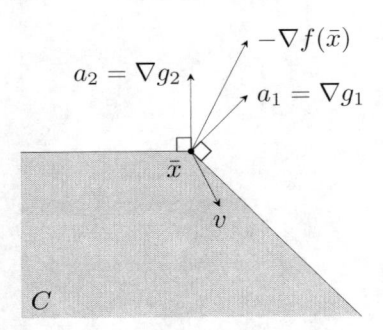

FIGURE 4.3: Gradient and feasible direction.

In general, the vector v is called a *feasible direction* if we can move a little bit toward the direction v from the point $\bar{x}$, so $\bar{x} + tv \in C$ for small enough $t > 0$. In our case, by (4.3), v is a feasible direction if $\langle a_i, v \rangle \leq 0$ for $i = 1, 2$. If v is a feasible direction and $\bar{x}$ is the minimum of f, the necessary condition

(4.4) is still valid. By looking at Figure 4.3, in order for $\bar{x}$ to be the minimum, it is necessary that $-\nabla f(\bar{x})$ lies between the vectors a_1 and a_2. This is true if and only if there are numbers $\lambda_1, \lambda_2 \geq 0$ such that

$$-\nabla f(\bar{x}) = \lambda_1 a_1 + \lambda_2 a_2 \iff \nabla f(\bar{x}) + \lambda_1 \nabla g_1(\bar{x}) + \lambda_2 \nabla g_2(\bar{x}) = 0.$$

Although we have assumed that both constraints bind, this equation is true even if one (or both) of them does not bind by setting $\lambda_1 = 0$ and/or $\lambda_2 = 0$.

4.4 KARUSH-KUHN-TUCKER THEOREM

It is clear that the preceding argument holds for arbitrarily many linear constraints. Therefore we obtain the following general theorem.

Theorem 4.2 (Karush-Kuhn-Tucker theorem with linear constraints). *Consider the optimization problem*

$$\begin{aligned} &\text{minimize} && f(x) \\ &\text{subject to} && g_i(x) \leq 0 && (i = 1, \ldots, I), \end{aligned}$$

where f is differentiable and $g_i(x) = \langle a_i, x \rangle - c_i$ is affine with $a_i \neq 0$. If $\bar{x}$ is a local solution, then there exist $\lambda_1, \ldots, \lambda_I$ such that

$$\nabla f(\bar{x}) + \sum_{i=1}^{I} \lambda_i \nabla g_i(\bar{x}) = 0, \tag{4.6a}$$

$$(\forall i)\ \lambda_i \geq 0,\ g_i(\bar{x}) \leq 0,\ \lambda_i g_i(\bar{x}) = 0. \tag{4.6b}$$

Condition (4.6a) is called the *first-order condition*. Its interpretation is that at the minimum $\bar{x}$, the negative of the gradient $-\nabla f(\bar{x})$ must lie between all the normal vectors $a_i = \nabla g_i(\bar{x})$ corresponding to the active constraints (Figure 4.3). Condition (4.6b) is called the *complementary slackness condition*. The first-order and complementary slackness conditions are jointly called the *Karush-Kuhn-Tucker (KKT) conditions*. The numbers $\lambda_1, \ldots, \lambda_I$ in (4.6) are called *Lagrange multipliers*. The condition $\lambda_i \geq 0$ says that the Lagrange multiplier is nonnegative, and $g_i(\bar{x}) \leq 0$ says that the constraint is satisfied, which are not new. The condition $\lambda_i g_i(\bar{x}) = 0$ takes care of both the active (binding) and inactive (non-binding) cases. If the constraint i is active, then $g_i(\bar{x}) = 0$, so we have $\lambda_i g_i(\bar{x}) = 0$ automatically. If the constraint i is inactive, we have $\lambda_i = 0$, so again $\lambda_i g_i(\bar{x}) = 0$ automatically.

An easy way to remember the first-order condition (4.6a) is as follows. Given the objective function $f(x)$ and the constraints $g_i(x) \leq 0$, define the *Lagrangian*

$$L(x, \lambda) = f(x) + \sum_{i=1}^{I} \lambda_i g_i(x),$$

where $\lambda = (\lambda_1, \ldots, \lambda_I)$. The Lagrangian is the sum of the objective function $f(x)$ and the constraint functions $g_i(x)$ weighted by the Lagrange multipliers

λ_i. Pretend that λ is constant and you want to minimize $L(x, \lambda)$ with respect to x without any constraints. Then the first-order condition is

$$0 = \nabla L(x, \lambda) = \nabla f(x) + \sum_{i=1}^{I} \lambda_i \nabla g_i(x),$$

which is exactly (4.6a).

William Karush (1917-1997)

A version of Theorem 4.2 appeared in the 1939 master's thesis of William Karush (1917-1997) but received no attention. (Applied mathematics gained respect only after proving its usefulness during World War II.) The theorem became widely known after its rediscovery by Harold Kuhn (1925-2014) and Albert Tucker (1905-1995) in a conference paper in 1950. For this reason (and perhaps because Karush was a teaching professor at California State University whereas Kuhn and Tucker were research professors at Princeton), the KKT theorem is often called the "Kuhn-Tucker theorem". Obviously, we should give credit to Karush. See Kjeldsen (2000) for an interesting historical discussion.

4.5 INEQUALITY AND EQUALITY CONSTRAINTS

So far we have considered the case when all constraints are inequalities, but what if there are also equations? For example, consider the optimization problem

$$\begin{aligned}
&\text{minimize} && f(x) \\
&\text{subject to} && \langle a, x \rangle \le c, \\
& && \langle b, x \rangle = d,
\end{aligned}$$

where f is differentiable, a, b are nonzero vectors, and c, d are constants. We derive a necessary condition for optimality by turning this problem into one with only inequality constraints. Note that $\langle b, x \rangle = d$ is equivalent to $\langle b, x \rangle \le d$ and $\langle b, x \rangle \ge d$. Furthermore, $\langle b, x \rangle \ge d$ is equivalent to $\langle -b, x \rangle \le -d$. Therefore the problem is equivalent to:

$$\begin{aligned}
&\text{minimize} && f(x) \\
&\text{subject to} && \langle a, x \rangle - c \le 0, \\
& && \langle b, x \rangle - d \le 0, \\
& && \langle -b, x \rangle + d \le 0.
\end{aligned}$$

Setting $g_1(x) = \langle a, x \rangle - c$, $g_2(x) = \langle b, x \rangle - d$, and $g_3(x) = \langle -b, x \rangle + d$, this problem is exactly the form in Theorem 4.2. Therefore if $\bar{x}$ is a solution, there exist Lagrange multipliers $\lambda_1, \lambda_2, \lambda_3 \geq 0$ such that

$$\nabla f(\bar{x}) + \lambda_1 \nabla g_1(\bar{x}) + \lambda_2 \nabla g_2(\bar{x}) + \lambda_3 \nabla g_3(\bar{x}) = 0.$$

Substituting $\nabla g_i(\bar{x})$'s, we obtain

$$\nabla f(\bar{x}) + \lambda_1 a + \lambda_2 b + \lambda_3(-b) = 0.$$

Letting $\lambda = \lambda_1$ and $\mu = \lambda_2 - \lambda_3$, we obtain

$$\nabla f(\bar{x}) + \lambda a + \mu b = 0.$$

This equation is similar to the KKT condition (4.6), except that μ can be positive or negative. In general, we obtain the following theorem.

Theorem 4.3 (Karush-Kuhn-Tucker theorem with linear constraints). *Consider the optimization problem*

$$
\begin{aligned}
\text{minimize} \quad & f(x) \\
\text{subject to} \quad & g_i(x) \leq 0 && (i = 1, \ldots, I), \\
& h_j(x) = 0 && (j = 1, \ldots, J),
\end{aligned}
$$

where f is differentiable and $g_i(x) = \langle a_i, x \rangle - c_i$ and $h_j(x) = \langle b_j, x \rangle - d_j$ are affine with $a_i, b_j \neq 0$. If $\bar{x}$ is a local solution, then there exist Lagrange multipliers $\lambda_1, \ldots, \lambda_I$ and $\mu_1, \ldots, \mu_J$ such that

$$\nabla f(\bar{x}) + \sum_{i=1}^{I} \lambda_i \nabla g_i(\bar{x}) + \sum_{j=1}^{J} \mu_j \nabla h_j(\bar{x}) = 0, \tag{4.7a}$$

$$(\forall i) \; \lambda_i \geq 0, \; g_i(\bar{x}) \leq 0, \; \lambda_i g_i(\bar{x}) = 0, \tag{4.7b}$$

$$(\forall j) \; h_j(\bar{x}) = 0. \tag{4.7c}$$

An easy way to remember the KKT conditions (4.7) is as follows. As in the case with only inequality constraints, define the Lagrangian

$$L(x, \lambda, \mu) = f(x) + \sum_{i=1}^{I} \lambda_i g_i(x) + \sum_{j=1}^{J} \mu_j h_j(x).$$

Pretend that λ, μ are constants and you want to minimize L with respect to x. The first-order condition is $\nabla_x L(x, \lambda, \mu) = 0$, which is exactly (4.7a). The complementary slackness condition (4.7b) is the same as in the case with only inequality constraints. The new condition (4.7c) merely says that the solution $\bar{x}$ must satisfy the equality constraints $h_j(x) = 0$.

4.6   CONSTRAINED MAXIMIZATION

We briefly discuss maximization. Although maximization is equivalent to minimization by flipping the sign of the objective function, doing so every time is inefficient. So consider the maximization problem

$$
\begin{aligned}
&\text{maximize} && f(x) \\
&\text{subject to} && g_i(x) \geq 0 && (i = 1, \dots, I),
\end{aligned}
\qquad (4.8)
$$

where f is differentiable and g_i's are affine. Then (4.8) is equivalent to the minimization problem

$$
\begin{aligned}
&\text{minimize} && -f(x) \\
&\text{subject to} && -g_i(x) \leq 0 && (i = 1, \dots, I).
\end{aligned}
$$

Applying the KKT theorem 4.2, the necessary condition for optimality is

$$
-\nabla f(\bar{x}) - \sum_{i=1}^{I} \lambda_i \nabla g_i(\bar{x}) = 0, \qquad (4.9a)
$$

$$
(\forall i)\ \lambda_i(-g_i(\bar{x})) = 0. \qquad (4.9b)
$$

Obviously, (4.9) is equivalent to (4.6) by multiplying all terms by (-1). For this reason, it is customary to formulate a maximization problem as in (4.8) so that the inequality constraints are always "greater than or equal to zero".

Tips for formulating constrained optimization problems

- For minimization problems, use the format

$$
\begin{aligned}
&\text{minimize} && f(x) \\
&\text{subject to} && g(x) \leq 0.
\end{aligned}
$$

- For maximization problems, use the format

$$
\begin{aligned}
&\text{maximize} && f(x) \\
&\text{subject to} && g(x) \geq 0.
\end{aligned}
$$

- In either case, the Lagrangian is $L(x, \lambda) = f(x) + \lambda g(x)$ with $\lambda \geq 0$.

- First-order condition is $\nabla_x L(x, \lambda) = 0$.

To illustrate how to use the KKT theorem, we provide an example with a step-by-step analysis.

Example 4.1. Consider the utility maximization problem (4.2) with two goods ($N = 2$). Suppose the utility function $u : \mathbb{R}^2_+ \to [-\infty, \infty)$ is

$$u(x) = \alpha \log x_1 + (1 - \alpha) \log x_2, \tag{4.10}$$

where $0 < \alpha < 1$ and $x_1, x_2 \geq 0$ are consumption of goods 1 and 2. (The logarithmic utility function (4.10) is called a *Cobb-Douglas* utility function.) Let $p_1, p_2 > 0$ be the price of each good and $w > 0$ be the wealth. By convention, we define $\log 0 = -\infty$. The consumer's utility maximization problem (UMP) is

$$\begin{aligned} \text{maximize} \quad & \alpha \log x_1 + (1 - \alpha) \log x_2 \\ \text{subject to} \quad & p_1 x_1 + p_2 x_2 \leq w, \\ & x_1 \geq 0, x_2 \geq 0. \end{aligned}$$

Step 1. Existence of a solution.

Define the constraint set by

$$C = \left\{ (x_1, x_2) \in \mathbb{R}^2 : p_1 x_1 + p_2 x_2 \leq w, x_1 \geq 0, x_2 \geq 0 \right\}.$$

Since $p_1, p_2, w > 0$, it is easy to show that C is nonempty, closed, and bounded. The objective function u is continuous. Therefore by the extreme value theorem (Theorem 1.11), u achieves a maximum $\bar{x} = (\bar{x}_1, \bar{x}_2)$.

Step 2. Application of KKT theorem.

If $\bar{x}_n = 0$ for some n, then $u(\bar{x}) = -\infty$, which is clearly not an optimum. Therefore $\bar{x}_n > 0$ for all n. Since u is differentiable on the set $\mathbb{R}^2_{++} = \{ x = (x_1, x_2) \in \mathbb{R}^2 : x_1 > 0, x_2 > 0 \}$, we can apply the KKT theorem. To this end, rewrite the optimization problem as

$$\begin{aligned} \text{maximize} \quad & \alpha \log x_1 + (1 - \alpha) \log x_2 \\ \text{subject to} \quad & w - p_1 x_1 - p_2 x_2 \geq 0, \\ & x_1 \geq 0, \\ & x_2 \geq 0. \end{aligned}$$

Step 3. Derivation of KKT conditions.

Define the Lagrangian by

$$L(x, \lambda, \mu) = \alpha \log x_1 + (1 - \alpha) \log x_2 + \lambda(w - p_1 x_1 - p_2 x_2) + \mu_1 x_1 + \mu_2 x_2,$$

where $\lambda \geq 0$ is the Lagrange multiplier corresponding to the budget constraint and $\mu_n \geq 0$ is the Lagrange multiplier corresponding to the nonnegativity constraint $x_n \geq 0$ for $n = 1, 2$. The first-order conditions are

$$0 = \frac{\partial L}{\partial x_1} = \frac{\alpha}{x_1} - \lambda p_1 + \mu_1,$$

$$0 = \frac{\partial L}{\partial x_2} = \frac{1 - \alpha}{x_2} - \lambda p_2 + \mu_2.$$

The complementary slackness conditions are

$$\lambda(w - p_1 x_1 - p_2 x_2) = 0,$$
$$\mu_1 x_1 = 0,$$
$$\mu_2 x_2 = 0.$$

Step 4. Derivation of the solution.

Since the solution satisfies $x_1, x_2 > 0$, by complementary slackness we obtain $\mu_1 = \mu_2 = 0$. Then by the first-order condition we get $x_1 = \frac{\alpha}{\lambda p_1}$, $x_2 = \frac{1-\alpha}{\lambda p_2}$, so $\lambda > 0$ and hence $p_1 x_1 + p_2 x_2 = w$. Substituting the expressions for x_1, x_2 into $p_1 x_1 + p_2 x_2 = w$, we obtain

$$\frac{\alpha}{\lambda} + \frac{1-\alpha}{\lambda} = w \iff \lambda = \frac{1}{w}.$$

Therefore

$$(x_1, x_2) = \left(\frac{\alpha w}{p_1}, \frac{(1-\alpha)w}{p_2} \right).$$

Since we know that a solution exists, and we reached a unique candidate by using only necessary conditions, this x must be the unique solution.

4.7 DROPPING NONNEGATIVITY CONSTRAINTS

In many economic applications such as the utility maximization problem in Example 4.1, some of the constraints are nonnegative constraints: $x \geq 0$. In Example 4.1, we used the fact $\log 0 = -\infty$ to rule out solutions of the form $x_1 = 0$ or $x_2 = 0$. The following proposition provides a more general sufficient condition for dropping nonnegativity constraints.

Proposition 4.4. *Consider the minimization problem* (4.1), *where* $f : \mathbb{R}^N_+ \to (-\infty, \infty]$ *is continuous and* $C \subset \mathbb{R}^N_+$. *Suppose that*

(i) C is a convex set, so $x_1, x_2 \in C$ and $t \in [0,1]$ imply $(1-t)x_1 + tx_2 \in C$; furthermore, there exists $x_0 \gg 0$ such that $x_0 \in C$,

(ii) f is differentiable on $\mathbb{R}^N_{++}$ with partial derivatives that are uniformly bounded above, so there exists $b \geq 0$ such that $\max_n \sup_{x \in C} \frac{\partial f}{\partial x_n} \leq b$,

(iii) f satisfies the Inada condition *with respect to x_n, so*

$$\lim_{y \to x} \frac{\partial f}{\partial x_n}(y) = -\infty \qquad (4.11)$$

whenever $x = (x_1, \ldots, x_N)$ satisfies $x_n = 0$.

If $\bar{x} \in C$ is a solution, then $\bar{x}_n > 0$.

Proof. Suppose $\bar{x} \in C$ is a solution to the minimization problem (4.1). Since C is convex and $x_0 \in C$, we may define $g : [0,1] \to (-\infty, \infty]$ by $g(t) = f(x(t))$, where $x(t) := (1-t)\bar{x} + tx_0$. By assumption, g is continuous on $[0,1]$ and differentiable on $(0,1]$. Applying the chain rule and using the uniform boundedness of partial derivatives, for $t \in (0,1]$ we obtain

$$g'(t) = \sum_{n=1}^{N} \frac{\partial f}{\partial x_n}(x(t))(x_{0n} - \bar{x}_n)$$

$$\leq \frac{\partial f}{\partial x_n}(x(t))(x_{0n} - \bar{x}_n) + (N-1)b\,\|x_0 - \bar{x}\|, \qquad (4.12)$$

where the norm denotes the supremum (l^∞) norm.

Suppose to the contrary that $\bar{x}_n = 0$. Then $x_{0n} - \bar{x}_n > 0$, so letting $t \downarrow 0$ in (4.12) and using the Inada condition (4.11), we obtain $\lim_{t \downarrow 0} g'(t) = -\infty$. In particular, $g'(t) < 0$ for sufficiently small t. Since $\bar{x}$ is a solution, we have

$$-\infty < g(0) = f(\bar{x}) \leq f(x_0) < \infty.$$

By the mean value theorem (Proposition 2.3), we can take $s \in (0,t)$ such that

$$g(t) - g(0) = g'(s)(t - 0) = g'(s)t < 0 \implies f(x(t)) = g(t) < g(0) = f(\bar{x}),$$

which is a contradiction because $\bar{x}$ is a solution. □

Remark. The condition of the form (4.11) was introduced by Inada (1963) to rule out corner solutions. If the Inada condition holds, because the nonnegativity constraint does not bind, the corresponding Lagrange multiplier must be zero. Therefore we may drop terms from the Lagrangian corresponding to these constraints outright, which significantly simplifies the analysis. (See Problem 4.2 as an application.)

PROBLEMS

4.1. Consider a consumer with utility function

$$u(x) = \sum_{n=1}^{N} \alpha_n \log x_n,$$

where $\alpha_n > 0$, $\sum_{n=1}^{N} \alpha_n = 1$, and $x_n \geq 0$ is the consumption of good n. Let $p = (p_1, \ldots, p_N)$ be a price vector with $p_n > 0$ and $w > 0$ be the wealth.

(i) Formulate the consumer's utility maximization problem.

(ii) Compute the solution.

4.2. Solve the same problem as above for the case

$$u(x) = \sum_{n=1}^{N} \alpha_n \frac{x_n^{1-\gamma}}{1-\gamma},$$

where $0 < \gamma \neq 1$.

II

Matrix and Nonlinear Analysis

CHAPTER 5

Vector Space, Matrix, and Determinant

5.1 INTRODUCTION

When dealing with the calculus of functions with multiple variables, linear algebra becomes indispensable. We have already encountered some of the results in Chapters 1 and 3. The next few chapters cover additional results and related topics that will be subsequently applied. Because linear algebra itself is not the main goal of this book, the treatment is not comprehensive. Jänich (1994) and Axler (2024) cover basic topics with proofs, while Lax (2007) focuses more on the analytical aspects.

5.2 VECTOR SPACE

Roughly speaking, a *linear space* (more commonly *vector space*) is a set on which addition and scalar multiplication are defined. Thus if V is a vector space, for each vector $v, w \in \mathsf{V}$, there corresponds the sum $v + w \in \mathsf{V}$, and for each $v \in \mathsf{V}$ and scalar α, there corresponds the scalar multiplication $\alpha v \in \mathsf{V}$. By "scalar", for practical purposes, we use either the set of real numbers $\mathbb{R}$ or the set of complex numbers $\mathbb{C}$. Unless otherwise stated, the scalar field is $\mathbb{R}$. We omit the precise axioms as they are well known.

A typical example of a vector space is the N-dimensional Euclidean space $\mathbb{R}^N$ defined in Chapter 1. Other examples are

$$\mathsf{V}_1 := \{v : \mathbb{R} \to \mathbb{R} : v \text{ is a continuous function}\}, \tag{5.1a}$$

$$\mathsf{V}_2 := \{v : \mathbb{R} \to \mathbb{R} : v \text{ is a bounded continuous function}\}, \tag{5.1b}$$

$$\mathsf{V}_3 := \{v : \mathbb{R} \to \mathbb{R} : v \text{ is a polynomial}\}, \tag{5.1c}$$

$$\mathsf{V}_4 := \{v : \mathbb{R} \to \mathbb{R} : v \text{ is a polynomial of degree} \leq N - 1\}, \tag{5.1d}$$

etc., where addition and scalar multiplication of functions are defined pointwise. If the subset $\mathsf{W} \subset \mathsf{V}$ is itself a vector space, we say that W is a *subspace*

DOI: 10.1201/9781032698953-5

of V. Obviously, in (5.1), V_2, V_3 are subspaces of V_1 and V_4 is a subspace of V_3.

Let V be a vector space, $v_1, \ldots, v_K \in V$, and $\alpha_1, \ldots, \alpha_K \in \mathbb{R}$. Then the vector

$$v := \alpha_1 v_1 + \cdots + \alpha_K v_K = \sum_{k=1}^{K} \alpha_k v_k \in V$$

is called a *linear combination* of $\{v_k\}$ with coefficients $\{\alpha_k\}$. The set

$$\mathrm{span}[v_1, \ldots, v_K] := \left\{ v = \sum_{k=1}^{K} \alpha_k v_k : (\forall k)\alpha_k \in \mathbb{R} \right\}$$

is called the *span* of $\{v_k\}$, which is clearly a subspace of V. When $\mathrm{span}[v_1, \ldots, v_K] = V$, that is, if any $v \in V$ can be expressed as a linear combination of $\{v_k\}$, we say that $\{v_k\}$ *spans* V. If V has a finite set of vectors $\{v_k\}$ that spans V, we say that V is *finite-dimensional*. Otherwise, we say that V is *infinite-dimensional*. Clearly, $\mathbb{R}^N$ is finite-dimensional because it can be spanned by the unit vectors $\{e_n\}_{n=1}^{N}$ defined by $e_n = (0, \ldots, 1, \ldots, 0)$. In contrast, the spaces V_1, V_2, V_3 in (5.1) are infinite-dimensional.

We say that the set of vectors $\{v_k\}$ is *linearly dependent* (or the vectors are linearly dependent) if there exists $0 \neq \alpha = (\alpha_k) \in \mathbb{R}^K$ such that $\sum_{k=1}^{K} \alpha_k v_k = 0$, that is, there is a nontrivial linear combination that generates 0. Otherwise, we say that $\{v_k\}$ is *linearly independent*. By definition, if $\{v_k\}$ is linearly independent, then $\sum_{k=1}^{K} \alpha_k v_k = 0$ implies $\alpha_k = 0$ for all k. If $\{v_k\}_{k=1}^{K}$ is linearly independent and spans V, we say that $\{v_k\}$ is a *basis* of V. Then we say that the *dimension* of V is K and write $\dim V = K$. Clearly $\dim \mathbb{R}^N = N$. In (5.1), any $v \in V_4$ can be uniquely expressed as

$$v(x) = \sum_{n=1}^{N} \alpha_n x^{n-1}.$$

Therefore V_4 is spanned by the monomials $1, x, \ldots, x^{N-1}$. It is straightforward to show that they are linearly independent (by applying the fundamental theorem of algebra; see Problem 5.1), so $\dim V_4 = N$.

For general sets V, W, we say that $\phi : V \to W$ is *one-to-one* (or *injective*) if $v_1 \neq v_2$ implies $\phi(v_1) \neq \phi(v_2)$. We say that ϕ is *onto* (or *surjective*) if, for all $w \in W$, there exists $v \in V$ such that $\phi(v) = w$. When ϕ is both one-to-one and onto, we say that it is *bijective*. In that case for each $w \in W$, there exists a unique $v \in V$ such that $\phi(v) = w$, which we denote as $v = \phi^{-1}(w)$. The map $\phi^{-1} : W \to V$ is called the *inverse* of ϕ. Roughly speaking, when a bijective map (or *bijection*) $\phi : V \to W$ preserves properties that we are interested in, we call it an *isomorphism*. For instance, if V, W are vector spaces (which are characterized by linearity), a bijection $\phi : V \to W$ is an isomorphism if it is linear:

$$\phi(\alpha_1 v_1 + \alpha_2 v_2) = \alpha_1 \phi(v_1) + \alpha_2 \phi(v_2).$$

Two sets that are isomorphic (that is, those mapped by an isomorphism) can be regarded as identical, as long as we are concerned with the properties that we are interested in. For example, let V be a vector space with $\dim V = N$. By definition, we can take a basis $\{v_n\}_{n=1}^N$, and for any $v \in V$, we can uniquely express it as $v = \sum_{n=1}^N x_n v_n$ for some $x_1, \ldots, x_N \in \mathbb{R}$. Thus we can define $\phi : V \to \mathbb{R}^N$ by $\phi(v) = x = (x_1, \ldots, x_N)$. This ϕ is an isomorphism (see Problem 5.2 for details), so any N-dimensional (real) vector space is isomorphic to $\mathbb{R}^N$. For instance, V_4 in (5.1) is isomorphic to $\mathbb{R}^N$ by identifying

$$V_4 \ni v(x) = \sum_{n=1}^N \alpha_n x^{n-1} \longleftrightarrow \alpha = (\alpha_1, \ldots, \alpha_N) \in \mathbb{R}^N.$$

5.3   SOLVING LINEAR EQUATIONS

In practice, we often want to solve the linear equation

$$Ax = b, \tag{5.2}$$

where A is an $N \times N$ matrix, $b \in \mathbb{R}^N$, and $x \in \mathbb{R}^N$. If we define $\phi : \mathbb{R}^N \to \mathbb{R}^N$ by $\phi(x) = Ax$, then (5.2) can be rewritten as $\phi(x) = b$. Obviously, if ϕ is bijective, we may solve $x = \phi^{-1}(b)$. Clearly ϕ is linear, so if ϕ is bijective, ϕ^{-1} is also linear and admits a matrix representation by the discussion in Chapter 3. In that case, this matrix is called the *inverse* of A and is denoted by A^{-1}. Thus we may write the solution of (5.2) as $x = A^{-1}b$. A matrix that admits an inverse is called *nonsingular* or *invertible*. If A is invertible (so ϕ is bijective), clearly $AA^{-1} = A^{-1}A = I$, where I denotes the identity matrix. The inverse of A, if it exists, is unique. To see this, suppose that B, C are both inverses of A. Then $AB = BA = I$ and $AC = CA = I$, so

$$B = BI = B(AC) = (BA)C = IC = C.$$

All this argument is vacuous unless we can characterize conditions under which A is nonsingular or provide an algorithm to compute A^{-1} or $x = A^{-1}b$, which we turn to next. If $N = 1$, then (5.2) may be written as $ax = b$ (where all quantities are real numbers) and we can solve $x = b/a$ provided $a \neq 0$. If $N = 2$, (5.2) may be written as

$$a_{11}x_1 + a_{12}x_2 = b_1,$$
$$a_{21}x_1 + a_{22}x_2 = b_2,$$

and we can solve it by eliminating one variable from the two equations. This process involves (i) swapping two equations, (ii) multiplying an equation by a nonzero scalar, and (iii) adding a scalar multiple of an equation to another.

These operations can be expressed as matrix multiplication. Fix N and let $1 \leq i \neq j \leq N$ and $c \neq 0$. Let $P = I$ (identity matrix), and define

$P(i,j) = (p_{mn})$ by setting $p_{ii} = p_{jj} = 0$ and $p_{ij} = p_{ji} = 1$ in P. For instance, if $N = 3$ and $(i,j) = (2,3)$, we have

$$P(i,j) = \begin{bmatrix} 1 & 0 & 0 \\ 0 & 0 & 1 \\ 0 & 1 & 0 \end{bmatrix}.$$

Then (i) swapping rows i and j of (5.2) corresponds to the equation

$$P(i,j)Ax = P(i,j)b. \tag{5.3}$$

Note that $P(i,j)^2 = I$, so multiplying $P(i,j)$ from left to (5.3), we recover (5.2). Thus these equations are equivalent.

Next, let $Q = I$, and define $Q(i;c) = (q_{mn})$ by setting $q_{ii} = c$ in Q. For instance, if $N = 3$ and $i = 2$, we have

$$Q(i;c) = \begin{bmatrix} 1 & 0 & 0 \\ 0 & c & 0 \\ 0 & 0 & 1 \end{bmatrix}.$$

Then (ii) multiplying row i of (5.2) by $c \neq 0$ corresponds to the equation

$$Q(i;c)Ax = Q(i;c)b. \tag{5.4}$$

Note that $Q(i;1/c)Q(i;c) = I$, so multiplying $Q(i;1/c)$ from left to (5.4), we recover (5.2).

Finally, let $R = I$, and define $R(i,j;c) = (r_{mn})$ by setting $r_{ij} = c$ in R. For instance, if $N = 3$ and $(i,j) = (2,3)$, we have

$$R(i,j;c) = \begin{bmatrix} 1 & 0 & 0 \\ 0 & 1 & c \\ 0 & 0 & 1 \end{bmatrix}.$$

Then (iii) adding c times row j of (5.2) to row i corresponds to the equation

$$R(i,j;c)Ax = R(i,j;c)b. \tag{5.5}$$

Note that $R(i,j;-c)R(i,j;c) = I$, so multiplying $R(i,j;-c)$ from left to (5.5), we recover (5.2).

Thus multiplying any of these matrices P, Q, R from left to (5.2) leaves the system of equations equivalent. We can now provide an algorithm to solve the system of linear equations (5.2), called *Gaussian elimination*.

Solving linear equations by Gaussian elimination

(i) If $A = 0$ (zero matrix), then either (5.2) holds for all x (if $b = 0$) or no x (if $b \neq 0$). Hence assume $A \neq 0$.

(ii) Find (i, j) such that $a_{ij} \neq 0$. If $j \neq 1$, consider the equation $AP(1, j)P(1, j)x = b$. By redefining $AP(1, j)$ as A and $P(1, j)x$ as x (swapping x_1 and x_j), we may assume $a_{i1} \neq 0$ for some i.

(iii) Find i such that $a_{i1} \neq 0$. If $i \neq 1$, consider the equation $P(i, 1)Ax = P(i, 1)b$. By redefining $P(i, 1)A$ as A and $P(i, 1)b$ as b (swapping rows 1 and i), we may assume $a_{11} \neq 0$.

(iv) Multiply $Q(1, 1; 1/a_{11})$ from left to $Ax = b$. Then we may assume $a_{11} = 1$.

(v) For each $m = 2, \ldots, N$, multiply $R(m, 1; -a_{m1})$ from left to $Ax = b$. Then we may assume $a_{m1} = 0$ for all $m > 1$.

(vi) The system of equations can now be written as

$$\begin{bmatrix} 1 & A_{12} \\ 0 & \tilde{A} \end{bmatrix} \begin{bmatrix} x_1 \\ \tilde{x} \end{bmatrix} = \begin{bmatrix} b_1 \\ \tilde{b} \end{bmatrix},$$

where A_{12} is $1 \times (N-1)$, $\tilde{x}$ is $(N-1) \times 1$, etc. This equation reduces to $\tilde{A}\tilde{x} = \tilde{b}$ and $x_1 = b_1 - A_{12}\tilde{x}$, so if we can solve the former, we are done. However, note that the dimension has been reduced by 1, so we may repeat this process until we can no longer continue.

(vii) By induction, by multiplying appropriate P, Q, R from left to $Ax = b$ or by rewriting $Ax = b$ as $APPx = b$, we may write $Ax = b$ equivalently as

$$(LAP)Px = Lb, \tag{5.6}$$

where L is the product of finitely many $P(i, j)$, $Q(i; c)$, $R(i, j; c)$ matrices, P is the product of finitely many $P(i, j)$ matrices, and

$$LAP = \begin{bmatrix} I_r & B \\ 0_{N-r,r} & 0_{N-r,N-r} \end{bmatrix}$$

for some $0 \leq r \leq N$ and $B \in \mathbb{R}^{r \times (N-r)}$.

(viii) Write $y = Px$, $c = Lb$, and partition (5.6) as

$$\begin{bmatrix} I & B \\ 0 & 0 \end{bmatrix} \begin{bmatrix} y_1 \\ y_2 \end{bmatrix} = \begin{bmatrix} c_1 \\ c_2 \end{bmatrix},$$

which is equivalent to $y_1 + By_2 = c_1$ and $c_2 = 0$. Therefore, there exists a solution if and only if $c_2 = 0$, in which case the solution takes the form $y_1 = c_1 - By_2$ for any $y_2 \in \mathbb{R}^{N-r}$.

(ix) There exists a unique solution if and only if $r = N$, in which case $y = Px = Lb \iff x = PLb$ (because $P^2 = I$).

Remark. Let $P = (p_{mn})$ be as in (5.6), which is the product of finitely many $P(i, j)$ matrices. Then for each m, we have $p_{mn} = 1$ for exactly one n and $p_{mn} = 0$ for all other n. Similarly, for each n, we have $p_{mn} = 1$ for exactly one m and $p_{mn} = 0$ for all other m. Such a matrix is called a *permutation matrix*.

Remark. Gaussian elimination also provides an algorithm to compute the inverse matrix. To see this, note that $X = A^{-1}$ satisfies $AX = I$. Thus replacing x, b in (5.2) with X, I and applying Gaussian elimination, we obtain $X = A^{-1}$.

The number r in the Gaussian elimination algorithm is called the *rank* of the matrix A, which is uniquely determined by A (Problem 5.5).

In the Gaussian elimination algorithm, we implicitly assumed A is a square matrix, but this is obviously not necessary (except for the obvious change of notation and the last statement on uniqueness). If A is $M \times N$, we say that A has *full row rank* if $r = M$ and *full column rank* if $r = N$. If $r = M = N$, we say A has full rank. The following corollary is obvious from the definition of invertibility and the Gaussian elimination algorithm.

Corollary 5.1. *Let $A \in \mathbb{R}^{N \times N}$. Then A is invertible if and only if it has full rank.*

5.4 DETERMINANT

Although Gaussian elimination is practical for computational purposes, it does not provide theoretical insights. To this end, we define the determinant of square matrices.

An $N \times N$ matrix can be written as $A = [a_1, \ldots, a_N]$, where $a_n \in \mathbb{R}^N$ is the n-th column vector. Consider the function $D : \mathbb{R}^{N \times N} \to \mathbb{R}$ satisfying the following properties.

(i) (Multi-linearity) For each n, $D(\ldots, x_n, \ldots)$ is linear in $x_n \in \mathbb{R}^N$, that is, for all $x_n, y_n \in \mathbb{R}^N$ and $\alpha, \beta \in \mathbb{R}$, we have

$$D(\ldots, \alpha x_n + \beta y_n, \ldots) = \alpha D(\ldots, x_n, \ldots) + \beta D(\ldots, y_n, \ldots).$$

(ii) (Alternation) For each $m < n$, the sign of D flips whenever we flip columns m, n:

$$D(\ldots, x_m, \ldots, x_n, \ldots) = -D(\ldots, x_n, \ldots, x_m, \ldots).$$

(iii) (Normalization) $D(I) = 1$.

It turns out that properties (i)–(iii) define a unique function D. Let us consider a few special cases. For $N = 1$, we can write $A = (a)$ (scalar), so it must be

$$D(A) = D(a) = D(aI) = aD(I) = a.$$

Clearly, this function satisfies (i)–(iii). Before considering the case $N = 2$, we note a few lemmas.

Lemma 5.2. *Let $A = [a_1, \ldots, a_N]$. If D satisfies (ii) and $a_m = a_n$ for some $m \neq n$, then $D(A) = 0$.*

Proof. Let $\tilde{A}$ be the matrix obtained by flipping the columns m, n of A. Since $a_m = a_n$, we have $\tilde{A} = A$. Hence using (ii), we obtain $D(A) = D(\tilde{A}) = -D(A)$, so $D(A) = 0$. $\qquad\square$

Lemma 5.3. *Let $A = [a_1, \ldots, a_N]$. If D satisfies (i), (ii) and $\{a_n\}$ is linearly dependent, then $D(A) = 0$.*

Proof. Since $\{a_n\}$ is linearly dependent, we have $\sum_{n=1}^{N} \alpha_n a_n = 0$ for some $0 \neq \alpha \in \mathbb{R}^N$. Suppose $\alpha_j \neq 0$. Then $a_j = -\frac{1}{\alpha_j} \sum_{n \neq j} \alpha_n a_n$. Using (i), (ii), we obtain

$$D(A) = D\left(\ldots, -\frac{1}{\alpha_j} \sum_{n \neq j} \alpha_n a_n, \ldots\right) = -\sum_{n \neq j} \frac{\alpha_n}{\alpha_j} D(\ldots, a_n, \ldots).$$

In the last expression, because columns j, n are both a_n, by Lemma 5.2, we have $D(\ldots, a_n, \ldots) = 0$. Therefore $D(A) = 0$. $\qquad\square$

Now suppose $N = 2$ and $A = \begin{bmatrix} a & b \\ c & d \end{bmatrix}$. If D satisfies (i)–(iii), then

$$D(A) = aD\begin{pmatrix} 1 & b \\ 0 & d \end{pmatrix} + cD\begin{pmatrix} 0 & b \\ 1 & d \end{pmatrix}$$

$$= abD\begin{pmatrix} 1 & 1 \\ 0 & 0 \end{pmatrix} + adD\begin{pmatrix} 1 & 0 \\ 0 & 1 \end{pmatrix} + bcD\begin{pmatrix} 0 & 1 \\ 1 & 0 \end{pmatrix} + cdD\begin{pmatrix} 0 & 0 \\ 1 & 1 \end{pmatrix}$$

$$= adD\begin{pmatrix} 1 & 0 \\ 0 & 1 \end{pmatrix} - bcD\begin{pmatrix} 1 & 0 \\ 0 & 1 \end{pmatrix}$$

$$= ad - bc,$$

where we have used Lemma 5.2. Thus D is uniquely determined.

The general case proceeds by induction. Suppose that for each $n = 1, \ldots, N-1$, there exists a unique function $D_n : \mathbb{R}^{n \times n} \to \mathbb{R}$ satisfying properties (i)–(iii). Let $A = (a_{mn}) \in \mathbb{R}^{N \times N}$. For fixed i, define

$$D_N(A) = \sum_{m=1}^{N} (-1)^{m+i} a_{mi} D_{N-1}(A_{mi}), \tag{5.7}$$

where A_{mi} is the $(N-1) \times (N-1)$ submatrix of A obtained by removing row m and column i. Then we can show that $D_N(A)$ does not depend on i and that it is the unique function satisfying (i)–(iii). For a proof (which uses Lemma 5.3), see for instance Jänich (1994, Chapter 6). The unique value $D(A)$ is called the *determinant* of A and is denoted by $\det A$ or $|A|$.

The formula (5.7) is called the *Laplace expansion* of the determinant. For instance, for $N = 2$ and $i = 1$, we may compute

$$\begin{vmatrix} a & b \\ c & d \end{vmatrix} = a(d) - c(b) = ad - bc.$$

For $N = 3$ and $i = 1$, we may compute

$$\begin{vmatrix} a & b & c \\ d & e & f \\ g & h & i \end{vmatrix} = a \begin{vmatrix} e & f \\ h & i \end{vmatrix} - d \begin{vmatrix} b & c \\ h & i \end{vmatrix} + g \begin{vmatrix} b & c \\ e & f \end{vmatrix}$$

$$= a(ei - fh) - d(bi - ch) + g(bf - ce),$$

etc.

The following lemma shows that properties (i) and (ii) characterize the determinant up to normalization, which is useful for deriving properties of the determinant.

Lemma 5.4. *If $F : \mathbb{R}^{N \times N} \to \mathbb{R}$ satisfies (i), (ii), then $F(A) = |A| \, F(I)$.*

Sketch of proof. Repeatedly using (i), (ii) as we did for the 2×2 case, we may write $F(A) = g(A)F(I)$ for some function g independent of F. If $F(I) = 1$, then by uniqueness it must be $F = \det$, so $g(A) = \det A = |A|$. Hence $F(A) = |A| \, F(I)$. $\qquad \square$

Proposition 5.5. *If $A, B \in \mathbb{R}^{N \times N}$, then $|AB| = |A| \, |B| = |BA|$.*

Proof. Fix $A \in \mathbb{R}^{N \times N}$ and define $F : \mathbb{R}^{N \times N} \to \mathbb{R}$ by $F(X) = |AX|$. Using the linearity of $X \mapsto AX$, we can see that F satisfies properties (i), (ii). Hence by Lemma 5.4, we obtain

$$|AX| = F(X) = |X| \, F(I) = |X| \, |A| = |A| \, |X| \, .$$

Setting $X = B$, we obtain $|AB| = |A| \, |B|$. Interchanging the roles of A, B, we obtain $|BA| = |B| \, |A| = |A| \, |B|$. $\qquad \square$

We say that a square matrix A is *block upper triangular* if it can be written as

$$A = \begin{bmatrix} A_{11} & A_{12} \\ 0 & A_{22} \end{bmatrix}, \tag{5.8}$$

where A_{11}, A_{22} are square matrices (that need not have the same size) called diagonal blocks. If in addition $A_{12} = 0$, we say that A is *block diagonal*. In this example, there are two diagonal blocks, but there could be any number M, for instance

$$A = \begin{bmatrix} A_{11} & \cdots & A_{1M} \\ \vdots & \ddots & \vdots \\ 0 & \cdots & A_{MM} \end{bmatrix}.$$

The following proposition facilitates the calculation of the determinant of block upper triangular matrices.

Proposition 5.6. *If A is block upper triangular and is given by (5.8), then $|A| = |A_{11}||A_{22}|$.*

Proof. Let $A_{11} \in \mathbb{R}^{r \times r}$. For a general matrix $X \in \mathbb{R}^{r \times r}$, define

$$F(X) = \begin{vmatrix} X & A_{12} \\ 0 & A_{22} \end{vmatrix}.$$

Then F satisfies properties (i), (ii) of the determinant, so by Lemma 5.4 we have $F(X) = |X| F(I)$. Hence it suffices to show $F(I) = |A_{22}|$. Now

$$F(I) = \begin{vmatrix} I & A_{12} \\ 0 & A_{22} \end{vmatrix} = \begin{vmatrix} I & 0 \\ 0 & A_{22} \end{vmatrix}$$

by subtracting some multiples of the first r columns from the last $N - r$ columns and applying Lemma 5.2. If we view the last expression as a function of A_{22}, it satisfies properties (i), (ii) of the determinant, so by Lemma 5.4 and property (iii) we have $F(I) = |A_{22}|$. □

Remark. Block lower triangular matrices are defined in the obvious way, and Proposition 5.6 remains true.

We say that a square matrix $A = (a_{mn})$ is *upper triangular* if $a_{mn} = 0$ whenever $m > n$, so A can be written as

$$A = \begin{bmatrix} a_{11} & \cdots & a_{1N} \\ \vdots & \ddots & \vdots \\ 0 & \cdots & a_{NN} \end{bmatrix}.$$

Similarly, we say $A = (a_{mn})$ is *lower triangular* if $a_{mn} = 0$ whenever $m < n$. Obviously, an upper triangular matrix is block upper triangular with N diagonal blocks of size 1×1.

Corollary 5.7. *If $A = (a_{mn})$ is upper triangular, then its determinant equals the product of its diagonal entries: $|A| = a_{11} \cdots a_{NN} = \prod_{n=1}^{N} a_{nn}$.*

Proof. Apply Proposition 5.6 and induction. □

An important implication of the Laplace expansion (5.7) is that it provides an explicit formula for the inverse matrix. To this end, we introduce some definitions. Let $A = (a_{mn})$ be a square matrix. Let A_{mn} be the submatrix of A obtained by removing row m and column n. Then $c_{mn} := (-1)^{m+n} |A_{mn}|$ is called the (m, n) *cofactor* of A. The matrix $C = (c_{mn})$ is called the *cofactor matrix*.

Proposition 5.8. *Let A be a square matrix and C be its cofactor matrix. Then A is invertible if and only if $|A| \neq 0$, in which case*

$$A^{-1} = \frac{1}{|A|} C'. \tag{5.9}$$

Proof. By the definition of the cofactor, for each i the Laplace expansion formula (5.7) implies

$$|A| = \sum_{m=1}^{N} a_{mi} c_{mi}.$$

Let $A[i \leftarrow j]$ be the matrix obtained by replacing column i with column j. If $i \neq j$, since column j appears twice in $A[i \leftarrow j]$, by Lemma 5.2 and (5.7) we have

$$0 = |A[i \leftarrow j]| = \sum_{m=1}^{N} a_{mj} c_{mi}.$$

Define Kronecker's delta by $\delta_{ij} = 1$ if $i = j$ and $\delta_{ij} = 0$ if $i \neq j$. Combining the cases $i = j$ (hence $A[i \leftarrow j] = A$) and $i \neq j$, we obtain

$$\delta_{ij} |A| = \sum_{m=1}^{N} c_{mi} a_{mj}.$$

Collecting terms into a matrix, we obtain $|A| I = C' A$. Therefore if $|A| \neq 0$, then A is invertible and (5.9) holds. Conversely, if A is invertible, then by Proposition 5.5, we obtain $1 = |I| = |AA^{-1}| = |A||A^{-1}|$, so it must be $|A| \neq 0$. □

Example 5.1. Let A be 2×2 and

$$A = \begin{bmatrix} a & b \\ c & d \end{bmatrix}.$$

The cofactor matrix is

$$C = \begin{bmatrix} d & -c \\ -b & a \end{bmatrix},$$

so the inverse matrix is

$$A^{-1} = \frac{1}{|A|} C' = \frac{1}{ad - bc} \begin{bmatrix} d & -b \\ -c & a \end{bmatrix}.$$

The following theorem provides equivalent conditions for the invertibility of a square matrix A.

Theorem 5.9. *Let A be a square matrix. Then the following conditions are equivalent.*

  (i) A is invertible.

  (ii) The column vectors of A are linearly independent.

  (iii) For any b, the equation $Ax = b$ has a unique solution.

  (iv) A has full rank.

  (v) $|A| \neq 0$.

Proof. $(i) \implies (ii)$: Let $A = [a_1, \ldots, a_N]$. Suppose $\sum_{n=1}^{N} x_n a_n = 0$ for some $x = (x_1, \ldots, x_N)$. Then $Ax = 0$. Since A is invertible, $x = A^{-1}Ax = 0$.

$(ii) \implies (iii)$: Let $A = [a_1, \ldots, a_N]$. Since $\{a_n\}$ is linearly independent, the vector space $\mathsf{V} := \mathrm{span}[a_1, \ldots, a_N]$ has dimension N. Since $\mathsf{V} \subset \mathbb{R}^N$, it must be $\mathsf{V} = \mathbb{R}^N$. Hence the equation $Ax = b$ has a solution. Uniqueness follows by linear independence.

$(iii) \implies (iv)$: Obvious from Gaussian elimination and the definition of the rank.

$(iv) \implies (v)$: If A has full rank, by applying Gaussian elimination, we may write $LAP = I$, where L is the product of finitely many matrices of the form P, Q, R. By Proposition 5.5, we obtain $1 = |I| = |LAP| = |L| |A| |P|$. Therefore $|A| \neq 0$.

$(v) \implies (i)$: Obvious from Proposition 5.8. $\qquad\qquad\qquad\square$

Order of operations

Let us evaluate how many algebraic operations are required to solve the linear equation $Ax = b$. (i) If we use Gaussian elimination, for each i and $m \neq i$, we subtract a constant multiple of row i from row m, which involves N numbers. Repeating this for each m and iterating over i, the order of operations is $N \times N \times N = N^3$. (ii) If we use Gaussian elimination to compute A^{-1} first (so applying Gaussian elimination to $b = e_n$ for each n) and compute $x = A^{-1}b$, the order of operations is $N^3 \times N = N^4$. (iii) Suppose we use the Laplace expansion to compute $|A|$. Letting $o(n)$ be the order for computing the determinant of $A \in \mathbb{R}^{n \times n}$, then Laplace expansion implies $o(n) = no(n-1)$, so $o(n) = n!$. Thus computing A^{-1} requires $N^2 \times (N-1)! \sim (N+1)!$ operations. We conclude that Laplace expansion is not practical. Furthermore, when solving linear equations, it is better to avoid computing the inverse. (In Matlab, use `x = A\b` instead of `x = inv(A)*b`.)

PROBLEMS

5.1. This problem asks you to show that the space of polynomials of degree up to $N-1$ (V_4 in (5.1)) has dimension N. It is clear that the monomials $1, x, \ldots, x^{N-1}$ span V_4, so it suffices to show that these monomials are linearly independent. To show this, let

$$v(x) = \sum_{n=1}^{N} \alpha_n x^{n-1}$$

and suppose $v = 0$ (the function identically equal to zero). By applying the fundamental theorem of algebra, prove that $\alpha_1 = \cdots = \alpha_N = 0$.

5.2. Let V be an N-dimensional real vector space. By definition, there exists a basis $\{v_n\}_{n=1}^N$, which means that $\{v_n\}$ is linearly independent and spans V.

   (i) Prove that for each $v \in V$, there exists a unique $x = (x_1, \ldots, x_N) \in \mathbb{R}^N$ such that $v = \sum_{n=1}^N x_n v_n$.

  (ii) Define $\phi : V \to \mathbb{R}^N$ by $\phi(v) = x$, where x is as in the previous question. Prove that ϕ is an isomorphism. More precisely, prove that ϕ is (a) one-to-one, (b) onto, and (c) linear.

5.3. This problem asks you to prove that any subspace W of $V = \mathbb{R}^N$ (or more generally, a subspace of any finite-dimensional space) is closed.

    Since W is a subspace of V, we can take a basis $\{a_n\}_{n=1}^N$ of V such that $\{a_n\}_{n=1}^M$ is a basis of W, where $M = \dim W \le N$. For any $x \in V$, there exist unique numbers $x_1, \ldots, x_N$ such that $x = \sum_{n=1}^N x_n a_n$. Define

$$\|x\| = \max_n |x_n|.$$

   (i) Prove that $\|\cdot\|$ is a norm on V.

  (ii) Show that W is closed. (Hint: use Theorem 1.3.)

  (iii) Let V be the space of bounded continuous functions defined on $[-1, 1]$ and $W \subset V$ be the space of polynomials. (Convergence is defined by the sup norm $\|f\| = \sup_{x \in [-1,1]} |f(x)|$.) Show that W is not closed. Hence the assumption of finite dimension is essential.

5.4. Let A, B, C be matrices with appropriate dimensions so that the following expressions are well defined. Prove that $A(B + C) = AB + AC$, $A(BC) = (AB)C$, $(AB)^{-1} = B^{-1}A^{-1}$, and $(AB)' = B'A'$.

5.5. Suppose there are two ways to write (5.6) as

$$L_1 A P_1 = \begin{bmatrix} I_{r_1} & B_1 \\ 0 & 0 \end{bmatrix}, \quad L_2 A P_2 = \begin{bmatrix} I_{r_2} & B_2 \\ 0 & 0 \end{bmatrix}.$$

Prove that $r_1 = r_2$.

5.6.   (i) Let A be a 2×2 block upper triangular matrix

$$A = \begin{bmatrix} A_{11} & A_{12} \\ 0 & A_{22} \end{bmatrix}.$$

    If A is invertible, explicitly compute A^{-1}.

  (ii) Repeat the above problem if A is 3×3 block upper triangular. What if A is $N \times N$ block upper triangular?

5.7. The Fibonacci sequence is defined by $f_0 = 0$, $f_1 = 1$, and $f_n = f_{n-1} + f_{n-2}$ for $n \ge 2$. The first few terms are $0, 1, 1, 2, 3, 5, 8, 13, \ldots$.

(i) Show that

$$\begin{bmatrix} f_{n+1} \\ f_n \end{bmatrix} = \begin{bmatrix} 1 & 1 \\ 1 & 0 \end{bmatrix} \begin{bmatrix} f_n \\ f_{n-1} \end{bmatrix}.$$

(ii) Show that

$$\begin{bmatrix} f_{n+1} & f_n \\ f_n & f_{n-1} \end{bmatrix} = \begin{bmatrix} 1 & 1 \\ 1 & 0 \end{bmatrix}^n.$$

(iii) Show that $f_{n+1}f_{n-1} - f_n^2 = (-1)^n$.

CHAPTER 6

Spectral Theory

6.1 INTRODUCTION

In economic analysis, we often want to know the behavior of the matrix power A^k as $k \to \infty$. For instance, the linearization of economic models often implies the dynamics

$$x_t = Ax_{t-1} + u_t, \tag{6.1}$$

where x_t is a vector of state variables, A is a square matrix, and u_t is a vector of shocks. (Although not a topic of this book, an equation of the form (6.1) is called a *vector autoregression* or VAR.) Iterating (6.1), we obtain

$$x_t = u_t + Au_{t-1} + \cdots + A^{t-1}u_1 + A^t x_0. \tag{6.2}$$

Thus if $\lim_{t \to \infty} A^t = 0$, then the term $A^t x_0$ in (6.2) converges to 0, so the initial condition becomes irrelevant as time goes by.

We say that a square matrix $A = (a_{mn})$ is *diagonal* if $a_{mn} = 0$ whenever $m \neq n$, so we can write

$$A = \text{diag}[d_1, \ldots, d_N] := \begin{bmatrix} d_1 & \cdots & 0 \\ \vdots & \ddots & \vdots \\ 0 & \cdots & d_N \end{bmatrix}.$$

If A is diagonal, a straightforward calculation shows $A^k = \text{diag}[d_1^k, \ldots, d_N^k]$ for all $k \in \mathbb{N}$, so $A^k \to 0$ as $k \to \infty$ if and only if $|d_n| < 1$ for all n. This chapter generalizes this argument for any square matrix.

6.2 EIGENVALUE AND EIGENVECTOR

Let A be a square matrix, which could be real or complex. If there is a vector $v \neq 0$ and scalar α such that $Av = \alpha v$, we say that α is an *eigenvalue* of A and v is an *eigenvector* corresponding to α. In that case, by iteration we may compute $A^k v = \alpha^k v$, so we can easily understand the behavior of $A^k v$ as $k \to \infty$.

DOI: 10.1201/9781032698953-6

We may characterize all eigenvalues of a square matrix $A \in \mathbb{C}^{N \times N}$ as follows. By definition, α is an eigenvalue if and only if there exists $v \neq 0$ such that

$$Av = \alpha v \iff (\alpha I - A)v = 0.$$

By Theorem 5.9, such $v \neq 0$ exists if and only if $|\alpha I - A| = 0$. For any complex number $z \in \mathbb{C}$, define the function $\Phi_A : \mathbb{C} \to \mathbb{C}$ by $\Phi_A(z) = |zI - A|$. Then by applying the Laplace expansion of the determinant and induction, we can see that Φ_A is a polynomial of degree N with leading coefficient 1. By the fundamental theorem of algebra, the equation $\Phi_A(z) = 0$ has exactly N roots if we count multiplicity. Thus, any $A \in \mathbb{C}^{N \times N}$ has exactly N eigenvalues. The polynomial Φ_A is called the *characteristic polynomial* of A.

Example 6.1. If A is 2×2 and

$$A = \begin{bmatrix} a & b \\ c & d \end{bmatrix},$$

then

$$\Phi_A(z) = |zI - A| = \begin{vmatrix} z - a & -b \\ -c & z - d \end{vmatrix} = z^2 - (a + d)z + ad - bc.$$

The equation $\Phi_A(z) = 0$ is called the *characteristic equation* of A, and its roots are called *characteristic roots*. By the previous argument, characteristic roots and eigenvalues of A are identical. Note that even if A is a real matrix, the eigenvalues (hence eigenvectors) need not be real.

Example 6.2. If

$$A = \begin{bmatrix} \cos\theta & -\sin\theta \\ \sin\theta & \cos\theta \end{bmatrix},$$

the characteristic equation and roots are

$$z^2 - 2(\cos\theta)z + 1 = 0 \iff z = \cos\theta \pm i\sin\theta,$$

which are complex whenever $\sin\theta \neq 0$.

Thus when we discuss eigenvalues and eigenvectors, we always consider the complex vector space $\mathbb{C}^N$ unless otherwise specified.

The characteristic polynomial of a block upper triangular matrix is the product of the characteristic polynomials of the diagonal blocks.

Proposition 6.1. *If*

$$A = \begin{bmatrix} A_{11} & A_{12} \\ 0 & A_{22} \end{bmatrix}$$

is block upper triangular, then $\Phi_A(z) = \Phi_{A_{11}}(z)\Phi_{A_{22}}(z)$.

Proof. Immediate from the definition of the characteristic polynomial and Proposition 5.6. $\qquad\square$

For upper triangular matrix, the eigenvalues are given by diagonal entries.

Proposition 6.2. *If $A = (a_{mn})$ is upper triangular (so $a_{mn} = 0$ whenever $m > n$), then the eigenvalues of A are the diagonal entries $a_{11}, \ldots, a_{NN}$.*

Proof. If A is upper triangular, so is $zI - A$, whose n-th diagonal entry is $z - a_{nn}$. By Corollary 5.7, we have

$$\Phi_A(z) = |zI - A| = (z - a_{11}) \cdots (z - a_{NN}). \qquad \square$$

6.3 DIAGONALIZATION

We usually take the standard basis $\{e_1, \ldots, e_N\}$ in $\mathbb{R}^N$ or $\mathbb{C}^N$, but that is not necessary. Suppose we take a different basis $\{p_1, \ldots, p_N\}$, so by definition the vectors $\{p_n\}$ are linearly independent. By Theorem 5.9, the matrix $P = [p_1, \ldots, p_N]$ is invertible. Let x be any vector and $y = P^{-1}x$. Then

$$x = PP^{-1}x = Py = y_1 p_1 + \cdots + y_N p_N,$$

so the entries of y can be interpreted as the coordinates of x when expressed with the basis P. How does a matrix A look when we use the basis P? Consider the linear map $x \mapsto Ax$. Then

$$y = P^{-1}x \mapsto P^{-1}Ax = (P^{-1}AP)(P^{-1}x) = (P^{-1}AP)y,$$

so the linear map $x \mapsto Ax$ has the matrix representation $B = P^{-1}AP$ under the basis P. In general, when there exists an invertible matrix P such that $B = P^{-1}AP$, we say that A, B are *similar*. When A, B are similar, they can be regarded as identical because they can be mapped to each other by a change of basis. For instance, using Proposition 5.5, the characteristic polynomial of $B = P^{-1}AP$ is

$$\Phi_B(z) = |zI - B| = \left|zI - P^{-1}AP\right| = \left|P^{-1}(zI - A)P\right| = |zI - A| = \Phi_A(z),$$

so A, B have identical eigenvalues.

For analysis, it is oftentimes useful to find a matrix P such that $P^{-1}AP$ is a simple matrix. For instance, let $B = P^{-1}AP$ and suppose that computing B^k is easy (which is the case if B is diagonal). Then $B^k = (P^{-1}AP)^k = P^{-1}A^kP$, so we may compute $A^k = PB^kP^{-1}$. The simplest matrices of all are diagonal ones. When $D := P^{-1}AP$ is diagonal, we say that A is *diagonalizable*. The following proposition provides a sufficient condition for diagonalizability.

Proposition 6.3. *If the eigenvalues of the square matrix A are distinct, A is diagonalizable.*

Proof. Let $\{\alpha_n\}_{n=1}^{N}$ be the eigenvalues of A. For each n, let p_n be an eigenvector of A corresponding to α_n. Then $Ap_n = \alpha_n p_n$ for all n.

Let us show that $\{p_n\}$ are linearly independent. Suppose $\sum_{n=1}^{N} x_n p_n = 0$. Fix m, and multiply both sides by $B_m := \prod_{n \neq m} (A - \alpha_n I)$. Since

$$(A - \alpha I)(A - \beta I) = A^2 - (\alpha + \beta) A + \alpha \beta I = (A - \beta I)(A - \alpha I),$$

it does not matter the order we apply the product. Since p_n is an eigenvector, we have $(A - \alpha_n I) p_n = A p_n - \alpha_n p_n = 0$. Therefore we obtain

$$0 = B_m 0 = B_m \sum_{n=1}^{N} x_n p_n = x_m \left(\prod_{n \neq m} (\alpha_m - \alpha_n) \right) p_m.$$

Since $\{\alpha_n\}$ are distinct and $p_m \neq 0$, we obtain $x_m = 0$. Since this holds for all m, it follows that $\{p_n\}$ are linearly independent.

Now define the matrix $P = [p_1, \ldots, p_N]$. By Theorem 5.9, P is invertible. Stacking $A p_n = \alpha_n p_n$ as column vectors, we obtain

$$AP = A[p_1, \ldots, p_N] = [\alpha_1 p_1, \ldots, \alpha_N p_N] = P \operatorname{diag}[\alpha_1, \ldots, \alpha_N].$$

Multiplying P^{-1} from left, we obtain $P^{-1} A P = \operatorname{diag}[\alpha_1, \ldots, \alpha_N]$. □

6.4   INNER PRODUCT AND NORM

When the eigenvalues are not distinct, a matrix may not be diagonalizable (Problem 6.4). To treat such cases, we need additional structure.

Let V be a real vector space. We say that a function $\langle \cdot, \cdot \rangle : V \times V \to \mathbb{R}$ is an *inner product* if it satisfies the following conditions.

(i) (Nonnegativity) $\langle x, x \rangle \geq 0$ for all $x \in V$, with equality if and only if $x = 0$,

(ii) (Symmetry) $\langle x, y \rangle = \langle y, x \rangle$ for all $x, y \in V$,

(iii) (Linearity) $\langle x, y \rangle$ is linear in y.[1]

A real vector space equipped with an inner product $\langle \cdot, \cdot \rangle$ is called an inner product space. An obvious example is $\mathbb{R}^N$, but there are many others.

Example 6.3. Let $a < b$ and $w : [a, b] \to (0, \infty)$ be a positive continuous function. Let V be the space of continuous functions defined on $[a, b]$. For $f, g \in V$, define

$$\langle f, g \rangle = \int_a^b f(x) g(x) w(x) \, dx.$$

Then V is an inner product space (Problem 6.1).

---

[1] Some authors require linearity in the first argument x instead of the second argument y. For real vector spaces, the two definitions are equivalent due to symmetry. For complex vector spaces, they are equivalent up to complex conjugacy.

As in $\mathbb{R}^N$, if V is an inner product space, for each $x \in \mathsf{V}$ we may define $\|x\| := \sqrt{\langle x, x \rangle} \geq 0$. Then for any $x, y \in \mathsf{V}$, the Cauchy-Schwarz inequality

$$\|x\| \, \|y\| \geq |\langle x, y \rangle| \tag{6.3}$$

and the triangle inequality

$$\|x + y\| \leq \|x\| + \|y\| \tag{6.4}$$

hold (Problem 6.2). Thus an inner product space is automatically a normed space.

When V is a complex vector space, symmetry is replaced with

(ii)' (Conjugate symmetry) $\langle x, y \rangle = \overline{\langle y, x \rangle}$,

where $\bar{\alpha}$ denotes the complex conjugate of the scalar $\alpha \in \mathbb{C}$. For example, if $\mathsf{V} = \mathbb{C}^N$ and $x, y \in \mathbb{C}^N$, the inner product is defined by

$$\langle x, y \rangle = x^* y = \bar{x}' y = \sum_{n=1}^{N} \bar{x}_n y_n,$$

where $x^* = \bar{x}'$ is the transpose of the complex conjugate of x, or *conjugate transpose* for short.

Let V be a (real or complex) inner product space. Two vectors $x, y \in \mathsf{V}$ satisfying $\langle x, y \rangle = 0$ are called *orthogonal*. The set of vectors $\{v_k\}_{k=1}^{K}$ is called orthogonal if any two vectors are orthogonal. If in addition $\|v_k\| = 1$ for all k, we say that $\{v_k\}_{k=1}^{K}$ is *orthonormal*. If $\{v_k\}$ spans V, we call it an *orthonormal basis*.

Let V be an inner product space and $\{v_k\}_{k=1}^{K}$ be linearly independent. Then we may construct orthonormal vectors $\{u_k\}_{k=1}^{K}$ such that

$$\mathrm{span}[u_1, \ldots, u_K] = \mathrm{span}[v_1, \ldots, v_K],$$

as follows. First, take v_1. Since $\{v_k\}$ is linearly independent, clearly $v_1 \neq 0$. Define $u_1 = v_1 / \|v_1\|$. Then clearly $\|u_1\| = 1$. We proceed by induction. Suppose $u_1, \ldots, u_k$ have already been defined and $\mathrm{span}[u_1, \ldots, u_k] = \mathrm{span}[v_1, \ldots, v_k]$. Define $v = v_{k+1} - \sum_{l=1}^{k} \langle v_{k+1}, u_l \rangle u_l$. Since $\{v_k\}$ is linearly independent, we have $v_{k+1} \notin \mathrm{span}[v_1, \ldots, v_k] = \mathrm{span}[u_1, \ldots, u_k]$, so $v \neq 0$. Define $u_{k+1} = v / \|v\|$. Then clearly $\|u_{k+1}\| = 1$ and $\langle u_{k+1}, u_l \rangle = 0$ for all $l = 1, \ldots, k$. Continuing this process, we obtain the desired orthonormal vectors $\{u_k\}$. This process is called the *Gram-Schmidt orthonormalization*.

6.5   UPPER TRIANGULARIZATION

We now show that any complex square matrix A can be upper triangularized, so we can find an invertible matrix P such that $P^{-1}AP$ is upper triangular.

To this end, we introduce some definitions. For a complex (not necessarily square) matrix A, we define its *conjugate transpose* A^* by the complex conjugate of the transpose. Therefore if $A = (a_{mn})$, then $A^* = (\bar{a}_{nm})$. Using the properties of the inner product, we have

$$\langle A^* x, y \rangle = (A^* x)^* y = x^* (A^*)^* y = x^* A y = \langle x, A y \rangle .$$

Take an arbitrary basis in $\mathbb{C}^N$. Starting from this basis, applying the Gram-Schmidt orthonormalization, we may construct an orthonormal basis $\{u_1, \ldots, u_N\}$. Define the matrix U by $U = [u_1, \ldots, u_N]$. Noting that $\{u_n\}$ is orthonormal and using the definition of the inner product, the (m, n) entry of the matrix $U^* U$ is

$$\langle u_m, u_n \rangle = \delta_{mn} = \begin{cases} 1, & (m = n) \\ 0. & (m \neq n) \end{cases}$$

Therefore $U^* U = I$. A matrix $U \in \mathbb{C}^{N \times N}$ is called *unitary* if $U^* U = U U^* = I$, or equivalently $U^* = U^{-1}$. A real unitary matrix is called *orthogonal*. By definition, $P \in \mathbb{R}^{N \times N}$ is orthogonal if $P'P = PP' = I$ or $P' = P^{-1}$. If U_1, U_2 are unitary matrices and $U = U_1 U_2$, then

$$U^* U = (U_1 U_2)^* (U_1 U_2) = U_2^* U_1^* U_1 U_2 = U_2^* U_2 = I,$$

so U is also unitary. Thus the set of unitary matrices is closed under multiplication.

The following theorem shows that any square matrix can be upper triangularized by a unitary matrix.

Theorem 6.4 (Schur triangularization theorem). *For any $A \in \mathbb{C}^{N \times N}$, there exists a unitary matrix U such that $U^{-1} A U = U^* A U$ is upper triangular.*

Proof. We prove the claim by mathematical induction on the dimension N of A. If $N = 1$, the claim is trivial by setting $U = (1)$.

Suppose that the claim is true up to dimension $N - 1$. Let α_1 be an eigenvalue of A and u_1 be a corresponding eigenvector, so $A u_1 = \alpha_1 u_1$. Without loss of generality, assume $\|u_1\| = 1$. Applying the Gram-Schmidt orthonormalization, construct an orthonormal basis $\{u_n\}$ and set $U_0 = [u_1, \ldots, u_N]$. Then U_0 is unitary. Consider the matrix $U_0^* A U_0$. Its $(m, 1)$ entry is

$$e_m^* U_0^* A U_0 e_1 = u_m^* A u_1 = \alpha_1 u_m^* u_1 = \alpha_1 \langle u_m, u_1 \rangle = \alpha_1 \delta_{m1}.$$

Therefore we can take $A_1 \in \mathbb{C}^{(N-1) \times (N-1)}$ and $b_1 \in \mathbb{C}^{N-1}$ such that

$$U_0^* A U_0 = \begin{bmatrix} \alpha_1 & b_1^* \\ 0 & A_1 \end{bmatrix}. \tag{6.5}$$

By the induction hypothesis, we can take a unitary matrix U_1 such that $T_1 := U_1^* A_1 U_1$ is upper triangular. Let

$$V := \begin{bmatrix} 1 & 0 \\ 0 & U_1 \end{bmatrix}.$$

Since U_1 is unitary, we have $V^*V = I$, so V is unitary. Furthermore, we can rewrite (6.5) as

$$U_0^* A U_0 = \begin{bmatrix} \alpha_1 & b_1^* \\ 0 & U_1 T_1 U_1^* \end{bmatrix} = V \begin{bmatrix} \alpha_1 & b_1^* U_1 \\ 0 & T_1 \end{bmatrix} V^*. \tag{6.6}$$

Let $U := U_0 V$, which is unitary. Multiplying V^* (V) from left (right) to (6.6), we obtain

$$U^* A U = V^* U_0^* A U_0 V = \begin{bmatrix} \alpha_1 & b_1^* U_1 \\ 0 & T_1 \end{bmatrix},$$

which is upper triangular. □

The Schur triangularization theorem has many applications. One of them is to provide a class of matrices for which diagonalization is always possible. Matrices satisfying $A^* = A$ are called *Hermitian* or *self-adjoint*.[2] Real self-adjoint matrices are commonly called *symmetric*. Note that if $A = (a_{mn})$ is real symmetric, then $A' = A$ and $a_{mn} = a_{nm}$.

Corollary 6.5 (Spectral theorem). *A self-adjoint matrix is diagonalizable by a unitary matrix.*

Proof. Let A be self-adjoint. By Theorem 6.4, we can take a unitary U such that $T := U^* A U$ is upper triangular. Therefore its conjugate transpose T^* is lower triangular. Since $A^* = A$, we have

$$T = U^* A U = U^* A^* U = (U^* A U)^* = T^*,$$

so T is both upper and lower triangular, hence diagonal. □

The eigenvalues of self-adjoint matrices are all real.

Proposition 6.6. *If $A \in \mathbb{C}^{N \times N}$ is self-adjoint, the following statements are true.*

(i) For any $x \in \mathbb{C}^N$, the quadratic form $\langle x, Ax \rangle$ is real.

(ii) All eigenvalues of A are real.

Proof. (i) $\overline{\langle x, Ax \rangle} = \langle Ax, x \rangle = \langle A^* x, x \rangle = \langle x, Ax \rangle$, so $\langle x, Ax \rangle \in \mathbb{R}$.

(ii) Let $\alpha \in \mathbb{C}$ be an eigenvalue of A, so $Av = \alpha v$ for some $v \neq 0$. Then by (i) we have

$$\mathbb{R} \ni \langle v, Av \rangle = \langle v, \alpha v \rangle = \alpha \langle v, v \rangle = \alpha \|v\|^2,$$

so $\alpha = \langle v, Av \rangle / \|v\|^2$ is also real. □

Since real symmetric matrices are self-adjoint, the eigenvalues of real symmetric matrices are all real (and so are eigenvectors).

---

[2]The transpose of the cofactor matrix is sometimes called the (classical) adjoint matrix or the adjugate matrix, which should not be confused. The term "self-adjoint" is commonly used in functional analysis.

Corollary 6.7. *A real symmetric matrix is diagonalizable by an orthogonal matrix.*

Proof. Immediate from Corollary 6.5 and Proposition 6.6. □

6.6 POSITIVE DEFINITE MATRICES

For $A \in \mathbb{R}^{N \times N}$ and $x \in \mathbb{R}^N$, the inner product $\langle x, Ax \rangle$ is called a *quadratic form*. Such expressions often appear in applications; see for instance Problem 3.7. Without loss of generality, we may assume A is symmetric. To see this, noting that $\langle x, Ax \rangle$ is a scalar, we have $\langle x, Ax \rangle = \langle Ax, x \rangle = \langle x, A'x \rangle$, so

$$\langle x, Ax \rangle = \frac{1}{2}(\langle x, Ax \rangle + \langle Ax, x \rangle) = \left\langle x, \left(\frac{A + A'}{2} \right) x \right\rangle.$$

Thus we may replace the matrix A with the symmetric matrix $(A + A')/2$ without affecting the value of the quadratic form.

In many applications, it is important to know the sign of the quadratic form $\langle x, Ax \rangle$. We say that a symmetric matrix A is *positive semidefinite* (psd) if $\langle x, Ax \rangle \geq 0$ for all x. If the inequality is strict whenever $x \neq 0$, we say that A is *positive definite* (pd). Negative (semi)definite matrices are defined analogously. Clearly, A is negative (semi)definite if and only if $-A$ is positive (semi)definite. We may provide a complete characterization of positive (semi)definite matrices by applying the spectral theorem.

Proposition 6.8. *A real symmetric matrix is positive semidefinite (definite) if and only if all eigenvalues are nonnegative (positive).*

Proof. By Corollary 6.7, we can take an orthogonal matrix P such that $P'AP = \text{diag}[\alpha_1, \ldots, \alpha_N]$. For any x, let $y = P'x$. Since $PP' = I$, we have

$$\langle x, Ax \rangle = x'Ax = x'PP'APP'x = y' \text{diag}[\alpha_1, \ldots, \alpha_N]y = \sum_{n=1}^{N} \alpha_n y_n^2.$$

The last expression is nonnegative (positive) for all x (hence for all y) if and only if all α_n's are nonnegative (positive). □

There is a simple test for positive definiteness that does not involve solving for eigenvalues. Let A be a square matrix. The determinant of the matrix obtained by keeping the first k rows and columns of A is called the k-th *principal minor* of A. For example, if $A = (a_{mn})$ is $N \times N$, then the first principal minor is a_{11}, the second principal minor is $a_{11}a_{22} - a_{12}a_{21}$, and the N-th principal minor is $|A|$, etc.

Proposition 6.9. *A real symmetric matrix is positive definite if and only if its principal minors are all positive.*

Proof. We prove by mathematical induction on the dimension N of the matrix A. If $N = 1$, the claim is trivial.

Suppose the claim is true up to dimension $N - 1$, and let $A \in \mathbb{R}^{N \times N}$. Partition A as

$$A = \begin{bmatrix} A_1 & b \\ b' & c \end{bmatrix},$$

where $A_1 \in \mathbb{R}^{(N-1) \times (N-1)}$ is symmetric, $b \in \mathbb{R}^{N-1}$, and $c \in \mathbb{R}$. Let

$$P = \begin{bmatrix} I & -A_1^{-1}b \\ 0 & 1 \end{bmatrix}.$$

Then by simple algebra we get

$$P'AP = \begin{bmatrix} A_1 & 0 \\ 0 & c - b'A_1^{-1}b \end{bmatrix}.$$

By Proposition 5.6, we have $|P| = 1$, so P is invertible. Since

$$\langle x, Ax \rangle = x'Ax = (P^{-1}x)'(P'AP)(P^{-1}x),$$

A is pd if and only if $P'AP$ is. But since $P'AP$ is block diagonal, $P'AP$ is pd if and only if A_1 is pd and $c - b'A^{-1}b > 0$. By the inductive hypothesis, A_1 is pd if and only if its principal minors are all positive. Furthermore, since $|P| = 1$, by Propositions 5.5 and 5.6 we have

$$|A| = |P'AP| = |A_1|\,(c - b'A_1^{-1}b).$$

Therefore

$$A \text{ is pd} \iff \text{all principal minors of } A_1 \text{ are positive and } c - b'A_1^{-1}b > 0$$
$$\iff \text{all principal minors of } A_1 \text{ are positive and } |A| > 0$$
$$\iff \text{all principal minors of } A \text{ are positive,}$$

so the claim is true for N as well. $\qquad\qquad\square$

6.7 SECOND-ORDER OPTIMALITY CONDITION

The astute reader may notice that we have provided a second-order characterization of local minima of one-variable functions in Proposition 2.6, but we have not done so for multi-variable functions in Chapter 3. The reason is that it requires knowledge of positive definite matrices. We now have all tools to study second-order conditions for optimality.

Let $U \subset \mathbb{R}^N$ be open and $f : U \to \mathbb{R}$ be C^2 (twice continuously differentiable). Fix some $a \in U$, let $x \in U$ be sufficiently close to a, and define the one-variable function $g : [0, 1] \to \mathbb{R}$ by $g(t) = f(a + t(x - a))$. Then $g(0) = f(a)$ and $g(1) = f(x)$. Now apply Taylor's theorem to g and set $t = 1$. The result is Taylor's theorem for the multi-variable function $f(x)$. The multi-variable version of Taylor's theorem is most useful in the second-order approximation:

$$f(x) = f(a) + \langle \nabla f(a), x - a \rangle + \frac{1}{2} \langle x - a, \nabla^2 f(\xi)(x - a) \rangle, \qquad (6.7)$$

where $\xi = (1 - \theta)a + \theta x$ for some $0 < \theta < 1$ and

$$\nabla^2 f = \left(\frac{\partial^2 f}{\partial x_m \partial x_n} \right)$$

is the matrix of second partial derivatives of f, known as the *Hessian*.

Although we do not prove it (see Theorem 9.41 of Rudin (1976)), for C^2 functions, the order of the partial derivatives can be exchanged: $\frac{\partial^2 f}{\partial x_m \partial x_n} = \frac{\partial^2 f}{\partial x_n \partial x_m}$. Thus the Hessian is a symmetric matrix.

The following proposition provides a second-order characterization of local minima, which generalizes Proposition 2.6.

Proposition 6.10. *Let $U \subset \mathbb{R}^N$ be open and $f : U \to \mathbb{R}$ be C^2. Then the following statements are true.*

(i) *If $\bar{x} \in U$ is a local minimum, then $\nabla f(\bar{x}) = 0$ and $\nabla^2 f(\bar{x})$ is positive semidefinite.*

(ii) *If $\nabla f(\bar{x}) = 0$ and $\nabla^2 f(\bar{x})$ is positive definite, then $\bar{x}$ is a strict local minimum.*

Proof. Suppose $\bar{x}$ is a local minimum. By Proposition 3.2, we have $\nabla f(\bar{x}) = 0$. Take any $v \in \mathbb{R}^N$. Then for small enough $t > 0$, letting $a = \bar{x}$ and $x = a + tv$ in (6.7), we obtain

$$f(\bar{x}) \leq f(x) = f(\bar{x}) + t \langle \nabla f(\bar{x}), v \rangle + \frac{1}{2} t^2 \langle v, \nabla^2 f(\bar{x} + \theta tv)v \rangle$$
$$\implies 0 \leq \langle v, \nabla^2 f(\bar{x} + \theta tv)v \rangle.$$

Letting $t \to 0$ and noting that f is C^2, we obtain $\langle v, \nabla^2 f(\bar{x})v \rangle \geq 0$. Since v is arbitrary, $\nabla^2 f(\bar{x})$ is positive semidefinite.

Conversely, suppose that $\nabla f(\bar{x}) = 0$ and $\nabla^2 f(\bar{x})$ is positive definite. Since the determinant of a matrix is continuous in its entries, the signs of principal minors of $\nabla^2 f(x)$ remain the same if x is sufficiently close to $\bar{x}$. Hence by Proposition 6.9, $\nabla^2 f(x)$ is positive definite in the neighborhood of $\bar{x}$. Let $\|v\| = 1$ and $x = \bar{x} + tv$ for sufficiently small $t > 0$. By Taylor's theorem, we have

$$f(x) = f(\bar{x}) + t \langle \nabla f(\bar{x}), v \rangle + \frac{1}{2} t^2 \langle v, \nabla^2 f(\bar{x} + \theta tv)v \rangle$$
$$= f(\bar{x}) + \frac{1}{2} t^2 \langle v, \nabla^2 f(\bar{x} + \theta tv)v \rangle > f(\bar{x}),$$

so $\bar{x}$ is a strict local minimum. □

6.8   MATRIX NORM AND SPECTRAL RADIUS

In Chapter 1, we defined the norm on a vector space by a real function satisfying nonnegativity, positive homogeneity, and triangle inequality. Since $N \times N$ matrices can be viewed as N^2-dimensional vectors, we can also define norms for matrices.

However, a distinctive property of matrices is that they can be multiplied. We thus define the *matrix norm* by a function satisfying the following four properties:

(i) (Nonnegativity) $\|A\| \geq 0$, with equality if and only if $A = 0$,

(ii) (Positive homogeneity) $\|\alpha A\| = |\alpha| \, \|A\|$,

(iii) (Triangle inequality) $\|A + B\| \leq \|A\| + \|B\|$,

(iv) (Submultiplicativity) $\|AB\| \leq \|A\| \, \|B\|$.

When submultiplicativity is dropped, we call $\|\cdot\|$ a *vector norm* for matrices. With a (vector) norm on the set of matrices, we may talk about the convergence of sequences of matrices. By the norm equivalence theorem (Theorem 1.3), all vector norms (and hence matrix norms) define the same topology.

Any norm $\|\cdot\|$ on $\mathbb{R}^N$ induces a matrix norm.

Proposition 6.11. *Let $\|\cdot\|$ be a norm on $\mathbb{R}^N$. For any $A \in \mathbb{R}^{N \times N}$, define*

$$\|A\| = \sup_{x \neq 0} \frac{\|Ax\|}{\|x\|}. \tag{6.8}$$

Then $\|\cdot\|$ is a matrix norm on $\mathbb{R}^{N \times N}$.

Proof. We first show that (6.8) is well-defined. Using the positive homogeneity of the norm, we have $\|A(\alpha x)\| / \|\alpha x\| = \|Ax\| / \|x\|$ for all $\alpha \neq 0$ and $x \neq 0$. Therefore by setting $\alpha = 1/\|x\|$, without loss of generality, we may assume $\|x\| = 1$. Then (6.8) becomes

$$\|A\| = \sup_{\|x\|=1} \|Ax\|. \tag{6.9}$$

Since the unit sphere $\{x \in \mathbb{R}^N : \|x\| = 1\}$ is nonempty, closed, bounded, and the norm is continuous, it follows from the extreme value theorem (Theorem 1.11) that the maximum in (6.9) is achieved and is finite. Therefore $\|A\| \in [0, \infty)$ is well defined.

(Nonnegativity) Clearly $\|A\| \geq 0$. If $\|A\| = 0$, then $\|Ax\| = 0$ for all $x \in \mathbb{R}^N$. Since $\|\cdot\|$ is a norm on $\mathbb{R}^N$, we have $Ax = 0$ for all x, so $A = 0$.

(Positive homogeneity) Let $\alpha \in \mathbb{R}$. Then (6.8) implies

$$\|\alpha A\| = \sup_{x \neq 0} \frac{\|\alpha Ax\|}{\|x\|} = |\alpha| \sup_{x \neq 0} \frac{\|Ax\|}{\|x\|} = |\alpha| \, \|A\|.$$

(Triangle inequality) Note that (6.8) implies $\|Ax\| \leq \|A\| \, \|x\|$ for all x. Therefore

$$\|(A+B)x\| = \|Ax + Bx\| \leq \|Ax\| + \|Bx\| \leq (\|A\| + \|B\|) \, \|x\| \, .$$

Dividing both sides by $\|x\|$ and taking the supremum, we obtain $\|A + B\| \leq \|A\| + \|B\|$.

(Submultiplicativity) For all x, we have

$$\|ABx\| = \|A(Bx)\| \leq \|A\| \, \|Bx\| \leq \|A\| \, \|B\| \, \|x\| \, .$$

Dividing both sides by $\|x\|$ and taking the supremum, we obtain $\|AB\| \leq \|A\| \, \|B\|$. $\qquad\square$

The matrix norm $\|\cdot\|$ in Proposition 6.11 is called the *operator norm*.

Example 6.4. If $\|\cdot\|$ denotes the ℓ^∞ norm and $A = (a_{mn})$, then

$$\|Ax\| = \max_m \left| \sum_{n=1}^{N} a_{mn} x_n \right| .$$

Taking the maximum over all x with $\|x\| = \max_n |x_n| = 1$, it follows from (6.9) that

$$\|A\| = \max_m \sum_{n=1}^{N} |a_{mn}| \, .$$

Remark. The proof of Proposition 6.11 does not use the property of $\mathbb{R}$, so we can also define the operator norm on $\mathbb{C}^{N \times N}$. Furthermore, except submultiplicativity, we have not used the fact that A, B are square matrices, so we may define a vector norm on $\mathbb{C}^{M \times N}$ induced by any norms defined on $\mathbb{C}^N$ and $\mathbb{C}^M$ using (6.8).

If $A \in \mathbb{C}^{N \times N}$, the set of eigenvalues $\{\alpha_n\}_{n=1}^{N}$ is called the *spectrum* of A. The largest absolute value of all eigenvalues,

$$\rho(A) := \max_n |\alpha_n| \, , \tag{6.10}$$

is called the *spectral radius* of A.

As another application of the Schur triangularization theorem, we can show that the eigenvalues and the spectral radius of a matrix are continuous in the entries.

Proposition 6.12 (Continuity of eigenvalues). *Let $\{A_k\}_{k=1}^{\infty} \subset \mathbb{C}^{N \times N}$ be a sequence such that $A := \lim_{k \to \infty} A_k$ exists. Then there exist a subsequence $\{A_{k_l}\}_{l=1}^{\infty}$ and an ordered list $(\alpha_{nk_l})_{n=1}^{N}$ of eigenvalues of A_{k_l} such that $\alpha_n := \lim_{l \to \infty} \alpha_{nk_l}$ exists for all n and $\{\alpha_n\}_{n=1}^{N}$ is the spectrum of A.*

Proof. For each k, by Theorem 6.4, we can take a unitary matrix U_k such that $T_k := U_k^* A_k U_k$ is upper triangular. Since the column vectors of unitary matrices form an orthonormal basis, they are bounded. Therefore by Theorem 1.10, we can take a convergent subsequence $\{U_{k_l}\}$. Let $U = \lim_{l\to\infty} U_{k_l}$. Since each U_{k_l} is unitary, so is U. Let $T := U^* A U$. Since $U_{k_l} \to U$ and $A_k \to A$, we have $T_{k_l} \to T$. Let α_{nk_l} be the n-th diagonal entry of T_{k_l}. Since T_{k_l} is upper triangular, by Proposition 6.2 $(\alpha_{nk_l})_{n=1}^N$ is an ordered list of eigenvalues of T_{k_l} and hence of A_{k_l}. Since $T_{k_l} \to T$, $\alpha_n := \lim_{l\to\infty} \alpha_{nk_l}$ exists for all n and T is upper triangular. Since $T = U^* A U$, $\{\alpha_n\}_{n=1}^N$ is the spectrum of A. $\qquad\square$

Corollary 6.13. *The spectral radius is continuous in the entries of the matrix.*

Recall that if $A = \mathrm{diag}[d_1, \dots, d_N]$ is diagonal, we have $A^k \to 0$ as $k \to 0$ if and only if $|d_n| < 1$ for all n. (Here we implicitly assume entrywise convergence, but we can use any vector norm by Theorem 1.3.) By Proposition 6.2, the spectrum of A is $\{d_1, \dots, d_N\}$, and hence $\rho(A) = \max_n |d_n|$. Thus, for diagonal matrices, we have $A^k \to 0$ if and only if $\rho(A) < 1$. This property is in fact true for all matrices. Before we state the result, to simplify notation, for a general matrix $A = (a_{mn})$, denote the matrix of absolute values by $|A| = (|a_{mn}|)$. (Although we use the same notation as the determinant, the meaning should be clear from the context.)

Proposition 6.14. *Let $A \in \mathbb{C}^{N\times N}$. Then $\lim_{k\to\infty} A^k = 0$ if and only if $\rho(A) < 1$.*

Proof. By the Schur triangularization theorem (Theorem 6.4), without loss of generality, we may assume that A is upper triangular.

Suppose that A is upper triangular and $A^k \to 0$. By Proposition 6.2, the diagonal entries of A are eigenvalues of A denoted by $\{\alpha_n\}$. Therefore the diagonal entries of A^k are $\{\alpha_n^k\}$. Since $A^k \to 0$, we have $\alpha_n^k \to 0$ as $k \to \infty$. Therefore $|\alpha_n| < 1$ for all n, so $\rho(A) < 1$.

Conversely, suppose A is upper triangular and $r := \rho(A) < 1$. Since A is upper triangular, we may uniquely write $A = D + T$, where D is diagonal and T is upper triangular with $T_{mn} = 0$ for all $m \geq n$. Then we have the entrywise inequality
$$|A| = |D| + |T| \leq rI + |T|.$$
Since $T \in \mathbb{C}^{N\times N}$ is upper triangular with zero diagonal entries, we can easily check that $|T|^N = 0$ (Problem 6.15). Therefore by the triangle inequality for complex numbers and the binomial theorem, for $k \geq N$ we have
$$0 \leq |A^k| \leq |A|^k \leq (rI + |T|)^k = \sum_{l=0}^k \binom{k}{l} r^{k-l} |T|^l = \sum_{l=0}^{N-1} \binom{k}{l} r^{k-l} |T|^l.$$

The binomial coefficient in the last expression can be bounded as
$$\binom{k}{l} = \frac{k(k-1)\cdots(k-l+1)}{l!} \leq \frac{k^l}{l!},$$

which is a polynomial in k. Since $0 \le r < 1$, for all $l = 0, \ldots, N-1$ we have $\binom{k}{l} r^{k-l} \to 0$ as $k \to \infty$, so $A^k \to 0$. $\qquad\square$

The spectral radius and the matrix norm are related as follows.

Theorem 6.15 (Gelfand spectral radius formula). *Let $\|\cdot\|$ be any matrix norm on $\mathbb{C}^{N \times N}$. Then $\rho(A) \le \left\|A^k\right\|^{1/k}$ and $\rho(A) = \lim_{k \to \infty} \left\|A^k\right\|^{1/k}$.*

Proof. Let α be an eigenvalue of A and $v \ne 0$ be a corresponding eigenvector. Then $A^k v = \alpha^k v$ for all k. Let $V = (v, \ldots, v)$ be the matrix obtained by replicating v. Then $A^k V = \alpha^k V$. Taking the norm of both sides, we obtain

$$|\alpha|^k \, \|V\| = \left\|A^k V\right\| \le \left\|A^k\right\| \, \|V\| \implies |\alpha|^k \le \left\|A^k\right\|.$$

Since α is any eigenvalue, it follows that $\rho(A) \le \left\|A^k\right\|^{1/k}$.

Take any $\epsilon > 0$ and define $\tilde{A} = \frac{1}{\rho(A)+\epsilon} A$. Then $\rho(\tilde{A}) = \frac{\rho(A)}{\rho(A)+\epsilon} < 1$, so $\lim_{k \to \infty} \tilde{A}^k = 0$ by Proposition 6.14. Therefore $\left\|\tilde{A}^k\right\| < 1$ for large enough k, and hence $\left\|A^k\right\| \le (\rho(A)+\epsilon)^k$. Taking the k-th root, letting $k \to \infty$, and $\epsilon \downarrow 0$, we obtain $\limsup_{k \to \infty} \left\|A^k\right\|^{1/k} \le \rho(A)$. Since $\rho(A) \le \left\|A^k\right\|^{1/k}$, it follows that $\rho(A) = \lim_{k \to \infty} \left\|A^k\right\|^{1/k}$. $\qquad\square$

Remark. Although the above proof of Theorem 6.15 uses the submultiplicativity of the matrix norm, this condition is actually not necessary. For a proof of Gelfand's formula that does not require submultiplicativity, see Horn and Johnson (2013, Theorem 5.7.10).

An important implication of Theorem 6.15 is that the "size" of the matrix power A^k is approximately $\rho(A)^k$. Recall that in complex analysis we study the convergence of power series

$$f(z) = \sum_{k=0}^{\infty} a_k z^k.$$

If this series converges for $|z| < r$ and a matrix satisfies $\rho(A) < r$, then we may unambiguously define the matrix series

$$f(A) = \sum_{k=0}^{\infty} a_k A^k.$$

See Problems 6.16 and 6.17 for concrete examples.

PROBLEMS

6.1. Verify the claim in Example 6.3.

6.2. Let V be a real inner product space. For $x \in \mathsf{V}$, define $\|x\| = \sqrt{\langle x, x \rangle} \ge 0$.

(i) For any $0 \neq x \in V$ and $y \in V$, define the function $f : \mathbb{R} \to \mathbb{R}$ by $f(t) = \|tx - y\|^2$. Solve $\min_t f(t)$.

(ii) By evaluating f at the minimum value, prove the Cauchy-Schwarz inequality (6.3).

(iii) By using the Cauchy-Schwarz inequality, prove the triangle inequality (6.4).

6.3. Generalize the Cauchy-Schwarz inequality for a complex inner product space.

6.4. Prove that the matrix $A = \begin{bmatrix} 1 & 1 \\ 0 & 1 \end{bmatrix}$ is not diagonalizable. (Hint: Proposition 6.2.)

6.5. Let A be real symmetric and positive semidefinite. Show that there exists a real symmetric and positive semidefinite matrix B such that $A = B^2$.

6.6. Let A be real symmetric with eigenvalues $\alpha_1, \ldots, \alpha_N$, where $|\alpha_1| \leq \cdots \leq |\alpha_N|$. Let $\|\cdot\|$ be the Euclidean norm. Show that for any nonzero vector $x \in \mathbb{R}^N$, we have $|\alpha_1| \leq \|Ax\| / \|x\| \leq |\alpha_N|$.

6.7. Let $A = [a_1, \ldots, a_N] \in \mathbb{R}^{M \times N}$, where a_n is the n-th column vector of A. Show that $A'A$ is positive definite if and only if $\{a_1, \ldots, a_N\}$ is linearly independent.

6.8. Let V be a real inner product space. Let $\{v_n\}_{n=1}^N \subset V$, and define the $N \times N$ matrix $A = (a_{mn})$ by $a_{mn} = \langle v_m, v_n \rangle$.

(i) Show that A is positive semidefinite.

(ii) Show that A is positive definite if and only if the vectors $\{v_n\}_{n=1}^N$ are linearly independent.

(iii) For the inner product space V, consider the space of continuous functions $f : [0, 1] \to \mathbb{R}$ with inner product defined by

$$\langle f, g \rangle = \int_0^1 f(x) g(x) \, \mathrm{d}x.$$

Show that $\langle \cdot, \cdot \rangle$ is indeed an inner product.

(iv) Let V be as in the previous question. For $n = 1, \ldots, N$, let $v_n(x) = x^{n-1}$. Show that $\{v_n\}_{n=1}^N$ is linearly independent.

(v) Define the matrix $A = (a_{mn})$ by $a_{mn} = \frac{1}{m+n-1}$. Prove that A is positive definite.

6.9. Compute the partial derivatives, the gradient, and the Hessian of the following functions.

(i) $f(x_1, x_2) = a_1 x_1 + a_2 x_2$, where a_1, a_2 are constants.

(ii) $f(x_1, x_2) = ax_1^2 + 2bx_1 x_2 + cx_2^2$, where a, b, c are constants.

(iii) $f(x_1, x_2) = x_1 x_2$.

(iv) $f(x_1, x_2) = x_1 \log x_2$, where $x_2 > 0$.

6.10. Compute the gradient and the Hessian of the following functions.

(i) $f(x) = \langle a, x \rangle$, where a, x are vectors of the same dimensions and $\langle a, x \rangle = a \cdot x$ is the inner product of a and x.

(ii) $f(x) = \langle x, Ax \rangle$, where A is a square matrix of the same dimension as the vector x.

6.11. Let $f(x_1, x_2) = x_1^3 + 3x_1^2 + x_1 x_2 + x_2^2 - 5x_2 + 6$. Compute all points with $\nabla f(x) = 0$, and determine whether each is a local minimum, local maximum, or neither.

6.12. For $A = (a_{mn}) \in \mathbb{C}^{N \times N}$, define

$$\|A\| = \left(\sum_{m,n=1}^{N} |a_{mn}|^2 \right)^{1/2}.$$

Show that $\|\cdot\|$ is a matrix norm.

6.13. For $A = (a_{mn}) \in \mathbb{C}^{N \times N}$, define

$$\|A\| = \sum_{m,n=1}^{N} |a_{mn}|.$$

Show that $\|\cdot\|$ is a matrix norm.

6.14. Let $\|\cdot\|$ be the Euclidean norm on $\mathbb{C}^N$ and let $A \in \mathbb{C}^{N \times N}$.

(i) Show that $\|Ax\|^2 = \langle x, A^* Ax \rangle$.

(ii) Show that $\max_{\|x\|=1} \langle x, A^* Ax \rangle = \rho(A^* A)$.

(iii) Show that $\|A\| = \sqrt{\rho(A^* A)}$.

6.15. For $1 \le p \le N$, let $\mathcal{T}_N^p$ be the set of $N \times N$ upper triangular matrices $A = (a_{mn})$ with $a_{mn} = 0$ whenever $n - m < p$.

(i) Show that if $A \in \mathcal{T}_N^p$ and $B \in \mathcal{T}_N^q$, then $AB \in \mathcal{T}_N^{p+q}$.

(ii) Show that if $A \in \mathcal{T}_N^1$, then $A^N = 0$.

6.16. If $\rho(A) < 1$, prove that the matrix series $\sum_{k=0}^{\infty} A^k$ is well defined and equals $(I - A)^{-1}$. (Hint: use $(1 - z)(1 + z + \cdots + z^k) = 1 - z^{k+1}$.)

6.17. Prove that the matrix series

$$\exp(A) := \sum_{k=0}^{\infty} \frac{1}{k!} A^k$$

is well defined. (Hint: use the Cauchy criterion for convergence.) We can thus define the matrix exponential.

CHAPTER 7

Metric Space and Contraction

7.1 METRIC SPACE

Recall that a normed space is a vector space V equipped with a norm $\|\cdot\|$. For any two elements v_1, v_2 of V, we may define their distance by

$$d(v_1, v_2) := \|v_1 - v_2\|.$$

Using the properties of the norm, we can easily show (Problem 7.1) that d satisfies the following three properties:

(i) (Nonnegativity) $d(v_1, v_2) \geq 0$, with equality if and only if $v_1 = v_2$,

(ii) (Symmetry) $d(v_1, v_2) = d(v_2, v_1)$,

(iii) (Triangle inequality) $d(v_1, v_3) \leq d(v_1, v_2) + d(v_2, v_3)$.

In general, if a set V is equipped with a function $d : V \times V \to \mathbb{R}$ satisfying these three properties, we say that (V, d) is a *metric space* and refer to the function d as the *metric* or the *distance*. When the metric d is understood, we often just say V is a metric space, omitting the reference to d.

If (V, d) is a metric space and $V_1 \subset V$, the pair (V_1, d) is obviously a metric space. This property allows us to construct many metric spaces. In contrast, if $(V, \|\cdot\|)$ is a normed space and $V_1 \subset V$, the pair $(V_1, \|\cdot\|)$ is a normed space if and only if V_1 is a subspace (has the vector space structure). For instance, let V be the set of functions from $\mathbb{R}$ to $\mathbb{R}$, which is a vector space by defining addition and scalar multiplication pointwise. Let $V_1 \subset V$ be the set of increasing functions. Then V_1 can never be a normed space because it is not a vector space (since the difference of two increasing functions need not be increasing). But V_1 could be a metric space with a suitable metric.

We provide several examples.

DOI: 10.1201/9781032698953-7

Example 7.1. Let $X \subset \mathbb{R}^N$ be nonempty and V be the space of bounded functions on X:
$$\mathsf{V} = \{v : X \to \mathbb{R} : v \text{ is bounded}\} .$$

For $v \in \mathsf{V}$, define
$$\|v\| = \sup_{x \in X} |v(x)| .$$

Then $(\mathsf{V}, \|\cdot\|)$ is a normed space.

Proof. Since $v \in \mathsf{V}$ is bounded, clearly $0 \leq \|v\| < \infty$. If $\|v\| = 0$, then $|v(x)| = 0$ for all $x \in X$, so $v = 0$. If $\alpha \in \mathbb{R}$ and $v \in \mathsf{V}$, then
$$\|\alpha v\| = \sup_{x \in X} |\alpha v(x)| = |\alpha| \sup_{x \in X} |v(x)| = |\alpha| \|v\| .$$

Noting that $|v(x)| \leq \|v\|$ for all $x \in X$, for $v_1, v_2 \in \mathsf{V}$, we have
$$|v_1(x) + v_2(x)| \leq |v_1(x)| + |v_2(x)| \leq \|v_1\| + \|v_2\| .$$

Taking the supremum of the left-hand side over $x \in X$, we obtain
$$\|v_1 + v_2\| \leq \|v_1\| + \|v_2\| .$$

Therefore $\|\cdot\|$ is a norm. □

The norm $\|\cdot\|$ in Example 7.1 is called the *supremum norm* or the *sup norm*.

Example 7.2. Let $(\mathsf{V}, \|\cdot\|)$ be as in Example 7.1. For $v_1, v_2 \in \mathsf{V}$, define
$$d(v_1, v_2) = \|v_1 - v_2\| = \sup_{x \in X} |v_1(x) - v_2(x)| .$$

Then for any $\mathsf{V}_1 \subset \mathsf{V}$, the pair (V_1, d) is a metric space.

The distance d in Example 7.2 is called the *sup distance*. For instance, the set of bounded increasing (or continuous or convex) functions from $\mathbb{R}$ to $\mathbb{R}$ equipped with the sup distance is a metric space but not a normed space.

If (V, d) is a metric space, we define the (open) *ball* with center $v \in \mathsf{V}$ and radius $\epsilon > 0$ by the set
$$B_\epsilon(v) := \{w \in \mathsf{V} : d(v, w) < \epsilon\} .$$

Then we may define the convergence of sequences in V and the topology (open sets) of V exactly as in Chapter 1. For instance, a set $U \subset \mathsf{V}$ is *open* if and only if for any $v \in U$, we can take $\epsilon > 0$ such that $B_\epsilon(v) \subset U$. Similarly, a sequence $\{v_k\}_{k=1}^\infty \subset \mathsf{V}$ *converges* to $v \in \mathsf{V}$ if and only if $d(v_k, v) \to 0$ as $k \to \infty$. All results in §1.5 generalize to metric spaces, and the proofs are identical.

7.2 COMPLETENESS AND BANACH SPACE

Let (V, d) be a metric space. We say that a sequence $\{v_k\}_{k=1}^{\infty} \subset V$ is *Cauchy* if

$$(\forall \epsilon > 0)(\exists K > 0)(\forall k, l \geq K) \quad d(v_k, v_l) < \epsilon. \tag{7.1}$$

We know from Problem 1.10 that Cauchy sequences in $\mathbb{R}^N$ are convergent. This property is called the *completeness* of $\mathbb{R}^N$. When the metric space (V, d) is complete, we call it a *complete metric space*. A normed space $(V, \|\cdot\|)$ can be viewed as a metric space with distance $d(v_1, v_2) = \|v_1 - v_2\|$. A complete normed space is called a *Banach space*. The following proposition provides an example.

Proposition 7.1. *The normed space $(V, \|\cdot\|)$ in Example 7.1 is a Banach space. If $V_1 \subset V$ is closed, the metric space (V_1, d) in Example 7.2 is complete.*

Proof. Let V be the space of bounded functions on X with sup norm $\|\cdot\|$. Let $\{v_k\}_{k=1}^{\infty} \subset V$ be Cauchy. By definition, (7.1) holds. Since $|v(x)| \leq \|v\|$ for all x, we have

$$(\forall \epsilon > 0)(\exists K > 0)(\forall k, l \geq K)(\forall x \in X) \quad |v_k(x) - v_l(x)| < \epsilon. \tag{7.2}$$

Therefore for fixed $x \in X$, the real sequence $\{v_k(x)\}$ is Cauchy. By Problem 1.10, $\{v_k(x)\}$ is convergent; let $v(x)$ be its limit. Letting $l \to \infty$ in (7.2), we obtain

$$(\forall \epsilon > 0)(\exists K > 0)(\forall k \geq K)(\forall x \in X) \quad |v_k(x) - v(x)| \leq \epsilon.$$

Taking the supremum over $x \in X$, we obtain

$$(\forall \epsilon > 0)(\exists K > 0)(\forall k \geq K) \quad \|v_k - v\| \leq \epsilon.$$

This implies that $v_k - v \in V$, and hence $v = v_k - (v_k - v) \in V$. Furthermore, by the definition of convergence, we have $v_k \to v$ as $k \to \infty$. Therefore V is complete and $(V, \|\cdot\|)$ is a Banach space.

Let $V_1 \subset V$ be closed. If $\{v_k\}_{k=1}^{\infty} \subset V_1$ is Cauchy, then in particular it is Cauchy in V. Since V is complete, $\{v_k\}_{k=1}^{\infty}$ converges to some $v \in V$. Since $V_1 \subset V$ is closed, we have $v \in V_1$. Therefore (V_1, d) is a complete metric space. $\qquad\square$

Since monotonicity and convexity are preserved by taking limits, it follows that the spaces of bounded increasing functions, bounded convex functions, and bounded increasing convex functions are all complete metric spaces.

Corollary 7.2. *The space of bounded continuous functions is Banach. Any closed subset of it is a complete metric space.*

Proof. Let $X \subset \mathbb{R}^N$ and bX be the space of bounded functions on X with sup norm $\|\cdot\|$. By Proposition 7.1, bX is Banach. Let bcX be the space of bounded continuous functions on X. Since $bcX \subset bX$ is a vector space and $(bX, \|\cdot\|)$ is Banach (hence normed space), $(bcX, \|\cdot\|)$ is a normed space. Let $\{v_k\}_{k=1}^{\infty}$ be Cauchy in bcX. Then it is Cauchy in bX, and since bX is Banach, we can take $v \in bX$ such that $\|v_k - v\| \to 0$ as $k \to \infty$. Hence to show the completeness of bcX, it suffices to show that v is continuous.

Take any $\epsilon > 0$. Since $v_k \to v$ in bX, we can take K such that $\|v - v_k\| < \epsilon/3$ for $k > K$. Fix such k and take any $x \in X$. Since v_k is continuous, we can take a neighborhood U of x such that $|v_k(y) - v_k(x)| < \epsilon/3$ for $y \in U$. Then

$$
\begin{aligned}
|v(y) - v(x)| &= |v(y) - v_k(y) + v_k(y) - v_k(x) + v_k(x) - v(x)| \\
&\leq |v(y) - v_k(y)| + |v_k(y) - v_k(x)| + |v_k(x) - v(x)| \\
&\leq \|v - v_k\| + \frac{\epsilon}{3} + \|v - v_k\| < \epsilon,
\end{aligned}
$$

so v is continuous. $\qquad\square$

Convergence with respect to the supremum norm as in Proposition 7.1 is sometimes called *uniform convergence*. Corollary 7.2 states that the uniform limit of continuous functions on a compact set is continuous, a well-known result in real analysis.

7.3 CONTRACTION MAPPING THEOREM

In general, if V is a set and T is a function from V to itself ($T : \mathsf{V} \to \mathsf{V}$), we say that T is a *self-map* or sometimes an *operator*. If T is a self-map on V and $v \in \mathsf{V}$ satisfies $T(v) = v$, so v remains unchanged by applying T, we say that v is a *fixed point* of T. In what follows, we often write Tv for $T(v)$ to simplify notation, just like we did for matrix multiplication.

Let (V, d) be a metric space. A self-map $T : \mathsf{V} \to \mathsf{V}$ is called a *contraction mapping* (or simply a *contraction*) with modulus β if $\beta \in [0, 1)$ and

$$
d(Tv_1, Tv_2) \leq \beta d(v_1, v_2) \tag{7.3}
$$

for all $v_1, v_2 \in \mathsf{V}$. Intuitively, the condition (7.3) means that when we apply T, the distance between two points shrinks by a factor $\beta < 1$. The following contraction mapping theorem (also called the Banach fixed point theorem) is elementary but has many important applications, as we shall see below.

Theorem 7.3 (Contraction mapping theorem). *Let (V, d) be a complete metric space and $T : \mathsf{V} \to \mathsf{V}$ be a contraction with modulus $\beta \in [0, 1)$. Then*

(i) T has a unique fixed point $v^* \in \mathsf{V}$,

(ii) for any $v_0 \in \mathsf{V}$, we have $v^* = \lim_{k \to \infty} T^k v_0$, and

(iii) the approximation error $d(T^k v_0, v^*)$ has order of magnitude β^k.

Proof. First note that a contraction is continuous (indeed, uniformly continuous) because for any $\epsilon > 0$, if $d(v_1, v_2) < \epsilon$ then

$$d(Tv_1, Tv_2) \leq \beta d(v_1, v_2) \leq \beta\epsilon \leq \epsilon.$$

Take any $v_0 \in \mathsf{V}$ and define $v_k = Tv_{k-1}$ for $k \geq 1$. Then $v_k = T^k v_0$. Since T is a contraction, we have

$$d(v_k, v_{k-1}) = d(Tv_{k-1}, Tv_{k-2}) \leq \beta d(v_{k-1}, v_{k-2}) \leq \cdots \leq \beta^{k-1} d(v_1, v_0).$$

If $k > l \geq K$, then by the triangle inequality we have

$$\begin{aligned}
d(v_k, v_l) &\leq d(v_k, v_{k-1}) + \cdots + d(v_{l+1}, v_l) \\
&\leq (\beta^{k-1} + \cdots + \beta^l) d(v_1, v_0) \\
&= \frac{\beta^l - \beta^k}{1 - \beta} d(v_1, v_0) \leq \frac{\beta^l}{1 - \beta} d(v_1, v_0) \leq \frac{\beta^K}{1 - \beta} d(v_1, v_0).
\end{aligned}$$

Since $0 \leq \beta < 1$, we have $\beta^K \to 0$ as $K \to \infty$, so $\{v_k\}$ is Cauchy. Since V is complete, $v^* = \lim_{k \to \infty} v_k$ exists. By the triangle inequality, we have

$$\begin{aligned}
d(Tv^*, v^*) &\leq d(Tv^*, Tv_k) + d(Tv_k, v_k) + d(v_k, v^*) \\
&\leq \beta d(v^*, v_k) + d(v_{k+1}, v_k) + d(v_k, v^*) \\
&\leq (1 + \beta) d(v_k, v^*) + \beta^k d(v_1, v_0) \to 0
\end{aligned}$$

as $k \to \infty$, so $d(Tv^*, v^*) = 0$. Since d is a metric, we have $Tv^* = v^*$, so v^* is a fixed point of T.

To show uniqueness, suppose that v_1, v_2 are fixed points of T, so $Tv_1 = v_1$ and $Tv_2 = v_2$. Since T is a contraction, we have

$$0 \leq d(v_1, v_2) = d(Tv_1, Tv_2) \leq \beta d(v_1, v_2) \implies (\beta - 1) d(v_1, v_2) \geq 0.$$

Since $\beta < 1$, it must be $d(v_1, v_2) = 0$ and hence $v_1 = v_2$. Therefore the fixed point is unique.

Finally, let v^* be the fixed point of T, v_0 be any point, and $v_k = T^k v_0$. Then

$$d(v_k, v^*) = d(Tv_{k-1}, Tv^*) \leq \beta d(v_{k-1}, v^*) \leq \cdots \leq \beta^k d(v_0, v^*).$$

Letting $k \to \infty$ we have $v_k \to v^*$, and the error has an order of magnitude β^k. $\square$

Sometimes, we need to work with self-maps T such that T^m is a contraction for some $m \in \mathbb{N}$, although T itself may not be a contraction. The following theorem extends Theorem 7.3 to such a case. (See Problem 7.3 for an example.)

Theorem 7.4. *Let (V, d) be a complete metric space and $T : \mathsf{V} \to \mathsf{V}$ be such that T^m is a contraction for some $m \in \mathbb{N}$. Then T has a unique fixed point $v^* \in \mathsf{V}$ and we have $v^* = \lim_{k \to \infty} T^k v_0$ for any $v_0 \in \mathsf{V}$.*

Proof. By the contraction mapping theorem, T^m has a unique fixed point $v^* \in \mathsf{V}$, so $T^m v^* = v^*$. Since

$$Tv^* = TT^m v^* = T^{m+1} v^* = T^m Tv^*,$$

Tv^* is also a fixed point of T^m. Since the fixed point of T^m is unique, it must be $Tv^* = v^*$, so v^* is a fixed point of T. If v_1, v_2 are fixed points of T, then $v_1 = Tv_1 = \cdots = T^m v_1$ and $v_2 = Tv_2 = \cdots = T^m v_2$, so v_1, v_2 are also fixed points of T^m. Since T^m is a contraction, it must be $v_1 = v_2$. Therefore the fixed point of T is unique.

To show $T^k v_0 \to v^*$ for any $v_0 \in \mathsf{V}$, express any $k \in \mathbb{N}$ uniquely as $k = mq_k + r_k$, where $q_k n \in \mathbb{Z}_+$ and $r_k \in \{0, \dots, m-1\}$. Then for each fixed $r \in \{0, \dots, m-1\}$, applying Theorem 7.3 to the initial value $T^r v_0$, we have $v^* = \lim_{q \to \infty} (T^m)^q T^r v_0 = \lim_{q \to \infty} T^{mq+r} v_0$. Since $r \in \{0, \dots, m-1\}$ is arbitrary, we obtain $T^k v_0 \to v^*$. □

7.4 BLACKWELL'S SUFFICIENT CONDITION

It would be convenient if there is a sufficient condition for contraction that is easily verifiable. The following proposition provides a sufficient condition for a contraction. Below, for functions v_1, v_2 defined on a set X, we write $v_1 \le v_2$ if $v_1(x) \le v_2(x)$ for all $x \in X$.

Proposition 7.5 (Blackwell's sufficient condition). *Let X be a set and V be a space of functions on X with the following properties:*

(a) *(Upward shift) For $v \in \mathsf{V}$ and $c \in \mathbb{R}_+$, we have $v + c \in \mathsf{V}$.*

(b) *(Bounded difference) For all $v_1, v_2 \in \mathsf{V}$, we have*

$$d(v_1, v_2) := \sup_{x \in X} |v_1(x) - v_2(x)| < \infty.$$

Suppose that (V, d) is a complete metric space and $T : \mathsf{V} \to \mathsf{V}$ satisfies

(i) *(Monotonicity) $v_1 \le v_2$ implies $Tv_1 \le Tv_2$,*

(ii) *(Discounting) there exists $\beta \in [0, 1)$ such that, for all $v \in \mathsf{V}$ and $c \in \mathbb{R}_+$, we have $T(v + c) \le Tv + \beta c$.*

Then T is a contraction with modulus β.

Proof. Take any $v_1, v_2 \in \mathsf{V}$ and let $c = d(v_1, v_2) \ge 0$. For any $x \in X$, we have

$$v_1(x) = v_1(x) - v_2(x) + v_2(x) \le v_2(x) + c,$$

so $v_1 \le v_2 + c \in \mathsf{V}$ by the upward shift property. Using monotonicity and discounting, we obtain

$$Tv_1 \le T(v_2 + c) \le Tv_2 + \beta c \implies Tv_1 - Tv_2 \le \beta c.$$

Interchanging the role of v_1, v_2, we obtain $Tv_2 - Tv_1 \leq \beta c$. This shows that $|(Tv_1)(x) - (Tv_2)(x)| \leq \beta d(v_1, v_2)$ for any $x \in X$. Taking the supremum over x, we obtain $d(Tv_1, Tv_2) \leq \beta d(v_1, v_2)$, so T is a contraction with modulus β. $\qquad\square$

7.5   PEROV CONTRACTION

There is a useful generalization of the contraction mapping theorem to what is called vector-valued metric spaces.

Let V be a set, $N \in \mathbb{N}$, and $d : V \times V \to \mathbb{R}^N$. We say that d is a *vector-valued metric* if the following conditions hold:

(i) (Nonnegativity) $d(v_1, v_2) \geq 0$, with equality if and only if $v_1 = v_2$,

(ii) (Symmetry) $d(v_1, v_2) = d(v_2, v_1)$,

(iii) (Triangle inequality) $d(v_1, v_3) \leq d(v_1, v_2) + d(v_2, v_3)$.

In conditions (i) and (iii), note that for $a = (a_1, \ldots, a_N) \in \mathbb{R}^N$ and $b = (b_1, \ldots, b_N) \in \mathbb{R}^N$, we write $a \leq b$ if and only if $a_n \leq b_n$ for all n. A set V endowed with a vector-valued metric d is called a *vector-valued metric space*. Obviously, a metric space is a special case of a vector-valued metric space by setting $N = 1$.

Let $\|\cdot\|$ denote the supremum norm on $\mathbb{R}^N$, so $\|a\| = \max_n |a_n|$ for $a = (a_1, \ldots, a_N) \in \mathbb{R}^N$. Note that the supremum norm satisfies the following monotonicity property: if $a, b \in \mathbb{R}^N$ and $0 \leq a \leq b$, then

$$\|a\| = \max_n a_n \leq \max_n b_n = \|b\|.$$

The monotonicity will be repeatedly used in the subsequent discussion. If (V, d) is a vector-valued metric space and we define $\|d\| : V \times V \to \mathbb{R}$ by

$$\|d\|(v_1, v_2) = \|d(v_1, v_2)\| = \max_n d_n(v_1, v_2),$$

then $(V, \|d\|)$ is a metric space in the usual sense. To see this, conditions (i) and (ii) are trivial, and condition (iii) holds because

$$\|d\|(v_1, v_3) = \|d(v_1, v_3)\| \leq \|d(v_1, v_2) + d(v_2, v_3)\|$$
$$\leq \|d(v_1, v_2)\| + \|d(v_2, v_3)\| = \|d\|(v_1, v_2) + \|d\|(v_2, v_3),$$

where the first inequality uses condition (iii) for d and the monotonicity of the supremum norm $\|\cdot\|$. We say that the vector-valued metric space (V, d) is *complete* if the metric space $(V, \|d\|)$ is complete.

Below, let $\|\cdot\|$ also denote the operator norm for $N \times N$ matrices induced by the supremum norm (Proposition 6.11). Recall that for a square matrix A, the spectral radius $\rho(A)$ is defined by the largest absolute value of all eigenvalues (see (6.10)). We extend the notion of contractions as follows. Let (V, d) be a vector-valued metric space. We say that a self-map $T : \mathsf{V} \to \mathsf{V}$ is a *Perov contraction* with coefficient matrix $B \geq 0$ if $\rho(B) < 1$ and

$$d(Tv_1, Tv_2) \leq Bd(v_1, v_2) \tag{7.4}$$

for all $v_1, v_2 \in \mathsf{V}$. Here $B \geq 0$ means that the matrix $B = (b_{mn})$ is nonnegative: $b_{mn} \geq 0$ for all m, n. (We have much more to say about nonnegative matrices in Chapter 9.) We can now generalize the contraction mapping theorem (Theorem 7.3) as follows.

Theorem 7.6 (Perov contraction theorem). *Let (V, d) be a complete vector-valued metric space and $T : \mathsf{V} \to \mathsf{V}$ be a Perov contraction with coefficient matrix $B \geq 0$. Then*

(i) T has a unique fixed point $v^* \in \mathsf{V}$,

(ii) for any $v_0 \in \mathsf{V}$, we have $v^* = \lim_{k \to \infty} T^k v_0$, and

(iii) for any $\beta \in (\rho(B), 1)$, the approximation error $d(T^k v_0, v^*)$ has order of magnitude β^k.

Proof. Because the proof of Theorem 7.6 is similar to Theorem 7.3, we only provide a sketch and leave the details to Problem 7.4. Take any $v_0 \in \mathsf{V}$ and define $v_k = Tv_{k-1}$ for $k \geq 1$. Then $v_k = T^k v_0$. Repeatedly applying the triangle inequality and (7.4), for $k > l$, we obtain

$$d(v_k, v_l) \leq (B^{k-1} + \cdots + B^l)d(v_1, v_0).$$

Applying the sup norm $\|\cdot\|$ and using its monotonicity, we obtain

$$\|d(v_k, v_l)\| \leq (\|B^{k-1}\| + \cdots + \|B^l\|) \|d(v_1, v_0)\|.$$

Take any $\beta \in (\rho(B), 1)$. By the Gelfand spectral radius formula (Theorem 6.15), we have $\|B^k\| \leq \beta^k$ for sufficiently large k, so

$$\|d(v_k, v_l)\| \leq (\beta^{k-1} + \cdots + \beta^l) \|d(v_1, v_0)\| \leq \frac{\beta^l}{1 - \beta} \|d(v_1, v_0)\| \to 0$$

as $l \to \infty$. Therefore $\{v_k\}$ is Cauchy in the complete metric space $(\mathsf{V}, \|d\|)$ and hence convergent. The rest of the proof is the same as Theorem 7.3. $\square$

The following proposition generalizes Blackwell's sufficient condition to Perov contractions.

Proposition 7.7. *Let X be a set and V be a space of functions $v : X \to \mathbb{R}^N$ with the following properties:*

(a) (Upward shift) For $v \in \mathsf{V}$ and $c \in \mathbb{R}_+^N$, we have $v + c \in \mathsf{V}$.

(b) (Bounded difference) For all $u, v \in \mathsf{V}$ and n, we have

$$d_n(u, v) := \sup_{x \in X} |u_n(x) - v_n(x)| < \infty.$$

Let $d = (d_1, \ldots, d_N)$. Suppose that (V, d) is a complete vector-valued metric space and $T : \mathsf{V} \to \mathsf{V}$ satisfies

(i) (Monotonicity) $u \leq v$ implies $Tu \leq Tv$,

(ii) (Discounting) there exists a nonnegative matrix $B \in \mathbb{R}^{N \times N}$ with $\rho(B) < 1$ such that, for all $v \in \mathsf{V}$ and $c \in \mathbb{R}_+^N$, we have $T(v + c) \leq Tv + Bc$.

Then T is a Perov contraction with coefficient matrix B.

The proof is similar to Proposition 7.5 (Problem 7.5).

7.6 PARAMETRIC CONTINUITY OF FIXED POINT

Let (V, d) be a complete metric space. In some applications, the self-map $T : \mathsf{V} \to \mathsf{V}$ itself may depend on some parameter $\theta \in \Theta$, or more precisely, $T : \mathsf{V} \times \Theta \to \mathsf{V}$. Fixing $\theta \in \Theta$, we may define the self-map $T_\theta : \mathsf{V} \to \mathsf{V}$ by $T_\theta(v) = T(v, \theta)$. If for each θ the self-map T_θ is a contraction, then by the contraction mapping theorem, there exists a unique fixed point $v^*(\theta) \in \mathsf{V}$. A natural question is how $v^*(\theta)$ depends on the parameter $\theta \in \Theta$. The following proposition shows that v^* is continuous if T is continuous.

Proposition 7.8. *Let (V, d) be a complete metric space and Θ be a topological space. Suppose $T : \mathsf{V} \times \Theta \to \mathsf{V}$ is continuous and there exists $\beta \in [0, 1)$ such that for all $\theta \in \Theta$, the self-map $T_\theta : \mathsf{V} \to \mathsf{V}$ defined by $T_\theta v = T(v, \theta)$ is a contraction with modulus β. Then*

(i) for each $\theta \in \Theta$, there exists a unique fixed point $v^*(\theta)$ of T_θ, and

(ii) $v^* : \Theta \to \mathsf{V}$ is continuous.

Proof. The first claim is immediate from the contraction mapping theorem.

To show the second claim, fix any $(v_0, \theta) \in \mathsf{V} \times \Theta$ and define $v_k = T_\theta^k v_0$ for $k \in \mathbb{N}$. Then by the triangle inequality and the contraction property, we have

$$\begin{aligned}
d(v_k, v_0) &\leq d(v_n, v_{k-1}) + \cdots + d(v_1, v_0) \\
&\leq (\beta^{k-1} + \cdots + 1)d(v_1, v_0) \\
&\leq \frac{1}{1 - \beta} d(v_1, v_0) = \frac{1}{1 - \beta} d(T_\theta v_0, v_0).
\end{aligned}$$

Letting $k \to \infty$ and noting that $v_k \to v^*(\theta)$ by the contraction mapping theorem, we have

$$d(v^*(\theta), v_0) \leq \frac{1}{1 - \beta} d(T_\theta v_0, v_0). \tag{7.5}$$

Since $v_0 \in \mathsf{V}$ and $\theta \in \Theta$ are arbitrary in (7.5), set $\theta = \theta'$ and $v_0 = v^*(\theta)$, where $\theta, \theta' \in \Theta$ are arbitrary. Since by definition $T_\theta v_0 = v_0$, it follows that

$$d(v^*(\theta'), v^*(\theta)) \le \frac{1}{1-\beta} d(T_{\theta'} v_0, v_0) = \frac{1}{1-\beta} d(T_{\theta'} v_0, T_\theta v_0)$$
$$= \frac{1}{1-\beta} d(T(v_0, \theta'), T(v_0, \theta)), \tag{7.6}$$

where $v_0 = v^*(\theta)$. Since T is continuous and $v_0 = v^*(\theta)$ depends only on θ, for any $\epsilon > 0$ there exists an open neighborhood U of θ such that

$$d(T(v_0, \theta'), T(v_0, \theta)) < (1-\beta)\epsilon \tag{7.7}$$

whenever $\theta' \in U$. Combining (7.6) and (7.7), for all $\theta' \in U$ we have

$$d(v^*(\theta'), v^*(\theta)) < \epsilon,$$

so $v^* : \Theta \to \mathsf{V}$ is continuous. □

Remark. If $T : \mathsf{V} \times \Theta \to \mathsf{V}$ satisfies the assumption of Proposition 7.8, we say that T is a *uniform contraction* with modulus β. Chicone (2006, Theorem 1.244) shows that the fixed point of a uniform contraction is not just continuous but also smooth if T is smooth.

NOTES

Blackwell's sufficient condition (Proposition 7.5) is essentially Theorem 5 of Blackwell (1965), who imposes stronger assumptions. The Perov contraction theorem (Theorem 7.6) appeared in Perov (1964) to study a system of ordinary differential equations. The exposition in §7.5 largely follows Toda (2021b).

PROBLEMS

7.1. Let $(\mathsf{V}, \|\cdot\|)$ be a normed space and define $d : \mathsf{V} \times \mathsf{V} \to \mathbb{R}$ by $d(v_1, v_2) = \|v_1 - v_2\|$. For any set $\mathsf{V}_1 \subset \mathsf{V}$, prove that (V_1, d) is a metric space.

7.2. Let (V, d) be a complete metric space, $T : \mathsf{V} \to \mathsf{V}$ a contraction with a unique fixed point $v^* \in \mathsf{V}$, and let $\mathsf{V}_1 \subset \mathsf{V}$ be a nonempty closed set such that $T\mathsf{V}_1 \subset \mathsf{V}_1$. Show that $v^* \in \mathsf{V}_1$.

7.3. Consider the integral equation

$$f(x) = \lambda \int_a^x K(x, y) f(y) \, \mathrm{d}y + \phi(x), \tag{7.8}$$

where $\phi : [a, b] \to \mathbb{R}$ and $K : [a, b]^2 \to \mathbb{R}$ are given continuous functions and $\lambda \in \mathbb{R}$.

(i) Let V be the space of continuous functions $f : [a, b] \to \mathbb{R}$ equipped with the supremum norm $\|\cdot\|$. For each $x \in [a, b]$, define

$$(Tf)(x) = \lambda \int_a^x K(x, y) f(y) \, dy + \phi(x).$$

Show that $T : V \to V$.

(ii) Let $M := \sup_{(x,y) \in [a,b]^2} |K(x, y)|$. For any $f, g \in V$, show that

$$|(Tf)(x) - (Tg)(x)| \le |\lambda| M (x - a) \|f - g\|.$$

(iii) Show that there exists a unique solution f to (7.8) by showing that T^m is a contraction for some $m \in \mathbb{N}$.

7.4. Complete the proof of Theorem 7.6.

7.5. Prove Proposition 7.7.

7.6. Define the 2×2 upper triangular matrix T by

$$T = \begin{bmatrix} a & b \\ 0 & a \end{bmatrix},$$

where $a, b \ge 0$. We also use the notation T for the operator $T : \mathbb{R}^2 \to \mathbb{R}^2$ defined by $x \mapsto Tx$. Endow $\mathbb{R}^2$ with the supremum norm, so write $\|x\| = \max\{|x_1|, |x_2|\}$ for $x = (x_1, x_2)'$.

(i) Compute the eigenvalues and spectral radius of T.

(ii) Compute the operator norm of T induced by $\|\cdot\|$.

(iii) Show that T is not a contraction if $a + b \ge 1$.

(iv) Show that T is a Perov contraction if $a < 1$.

CHAPTER 8

Implicit Function and Stable Manifold Theorem

8.1 INTRODUCTION

When solving economic problems, we often encounter equations like

$$f(x, y) = 0, \tag{8.1}$$

where y is an endogenous variable and x is an exogenous variable. Oftentimes y does not have an explicit expression, but nevertheless we might be interested in how y changes with x, that is, $\mathrm{d}y/\mathrm{d}x$. Such an exercise is called *comparative statics*. The implicit function theorem, which is one of the most useful theorems for economic analysis, allows us to compute this derivative as follows. Let $y = g(x)$. Substituting this into (8.1), we obtain

$$f(x, g(x)) = 0. \tag{8.2}$$

Differentiating both sides of (8.2) with respect to x and using the chain rule, we get $f_x + f_y g'(x) = 0$, where f_x is the shorthand for $\partial f/\partial x$. Solving this equation, we obtain $g'(x) = -f_x/f_y$. This is the essence of the implicit function theorem (Theorem 8.3).

The analysis of dynamic economic models often reduces to the nonlinear implicit difference equation of the form

$$f(x_t, x_{t+1}) = 0$$

for $t = 0, 1, \ldots$. We say that x^* is a *steady state* if $f(x^*, x^*) = 0$. The local stable manifold theorem (Theorem 8.9) allows us to study the local behavior of the solution $\{x_t\}_{t=0}^{\infty}$ around the steady state x^* by linearization.

To illustrate the usefulness of these techniques, we discuss applications to optimal savings problem, optimal portflio problem, and the overlapping generations model.

DOI: 10.1201/9781032698953-8

8.2 INVERSE FUNCTION THEOREM

To prove the implicit function theorem, we need the following inverse function theorem.

Theorem 8.1 (Inverse function theorem). *Let $f : \mathbb{R}^N \to \mathbb{R}^N$ be C^1. If $Df(x_0)$ is invertible, then there exists a neighborhood V of $y_0 = f(x_0)$ such that*

(i) $f : U := f^{-1}(V) \to V$ is bijective,

(ii) $g = f^{-1}$ is C^1, and

(iii) $Dg(y) = [Df(g(y))]^{-1}$ on V.

If f is affine, so $f(x) = y_0 + A(x - x_0)$ for some matrix A, then we can find the inverse function by solving

$$y = y_0 + A(x - x_0) \iff x = x_0 + A^{-1}(y - y_0)$$

provided that A is invertible. The idea to prove the general case is to linearize f around x_0. Since f is differentiable, we have

$$y = f(x) \approx f(x_0) + Df(x_0)(x - x_0).$$

Solving this equation for x, we obtain

$$x \approx x_0 + Df(x_0)^{-1}(y - f(x_0)). \tag{8.3}$$

Therefore, given an approximate solution x_0 of $f(x) = y$, the solution can be approximated further by (8.3) (which is essentially the Newton method for solving the nonlinear equation $f(x) = y$ discussed in Appendix A.2). This intuition is helpful for understanding the proof below.

To prove the inverse function theorem, we need the following result.

Proposition 8.2 (Mean value inequality). *Let $f : \mathbb{R}^N \to \mathbb{R}^M$ be differentiable and $\|\cdot\|$ denote the Euclidean norm (as well as the operator norm induced by $\|\cdot\|$). Then*

$$\|f(x_2) - f(x_1)\| \leq \sup_{t \in [0,1]} \|Df(x_1 + t(x_2 - x_1))\| \, \|x_2 - x_1\|.$$

Proof. The claim is trivial if $f(x_1) = f(x_2)$, so assume $f(x_1) \neq f(x_2)$. Take any $v \in \mathbb{R}^M$ with $\|v\| = 1$. Define $\phi : [0, 1] \to \mathbb{R}$ by

$$\phi(t) = \langle v, f(x_1 + t(x_2 - x_1)) - f(x_1) \rangle.$$

Then $\phi(0) = 0$ and $\phi(1) = \langle v, f(x_2) - f(x_1) \rangle$. By the mean value theorem (Proposition 2.3), there exists $t \in (0, 1)$ such that

$$\langle v, f(x_2) - f(x_1) \rangle = \phi(1) - \phi(0)$$

$$= \phi'(t) = \langle v, Df(x_1 + t(x_2 - x_1))(x_2 - x_1) \rangle,$$

where the last equality follows from the chain rule. Taking the absolute value of both sides and applying the Cauchy-Schwarz inequality, we obtain

$$|\langle v, f(x_2) - f(x_1)\rangle| = |\langle v, Df(x_1 + t(x_2 - x_1))(x_2 - x_1)\rangle|$$
$$\leq \|Df(x_1 + t(x_2 - x_1))(x_2 - x_1)\|$$
$$\leq \|Df(x_1 + t(x_2 - x_1))\| \|x_2 - x_1\|,$$

where the last inequality follows from $\|v\| = 1$ and the property of the matrix norm; see (6.9). Taking the supremum over $t \in [0, 1]$ and setting

$$v = \frac{f(x_2) - f(x_1)}{\|f(x_2) - f(x_1)\|},$$

we obtain the desired inequality. □

Proof of Theorem 8.1. Fix $y \in \mathbb{R}^N$ and define $T : \mathbb{R}^N \to \mathbb{R}^N$ by

$$T(x) = x + Df(x_0)^{-1}(y - f(x)),$$

which is well-defined because $Df(x_0)$ is invertible. To simplify notation, let $A = Df(x_0)^{-1}$. For any x_1, x_2, let $x(t) = x_1 + t(x_2 - x_1)$. Applying the mean value inequality (Proposition 8.2) to $T(x)$, we have

$$\|T(x_2) - T(x_1)\| \leq \sup_{t \in [0,1]} \|I - ADf(x(t))\| \|x_2 - x_1\|.$$

Since f is C^1 and $A = Df(x_0)^{-1}$, we can take $\epsilon > 0$ such that $\|I - ADf(x)\| \leq 1/2$ whenever $\|x - x_0\| \leq \epsilon$. Noting that y cancels out in $T(x_2) - T(x_1)$, the choice of ϵ does not depend on y. Let $B = \{x : \|x - x_0\| \leq \epsilon\}$ be the closed ball with center x_0 and radius ϵ. If $x_1, x_2 \in B$, then

$$\|x(t) - x_0\| \leq (1 - t)\|x_1 - x_0\| + t\|x_2 - x_0\| \leq \epsilon,$$

so $x(t) \in B$. Therefore if $x_1, x_2 \in B$, we have

$$\|T(x_2) - T(x_1)\| \leq \frac{1}{2}\|x_2 - x_1\|. \tag{8.4}$$

Let us show that $T(B) \subset B$ if y is sufficiently close to $y_0 = f(x_0)$. To see this, note that

$$T(x) - x_0 = x - x_0 + A(f(x_0) - f(x)) + A(y - y_0).$$

Using the mean value inequality to $x \mapsto x - Af(x)$, we obtain

$$\|T(x) - x_0\| \leq \sup_{t \in [0,1]} \|I - ADf(x_0 + t(x - x_0))\| \|x - x_0\| + \|A(y - y_0)\|.$$

Take a neighborhood V of y_0 such that $\|A(y - y_0)\| \leq \frac{1}{2}\epsilon$ for all $y \in V$. If $y \in V$ and $x \in B$, then we have

$$\|T(x) - x_0\| \leq \frac{1}{2}\|x - x_0\| + \frac{1}{2}\epsilon \leq \epsilon,$$

so $T(x) \in B$. This shows that $T(B) \subset B$. Since $T : B \to B$ and (8.4) holds, T is a contraction with modulus $1/2$. Furthermore, since B is closed, by the contraction mapping theorem (Theorem 7.3), there exists a unique fixed point x of T. Since

$$x = T(x) = x + A(y - f(x)),$$

we have $y = f(x)$.

Let the unique $x \in B$ such that $y = f(x)$ for any $y \in V$ be denoted by $x = g(y)$. Since $f(x) = y$, we have $f(g(y)) = y$. Let us show that g is continuous on V. Suppose $y_k \to y$ and $x_k = g(y_k)$ but $x_k \not\to x$. Since B is closed and bounded, by taking a subsequence if necessary, we may assume that $x_k \to x'$, where $x \neq x' \in B$. Since $f(x_k) = f(g(y_k)) = y_k$, letting $k \to \infty$, since f is continuous we get $f(x') = y$, which is a contradiction because $f(x) = y$ has a unique solution on B. Therefore g is continuous.

To show the differentiability of g, for small enough $h \in \mathbb{R}^N$, let $k(h) := g(y+h) - g(y)$. Since g is continuous, so is k. Noting that $g(y+h) = g(y) + k(h) = x + k$ and f is differentiable, we obtain

$$y + h = f(g(y+h)) = f(x+k) = f(x) + Dfk + o(k).$$

Since $y = f(x)$, we get $h = Dfk + o(k)$, so h and k have the same order of magnitude. Finally,

$$g(y+h) = g(y) + k = g(y) + [Df]^{-1}(h - o(k)) = g(y) + [Df]^{-1}h + o(h),$$

so g is differentiable and $Dg(y) = [Df(g(y))]^{-1}$. □

Remark. Although Theorem 8.1 and Proposition 8.2 assume the domain of f is $\mathbb{R}^N$, because the proofs use only local arguments, the statements remain valid even if the domain is an arbitrary open set.

8.3 IMPLICIT FUNCTION THEOREM

Armed with the inverse function theorem, we can state and prove the implicit function theorem. In what follows, for a function $f(x, y)$, $D_x f(x, y)$ denotes the Jacobian of f with respect to x.

Theorem 8.3 (Implicit function theorem). *Let $f : \mathbb{R}^M \times \mathbb{R}^N \to \mathbb{R}^N$ be C^1. If $f(x_0, y_0) = 0$ and $D_y f(x_0, y_0)$ is invertible, then there exist neighborhoods U of x_0 and V of y_0 and a function $g : U \to V$ such that*

(i) for all $x \in U$, $f(x, y) = 0 \iff y = g(x)$,

(ii) g is C^1, and

(iii) $D_x g(x) = -[D_y f(x, y)]^{-1} D_x f(x, y)$, where $y = g(x)$.

Proof. (i) Define $F : \mathbb{R}^{M+N} \to \mathbb{R}^{M+N}$ by

$$F(x,y) = \begin{bmatrix} x \\ f(x,y) \end{bmatrix}.$$

Then F is C^1. Furthermore, since

$$DF(x,y) = \begin{bmatrix} I & 0 \\ D_x f(x,y) & D_y f(x,y) \end{bmatrix}$$

is block lower triangular, by Proposition 5.6 we have

$$|DF(x_0, y_0)| = |D_y f(x_0, y_0)| \neq 0,$$

so $DF(x_0, y_0)$ is invertible. Since $F(x_0, y_0) = (x_0, 0)$, by the inverse function theorem there exists a neighborhood V of $(x_0, 0)$ such that $F : F^{-1}(V) \to V$ is bijective. Let G be the inverse function of F. Then for any $(z, w) \in V$, we have

$$F(x,y) = (z,w) \iff (x,y) = G(z,w) = (G_1(z,w), G_2(z,w)).$$

Since by definition $F(x,y) = (x, f(x,y))$, we have $x = z$, so

$$f(x,y) = w \iff y = G_2(x,w).$$

Letting $w = 0$, we have

$$f(x,y) = 0 \iff y = g(x) := G_2(x,0).$$

(ii) Since G is continuously differentiable, so is g.

(iii) Differentiating both sides of $f(x, g(x)) = 0$ with respect to x and applying the chain rule, we get

$$D_x f + D_y f D_x g = 0 \iff D_x g = -[D_y f]^{-1} D_x f. \qquad \square$$

Remembering the implicit function theorem

A simple way to remember the assumption and the statement of the implicit function theorem is as follows. Start from the equation $f(x,y) = 0$. Set $y = g(x)$, differentiate $f(x, g(x)) = 0$ applying the chain rule, and derive (iii):

$$D_x f + D_y f D_x g = 0 \iff D_x g = -[D_y f]^{-1} D_x f.$$

For this equation to be meaningful, we need $D_y f$ to be invertible, which is exactly the assumption.

As mentioned in the introduction, the implicit function theorem is one of the most useful theorems for economic analysis. In what follows, we discuss several applications.

8.4   OPTIMAL SAVINGS PROBLEM

As the first application of the implicit function theorem, consider the following generalization of the optimal savings problem discussed in §2.6.

An agent lives for two dates indexed by $t = 1, 2$. The agent is endowed with initial wealth $w > 0$, and at $t = 1$ the agent needs to decide how much to consume or save. The gross interest rate on savings is $R > 0$. Thus if the agent consumes c at $t = 1$, savings is $w - c$, and the wealth at $t = 2$ is $R(w - c)$. Suppose that the agent wishes to maximize the utility

$$U(c_1, c_2) = u(c_1) + \beta v(c_2), \tag{8.5}$$

where u, v are period utility functions and $\beta > 0$ is the discount factor. Assume u is twice continuously differentiable on $(0, \infty)$ with $u' > 0$, $u'' < 0$, $\lim_{x \downarrow 0} u'(x) = \infty$ (which is the Inada condition discussed in Proposition 4.4), and likewise for v. Clearly, the model in §2.6 is a special case by setting $u(c) = v(c) = \frac{c^{1-\gamma}}{1-\gamma}$.

Letting $s = w - c$ be the savings, solving the optimal savings problem reduces to maximizing

$$u(w - s) + \beta v(Rs).$$

Applying the same argument as in §2.6, the first-order condition is

$$-u'(w - s) + \beta R v'(Rs) = 0. \tag{8.6}$$

Under the maintained assumption, it is straightforward to show that there exists a unique $s \in (0, w)$ satisfying (8.6). A natural question is how the optimal savings s depends on model parameters such as the initial wealth w or the gross interest rate R.

For instance, suppose we would like to compute $\partial s / \partial w$. To this end, define $f(w, s)$ by the left-hand side of (8.6), so

$$f(w, s) = -u'(w - s) + \beta R v'(Rs).$$

To compute $\partial s / \partial w$, we apply the implicit function theorem to $x = w$ and $y = s$. A straightforward calculation yields

$$f_w(w, s) = -u''(w - s) > 0,$$
$$f_s(w, s) = u''(w - s) + \beta R^2 v''(Rs) < 0.$$

Therefore by the implicit function theorem, we obtain

$$\frac{\partial s}{\partial w} = -\frac{f_w}{f_s} = \frac{u''(w - s)}{u''(w - s) + \beta R^2 v''(Rs)} \in (0, 1).$$

8.5   OPTIMAL PORTFOLIO PROBLEM

As the second application of the implicit function theorem, let us study how an investor's asset allocation is related to wealth. Consider an agent with a utility function u and initial wealth $w > 0$. Suppose that there are two assets, one risky (stock) with gross return $R > 0$ and the other risk-free (bond) with gross risk-free rate $R_f > 0$. If the investor invests x in the risky asset, the total wealth after investment is

$$R(x) := Rx + R_f(w - x).$$

Therefore the utility maximization problem is

$$\max_{x} \mathrm{E}[u(R(x))],$$

where E denotes the expectation. Suppose that $u' > 0$ and $u'' < 0$, so the utility function is strictly increasing and concave.

The following lemma shows that if the expected excess return of the risky asset is positive, then the investor always holds a positive amount of stocks.

Lemma 8.4. *Suppose that* $\mathrm{E}[R] > R_f$ *and a solution* x *to the utility maximization problem exists. Then* $x > 0$.

Proof. Let $f(x) = \mathrm{E}[u(R(x))]$ be the expected utility. Then by the chain rule we have

$$f'(x) = \mathrm{E}[u'(R(x))(R - R_f)],$$
$$f''(x) = \mathrm{E}[u''(R(x))(R - R_f)^2].$$

Since $u'' < 0$, and $R \neq R_f$ with positive probability because $\mathrm{E}[R] > R_f$, it follows that $f''(x) < 0$. Therefore f is strictly concave.

If x solves the utility maximization problem, by the first-order condition we have $f'(x) = 0$. Since

$$f'(0) = \mathrm{E}[u'(R_f w)(R - R_f)] = u'(R_f w)(\mathrm{E}[R] - R_f) > 0$$

because $u' > 0$ and $\mathrm{E}[R] > R_f$ and f' is strictly decreasing because $f'' < 0$, $f'(x) = 0 < f'(0)$ implies $x > 0$. $\qquad\square$

A measure of risk aversion known as the *absolute risk aversion* coefficient at wealth w is defined by the quantity $\alpha(w) = -u''(w)/u'(w)$. The following proposition shows that if investors' absolute risk aversion is decreasing, then investors hold more stocks as they get richer. The proof is an application of the implicit function theorem.

Proposition 8.5. *Suppose that* $\alpha(w) = -u''(w)/u'(w)$ *is decreasing,* $\mathrm{E}[R] > R_f$, *and let* $x > 0$ *be the optimal stock holdings. Then* $\partial x/\partial w \geq 0$.

Proof. By the first-order condition, we have

$$F(w, x) := \mathrm{E}[u'(R(x))(R - R_f)] = 0.$$

Assuming that the implicit function theorem is applicable, we have $\partial x/\partial w = -(\partial F/\partial w)/(\partial F/\partial x)$. The denominator is

$$\frac{\partial F}{\partial x} = \mathrm{E}[u''(R(x))(R - R_f)^2] < 0,$$

so we can apply the implicit function theorem. Using the definition of α, the numerator is

$$\frac{\partial F}{\partial w} = \mathrm{E}[u''(R(x))(R - R_f)R_f] = -\mathrm{E}[\alpha(R(x))u'(R(x))(R - R_f)R_f].$$

If $R \geq R_f$, since $x > 0$ we get

$$R(x) = Rx + R_f(w - x) = R_f w + (R - R_f)x \geq R_f w.$$

Since α is decreasing, we get $\alpha(R(x)) \leq \alpha(R_f w)$. Multiplying both sides by $R - R_f \geq 0$, we obtain

$$\alpha(R(x))(R - R_f) \leq \alpha(R_f w)(R - R_f).$$

If $R \leq R_f$, by a similar argument $R(x) \leq R_f$ and $\alpha(R(x)) \geq \alpha(R_f w)$, so again

$$\alpha(R(x))(R - R_f) \leq \alpha(R_f w)(R - R_f).$$

Since $u' > 0$, we obtain

$$\mathrm{E}[\alpha(R(x))u'(R(x))(R - R_f)R_f] \leq \mathrm{E}[\alpha(R_f w)u'(R(x))(R - R_f)R_f]$$
$$= \alpha(R_f w)R_f \mathrm{E}[u'(R(x))(R - R_f)] = 0$$

by the first-order condition, so $\partial F/\partial w \geq 0$. Hence by the implicit function theorem $\partial x/\partial w = -(\partial F/\partial w)/(\partial F/\partial x) \geq 0$. $\qquad\square$

For similar economic applications of the implicit function theorem, see for example Phelan and Toda (2019, Theorem 3), Toda and Walsh (2020, Lemma 1), and Beare and Toda (2022, Appendix B).

8.6 STABLE MANIFOLD THEOREM

In some economic applications, we would like to study the long-run behavior of the (potentially nonlinear) dynamics $x_t = f(x_{t-1})$ for $t = 1, 2, \ldots$. This section introduces some tools for that purpose.

We first consider the special case where f is linear, so $x_t = A x_{t-1}$ for some $A \in \mathbb{R}^{N \times N}$. Then by iteration $x_t = A^t x_0$, so by Proposition 6.14 we have $x_t \to 0$ as $t \to \infty$ for all x_0 if and only if $\rho(A) < 1$. However, we may be interested in under what conditions on x_0 we have $A^t x_0 \to 0$ without assuming $\rho(A) < 1$. The following theorem shows that the set of such x_0 is a subspace whose dimension is related to the number of particular eigenvalues.

Theorem 8.6 (Stable manifold theorem for linear operators). *Let $A \in \mathbb{R}^{N \times N}$ and define its stable manifold by*

$$E_s(A) := \left\{ x \in \mathbb{R}^N : \lim_{t \to \infty} A^t x = 0 \right\}. \tag{8.7}$$

Then $E_s(A)$ is a subspace with dimension equal to the number of eigenvalues of A with absolute values strictly less than 1.

The idea of the proof of Theorem 8.6 is to choose an invertible matrix P such that $P^{-1}AP$ is "simple" and to reduce to this case. Although the Schur triangularization theorem (Theorem 6.4) allows us to convert A to an upper triangular matrix, this argument cannot be applied because A may have complex eigenvalues. The following proposition allows us to stay in $\mathbb{R}^N$.

Proposition 8.7. *Let $A \in \mathbb{R}^{N \times N}$. Then there exists a real invertible matrix P such that $P^{-1}AP$ is block upper triangular, where each diagonal block is either 1×1 or 2×2 of the form*

$$\begin{bmatrix} r\cos\theta & -r\sin\theta \\ r\sin\theta & r\cos\theta \end{bmatrix} \tag{8.8}$$

with $r > 0$ and $\sin\theta \neq 0$.

Proof. The proof is by induction on N. If $N = 1$, the claim is trivial by setting $P = (1)$.

Suppose $N = 2$. Then A has either two real eigenvalues or two complex eigenvalues that are complex conjugates of each other. Suppose first that A has two real eigenvalues. Let α be one of them and $p_1 \in \mathbb{R}^2$ be a corresponding eigenvector, so $Ap_1 = \alpha p_1$. Take any $p_2 \in \mathbb{R}^2$ such that $\{p_1, p_2\}$ is linearly independent. Then we can take $\beta_1, \beta_2 \in \mathbb{R}$ such that $Ap_2 = \beta_1 p_1 + \beta_2 p_2$. Define the matrix $P = [p_1, p_2]$, which is invertible because $\{p_1, p_2\}$ is linearly independent (Theorem 5.9). Collecting vectors into a matrix, we obtain

$$AP = [Ap_1, Ap_2] = [\alpha p_1, \beta_1 p_1 + \beta_2 p_2] = P \begin{bmatrix} \alpha & \beta_1 \\ 0 & \beta_2 \end{bmatrix}$$

$$\iff P^{-1}AP = \begin{bmatrix} \alpha & \beta_1 \\ 0 & \beta_2 \end{bmatrix},$$

which is upper triangular and hence block upper triangular with 1×1 diagonal blocks. Suppose next that A has two complex eigenvalues $\alpha, \bar{\alpha} \in \mathbb{C}$. Let $v \in \mathbb{C}^2$ be an eigenvector corresponding to α. Since $\alpha \notin \mathbb{R}$, we can take $r > 0$ and $\theta \in \mathbb{R}$ such that $\sin\theta \neq 0$ and $\alpha = r(\cos\theta + i\sin\theta)$. Uniquely write $v = p_1 - ip_2$, where $p_1, p_2 \in \mathbb{R}^2$. To simplify notation, let $c = \cos\theta$ and $s = \sin\theta \neq 0$. Then

$$A(p_1 - ip_2) = Av = \alpha v = r(c + is)(p_1 - ip_2).$$

Comparing the real and imaginary parts, we obtain

$$Ap_1 = r(cp_1 + sp_2), \tag{8.9a}$$

$$Ap_2 = r(-sp_1 + cp_2). \tag{8.9b}$$

If $p_2 = 0$, then (8.9b) implies $rsp_1 = 0$. Since $r > 0$ and $s \neq 0$, we obtain $p_1 = 0$, so $v = p_1 - ip_2 = 0$, which contradicts that v is an eigenvector. Therefore $p_2 \neq 0$. Let us show that $\{p_1, p_2\}$ is linearly independent. If not, because $p_2 \neq 0$, we may write $p_1 = \beta p_2$ for some $\beta \in \mathbb{R}$. Then (8.9b) implies

$$Ap_2 = r(c - s\beta)p_2,$$

so $r(c - s\beta)$ is a real eigenvalue of A, which is a contradiction. Therefore $\{p_1, p_2\}$ is linearly independent and $P := [p_1, p_2]$ is invertible. Collecting the two vectors in (8.9) into a matrix, we obtain

$$AP = rP \begin{bmatrix} c & -s \\ s & c \end{bmatrix} \iff P^{-1}AP = r \begin{bmatrix} c & -s \\ s & c \end{bmatrix},$$

which takes the form (8.8).

Finally, suppose $N \geq 3$ and the claim is true up to dimension $N - 1$. The remaining proof is essentially the same as Theorem 6.4 so we only provide a sketch. If A has a real eigenvalue α_1, we can take a real eigenvector p_1, so $Ap_1 = \alpha p_1$. Construct a basis $\{p_n\}$ and set $P_0 = [p_1, \ldots, p_N]$. For each $n \geq 2$, we can take $\{\beta_{mn}\}_{m=1}^N \subset \mathbb{R}$ such that $Ap_n = \sum_{m=1}^N \beta_{mn} p_m$. Collecting these vectors into a matrix, we obtain

$$AP_0 = P_0 \begin{bmatrix} \alpha_1 & \beta_{12} & \cdots & \beta_{1N} \\ 0 & \beta_{22} & \cdots & \beta_{2N} \\ \vdots & \vdots & \ddots & \vdots \\ 0 & \beta_{N2} & \cdots & \beta_{NN} \end{bmatrix} \iff P_0^{-1}AP_0 = \begin{bmatrix} \alpha_1 & b_1' \\ 0 & A_1 \end{bmatrix}$$

for some $b_1 \in \mathbb{R}^{N-1}$ and $A_1 \in \mathbb{R}^{(N-1)\times(N-1)}$. Thus the analysis reduces to the case $N - 1$. If A has no real eigenvalues, by imitating the proof of the 2×2 case, we can take an invertible P_0 such that

$$P_0^{-1}AP_0 = \begin{bmatrix} r\cos\theta & -r\sin\theta & b_1' \\ r\sin\theta & r\cos\theta & b_2' \\ 0 & 0 & A_1 \end{bmatrix}$$

and the analysis reduces to the case $N - 2$. □

Proof of Theorem 8.6. Clearly $0 \in E_s(A)$. If $x, y \in E_s(A)$, by definition $A^t x, A^t y \to 0$ as $t \to \infty$. Then for any $\alpha, \beta \in \mathbb{R}$, we have

$$A^t(\alpha x + \beta y) = \alpha A^t x + \beta A^t y \to \alpha \cdot 0 + \beta \cdot 0 = 0$$

as $t \to \infty$, so $\alpha x + \beta y \in E_s(A)$. Therefore $E_s(A)$ is a subspace.

To determine the dimension of $E_s(A)$, let $N_s(A)$ and $N_u(A)$ be the number of eigenvalues of A that have absolute values less than (at least) 1. When the matrix is clear from the context, omit the reference to A. Then $N_s + N_u = N$. We prove the claim by induction on N_u. If $N_u = 0$, then $N_s = N$ and all eigenvalues of A have absolute values less than 1. Then $\rho(A) < 1$, so Proposition 6.14 implies $A^t x \to 0$ for any $x \in \mathbb{R}^N$. Clearly $E_s(A) = \mathbb{R}^N$ has dimension $N = N_s$, so the claim holds.

Let $j \geq 1$, suppose the claim holds for $N_u = 0, \ldots, j - 1$, and consider the case $N_u = j$. Let P be an invertible matrix and define $\tilde{A} = P^{-1}AP$ and $\tilde{x} = P^{-1}x$. Since $A^t x = P(P^{-1}AP)^t P^{-1}x = P\tilde{A}^t\tilde{x} \to 0$ if and only if $\tilde{A}^t\tilde{x} \to 0$, by Proposition 8.7, without loss of generality we may assume that A is block upper triangular where each diagonal block is either 1×1 or 2×2 of the form (8.8). Write

$$A = \begin{bmatrix} A_1 & \cdots & * \\ \vdots & \ddots & \vdots \\ 0 & \cdots & A_M \end{bmatrix} = \begin{bmatrix} B & C \\ 0 & A_M \end{bmatrix}, \tag{8.10}$$

where M is the number of diagonal blocks and B is defined by keeping the first $(M - 1) \times (M - 1)$ blocks of A. By interchanging rows and columns, without loss of generality, we may assume that diagonal blocks are ordered according to the spectral radius: $\rho(A_1) \leq \cdots \leq \rho(A_M)$.

By the induction hypothesis, we have $N_u = j \geq 1$, so $\rho(A_M) \geq 1$. Partition the vector x in accordance with the blocks of A in (8.10) such that

$$x = \begin{bmatrix} x_1 \\ \vdots \\ x_M \end{bmatrix} = \begin{bmatrix} y \\ x_M \end{bmatrix}. \tag{8.11}$$

Using (8.10) and (8.11), a straightforward calculation shows that

$$A^t x = \begin{bmatrix} B^t & \sum_{s=1}^t B^{t-s}CA_M^{s-1} \\ 0 & A_M^t \end{bmatrix} \begin{bmatrix} y \\ x_M \end{bmatrix}$$

$$= \begin{bmatrix} B^t y + \sum_{s=1}^t B^{t-s}CA_M^{s-1}x_M \\ A_M^t x_M \end{bmatrix}. \tag{8.12}$$

Let us show that $A_M^t x_M \to 0$ as $t \to \infty$ if and only if $x_M = 0$. If A_M is 1×1, since $\rho(A_M) \geq 1$, we can write $A_M = a$ with $|a| \geq 1$. Therefore $A_M^t x_M = a^t x_M \to 0$ if and only if $x_M = 0$. If A_M is 2×2, then A_M takes the form (8.8), so

$$A_M^t = r^t \begin{bmatrix} \cos t\theta & -\sin t\theta \\ \sin t\theta & \cos t\theta \end{bmatrix}.$$

Since $r = \rho(A_M) \geq 1$, the ℓ^2 norm of $A_M^t x_M$ is

$$\|A_M^t x_M\| = r^t \|x_M\| \to 0$$

if and only if $x_M = 0$.

Using (8.12), we have $A^t x \to 0$ if and only if $x_M = 0$ and $B^t y \to 0$. Therefore $\dim E_s(A) = \dim E_s(B)$. By Proposition 6.1, the spectrum of A is the union of the spectra of B and A_M. Thus $j = N_u(A) = N_u(B) + N_u(A_M)$. Since by assumption $N_u(A_M)$ equals either 1 or 2, it follows that $N_u(B) \leq j - 1$. Therefore we may apply the induction hypothesis to B and obtain $\dim E_s(B) = N_s(B)$. Since all eigenvalues of A_M have absolute values at least 1, we have $N_s(A) = N_s(B)$, so $\dim E_s(A) = N_s(A)$. $\qquad\square$

We next consider the general nonlinear case. Let $U \subset \mathbb{R}^N$ be a nonempty open set. We say that $f : U \to f(U)$ is a *homeomorphism* if $f^{-1} : f(U) \to U$ exists and f, f^{-1} are both continuous. Similarly, we say that f is a C^r-*diffeomorphism* if $f^{-1} : f(U) \to U$ exists and f, f^{-1} are both C^r. When $r = 1$, we simply say f is a diffeomorphism. Let $f : U \to f(U)$ be a homeomorphism. If $f(x^*) = x^*$ for some $x^* \in U$, we say that x^* is a *fixed point* or a *steady state* of f. If f is a diffeomorphism, x^* is a fixed point, and none of the eigenvalues of the Jacobian $Df(x^*)$ have an absolute value equal to 1, we say that x^* is a *hyperbolic fixed point* of f.

Let $\{x_t\}_{t=0}^{\infty}$ be a sequence satisfying $x_t = f(x_{t-1})$ for all t. If x^* is a fixed point of f and $x_0 = x^*$, then obviously $x_t = x^*$ for all t. Under some conditions, as long as x_0 is sufficiently close to x^*, we may expect that $\{x_t\}_{t=0}^{\infty}$ will converge to x^*. The following Hartman-Grobman theorem allows us to derive sufficient conditions.

Theorem 8.8 (Hartman-Grobman). *Let $0 \in U \subset \mathbb{R}^N$ be open and $f : U \to f(U)$ be a diffeomorphism such that 0 is a hyperbolic fixed point of f. Then there exists an open set V with $0 \in V \subset U$ and a homeomorphism $h : V \to h(V)$ with $h(0) = 0$ such that*

$$f(h(x)) = h(Df(0)x) \tag{8.13}$$

whenever $x \in V$ and both sides of the equation are defined.

Proof. See Chicone (2006, §4.3). $\qquad\square$

The Hartman-Grobman theorem implies that, if we let $A = Df(0)$ in (8.13), then $(h^{-1} \circ f \circ h)(x) = Ax$ for x sufficiently close to 0. Iterating both sides t times, we obtain

$$(h^{-1} \circ f^t \circ h)(y_0) = A^t y_0 \iff x_t = f^t(x_0) = h(A^t y_0) \tag{8.14}$$

for $y_0 = h^{-1}(x_0)$. Therefore whether $x_t \to 0$ or not reduces to $A^t y_0 \to 0$ or not, which we have already studied in Theorem 8.6. We thus obtain the following theorem.

Theorem 8.9 (Local stable manifold theorem). *Let everything be as in Theorem 8.8 and. Let $A = Df(0)$ and $E_s(A)$ be its stable manifold in (8.7). Then there exists an open neighborhood Ω of 0 such that, if $x_0 \in h(E_s(A) \cap \Omega)$, then $x_t := f^t(x_0) \to 0$ as $t \to \infty$.*

Proof. If $\dim E_s(A) = 0$, then $E_s(A) = \{0\}$ and the claim is obvious because $f(0) = h(0) = 0$. Suppose $\dim E_s(A) \geq 1$. Using the same notation as in the proof of Theorem 8.6, we have $N_s = \dim E_s(A) \geq 1$. Arrange the eigenvalues of A such that $|\alpha_1| \leq \cdots \leq |\alpha_N|$. Then by assumption $|\alpha_{N_s}| < 1 \leq |\alpha_{N_s+1}|$. Take $r \in (|\alpha_{N_s}|, 1)$. By Theorem 6.15 and the proof of Theorem 8.6, we can take a constant $C > 0$ such that $\|A^t y\| \leq Cr^t \|y\|$ for all t and $y \in E_s(A)$. Therefore if we take Ω to be the open ball $B_\epsilon(0)$ with center 0 and sufficiently small radius $\epsilon > 0$, for any $x_0 \in h(E_s(A) \cap \Omega)$, by setting $y_0 = h^{-1}(x_0)$, the sequence $\{A^t y_0\}$ remains arbitrarily close to 0. Therefore x_t in (8.14) is well defined, and since $A^t y_0 \to 0$ by Theorem 8.6 and $h(0) = 0$, we obtain $x_t \to 0$. □

Remark. If the fixed point x^* of f is different from the origin, we may apply Theorems 8.8 and 8.9 by considering the function $\tilde{f}(x) := f(x + x^*)$. For instance, the statement of Theorem 8.9 remains valid by changing 0 everywhere to x^* and letting $x_0 \in h((E_s(A) + x^*) \cap \Omega)$.

8.7 OVERLAPPING GENERATIONS MODEL

As an application of the local stable manifold theorem, we study a simple overlapping generations (OLG) model.

We embed the optimal savings problem studied in §8.4 into a dynamic model. Time is discrete and is indexed by $t = 0, 1, \ldots$. At any date, there are two agents, one young and one old. The young agent born at time t becomes old at time $t + 1$. The old agent exits the economy after consuming. At time t, the young and old are endowed with aG^t and bG^t units of consumption goods, where $a, b > 0$ and $G > 1$ is the economic growth rate. In addition, the initial old at $t = 0$ is endowed with one share of an asset that pays a constant dividend $D > 0$ (in units of the consumption good) every period. The utility function of an agent born at time t is

$$U(y_t, z_{t+1}) = u(y_t) + \beta u(z_{t+1}), \tag{8.15}$$

where (y_t, z_{t+1}) denotes the consumption when young and old, $\beta > 0$ is the discount factor, and the period utility function is the constant relative risk aversion (CRRA) specification

$$u(c) = \begin{cases} \frac{c^{1-\gamma}}{1-\gamma} & \text{if } 0 < \gamma \neq 1, \\ \log c & \text{if } \gamma = 1, \end{cases} \tag{8.16}$$

where the parameter $\gamma > 0$ governs risk aversion. The objective of the agents is to maximize utility subject to the budget constraints, taking prices as given. Let $\{P_t\}_{t=0}^{\infty}$ be the sequence of asset prices, to be determined. Letting x_t be the number of asset shares demanded by the young, the budget constraints of an agent born at time t are

$$\text{Young:} \qquad y_t + P_t x_t = aG^t, \tag{8.17a}$$

$$\text{Old:} \qquad z_{t+1} = bG^{t+1} + (P_{t+1} + D)x_t. \tag{8.17b}$$

That is, at time t the young decides to spend income aG^t on consumption y_t and asset purchase $P_t x_t$, and at time $t+1$ the old liquidates all wealth to consume.

Using the budget constraints (8.17) to solve for (y_t, z_{t+1}) and substituting into the utility function (8.15), the young seek to maximize utility

$$u(aG^t - P_t x) + \beta u(bG^{t+1} + (P_{t+1} + D)x) \tag{8.18}$$

over the number of shares held $x = x_t$. Applying the same argument as in §8.4, taking the derivative of (8.18) with respect to x and setting it to zero, we obtain the first-order condition

$$-P_t u'(aG^t - P_t x) + \beta(P_{t+1} + D)u'(bG^{t+1} + (P_{t+1} + D)x) = 0. \tag{8.19}$$

However, in the economy there is only one share of the asset, which needs to be held by somebody to equate demand and supply. Because the old exits the economy, the old sells the entire assets. This means the young must buy the asset, so in equilibrium we have $x_t = 1$. Therefore setting $x = 1$ in (8.19), using the functional form (8.15), and rearranging terms, we obtain

$$P_t = \beta \left(\frac{bG^{t+1} + P_{t+1} + D}{aG^t - P_t} \right)^{-\gamma} (P_{t+1} + D). \tag{8.20}$$

Thus an equilibrium is characterized by a sequence $\{P_t\}_{t=0}^{\infty}$ satisfying (8.20) for all t.

Note that (8.20) is a highly nonlinear difference equation in P_t and it may look hopeless to analyze it. However, for this purpose, the local stable manifold theorem (Theorem 8.9) is very useful. Because incomes are growing at rate $G > 1$ and the nonlinear difference equation (8.20) is non-autonomous (i.e., it explicitly depends on t), the first step is to detrend variables so that the system becomes autonomous. We thus define the detrended variable $\xi = (\xi_{1t}, \xi_{2t})$ by $\xi_{1t} := P_t/(aG^t)$ and $\xi_{2t} := D/(aG^t)$. Then (8.20) can be rewritten as the system of autonomous nonlinear implicit difference equations

$$F(\xi_t, \xi_{t+1}) = 0, \tag{8.21}$$

where $F : \mathbb{R}^4 \to \mathbb{R}^2$ is defined by

$$F_1(\xi, \eta) = \beta G^{1-\gamma} \left(\frac{w + \eta_1 + G\xi_2}{1 - \xi_1} \right)^{-\gamma} (\eta_1 + G\xi_2) - \xi_1, \tag{8.22a}$$

$$F_2(\xi, \eta) = \eta_2 - \frac{1}{G}\xi_2 \tag{8.22b}$$

with $w := b/a$. Let $\xi^* = (\xi_1^*, \xi_2^*)$ be a steady state of the difference equation (8.21), so $F(\xi^*, \xi^*) = 0$. Since $G > 1$ and hence $1/G \in (0, 1)$, (8.22b) implies that $\xi_2^* = 0$. Using (8.22a), we can solve for ξ_1^* as

$$\beta G^{1-\gamma} \left(\frac{w + \xi_1^*}{1 - \xi_1^*} \right)^{-\gamma} \xi_1^* - \xi_1^* = 0 \iff \xi_1^* = \frac{(\beta G^{1-\gamma})^{1/\gamma} - w}{1 + (\beta G^{1-\gamma})^{1/\gamma}}. \tag{8.23}$$

To guarantee that the steady state in (8.23) is positive, assume $w < (\beta G^{1-\gamma})^{1/\gamma}$.

We apply the implicit function theorem at $(\xi, \eta) = (\xi^*, \xi^*)$ to express (8.21) as $\xi_{t+1} = f(\xi_t)$ for ξ_t close to ξ^*. Noting that $\xi_2^* = 0$, a straightforward calculation using (8.22) and (8.23) implies that

$$D_\xi F(\xi^*, \xi^*) = \begin{bmatrix} F_{1,\xi_1} & F_{1,\xi_2} \\ 0 & -1/G \end{bmatrix} \quad \text{and} \quad D_\eta F(\xi^*, \xi^*) = \begin{bmatrix} F_{1,\eta_1} & 0 \\ 0 & 1 \end{bmatrix},$$

where

$$F_{1,\xi_1} = -\gamma \beta G^{1-\gamma}(w + \xi_1^*)^{-\gamma}(1 - \xi_1^*)^{\gamma-1}\xi_1^* - 1 = -1 - \gamma \frac{\xi_1^*}{1 - \xi_1^*},$$

$$F_{1,\eta_1} = \beta G^{1-\gamma} \left(\frac{w + \xi_1^*}{1 - \xi_1^*} \right)^{-\gamma} \left(1 - \gamma \frac{\xi_1^*}{w + \xi_1^*} \right) = 1 - \gamma \frac{\xi_1^*}{w + \xi_1^*},$$

and F_{1,ξ_2} is unimportant. Therefore except for the special case with $\gamma = 1 + w/\xi_1^*$, we may apply the implicit function theorem, and for (ξ, η) sufficiently close to (ξ^*, ξ^*), we have $F(\xi, \eta) = 0 \iff \eta = f(\xi)$ for some C^1 function f with

$$Df(\xi^*) = -[D_\eta F(\xi^*, \xi^*)]^{-1} D_\xi F(\xi^*, \xi^*) = \begin{bmatrix} \lambda_1 & * \\ 0 & \lambda_2 \end{bmatrix},$$

where

$$(\lambda_1, \lambda_2) = \left(\frac{1 + \gamma \frac{\xi_1^*}{1 - \xi_1^*}}{1 - \gamma \frac{\xi_1^*}{w + \xi_1^*}}, \frac{1}{G} \right). \tag{8.24}$$

We thus obtain the following proposition.

Proposition 8.10. *Let* $\kappa := (\beta G^{1-\gamma})^{1/\gamma} > b/a =: w$. *If* $\frac{1}{\gamma} \neq \frac{\kappa - w}{\kappa(1+w)}$, *then there exists an equilibrium such that* $P_t/(aG^t)$ *converges to* ξ_1^* *in (8.23). If in addition*

$$\frac{1}{\gamma} > \frac{1}{2} \frac{\kappa - w}{\kappa} \frac{1 - \kappa}{1 + w}, \tag{8.25}$$

then such an equilibrium is unique.

Proof. By the implicit function theorem, the equilibrium dynamics can be expressed as $\xi_{t+1} = f(\xi_t)$ if ξ_t is sufficiently close to ξ_1^*. To study the local stability, we apply the local stable manifold theorem (Theorem 8.9). Since

$G > 1$, one eigenvalue of $Df(\xi^*)$ is $\lambda_2 = 1/G \in (0, 1)$. If $1 - \gamma\frac{\xi_1^*}{w+\xi_1^*} > 0$, then clearly $\lambda_1 > 1$. If $1 - \gamma\frac{\xi_1^*}{w+\xi_1^*} < 0$, then

$$\lambda_1 = \frac{1 + \gamma\frac{\xi_1^*}{1-\xi_1^*}}{1 - \gamma\frac{\xi_1^*}{w+\xi_1^*}} < -1 \iff 1 + \gamma\frac{\xi_1^*}{1 - \xi_1^*} > -1 + \gamma\frac{\xi_1^*}{w + \xi_1^*}$$

$$\iff \frac{1}{\gamma} > \frac{(\kappa - w)(1 - \kappa)}{2\kappa(1 + w)}$$

using the definition of κ and ξ_1^*. Furthermore, we have

$$1 - \gamma\frac{\xi_1^*}{w + \xi_1^*} = 0 \iff \frac{1}{\gamma} = \frac{\kappa - w}{\kappa(1 + w)}.$$

Therefore if $\frac{1}{\gamma} \neq \frac{\kappa-w}{\kappa(1+w)}$, the eigenvalues of $Df(\xi^*)$ are not on the unit circle and at least one of them is inside, so Theorem 8.9 implies that for sufficiently large T (so that $\xi_{2T} = D/(aG^T)$ is sufficiently close to the steady state value 0), there exists $\xi_{1T} > 0$ such that the sequence $\{\xi_t\}_{t=T}^\infty$ defined by $\xi_{t+1} = f(\xi_t)$ for all $t \geq T$ converges to ξ^*. Once we construct such a sequence for $t \geq T$, it is straightforward to extend it backward to $t \geq 0$. To see why, since (8.21) holds, using (8.22b) we obtain $\xi_{2t} = G^{t-T}\xi_{2T}$ for $t = 0, 1, \ldots, T$. Using (8.22a), we see that $F_1(\xi, \eta)$ is strictly decreasing in ξ_1,

$$F_1(0, \xi_2, \eta_1, \eta_2) > 0,$$
$$F_1(1, \xi_2, \eta_1, \eta_2) = -1 < 0.$$

Therefore given $\xi_{2t}, \xi_{1,t+1}, \xi_{2,t+1}$, we can uniquely solve

$$F_1(\xi_{1t}, \xi_{2t}, \xi_{1,t+1}, \xi_{2,t+1}) = 0$$

for ξ_{1t}. Apply this argument backwards for $t = T - 1, \ldots, 0$, we obtain the entire sequence $\{\xi_t\}_{t=0}^\infty$.

Finally, if (8.25) holds, then $|\lambda_1| > 1 > \lambda_2 > 0$, so we have $\dim E_s(A) = 1$ using the notation in Theorem 8.6. Since the stable manifold is one-dimensional, given $\xi_{2T} = D/(aG^T)$, the choice of ξ_{1T} is unique. Therefore the equilibrium path $\{\xi_t\}_{t=0}^\infty$ is unique. □

Using the local stable manifold theorem

(i) Compute the steady state x^* of $F(x_t, x_{t+1}) = 0$.

(ii) Apply the implicit function theorem to locally solve as $x_{t+1} = f(x_t)$ and compute $Df(x^*)$.

(iii) Count the numbers N_s, N_u of stable (inside the unit circle) and unstable (outside the unit circle) eigenvalues of $Df(x^*)$.

(iv) If the number of exogenous initial conditions is at most N_s, then there exists a local solution $\{x_t\}_{t=0}^{\infty}$ converging to x^*; if the number of exogenous initial conditions equals N_s, then the local solution is unique.

PROBLEMS

8.1. Consider the optimal savings problem in §8.4.

(i) Applying the implicit function theorem, compute $\partial s/\partial R$.

(ii) Show that if $v(c) = \frac{c^{1-\gamma}}{1-\gamma}$ with $0 < \gamma < 1$, then $\partial s/\partial R > 0$.

8.2. Fill in the details of the proof of Proposition 8.7.

8.3. Show through a 2×2 example that the matrix P in Proposition 8.7 need not be orthogonal.

CHAPTER 9

Nonnegative Matrices

9.1 INTRODUCTION

Nonnegative matrices, although not usually treated in introductory textbooks on linear algebra, play an important role in economics. This chapter provides a brief introduction. For a more comprehensive treatment, see Horn and Johnson (2013, Ch. 8), Berman and Plemmons (1994), or Bapat and Raghavan (1997).

We first present a motivating example. Suppose a worker can be either employed or unemployed. If employed, the worker will be unemployed with probability $p \in (0, 1)$ next period. If unemployed, the worker will be employed with probability $q \in (0, 1)$ next period. Let $x_t = (e_t, u_t)$ be the (row) probability vector of being employed and unemployed at time t, where $u_t = 1 - e_t$. Then by assumption, we have

$$e_{t+1} = (1 - p)e_t + qu_t,$$
$$u_{t+1} = pe_t + (1 - q)u_t.$$

Collecting these equations into a vector, we obtain $x_{t+1} = x_t P$, where

$$P = \begin{bmatrix} 1 - p & p \\ q & 1 - q \end{bmatrix}.$$

Given the initial probability x_0, one might be interested in the probability vector x_t at time t and its behavior as $t \to \infty$. For this example, we can easily calculate these as follows. First, note that $x_t = x_0 P^t$, so it suffices to compute P^t. The characteristic polynomial of P is

$$\Phi_P(x) = |xI - P| = \begin{vmatrix} x - 1 + p & -p \\ -q & x - 1 + q \end{vmatrix}$$
$$= x^2 + (p + q - 2)x + 1 - p - q = (x - 1)(x + p + q - 1).$$

Therefore P has two eigenvalues 1 and $1 - p - q \in (-1, 1)$. We can find the eigenvectors as

$$P \begin{bmatrix} 1 \\ 1 \end{bmatrix} = \begin{bmatrix} 1 \\ 1 \end{bmatrix} \quad \text{and} \quad P \begin{bmatrix} p \\ -q \end{bmatrix} = (1 - p - q) \begin{bmatrix} p \\ -q \end{bmatrix}.$$

DOI: 10.1201/9781032698953-9

Therefore if we define the matrix of eigenvectors

$$S = \begin{bmatrix} 1 & p \\ 1 & -q \end{bmatrix},$$

by Proposition 6.3 we have

$$D := S^{-1}PS = \begin{bmatrix} 1 & 0 \\ 0 & 1-p-q \end{bmatrix}.$$

Therefore

$$P^t = SD^tS^{-1} = \frac{1}{p+q} \begin{bmatrix} 1 & p \\ 1 & -q \end{bmatrix} \begin{bmatrix} 1 & 0 \\ 0 & (1-p-q)^t \end{bmatrix} \begin{bmatrix} q & p \\ 1 & -1 \end{bmatrix}$$

$$= \frac{1}{p+q} \begin{bmatrix} q+p(1-p-q)^t & p(1-(1-p-q)^t) \\ q(1-(1-p-q)^t) & p+q(1-p-q)^t \end{bmatrix}.$$

Since $|1-p-q| < 1$, letting $t \to \infty$, we obtain

$$P^t \to \frac{1}{p+q} \begin{bmatrix} q & p \\ q & p \end{bmatrix}.$$

Noting that $e_0 + u_0 = 1$, regardless of the initial value $x_0 = (e_0, u_0)$, we obtain

$$x_t = x_0 P^t \to \begin{bmatrix} e_0 & u_0 \end{bmatrix} \frac{1}{p+q} \begin{bmatrix} q & p \\ q & p \end{bmatrix} = \frac{1}{p+q} \begin{bmatrix} q & p \end{bmatrix},$$

so the worker eventually becomes unemployed with probability $\frac{p}{p+q}$.

9.2 MARKOV CHAIN

When a random variable is indexed by time, it is called a *stochastic process*. Let $\{X_t\}_{t=0}^{\infty}$ be a stochastic process. When the distribution of X_t conditional on the past information $X_{t-1}, X_{t-2}, \dots$ depends only on the most recent past (i.e., X_{t-1}), $\{X_t\}$ is called a *Markov process*. For example, a vector autoregression (VAR)

$$X_t = AX_{t-1} + u_t$$

(where A is a matrix and the shock u_t is independent and identically distributed over time) is a Markov process. When the Markov process $\{X_t\}$ takes on finitely many values, it is called a *finite-state Markov chain*. Let $\{X_t\}$ be a (finite-state) Markov chain and $n = 1, \dots, N$ index the values $\{x_n\}_{n=1}^{N}$ the process can take. (We write $X_t = x_n$ when the state at t is n.) Since there are finitely many states, the distribution of X_t conditional on X_{t-1} is just a multinomial distribution. Therefore the Markov chain is completely characterized by the *transition probability (stochastic) matrix* $P = (p_{nn'})$, where $p_{nn'}$ is the probability of transitioning from state n to n'. Clearly, we have $p_{nn'} \ge 0$ and $\sum_{n'=1}^{N} p_{nn'} = 1$.

Suppose that X_0 is distributed according to the distribution represented by the row vector $\mu = (\mu_1, \ldots, \mu_N)$, where μ_n is the probability of being in state n. Then what is the distribution of X_1? Using transition probabilities, the probability of being in state n' at $t = 1$ is $\sum_{n=1}^{N} \mu_n p_{nn'}$, because the process must be in some state (say n) at $t = 0$ (which happens with probability μ_n) and conditional on being in state n at $t = 0$, the probability of moving to state n' at $t = 1$ is $p_{nn'}$. By the definition of matrix multiplication,

$$\sum_{n=1}^{N} \mu_n p_{nn'} = (\mu P)_{n'}$$

is the n'-th entry of the row vector μP, so μP is the distribution of X_1. Similarly, the distribution of X_2 is $(\mu P)P = \mu P^2$, and in general the distribution of X_t is μP^t.

As we let the system run for a long time, does the distribution settle down to some fixed distribution? That is, does $\lim_{t \to \infty} \mu P^t$ exist, and if so, is it unique? We can answer this question by using the contraction mapping theorem.

Theorem 9.1. *Let $P = (p_{nn'})$ be a stochastic matrix such that $p_{nn'} > 0$ for all n, n'. Then there exists a unique invariant distribution π such that $\pi = \pi P$, and $\lim_{t \to \infty} \mu P^t = \pi$ for all initial distribution μ.*

Proof. Let $\Delta = \left\{ x \in \mathbb{R}_+^N : \sum_{n=1}^{N} x_n = 1 \right\}$ be the set of all multinomial distributions. Since $\Delta \subset \mathbb{R}^N$ is closed and $\mathbb{R}^N$ is a complete metric space with the ℓ^1 norm (that is, $d(x, y) = \|x - y\|$ for $\|x\| = \sum_{n=1}^{N} |x_n|$), Δ is also a complete metric space.

View $x \in \mathbb{R}^N$ as a row vector and define $T : \Delta \to \Delta$ by $T(x) = xP$. To show that $T(x) \in \Delta$, note that if $x \in \Delta$, since $p_{nn'} \geq 0$ for all n, n', we have $xP \geq 0$, and since $\sum_{n'=1}^{N} p_{nn'} = 1$, we have

$$\sum_{n'=1}^{N} (xP)_{n'} = \sum_{n'=1}^{N} \sum_{n=1}^{N} x_n p_{nn'} = \sum_{n=1}^{N} x_n \sum_{n'=1}^{N} p_{nn'} = \sum_{n=1}^{N} x_n = 1.$$

Therefore $T(x) = xP \in \Delta$.

Next, let us show that T is a contraction. Since $p_{nn'} > 0$ and the number of states is finite, there exists $\epsilon > 0$ such that $p_{nn'} > \epsilon$ for all n, n'. Without loss of generality, we may assume $N\epsilon < 1$. Let $q_{nn'} = \frac{p_{nn'} - \epsilon}{1 - N\epsilon} > 0$ and $Q = (q_{nn'})$. Since $\sum_{n'} p_{nn'} = 1$, we obtain $\sum_{n'} q_{nn'} = 1$, so Q is also a stochastic matrix. Letting J be the matrix with all entries equal to 1, we have $P = (1 - N\epsilon)Q + \epsilon J$.

Now let $\mu, \nu \in \Delta$. Then

$$\mu P - \nu P = (1 - N\epsilon)(\mu Q - \nu Q) + \epsilon(\mu J - \nu J).$$

Since all entries of J are 1 and the vectors μ, ν sum to 1, we have $\mu J = \nu J = 1 = (1, \ldots, 1)$. Therefore letting $0 < \beta = 1 - N\epsilon < 1$, we get

$$\|T(\mu) - T(\nu)\| = \|\mu P - \nu P\| = \beta \|\mu Q - \nu Q\|$$

$$= \beta \sum_{n'=1}^{N} |(\mu Q)_{n'} - (\nu Q)_{n'}| = \beta \sum_{n'=1}^{N} \left| \sum_{n=1}^{N} (\mu_n - \nu_n) q_{nn'} \right|$$

$$\leq \beta \sum_{n'=1}^{N} \sum_{n=1}^{N} |\mu_n - \nu_n| q_{nn'} = \beta \sum_{n=1}^{N} |\mu_n - \nu_n| \sum_{n'=1}^{N} q_{nn'}$$

$$= \beta \sum_{n=1}^{N} |\mu_n - \nu_n| = \beta \|\mu - \nu\|.$$

Therefore T is a contraction. By the contraction mapping theorem, there exists a unique $\pi \in \Delta$ such that $\pi P = \pi$, and $\lim_{t \to \infty} \mu P^t = \pi$ for all $\mu \in \Delta$. □

Remark. By applying Theorem 7.4, the same conclusion holds if there exists $m \in \mathbb{N}$ such that P^m is a positive matrix.

The employment-unemployment example at the beginning of this chapter is clearly a special case of Theorem 9.1.

9.3 PERRON'S THEOREM

Recall the convention for vector inequalities: for real matrices $A = (a_{mn})$ and $B = (b_{mn})$ of the same size, we write $A \leq B$ ($A \ll B$) if $a_{mn} \leq b_{mn}$ ($a_{mn} < b_{mn}$) for all m, n. The reverse inequalities $\geq, \gg$ are defined analogously. If $A \geq 0$ ($A \gg 0$), we say that A is *nonnegative* (*positive*).[1] The set of $M \times N$ nonnegative (positive) matrices is denoted by $\mathbb{R}_+^{M \times N}$ ($\mathbb{R}_{++}^{M \times N}$). For example, stochastic matrices are nonnegative.

The following proposition provides inequalities for the spectral radius of nonnegative matrices. In what follows, for $A = (a_{mn}) \in \mathbb{C}^{M \times N}$, let $|A| = (|a_{mn}|)$ denote the matrix of absolute values.

Proposition 9.2. *For $A, B \in \mathbb{C}^{N \times N}$, the following statements are true.*

(i) If $0 \leq |A| \leq B$, then $\rho(A) \leq \rho(|A|) \leq \rho(B)$.

(ii) If $0 \ll A$, then $\rho(A) > 0$.

Proof. (i) Let $\|\cdot\|$ denote the supremum norm on $\mathbb{C}^N$ as well as the operator norm induced by it on $\mathbb{C}^{N \times N}$. Then by Example 6.4 and the triangle inequality for complex numbers, we have $\|A^k\| \leq \left\| |A|^k \right\| \leq \|B^k\|$. Taking the $1/k$-th

---

[1] Positive and positive definite matrices should not be confused. Positive matrices are matrices whose entries are all positive and need not be symmetric. Positive definite matrices are real symmetric matrices whose eigenvalues are all positive (Proposition 6.8) and may have negative entries.

power and letting $k \to \infty$, by the Gelfand spectral radius formula (Theorem 6.15) we obtain $\rho(A) \leq \rho(|A|) \leq \rho(B)$.

(ii) Suppose $A \gg 0$. Then we can take $\epsilon > 0$ such that $A \geq \epsilon I$. Applying (i), we obtain $\rho(A) \geq \rho(\epsilon I) = \epsilon > 0$. ☐

We can now generalize Theorem 9.1 as follows.

Theorem 9.3 (Perron's theorem). *If $A \in \mathbb{R}_{++}^{N \times N}$, the following statements are true.*

(i) $\rho(A) > 0$, which is an eigenvalue of A (called the Perron root).

(ii) There exist $x, y \gg 0$ (called the right and left Perron vectors) such that $Ax = \rho(A)x$ and $y'A = \rho(A)y'$.

(iii) The vectors x, y are unique up to scalar multiplication (in $\mathbb{C}^N$).

(iv) If x, y are chosen such that $y'x = 1$, then $\lim_{k \to \infty} [\frac{1}{\rho(A)} A]^k = xy'$.

Proof. (i)(ii) $\rho(A) > 0$ follows from Proposition 9.2. Let $\alpha = \rho(A)$. Let λ be an eigenvalue of A with $|\lambda| = \alpha > 0$ and $u = (u_1, \ldots, u_N)' \neq 0$ be a corresponding eigenvector. Let $v = (|u_1|, \ldots, |u_N|)' > 0$ be the vector of absolute values. Since $Au = \lambda u$, taking the absolute value of each entry and noting that A is positive, we obtain

$$\alpha |u_m| = \left| \sum_{n=1}^{N} a_{mn} u_n \right| \leq \sum_{n=1}^{N} a_{mn} |u_n| \iff \alpha v \leq Av.$$

Let us show that $Av = \alpha v$. Suppose to the contrary that $w := Av > \alpha v$. Then $w - \alpha v > 0$, so multiplying A from the left and noting that $A \gg 0$, we obtain

$$A(w - \alpha v) \gg 0 \iff Aw \gg \alpha Av = \alpha w.$$

Since A is finite-dimensional, we can take $\epsilon > 0$ such that $Aw \geq (1 + \epsilon)\alpha w$. Multiplying both sides from left by A^{k-1}, we obtain

$$A^k w \geq (1 + \epsilon)\alpha A^{k-1} w \geq \cdots \geq [(1 + \epsilon)\alpha]^k w. \tag{9.1}$$

Let $\|\cdot\|$ denote the supremum norm as well as the operator norm induced by it. Applying $\|\cdot\|$ to (9.1), we obtain

$$\|A^k\| \|w\| \geq \|A^k w\| \geq [(1 + \epsilon)\alpha]^k \|w\| \implies \|A^k\|^{1/k} \geq (1 + \epsilon)\alpha.$$

Letting $k \to \infty$, by the Gelfand spectral radius formula (Theorem 6.15), we obtain $\alpha \geq (1 + \epsilon)\alpha$, which is a contradiction since $\alpha > 0$. Therefore $Av = \alpha v$. Since $v > 0$, we have $Av \gg 0$, so $v = \frac{1}{\alpha} Av \gg 0$. The same argument applies to the left Perron vector.

(iv) Let $x \gg 0$ be a right Perron vector of A. Then for each m, we have $\sum_{n=1}^{N} a_{mn} x_n = \alpha x_m$. Define the diagonal matrix $D = \text{diag}[x_1, \ldots, x_N]$, which is invertible. Let $P = \frac{1}{\alpha} D^{-1} A D \gg 0$. Comparing the (m,n) entry, we obtain $p_{mn} = \frac{a_{mn} x_n}{\alpha x_m}$, so

$$\sum_{n=1}^{N} p_{mn} = \sum_{n=1}^{N} \frac{a_{mn} x_n}{\alpha x_m} = 1.$$

Thus P is a positive stochastic matrix. By Theorem 9.1, there exists a unique row vector $\pi \gg 0$ with $\sum_{n=1}^{N} \pi_n = 1$ such that

$$\pi = \pi P = \pi \frac{1}{\alpha} D^{-1} A D \iff y' A = \alpha y',$$

where $y' := \pi D^{-1} \gg 0$. Thus y is a left Perron vector. Letting $1 = (1, \ldots, 1)'$, we obtain

$$y'x = \pi D^{-1} x = \pi \, \text{diag}[x_1, \ldots, x_N]^{-1} x = \pi 1 = 1.$$

In Theorem 9.1, set $\mu = e'_n$ for each n to obtain

$$1\pi = \lim_{k \to \infty} P^k = \lim_{k \to \infty} D^{-1} \left[\frac{1}{\alpha} A \right]^k D$$

$$\iff \lim_{k \to \infty} \left[\frac{1}{\rho(A)} A \right]^k = D 1 \pi D^{-1} = x y'.$$

(iii) Let x be a right Perron vector of A, so $Ax = \alpha x$. Suppose there exists $u \in \mathbb{C}^N$ such that $Au = \alpha u$. Since A, α are both real, by taking the real and imaginary parts, $v = \text{Re}\, u, \text{Im}\, u$ both satisfy $Av = \alpha v$. Then

$$v = \left[\frac{1}{\alpha} A \right]^k v \to x y' v = (y' v) x,$$

so v is a scalar multiple of x. Therefore u is a scalar multiple of x. $\quad\square$

9.4   IRREDUCIBLE NONNEGATIVE MATRICES

Some properties of positive matrices generalize to nonnegative matrices.

Proposition 9.4. *If $A \in \mathbb{R}_+^{N \times N}$, then the spectral radius $\rho(A)$ is an eigenvalue of A and there exist $x, y > 0$ such that $Ax = \rho(A)x$ and $y' A = \rho(A) y'$.*

Proof. Let $A = (a_{mn})$ and $A(\epsilon) := (a_{mn} + \epsilon)$ for $\epsilon > 0$. Then $A(\epsilon)$ is positive, so by Theorem 9.3 $\rho(A(\epsilon))$ is an eigenvalue of A and there exists $x(\epsilon) \gg 0$ such that $A(\epsilon) x(\epsilon) = \rho(A(\epsilon)) x(\epsilon)$. Letting $\epsilon \downarrow 0$, applying Corollary 6.13, and passing to a subsequence, we obtain the claim. $\quad\square$

If A is nonnegative but not positive, the uniqueness of the eigenvector corresponding to $\rho(A)$ need not hold. For example, let

$$A(\epsilon) = \begin{bmatrix} 1 + \epsilon & \epsilon \\ \epsilon & 1 + \epsilon \end{bmatrix}.$$

If $\epsilon > 0$, then $A(\epsilon)$ is positive and we can easily see that $\rho(A(\epsilon)) = 1 + 2\epsilon$ and $(1,1)'$ is the right Perron vector. Letting $\epsilon \downarrow 0$, we obtain $A(\epsilon) \to A(0) = I$, and any $x \in \mathbb{R}^2$ is an eigenvector of $A(0) = I$.

However, the following proposition shows that if we can find a positive eigenvector, the eigenvalue must equal the spectral radius.

Proposition 9.5. *Let $A \in \mathbb{R}_+^{N \times N}$. If $v \gg 0$ satisfies $Av = \alpha v$ for some eigenvalue α, then $\alpha = \rho(A)$.*

Proof. By Proposition 9.4, we can take a left eigenvector $y > 0$ with $y'A = \rho(A)y'$. Multiplying v from right, we obtain

$$\rho(A)y'v = y'Av = y'(\alpha v) = \alpha y'v. \tag{9.2}$$

Since $v \gg 0$ and $y' > 0$, dividing both sides of (9.2) by the scalar $y'v > 0$, we obtain $\alpha = \rho(A)$. □

To recover the uniqueness of the Perron vector, we introduce the notion of *irreducible matrices*. Irreducibility is best understood with stochastic matrices. Let $\{X_t\}_{t=0}^\infty$ be a finite-state Markov chain with state space $\{x_1, \ldots, x_N\}$ and transition probability matrix $P = (p_{mn})$. Then for each (m, n) pair, by definition we have

$$\Pr(X_{t+1} = x_n \mid X_t = x_m) = p_{mn}.$$

If we write $P^k = (p_{mn}^{(k)})$ for $k = 1, 2, \ldots$, by the same calculation as before, we obtain

$$\Pr(X_{t+k} = x_n \mid X_t = x_m) = p_{mn}^{(k)}.$$

We say that the Markov chain is *irreducible* if for each (m, n) pair, we have $p_{mn}^{(k)} > 0$ for some k. In other words, irreducibility means that starting from any state m, we may transition to any other state n some time in the future with positive probability. Clearly, this definition depends only on the transition probability matrix P and not on the Markov chain itself, so we use expressions like "P is irreducible".

More generally, irreducibility is related to directed graphs or networks. Let $\{1, \ldots, N\}$ be a finite set, and for each (m, n) pair, suppose we can determine whether a property holds or not. For instance, the property may be "person m likes person n", "chapter m is required to understand chapter n", or "in a Markov chain, it is possible to transition from state m to n in one step", etc. For each (m, n) pair, define $a_{mn} = 1$ (0) if the property holds (does not hold). Mathematically, a directed graph is defined by a matrix (called *adjacency matrix*) $A = (a_{mn})$ such that $a_{mn} \in \{0, 1\}$ for all m, n: intuitively, we draw an arrow from point m to n if and only if $a_{mn} = 1$.

Example 9.1. Let $\{1, 2, 3, 4\}$ denote the four seasons (spring, summer, fall, winter). Let $a_{mn} = 1$ if season n immediately follows season m, and set $a_{mn} = 0$ otherwise. Thus the adjacency matrix is given by

$$A = \begin{bmatrix} 0 & 1 & 0 & 0 \\ 0 & 0 & 1 & 0 \\ 0 & 0 & 0 & 1 \\ 1 & 0 & 0 & 0 \end{bmatrix}$$

and the directed graph is shown in Figure 9.1a.

Example 9.2. Suppose an animal randomly crosses a river. Conditional on being on the left (right) side of the river, it attempts to cross the river with probability p (q). Each time the animal crosses the river, it drowns with probability r. Let $\{L, R, D\}$ denote the states left, right, and drown. The transition probability matrix P and the adjacency matrix A are given by

$$P = \begin{bmatrix} 1-p & p(1-r) & pr \\ q(1-r) & 1-q & qr \\ 0 & 0 & 1 \end{bmatrix} \quad \text{and} \quad A = \begin{bmatrix} 1 & 1 & 1 \\ 1 & 1 & 1 \\ 0 & 0 & 1 \end{bmatrix},$$

and the directed graph is shown in Figure 9.1b.

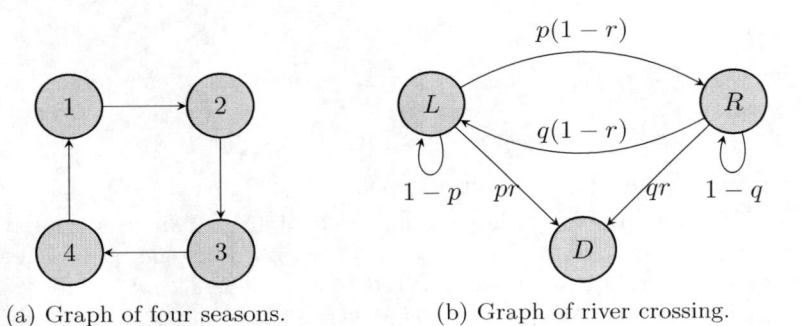

(a) Graph of four seasons. (b) Graph of river crossing.

FIGURE 9.1: Directed graphs.

We say that an adjacency matrix A is *irreducible* if in the corresponding graph, for any (m, n) pair, we can draw a path from m to n. More formally, for $A \in \mathbb{C}^{N \times N}$, we say that $A = (a_{mn})$ is *irreducible* if for all $m \neq n$, there exist $k \in \mathbb{N}$ and indices $m = i_0, i_1, \ldots, i_k = n$ such that $a_{i_l i_{l+1}} \neq 0$ for all $l = 0, \ldots, k-1$. Otherwise, we say that A is *reducible*.

There are many ways to characterize irreducibility.

Proposition 9.6. *For $A \in \mathbb{C}^{N \times N}$, the following conditions are equivalent.*

(i) The complex matrix A is irreducible.

(ii) The nonnegative matrix $|A|$ is irreducible.

(iii) For all $m \neq n$, there exist $k \in \{1, \ldots, N-1\}$ and indices $m = i_0 \neq i_1 \neq \cdots \neq i_k = n$ such that $a_{i_l i_{l+1}} \neq 0$ for all $l = 0, \ldots, k-1$.

(iv) $\sum_{k=0}^{N-1} |A|^k \gg 0$.

(v) $(I + |A|)^{N-1} \gg 0$.

Proof. (i) $\iff$ (ii) is obvious because $a_{mn} \neq 0 \iff |a_{mn}| \neq 0$.

Obviously (iii) $\implies$ (i). To show (i) $\implies$ (iii), suppose A is irreducible and for each $m \neq n$ take indices $m = i_0, i_1, \ldots, i_k = n$ such that $a_{i_l i_{l+1}} \neq 0$ for all $l = 0, \ldots, k-1$. If these indices contain i twice, say $i_{l_1} = i_{l_2} = i$ and $l_1 < l_2$, we may drop $i_{l_1+1}, \ldots, i_{l_2}$ from the list. Therefore without loss of generality, we may assume that $i_0, \ldots, i_k$ are all distinct. Since there are at most N distinct indices, we obtain $k + 1 \leq N \iff k \leq N - 1$. Thus (iii) holds.

To show (iii) $\implies$ (iv), suppose (iii) holds. Then we may replace the condition $a_{i_l i_{l+1}} \neq 0$ with $|a_{i_l i_{l+1}}| > 0$. However, the condition $m = i_0 \neq \cdots \neq i_k = n$ and $|a_{i_l i_{l+1}}| > 0$ for all l implies that the (m, n) entry of $|A|^k$ is positive. By taking such k for each $m \neq n$, it follows that $I + |A| + \cdots + |A|^k \gg 0$, so (iv) holds. Conversely, if (iv) holds, for each $m \neq n$ we can take $k \in \{1, \ldots, N-1\}$ such that the (m, n) entry of $|A|^k$ is positive, which implies (iii).

(iv) $\iff$ (v) is obvious by the binomial theorem $(I + |A|)^{N-1} = \sum_{k=0}^{N-1} \binom{N-1}{k} |A|^k$ and the fact that the coefficient $\binom{N-1}{k}$ does not affect positivity. $\square$

We can now generalize Perron's theorem to nonnegative matrices as follows.

Theorem 9.7 (Perron-Frobenius theorem). *If $A \in \mathbb{R}_+^{N \times N}$ is irreducible, the following statements are true.*

(i) $\rho(A)$ is an eigenvalue of A (called the Perron root).

(ii) There exist $x, y \gg 0$ (called the right and left Perron vectors) such that $Ax = \rho(A)x$ and $y'A = \rho(A)y'$.

(iii) The vectors x, y are unique up to scalar multiplication (in $\mathbb{C}^N$).

Proof. Let $\alpha = \rho(A)$. By Proposition 9.4, α is an eigenvalue of A and we can take $x > 0$ such that $Ax = \alpha x$. Define the matrix $B = I + A + \cdots + A^{N-1}$. Since A is nonnegative and irreducible, by Proposition 9.6, we have $B \gg 0$. Therefore

$$0 \ll Bx = (I + A + \cdots + A^{N-1})x = (1 + \alpha + \cdots + \alpha^{N-1})x =: \beta x,$$

so $x \gg 0$. Furthermore, since x is a positive eigenvector of B with eigenvalue β, by Proposition 9.5 it must be $\rho(B) = \beta$ and x is the right Perron vector of B, which is unique. The proof of the uniqueness of x in $\mathbb{C}^N$ is the same as Theorem 9.3. $\square$

Corollary 9.8. *An irreducible finite-state Markov chain has a unique invariant distribution.*

Proof. Let P be an irreducible stochastic matrix. Since P is a stochastic matrix, for $1 = (1, \ldots, 1)'$, we have $P1 = 1$. Hence by Proposition 9.5, we have $\rho(P) = 1$. By Theorem 9.7, there exists a unique left Perron vector $y \gg 0$, so $y'P = \rho(P)y' = y'$. Without loss of generality, we may assume $\sum_{n=1}^{N} y_n = 1$, which is the unique invariant distribution. □

Example 9.3 (PageRank). Suppose that there are N websites indexed by $n = 1, \ldots, N$. Define the adjacency matrix $A = (a_{mn})$ by $a_{mn} = 1$ if there is a link from site m to n and zero otherwise. From the adjacency matrix A, define the stochastic matrix P by $p_{mn} = a_{mn}/\sum_{n=1}^{N} a_{mn}$. If a Web surfer randomly clicks links on each page, then the location will evolve according to a Markov chain with transition probability matrix P. Assuming P is irreducible, by Corollary 9.8 the Markov chain has a unique invariant distribution π, which is the probability distribution of the location of the random Web surfer. The magnitude of π_n can be interpreted as the importance of site n. This method is exactly the PageRank algorithm proposed by Page et al. (1998).

9.5 METZLER MATRICES

In some applications, we need to deal with square matrices $A = (a_{mn})$ with nonnegative off-diagonal entries (so $a_{mn} \geq 0$ if $m \neq n$), although A may have negative diagonal entries. We call such matrices *essentially nonnegative* or *Metzler*. If A is Metzler, since by definition its off-diagonal entries are nonnegative, the matrix $A + dI$ becomes nonnegative if $d \geq 0$ is large enough. This observation enables us to establish properties of Metzler matrices using the Perron-Frobenius theorem. For Metzler matrices, the role of the spectral radius $\rho(A)$ is replaced with the *spectral abscissa*

$$\zeta(A) := \max\{\operatorname{Re}\alpha : \alpha \text{ is an eigenvalue of } A\},$$

which is the maximum real part of all eigenvalues.

The following theorem is the analogue of the Perron-Frobenius theorem for Metzler matrices.

Theorem 9.9. *Let A be a Metzler matrix. Then the spectral abscissa $\zeta(A)$ is an eigenvalue of A, and there exist nonnegative vectors x, y such that $Ax = \zeta(A)x$ and $y'A = \zeta(A)y'$. If in addition A is irreducible, then x, y are positive vectors and unique up to scalar multiplication.*

PROBLEMS

9.1. Let A be a square nonnegative matrix. Show that if $z > \rho(A)$, then the matrix $zI - A$ is invertible and $(zI - A)^{-1}$ is nonnegative. (Hint: let $B = \frac{1}{z}A$ and consider the identity $(I - B)(I + \cdots + B^{k-1}) = I - B^k$.)

9.2. Prove that $A \in \mathbb{C}^{N \times N}$ is reducible if and only if there exists a permutation matrix P such that

$$P'AP = \begin{bmatrix} A_{11} & A_{12} \\ 0 & A_{22} \end{bmatrix}$$

is block upper triangular.

9.3. Prove that for any $A \in \mathbb{C}^{N \times N}$, there exists a permutation matrix P such that

$$P'AP = \begin{bmatrix} A_{11} & \cdots & A_{1M} \\ \vdots & \ddots & \vdots \\ 0 & \cdots & A_{MM} \end{bmatrix}$$

is block upper triangular with $M \geq 1$ diagonal blocks, where each A_{mm} is irreducible.

9.4. If $\alpha_1, \ldots, \alpha_N$ are eigenvalues of a square matrix A, for any scalar z, show that the eigenvalues of $A + zI$ are $\alpha_1 + z, \ldots, \alpha_N + z$. Use this property to fill in the details of the proof of Theorem 9.9.

9.5. Let $A = (a_{nn'})$ be a Metzler matrix $d = (d_1, \ldots, d_N)' \gg 0$ such that

$$a_{nn} = -\frac{1}{d_n} \sum_{n' \neq n} a_{nn'} d_{n'}$$

for all n.

(i) Show that $Ad = 0$.

(ii) Show that the spectral abscissa of A is $\zeta(A) = 0$. (Hint: let $y > 0$ be a left eigenvector corresponding to $\zeta(A)$, and multiply y' from left to the identity $(A - \zeta(A)I)d = -\zeta(A)d$.)

III

Convex and Nonlinear Optimization

CHAPTER 10

Convex Sets

10.1 CONVEX SETS

A subset C of $\mathbb{R}^N$ (or of any vector space) is said to be *convex* if the line segment joining any two points in C is entirely included in C. More formally, C is convex if for any $x, y \in C$ and $\alpha \in [0, 1]$, we have $(1 - \alpha)x + \alpha y \in C$ (Figure 10.1). For example, a circle, a triangle, and a square are convex but a star shape is not (Figure 10.2).

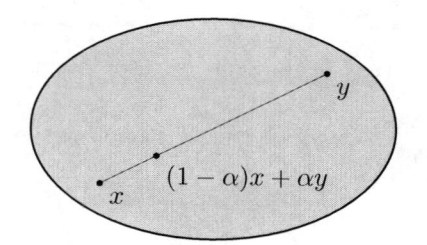

FIGURE 10.1: Definition of a convex set.

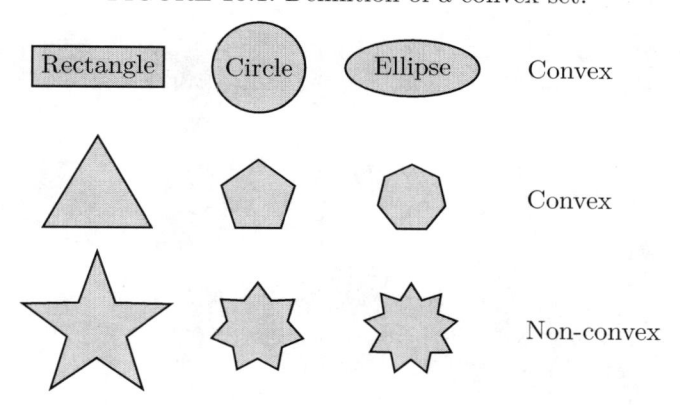

FIGURE 10.2: Examples of convex and non-convex sets.

DOI: 10.1201/9781032698953-10

10.2 CONVEX HULL

Let $A \subset \mathbb{R}^N$ be any set. The smallest convex set that includes A is called the *convex hull* of A and is denoted by co A. To see that co A is well defined, let $\{C_i\}_{i \in I}$ be the collection of all convex sets including A. There is at least one such C_i, namely the entire space $\mathbb{R}^N$. Define $C = \bigcap_{i \in I} C_i$. Take any $x, y \in C$ and $\alpha \in [0, 1]$. Since in particular $x, y \in C_i$ and C_i is convex, we have $(1 - \alpha)x + \alpha y \in C_i$. Since this is true for any i, we have $(1 - \alpha)x + \alpha y \in C$. Therefore, C is convex. But clearly $A \subset C$, and C was the intersection of all such convex sets, so C is the smallest convex set including A.

For example, in the left panel of Figure 10.3, the set A is not convex. (The shape of this set is the Chinese character for "convex", which is my favorite mathematical joke.) Its convex hull includes the light-shaded region in the right panel.

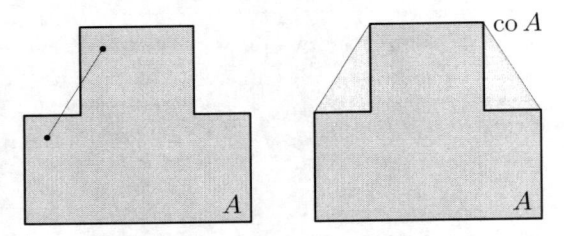

FIGURE 10.3: Non-convex set and convex hull.

Let $x_k \in \mathbb{R}^N$ for $k = 1, \ldots, K$. Take any numbers α_k for $k = 1, \ldots, K$ such that $\alpha_k \geq 0$ and $\sum_{k=1}^{K} \alpha_k = 1$. A point of the form

$$x = \sum_{k=1}^{K} \alpha_k x_k \tag{10.1}$$

is called a *convex combination* of the points $\{x_k\}_{k=1}^{K}$ with weights (or coefficients) $\{\alpha_k\}_{k=1}^{K}$. The following lemma provides a constructive way to obtain the convex hull of a set.

Lemma 10.1. *Let $A \subset \mathbb{R}^N$ be any set. Then co A consists of all convex combinations* (10.1) *of points of A.*

Proof. Problem 10.1. □

Actually, in Lemma 10.1 we may set $K = N + 1$ (so the number of points is at most the dimension plus one) when forming the convex combination as in (10.1). This result is known as the *Carathéodory theorem*, though it will not be used in this book.

10.3 HYPERPLANES AND HALF SPACES

As we know from analytic geometry, the equation of a line in $\mathbb{R}^2$ is

$$a_1 x_1 + a_2 x_2 = c$$

for some real numbers a_1, a_2, c, and the equation of a plane in $\mathbb{R}^3$ is

$$a_1 x_1 + a_2 x_2 + a_3 x_3 = c.$$

Letting $a = (a_1, \ldots, a_N)$ and $x = (x_1, \ldots, x_N)$ be vectors in $\mathbb{R}^N$, the equation $\langle a, x \rangle = c$ is a line if $N = 2$ and a plane if $N = 3$, where

$$\langle a, x \rangle = a_1 x_1 + \cdots + a_N x_N$$

is the inner product of the vectors a and x. In general, we say that the set

$$\left\{ x \in \mathbb{R}^N : \langle a, x \rangle = c \right\}$$

is a *hyperplane* if $a \neq 0$. The vector a is orthogonal to this hyperplane and is called a *normal vector*. To see this, let x_0 be a point in the hyperplane. Since $\langle a, x_0 \rangle = c$, by subtraction and linearity of the inner product, we get $\langle a, x - x_0 \rangle = 0$. This means that the vector a is orthogonal to the vector $x - x_0$, which can point to any direction in the plane by moving x. So it makes sense to say that a is orthogonal to the hyperplane $\langle a, x \rangle = c$.

The sets

$$H^+ = \left\{ x \in \mathbb{R}^N : \langle a, x \rangle \geq c \right\},$$
$$H^- = \left\{ x \in \mathbb{R}^N : \langle a, x \rangle \leq c \right\}$$

are called *half spaces*, since H^+ (H^-) is the portion of $\mathbb{R}^N$ separated by the hyperplane $\langle a, x \rangle = c$ toward the direction of a $(-a)$. It is easy to show that hyperplanes and half spaces are convex (Problem 10.2).

10.4 SEPARATION OF CONVEX SETS

Let C, D be two (not necessarily convex) sets. We say that the hyperplane H: $\langle a, x \rangle = c$ *separates* C, D if $C \subset H^-$ and $D \subset H^+$ (Figure 10.4), that is,

$$x \in C \implies \langle a, x \rangle \leq c,$$
$$x \in D \implies \langle a, x \rangle \geq c.$$

(The inequalities may be reversed.) When these inequalities hold, we call the hyperplane $\langle a, x \rangle = c$ a *separating hyperplane*.

Clearly C, D can be separated if and only if

$$\sup_{x \in C} \langle a, x \rangle \leq \inf_{x \in D} \langle a, x \rangle, \tag{10.2}$$

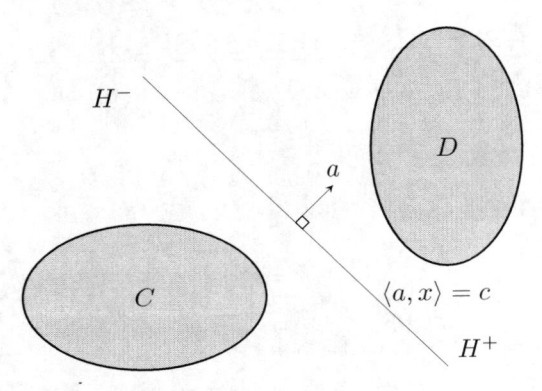

FIGURE 10.4: Separation of convex sets.

since we can take c between these two numbers. We say that C, D can be *strictly separated* if the inequality in (10.2) is strict, so

$$\sup_{x \in C} \langle a, x \rangle < \inf_{x \in D} \langle a, x \rangle. \tag{10.3}$$

The remarkable property of convex sets is that two disjoint convex sets can always be separated. This *separating hyperplane theorem* is one of the most important theorems applied in economics.

Theorem 10.2 (Separating hyperplane theorem). *Let $C, D \subset \mathbb{R}^N$ be nonempty, convex, and $C \cap D = \emptyset$. Then there exists a hyperplane that separates C, D, that is, there exists $0 \neq a \in \mathbb{R}^N$ such that (10.2) holds. If, in addition, C, D are closed and one of them is bounded, then they can be strictly separated, so (10.3) holds.*

Before proving the separating hyperplane theorem, we discuss why each assumption is necessary. In Figure 10.5, D is not convex, and it engulfs the (convex) set C. It is clear that C, D cannot be separated.

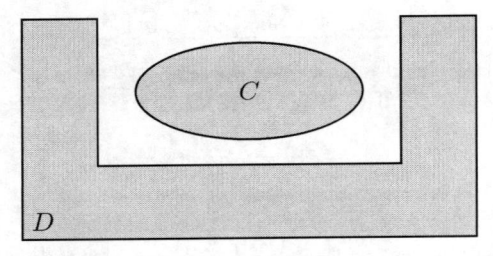

FIGURE 10.5: Necessity of convexity for separation.

In Figure 10.6, C, D are both straight lines (hence convex) but they intersect. It is clear that C, D cannot be separated.

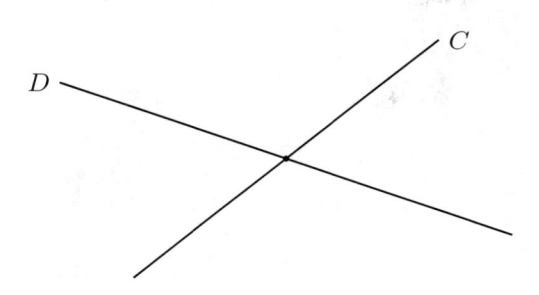

FIGURE 10.6: Necessity of empty intersection for separation.

In Figure 10.7, the sets C, D are defined by

$$C = \left\{(x,y) \in \mathbb{R}^2 : y \geq e^x\right\},$$
$$D = \left\{(x,y) \in \mathbb{R}^2 : y \leq 0\right\},$$

which are both nonempty, closed, convex, and do not intersect. Therefore, C, D satisfy the weak form of the separating hyperplane theorem and can be separated (by the horizontal line $y = 0$). However, they cannot be strictly separated because D includes this horizontal line. Strict separation fails because C, D are both unbounded.

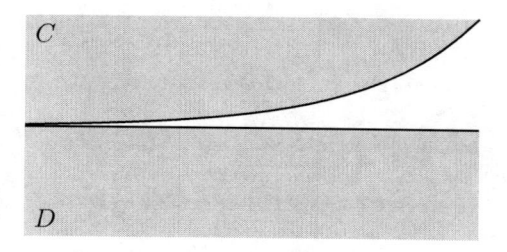

FIGURE 10.7: Necessity of boundedness for strict separation.

We prove Theorem 10.2 by establishing several intermediate results. In this chapter, $\|\cdot\|$ denotes the ℓ^2 (Euclidean) norm.

Lemma 10.3. *Let $C \subset \mathbb{R}^N$ be nonempty, closed, and convex. Then for any $x_0 \in \mathbb{R}^N$, the minimum distance problem*

$$\min_{x \in C} \|x - x_0\| \tag{10.4}$$

has a unique solution $x = \bar{x}$. Furthermore, for any $x \in C$ we have

$$\langle x_0 - \bar{x}, x - \bar{x} \rangle \leq 0. \tag{10.5}$$

The content of Lemma 10.3 can be understood from Figure 10.8.

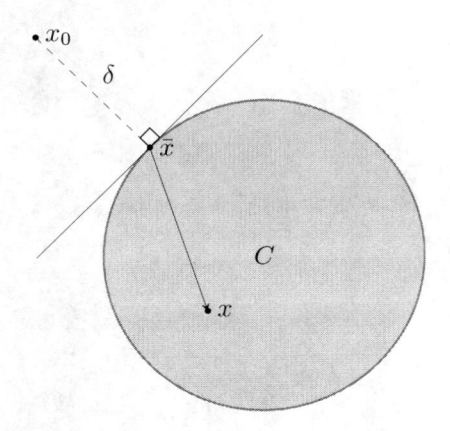

FIGURE 10.8: Projection on a convex set.

Proof. Let $\delta = \inf_{x \in C} \|x - x_0\| \geq 0$. Take a sequence $\{x_k\} \subset C$ such that $\|x_k - x_0\| \to \delta$. Then by simple algebra (Problem 10.4) we get

$$\|x_k - x_l\|^2 = 2\|x_0 - x_k\|^2 + 2\|x_0 - x_l\|^2 - 4\left\|x_0 - \frac{1}{2}(x_k + x_l)\right\|^2.$$

Since C is convex, we have $\frac{1}{2}(x_k + x_l) \in C$, so by the definition of δ we get

$$\|x_k - x_l\|^2 \leq 2\|x_0 - x_k\|^2 + 2\|x_0 - x_l\|^2 - 4\delta^2$$
$$\to 2\delta^2 + 2\delta^2 - 4\delta^2 = 0 \tag{10.6}$$

as $k, l \to \infty$. Since $\{x_k\} \subset C$ is Cauchy and C is closed, by Problem 1.10 and Proposition 1.6, $\{x_k\}$ converges to some $\bar{x} \in C$. Then

$$\delta \leq \|\bar{x} - x_0\| \leq \|\bar{x} - x_k\| + \|x_k - x_0\| \to 0 + \delta = \delta,$$

so $\|\bar{x} - x_0\| = \delta$ and $\bar{x}$ solves (10.4).

To show uniqueness, suppose there are two solutions x_1, x_2. Then setting $(k, l) = (1, 2)$ in (10.6) yields

$$0 \leq \|x_1 - x_2\|^2 \leq 2\delta^2 + 2\delta^2 - 4\delta^2 = 0,$$

so $x_1 = x_2$.

Finally, take any $x \in C$. Since C is convex, for any $0 < \alpha \leq 1$, we have $(1 - \alpha)\bar{x} + \alpha x \in C$. Therefore, by the definition of δ, we have

$$\delta^2 = \|x_0 - \bar{x}\|^2 \leq \|x_0 - (1 - \alpha)\bar{x} - \alpha x\|^2.$$

Expanding both sides, dividing by $\alpha > 0$, and letting $\alpha \to 0$, we obtain (10.5). □

The following proposition shows that a point that is not an interior point of a convex C can be separated from C.

Proposition 10.4. *Let $C \subset \mathbb{R}^N$ be nonempty and convex and $x_0 \notin \operatorname{int} C$. Then there exist $0 \neq a \in \mathbb{R}^N$ and $c \in \mathbb{R}$ such that*

$$\langle a, x \rangle \leq c \leq \langle a, x_0 \rangle \tag{10.7}$$

for any $x \in C$. If $x_0 \notin \operatorname{cl} C$, then the above inequalities can be made strict.

Proof. Suppose that $x_0 \notin \operatorname{cl} C$. Using Lemma 10.3, let $\bar{x}$ achieve the minimum distance to x_0 on $\operatorname{cl} C$. Then $x_0 \neq \bar{x}$ because $\bar{x} \in \operatorname{cl} C$ and $x_0 \notin \operatorname{cl} C$. Let $a = x_0 - \bar{x} \neq 0$. Then (10.5) implies

$$\langle a, x - \bar{x} \rangle \leq 0 \iff \langle a, x \rangle \leq \langle a, \bar{x} \rangle$$

for all $x \in \operatorname{cl} C$. The definition of a implies

$$0 < \|a\|^2 = \langle a, x_0 - \bar{x} \rangle \iff \langle a, x_0 \rangle = \langle a, \bar{x} \rangle + \|a\|^2 .$$

Therefore, (10.7) holds with strict inequalities if for example we set $c = \langle a, \bar{x} \rangle + \|a\|^2 / 2$.

If $x_0 \in \operatorname{cl} C$, since by assumption $x_0 \notin \operatorname{int} C$, we can take a sequence $\{x_k\}$ such that $x_k \notin \operatorname{cl} C$ and $x_k \to x_0$. Then for each k we can find a vector $a_k \neq 0$ and a number $c_k \in \mathbb{R}$ such that

$$\langle a_k, x \rangle \leq c_k \leq \langle a_k, x_k \rangle$$

for all $x \in C$. By dividing both sides by $\|a_k\| \neq 0$, without loss of generality we may assume $\|a_k\| = 1$. Since $x_k \to x_0$, the sequence $\{c_k\}$ is bounded. Therefore, we can find a convergent subsequence $(a_{k_l}, c_{k_l}) \to (a, c)$. Letting $l \to \infty$, obtain (10.7). □

We can now prove the separating hyperplane theorem.

Proof of Theorem 10.2. Define the set

$$E = C - D := \{z = x - y : x \in C, y \in D\} .$$

Since C, D are nonempty and convex, so is E. Since $C \cap D = \emptyset$, we have $0 \notin E$. In particular, $0 \notin \operatorname{int} E$. By Proposition 10.4, there exists $a \neq 0$ such that $\langle a, z \rangle \leq 0 = \langle a, 0 \rangle$ for all $z \in E$. By the definition of E, we have

$$\langle a, x - y \rangle \leq 0 \iff \langle a, x \rangle \leq \langle a, y \rangle$$

for all $x \in C$ and $y \in D$. Taking the supremum over $x \in C$ and infimum over $y \in D$, we obtain (10.2).

To show strict separation, suppose that C is closed and D is closed and bounded. Let us show that $E = C - D$ is closed. To this end, suppose that

$\{z_k\} \subset E$ and $z_k \to z$. Then we can take $\{x_k\} \subset C$ and $\{y_k\} \subset D$ such that $z_k = x_k - y_k$. Since D is closed and bounded and hence sequentially compact by Theorem 1.10, there is a subsequence such that $y_{k_l} \to y \in D$. Then $x_{k_l} = y_{k_l} + z_{k_l} \to y + z$, but since C is closed, $x = y + z \in C$. Therefore $z = x - y \in E$, so E is closed.

Since $E = C - D$ is closed and $0 \notin E$, by Proposition 10.4 there exists $a \neq 0$ such that $\langle a, 0 \rangle = 0 > \langle a, z \rangle$ for all $z \in E$. The rest of the proof is similar. $\qquad\square$

10.5   CONE AND DUAL CONE

A set $C \subset \mathbb{R}^N$ is said to be a *cone* if, whenever $x \in C$, the ray originating from 0 and passing through x is included in C. Formally, C is a cone if $x \in C$ and $\lambda > 0$ implies $\lambda x \in C$. An example is the nonnegative orthant

$$\mathbb{R}^N_+ := \left\{ x = (x_1, \dots, x_N) \in \mathbb{R}^N : (\forall n) x_n \geq 0 \right\}.$$

Another example is the set

$$C := \left\{ x = \sum_{k=1}^{K} \alpha_k a_k : (\forall k) \alpha_k \geq 0 \right\}, \tag{10.8}$$

where $a_1, \dots, a_K \in \mathbb{R}^N$. The set C in (10.8) is called the *polyhedral cone* generated by vectors $a_1, \dots, a_K$ and is denoted by $C = \text{cone}[a_1, \dots, a_K]$ (Figure 10.9). Clearly $\mathbb{R}^N_+ = \text{cone}[e_1, \dots, e_N]$, where $e_1, \dots, e_N$ are unit vectors of $\mathbb{R}^N$. When a cone is closed (convex), we say that it is a closed (convex) cone. A polyhedral cone is a closed convex cone (Problem 10.8).

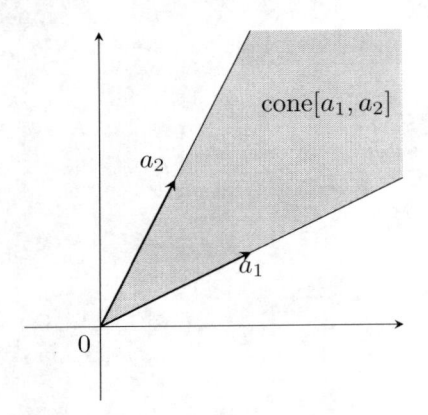

FIGURE 10.9: Polyhedral cone.

Let $C \subset \mathbb{R}^N$ be any nonempty set. The set

$$C^* = \left\{ y \in \mathbb{R}^N : (\forall x \in C) \langle x, y \rangle \leq 0 \right\} \tag{10.9}$$

is called the *dual cone* of C. Thus the dual cone C^* consists of all vectors that make an obtuse angle with any vector in C (Figure 10.10).

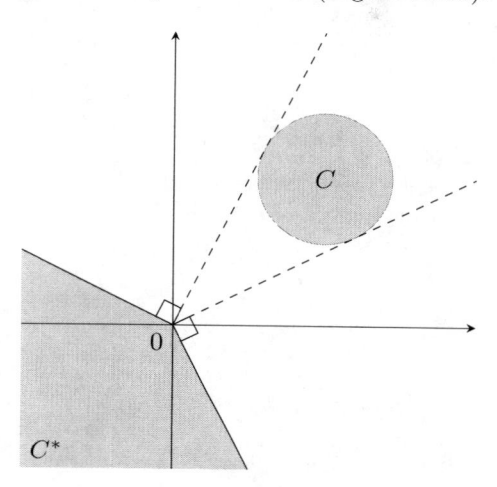

FIGURE 10.10: Cone and its dual.

Note that in the definition of the dual cone (10.9), the set C is arbitrary (not necessarily a cone). Yet, C^* is called the dual cone, which suggests that C^* is always a cone. The following proposition shows that this is indeed true.

Proposition 10.5. *Let $\emptyset \neq C \subset D$. Then (i) the dual cone C^* is a nonempty closed convex cone, (ii) $C^* \supset D^*$, and (iii) $C^* = (\mathrm{co}\, C)^*$.*

Proof. (i) C^* is nonempty since $0 \in C^*$. If $y \in C^*$, then by definition $\langle x, y \rangle \leq 0$ for all $x \in C$. Then for any $\lambda > 0$ and $x \in C$, we have $\langle x, \lambda y \rangle = \lambda \langle x, y \rangle \leq 0$, so $\lambda y \in C^*$. Therefore C^* is a cone. To show that C^* is closed and convex, note that (10.9) implies

$$C^* = \bigcap_{x \in C} \left\{ y \in \mathbb{R}^N : \langle x, y \rangle \leq 0 \right\}.$$

Since C^* is the intersection of half spaces (which are closed convex sets), by Corollary 1.5 and the remark in §10.2, it is a closed convex set.

(ii) If $y \in D^*$, then $\langle x, y \rangle \leq 0$ for all $x \in D$. Since $C \subset D$, we have $\langle x, y \rangle \leq 0$ for all $x \in C$. Therefore $y \in C^*$.

(iii) Since $C \subset \mathrm{co}\, C$, we have $C^* \supset (\mathrm{co}\, C)^*$ by letting $D = \mathrm{co}\, C$ in (ii). To prove the reverse inclusion, take any $x \in \mathrm{co}\, C$. By Lemma 10.1, there exists a convex combination $x = \sum_{k=1}^{K} \alpha_k x_k$ such that $x_k \in C$ for all k. If $y \in C^*$, it follows that

$$\langle x, y \rangle = \left\langle \sum \alpha_k x_k, y \right\rangle = \sum \alpha_k \langle x_k, y \rangle \leq 0,$$

so $y \in (\mathrm{co}\, C)^*$. Therefore $C^* \subset (\mathrm{co}\, C)^*$. $\qquad\square$

The dual cone of the dual cone C^*, namely $(C^*)^*$, is denoted by C^{**}. The following proposition shows that C^{**} is closely related to C.

Proposition 10.6. *Let $C \subset \mathbb{R}^N$ be a nonempty cone. Then $C^{**} = \mathrm{cl}\,\mathrm{co}\,C$.*

Proof. Let $x \in C$. For any $y \in C^*$, we have $\langle x, y \rangle \leq 0$. This implies $x \in C^{**}$. Hence $C \subset C^{**}$. Since by Proposition 10.5 the dual cone is closed and convex, we have $\mathrm{cl}\,\mathrm{co}\,C \subset C^{**}$.

To show the reverse inclusion, suppose that $x \notin \mathrm{cl}\,\mathrm{co}\,C$. Then by the strict version of the separating hyperplane theorem (Theorem 10.2), there exist a nonzero vector a and a constant c such that

$$\sup_{z \in \mathrm{cl}\,\mathrm{co}\,C} \langle a, z \rangle < c < \langle a, x \rangle.$$

In particular,

$$\sup_{z \in C} \langle a, z \rangle < c < \langle a, x \rangle.$$

Take any $z \in C$. Since C is a cone, we have $\lambda z \in C$ for any $\lambda > 0$, so

$$\lambda \langle a, z \rangle = \langle a, \lambda z \rangle < c < \langle a, x \rangle. \tag{10.10}$$

Letting $\lambda \to \infty$ in (10.10), it must be $\langle a, z \rangle \leq 0$. Therefore $a \in C^*$. Letting $\lambda \to 0$, we obtain $\langle a, x \rangle > c \geq 0$, so $x \notin C^{**}$. Therefore $C^{**} \subset \mathrm{cl}\,\mathrm{co}\,C$. □

The following proposition plays an important role in optimization theory.

Proposition 10.7 (Farkas' lemma). *Let $\{a_k\}_{k=1}^K \subset \mathbb{R}^N$ be vectors and define the sets $C, D \subset \mathbb{R}^N$ by*

$$C = \mathrm{cone}[a_1, \ldots, a_K],$$
$$D = \left\{ y \in \mathbb{R}^N : (\forall k) \langle a_k, y \rangle \leq 0 \right\}.$$

Then $D = C^*$ and $C = D^*$ (Figure 10.11).

Proof. Let $y \in D$. For any $x \in C$, by the definition of the polyhedral cone, we can take $\{\alpha_k\}_{k=1}^K \subset \mathbb{R}_+$ such that $x = \sum_k \alpha_k a_k$. Then

$$\langle x, y \rangle = \sum_k \alpha_k \langle a_k, y \rangle \leq 0,$$

so $y \in C^*$. Conversely, let $y \in C^*$. Since $a_k \in C$, we get $\langle a_k, y \rangle \leq 0$ for all k, so $y \in D$. Therefore $D = C^*$.

Since C is a closed convex cone, by Proposition 10.6, we get

$$C = \mathrm{cl}\,\mathrm{co}\,C = C^{**} = (C^*)^* = D^*. \qquad \square$$

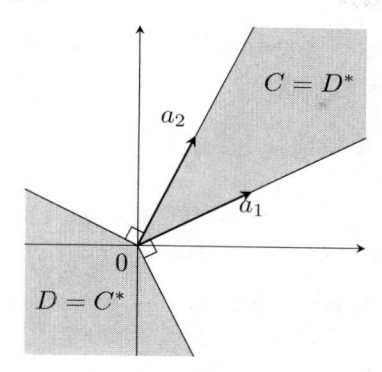

FIGURE 10.11: Farkas' lemma.

10.6   NO-ARBITRAGE ASSET PRICING

As an application of the separating hyperplane theorem, we briefly present the no-arbitrage asset pricing theory.

Consider an economy with two dates denoted by $t = 0, 1$. The economy features uncertainty, and let $s = 1, \ldots, S$ index the states that can realize at $t = 1$. Investors can trade J assets indexed by $j = 1, \ldots, J$. Asset j trades at price q_j at $t = 0$ and pays dividend $d_{sj} \in \mathbb{R}$ if state s realizes at $t = 1$. Let $q = (q_1, \ldots, q_J)$ be the vector of asset prices and $D = (d_{sj})$ the matrix of dividends. Let

$$A = (a_{sj}) := \begin{bmatrix} -q' \\ D \end{bmatrix} \tag{10.11}$$

be the $(1 + S) \times J$ payoff matrix. The (s, j) entry of the payoff matrix A in (10.11), denoted a_{sj}, is the payoff of one share of asset j in state s, where we define state 0 by the date $t = 0$. Note that because investors need to pay q_j to purchase one share of asset j at $t = 0$, the payoff is $a_{0j} = -q_j$.

Let $x = (x_1, \ldots, x_J) \in \mathbb{R}^J$ be a portfolio, where x_j denotes the number of shares of asset j an investor purchases. We allow shortsales, so $x_j < 0$ is possible. The net payments of the portfolio x is the vector

$$Ax = \begin{bmatrix} -q'x \\ Dx \end{bmatrix} \in \mathbb{R}^{1+S}.$$

Here the investor pays $q'x$ at $t = 0$ for buying the portfolio x and receives $(Dx)_s$ in state s at $t = 1$. We call the portfolio x an *arbitrage* if $Ax > 0$ because such a portfolio costs nothing at $t = 0$ ($q'x \leq 0$) and pays nonnegative amounts at $t = 1$ ($Dx \geq 0$), with at least one strict inequality. Thus an arbitrage is like a free lunch, which we expect not to happen under normal circumstances.

We define the *asset span* by the range of the payoff matrix A, or

$$V = \operatorname{range} A = \left\{ Ax : x \in \mathbb{R}^J \right\} \subset \mathbb{R}^{1+S},$$

which is the set of payoffs generated by all portfolios. We say that the asset span V exhibits *no-arbitrage* if no $x \in \mathsf{V}$ is an arbitrage, or equivalently,

$$\mathsf{V} \cap \mathbb{R}_+^{1+S} = \{0\}. \tag{10.12}$$

The idea of no-arbitrage is that it is impossible to find a portfolio that pays a nonnegative amount in every state and a positive amount in at least one state. With these definitions, we obtain the following result.

Theorem 10.8 (Fundamental Theorem of Asset Pricing). *The asset span* V *exhibits no-arbitrage if and only if there exists* $p = (p_1, \dots, p_S) \in \mathbb{R}_{++}^S$ *such that the asset pricing equation*

$$q_j = \sum_{s=1}^{S} p_s d_{sj} \tag{10.13}$$

holds for all j.

Proof. Suppose that there exists $p \in \mathbb{R}_{++}^S$ such that the asset pricing equation (10.13) holds, or equivalently $-q_j + \sum_{s=1}^{S} p_s d_{sj} = 0$. Collecting this equation into a row vector and using the definition of the payoff matrix A in (10.11), we obtain $[1, p']A = 0$. Suppose to the contrary that the asset span V exhibits arbitrage. Then we can take $x \in \mathbb{R}^J$ such that $v = Ax > 0$. Multiplying the positive row vector $[1, p']$ from left, we obtain

$$0 < v_0 + \sum_{s=1}^{S} p_s v_s = [1, p']v = [1, p']Ax = 0,$$

which is a contradiction. Therefore there is no arbitrage.

Conversely, suppose that there is no arbitrage. Letting

$$\Delta := \left\{ v \in \mathbb{R}_+^{1+S} : \sum_{s=0}^{S} v_s = 1 \right\}$$

denote the unit simplex and noting that $0 \notin \Delta \subset \mathbb{R}_+^{1+S}$, we have $\mathsf{V} \cap \Delta = \emptyset$. Clearly V, Δ are nonempty, closed, convex, and Δ is bounded. By the (strong version of) separating hyperplane theorem (Theorem 10.2), there exists a vector $0 \neq a \in \mathbb{R}^{1+S}$ such that

$$\sup_{u \in \mathsf{V}} \langle a, u \rangle < \inf_{v \in \Delta} \langle a, v \rangle. \tag{10.14}$$

Let us show that $a'A = 0$. Suppose not. Consider the portfolio $x = \lambda A'a \in \mathbb{R}^J$, where $\lambda > 0$. Then by (10.14), for $u = Ax$ we obtain

$$\langle a, v \rangle > \langle a, u \rangle = \langle a, A(\lambda A'a) \rangle = \lambda a'AA'a = \lambda \|a'A\|^2 \to \infty$$

as $\lambda \to \infty$ because $a'A \neq 0$, which is a contradiction. Therefore $a'A = 0$, so $\langle a, u \rangle = 0$ for all $u \in \mathsf{V}$. Then (10.14) becomes

$$0 < \inf_{v \in \Delta} \langle a, v \rangle .$$

Letting $v = e_s$ (the s-th unit vector) for $s = 0, 1, \ldots, S$, we get $a_s > 0$. Dividing both sides of $a'A = 0$ by $a_0 > 0$ and letting $p_s = a_s/a_0$ for $s = 1, \ldots, S$, the vector $p = (p_1, \ldots, p_S)$ satisfies $p \gg 0$ and $[1, p']A = 0$, which implies (10.13). □

Remark. The number $p_s > 0$ in Theorem 10.8 is called the *state price* of state s. It can be interpreted as the price of an insurance contract that pays 1 if state s realizes and 0 otherwise. The no-arbitrage asset pricing theory is fundamental for computing the prices of derivatives.

NOTES

A classic reference for convex analysis is Rockafellar (1970). Much of the theory of separation of convex sets can be generalized to infinite-dimensional spaces. The proof in this chapter generalizes to Hilbert spaces (spaces with an inner product), but for more general spaces (topological vector spaces) we need the Hahn-Banach theorem. See Berge (1963) and Luenberger (1969). The Fundamental Theorem of Asset Pricing (Theorem 10.8) is due to Harrison and Kreps (1979).

PROBLEMS

10.1. Let $A \subset \mathbb{R}^N$ be any set. Prove that co A consists of all convex combinations of points of A.

10.2.

(i) Let $0 \neq a \in \mathbb{R}^N$ and $c \in \mathbb{R}$. Show that the hyperplane and the half space defined by

$$H = \left\{ x \in \mathbb{R}^N : \langle a, x \rangle = c \right\},$$
$$H^- = \left\{ x \in \mathbb{R}^N : \langle a, x \rangle \leq c \right\}$$

are convex.

(ii) Let A be an $M \times N$ matrix and $b \in \mathbb{R}^M$. The set of the form

$$P = \left\{ x \in \mathbb{R}^N : Ax \leq b \right\}$$

is called a *polytope*. Show that a polytope is convex.

10.3. Let $A \subset \mathbb{R}^N$ be any nonempty set.

(i) Show that cl co A (the closure of the convex hull of A) is a closed convex set.

(ii) Show by example that co cl A (the convex hull of the closure of A) need not be closed.

10.4. Let $a, b \in \mathbb{R}^N$. Prove the following *parallelogram law*:

$$\|a + b\|^2 + \|a - b\|^2 = 2 \|a\|^2 + 2 \|b\|^2 .$$

10.5. Define the sets A, B by

$$A = \left\{ (x, y) \in \mathbb{R}^2 : y > x^3 \right\},$$
$$B = \left\{ (x, y) \in \mathbb{R}^2 : x \geq 1, y \leq 1 \right\}.$$

(i) Draw a picture of the sets A, B on the xy plane.

(ii) Can A, B be separated? If so, provide an equation of a straight line that separates them. If not, explain why.

10.6. Define the sets C, D by

$$C = \left\{ (x, y) \in \mathbb{R}^2 : y > e^x \right\},$$
$$D = \left\{ (x, y) \in \mathbb{R}^2 : y \leq 0 \right\}.$$

(i) Draw a picture of the sets C, D on the xy plane.

(ii) Provide an equation of a straight line that separates C, D.

(iii) Can C, D be strictly separated? Answer yes or no, then explain why.

10.7. This problem asks you to prove Stiemke's theorem: if A is an $M \times N$ matrix, then exactly one of the following statements is true:

(a) There exists $x \in \mathbb{R}^N_{++}$ such that $Ax = 0$.

(b) There exists $y \in \mathbb{R}^M$ such that $A'y > 0$.

Prove Stiemke's theorem using the following hints.

(i) Show that statements (a) and (b) cannot both be true.

(ii) Define the sets $C, D \subset \mathbb{R}^N$ by

$$C = \left\{ A'y : y \in \mathbb{R}^M \right\},$$
$$D = \left\{ x \in \mathbb{R}^N : x \geq 0, \sum_{n=1}^{N} x_n = 1 \right\}.$$

Show that C, D are nonempty, closed, convex, and D is bounded.

(iii) Show that if statement (b) does not hold, then statement (a) holds.

10.8. Let $a_1, \ldots, a_K$ be vectors. This problem asks you to prove that the polyhedral cone $C = \text{cone}[a_1, \ldots, a_K]$ is a closed convex cone.

(i) Prove that C is a nonempty convex cone.

(ii) Prove that if $x \in C$, then x can be expressed as $x = \sum_{j=1}^{J} \alpha_j a_{k_j}$, where $\alpha_j \geq 0$ and $a_{k_1}, \ldots, a_{k_J}$ are linearly independent. (Hint: among ways to express $x = \sum_{k=1}^{K} \alpha_k a_k$, consider the one with the minimum number of k's with $\alpha_k > 0$.)

(iii) Prove that C is closed. (Hint: use Problem 5.3.)

CHAPTER 11

Convex Functions

11.1   CONVEX AND QUASI-CONVEX FUNCTIONS

In Chapter 2 we introduced convex functions of a single variable and showed that the first-order necessary condition for optimality is actually sufficient (Proposition 2.5). In this chapter, we discuss the properties of convex and quasi-convex functions in a general setting.

Let $f : \mathbb{R}^N \to (-\infty, \infty]$ be a function. The set

$$\operatorname{epi} f := \left\{ (x, y) \in \mathbb{R}^N \times \mathbb{R} : f(x) \leq y \right\}$$

is called the *epigraph* of f, for the obvious reason that epi f is the set of points that lie on or above the graph of f. A function f is said to be *convex* if epi f is a convex set. It is straightforward to show (Problem 11.1) that a function f is convex if and only if for any $x_1, x_2 \in \mathbb{R}^N$ and $\alpha \in [0, 1]$, we have

$$f((1 - \alpha)x_1 + \alpha x_2) \leq (1 - \alpha)f(x_1) + \alpha f(x_2). \tag{11.1}$$

This inequality, sometimes called the *convex inequality*, is often used as the definition of a convex function. Note that because we adopt the convention $0 \times \infty = 0$, the right-hand side of (11.1) is unambiguous.

Figure 11.1 shows an example. The smooth curve is the graph of f. The epigraph is the region above the graph. The convex inequality (11.1) implies that the line segment joining the two points on the graph $(x_1, f(x_1))$ and $(x_2, f(x_2))$ is included in the epigraph.

The astute reader may wonder why we wrote $f : \mathbb{R}^N \to (-\infty, \infty]$, namely (i) why we let the domain of f to be the entire $\mathbb{R}^N$, and (ii) why we allow f to take the value ∞ but not $-\infty$. There are good reasons for doing so. Suppose for the moment that $f : C \to \mathbb{R}$ is a function in the usual sense, where $C \subset \mathbb{R}^N$ is the domain of f. If we require the convex inequality (11.1) to hold, for any $x_1, x_2 \in C$ and $\alpha \in [0, 1]$, the point $(1 - \alpha)x_1 + \alpha x_2$ must be in the domain of f. Therefore C must be a convex set. For $x \notin C$, define $f(x) = \infty$. Then f is defined on the entire $\mathbb{R}^N$. By the convention $0 \times \infty = 0$, clearly (11.1) holds if $\alpha = 0, 1$, so assume $\alpha \in (0, 1)$. Then whenever $f(x_1) = \infty$ or $f(x_2) = \infty$

DOI: 10.1201/9781032698953-11

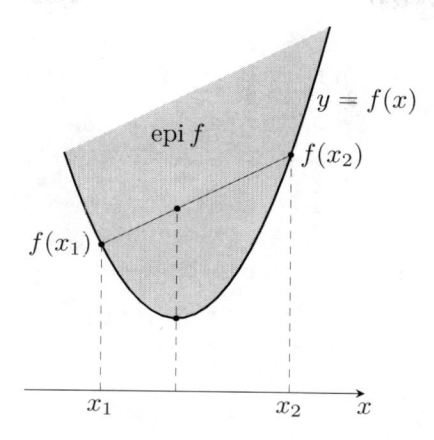

FIGURE 11.1: Convex function and its epigraph.

(so $x_1 \notin C$ or $x_2 \notin C$), (11.1) holds. Therefore starting from any real-valued convex function f defined on a convex set C, we may extend it to the entire $\mathbb{R}^N$ by letting f take the value ∞ outside the domain C. Finally, we exclude the value $-\infty$ from the range of the convex function to avoid the undefined expression $\infty - \infty$ on the right-hand side of (11.1). This argument shows why letting $f : \mathbb{R}^N \to (-\infty, \infty]$ is without loss of generality.

The set on which f takes finite values,

$$\operatorname{dom} f := \left\{ x \in \mathbb{R}^N : f(x) < \infty \right\},$$

is called the *effective domain* of f. If f is convex and $x_1, x_2 \in \operatorname{dom} f$, then

$$f((1 - \alpha)x_1 + \alpha x_2) \leq (1 - \alpha)f(x_1) + \alpha f(x_2) < \infty,$$

so $(1 - \alpha)x_1 + \alpha x_2 \in \operatorname{dom} f$. Therefore the effective domain of a convex function is a convex set. If the convex inequality (11.1) is strict whenever $x_1, x_2 \in \operatorname{dom} f$, $x_1 \neq x_2$, and $\alpha \in (0, 1)$, we say that f is *strictly convex*. A convex function is *proper* if $f(x) < \infty$ for some x, or equivalently, $\operatorname{dom} f \neq \emptyset$.

Another useful but weaker concept is quasi-convexity. The set

$$L_f(y) := \left\{ x \in \mathbb{R}^N : f(x) \leq y \right\} \tag{11.2}$$

is called the *lower contour set* of f at level y. We say that f is *quasi-convex* if lower contour sets are convex for all values of y. It is straightforward to show (Problem 11.2) that f is quasi-convex if and only if for any $x_1, x_2 \in \mathbb{R}^N$ and $\alpha \in [0, 1]$, we have

$$f((1 - \alpha)x_1 + \alpha x_2) \leq \max \left\{ f(x_1), f(x_2) \right\}. \tag{11.3}$$

Again, if the inequality (11.3) is strict whenever $x_1, x_2 \in \operatorname{dom} f$, $x_1 \neq x_2$, and $\alpha \in (0, 1)$, we say that f is *strictly quasi-convex*.

One reason why convex and quasi-convex functions are useful is that they guarantee the uniqueness of the solution to minimization problems.

Proposition 11.1. *If $C \subset \mathbb{R}^N$ is nonempty and convex and $f : C \to \mathbb{R}$ is strictly quasi-convex, then the solution to $\min_{x \in C} f(x)$ is unique.*

Proof. Suppose to the contrary that there are two solutions $x_1 \neq x_2$. Take any $\alpha \in (0, 1)$ and let $x = (1 - \alpha)x_1 + \alpha x_2$. Since C is convex, we have $x \in C$. Since f is strictly quasi-convex, using (11.3) we obtain

$$f(x) = f((1 - \alpha)x_1 + \alpha x_2) < \max\{f(x_1), f(x_2)\} = f(x_1) = \min_{x \in C} f(x),$$

which is a contradiction. □

A function f is said to be *concave* if $-f$ is convex, that is, f is a convex function flipped upside down. The definitions for strict concavity or quasi-concavity are similar. The algebraic definitions of concave and quasi-concave functions are given by flipping the inequalities (11.1) and (11.3).

Note that all convex functions are quasi-convex, but not vice versa. To see that all convex functions are quasi-convex, let $f : \mathbb{R}^N \to (-\infty, \infty]$ be convex. Take any $y \in (-\infty, \infty]$ and consider the lower contour set $L_f(y)$ in (11.2). Then if $x_1, x_2 \in L_f(y)$ and $\alpha \in [0, 1]$, we have

$$f((1 - \alpha)x_1 + \alpha x_2) \leq (1 - \alpha)f(x_1) + \alpha f(x_2)$$
$$\leq (1 - \alpha)y + \alpha y = y,$$

so by definition $(1 - \alpha)x_1 + \alpha x_2 \in L_f(y)$. Therefore $L_f(y)$ is convex, and hence f is quasi-convex. To see that not all quasi-convex functions are convex, consider the function $f : \mathbb{R} \to \mathbb{R}$ defined by $f(x) = x^3$. Then it is easy to see by drawing the graph that f is quasi-convex but not convex (Figure 11.2).

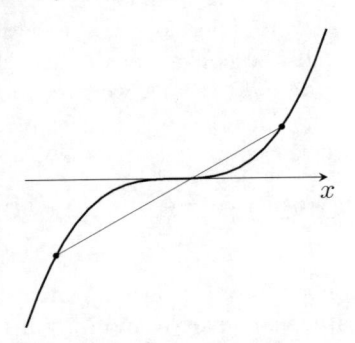

x

FIGURE 11.2: Quasi-convex but non-convex function.

If $f : \mathbb{R}^N \to \mathbb{R}$ is linear, then $f(x) = \langle a, x \rangle$ for some $a \in \mathbb{R}^N$ (Proposition 1.2). This f clearly satisfies the convex inequality (11.1) with equality, so all linear functions are convex. They are also concave.

11.2 CONVEXITY-PRESERVING OPERATIONS

There are certain operations that preserve the convexity of functions. These results allow us to construct many convex functions from functions that are already known to be convex (such as linear functions).

The following proposition shows that convexity is preserved by taking the weighted sum of functions.

Proposition 11.2. *For each $i = 1, \ldots, I$, let $f_i : \mathbb{R}^N \to (-\infty, \infty]$ be convex. Then for any $\beta_i \geq 0$, the function $f := \sum_{i=1}^{I} \beta_i f_i$ is convex.*

Proof. Take any x_1, x_2 and $\alpha \in [0, 1]$. Since f_i is convex, we have

$$f_i((1 - \alpha)x_1 + \alpha x_2) \leq (1 - \alpha)f_i(x_1) + \alpha f_i(x_2). \tag{11.4}$$

Multiplying both sides by $\beta_i \geq 0$ and summing across i, we obtain

$$f((1 - \alpha)x_1 + \alpha x_2) = \sum_{i=1}^{I} \beta_i f_i((1 - \alpha)x_1 + \alpha x_2)$$

$$\leq \sum_{i=1}^{I} \beta_i((1 - \alpha)f_i(x_1) + \alpha f_i(x_2))$$

$$= (1 - \alpha)f(x_1) + \alpha f(x_2),$$

so f is convex. $\qquad \square$

Similarly, if $f(x, y)$ is convex in y and $a < b$, then

$$F(y) := \int_a^b f(x, y) \, \mathrm{d}x$$

is convex in y. This is because integration can be thought of as the limit of summation. The proof of this statement is identical to Proposition 11.2.

The following proposition shows that (quasi-)convexity is preserved by taking the pointwise supremum of functions.

Proposition 11.3. *Let I be a nonempty set, and for each $i \in I$, suppose that $f_i : \mathbb{R}^N \to (-\infty, \infty]$ is (quasi-)convex. Then $f := \sup_{i \in I} f_i$ is (quasi-)convex.*

Proof. Suppose that each f_i is convex, so (11.4) holds. Since $f_i \leq f$, it follows that

$$f_i((1 - \alpha)x_1 + \alpha x_2) \leq (1 - \alpha)f(x_1) + \alpha f(x_2).$$

Taking the supremum over $i \in I$ in the left-hand side, we obtain

$$f((1 - \alpha)x_1 + \alpha x_2) \leq (1 - \alpha)f(x_1) + \alpha f(x_2),$$

so f is convex. The proof for quasi-convexity is similar. $\qquad \square$

Example 11.1. Let $\emptyset \neq A \subset \mathbb{R}^N$. For each $a \in A$, the linear function $f_a(x) := \langle a, x \rangle$ is clearly convex. Hence by Proposition 11.3, the function $h_A := \sup_{a \in A} f_a$ defined by $h_A(x) = \sup_{a \in A} \langle a, x \rangle$ is convex, which is called the *support function* of the set A.

The following proposition shows that (quasi-)convexity is preserved by a certain monotone transformation. We introduce some definitions to state this result. We say that $\phi : \mathbb{R}^N \to \mathbb{R}^M$ is a *monotone map* if

$$x_1 \leq x_2 \implies \phi(x_1) \leq \phi(x_2). \tag{11.5}$$

When $\phi : \mathbb{R}^N \to \mathbb{R}$, we say ϕ is a *monotone function* or simply *increasing*. We say that $f : \mathbb{R}^N \to \mathbb{R}^M$ is a *convex map* if $\alpha \in [0, 1]$ implies

$$f((1 - \alpha)x_1 + \alpha x_2) \leq (1 - \alpha)f(x_1) + \alpha f(x_2). \tag{11.6}$$

The inequalities in (11.5) and (11.6) are all vector inequalities.

Proposition 11.4. *If $f : \mathbb{R}^N \to \mathbb{R}^M$ is a convex map and $\phi : \mathbb{R}^M \to \mathbb{R}$ is a monotone (quasi-)convex function, then $g := \phi \circ f$ is (quasi-)convex.*

Proof. Suppose that ϕ is convex. Take any $x_1, x_2 \in \mathbb{R}^N$ and $\alpha \in [0, 1]$. Since f is a convex map, (11.6) holds. Applying ϕ to both sides, we obtain

$$
\begin{aligned}
g((1 - \alpha)x_1 + \alpha x_2) &= \phi(f((1 - \alpha)x_1 + \alpha x_2)) \\
&\leq \phi((1 - \alpha)f(x_1) + \alpha f(x_2)) && (\because \phi \text{ monotone}) \\
&\leq (1 - \alpha)\phi(f(x_1)) + \alpha\phi(f(x_2)) && (\because \phi \text{ convex}) \\
&= (1 - \alpha)g(x_1) + \alpha g(x_2),
\end{aligned}
$$

so g is convex. The proof when ϕ is quasi-convex is similar. $\square$

Remark. Obviously, the domains of f or ϕ need not be the entire $\mathbb{R}^N$ or $\mathbb{R}^M$. All we need is that the expressions appearing in the proof of Proposition 11.4 are well defined. The statements also hold for arbitrary vector spaces, not necessarily $\mathbb{R}^N$.

Remark. Proposition 11.2 is a special case of Proposition 11.4 by setting $\phi(y) = \sum_{i=1}^{I} \beta_i y_i$. Proposition 11.3 (with finite I) is also a special case by setting $\phi(y) = \max_i y_i$.

Remark. There are many variants of Proposition 11.4. For instance, the right inequality of (11.5) could be flipped (so ϕ is monotone decreasing) and/or f or ϕ could be (quasi-)convex/concave. Depending on the specification, $g = \phi \circ f$ could be (quasi-)convex/concave. We shall not exhaust all possibilities but the statement of the proposition and its proof are analogous.

If $\phi : \mathbb{R} \to \mathbb{R}$ is increasing, then it is quasi-convex. To see this, noting that $(1 - \alpha)x_1 + \alpha x_2 \leq \max\{x_1, x_2\}$ and applying ϕ to both sides, we obtain

$$\phi((1 - \alpha)x_1 + \alpha x_2) \leq \phi(\max\{x_1, x_2\}) = \max\{\phi(x_1), \phi(x_2)\},$$

so ϕ is quasi-convex by (11.3). Therefore by setting $M = 1$ in Proposition 11.4, we obtain the following corollary, which states that quasi-convexity is preserved by monotonic transformations.

Corollary 11.5. *Let* $f : \mathbb{R}^N \to (-\infty, \infty]$ *be quasi-convex and* $\phi : (-\infty, \infty] \to (-\infty, \infty]$ *be increasing. Then* $g = \phi \circ f$ *is quasi-convex.*

In contrast, convexity is not necessarily preserved by monotonic transformations. For instance, define $f : \mathbb{R} \to \mathbb{R}$ by $f(x) = |x|$ and $\phi : [0, \infty) \to \mathbb{R}$ by $\phi(y) = \sqrt{y}$. Then f is convex and ϕ is increasing, but $g(x) = \phi(f(x)) = \sqrt{|x|}$ is not convex, as we see in Figure 11.2. To preserve convexity, we need additional assumptions as in Proposition 11.4. We shall see many applications of Proposition 11.4 and Corollary 11.5 later.

Proposition 11.3 shows that taking the pointwise supremum of functions preserves convexity. This is not true for pointwise infimum. For example, if we define $f_1, f_2 : \mathbb{R} \to \mathbb{R}$ by $f_1(x) = x$ and $f_2(x) = -x$, then f_1, f_2 are both linear and hence convex, but $f(x) = \min\{f_1(x), f_2(x)\} = -|x|$ is not convex. However, the following propositions show that functions obtained as a certain parametric minimization problem are convex.

Proposition 11.6. *Let* X, Y *be vector spaces,* $f : X \times Y \to (-\infty, \infty]$ *be (quasi-)convex, and let* $g(y) := \inf_{x \in X} f(x, y)$. *If* $g(y) > -\infty$ *for all* $y \in Y$, *then* $g : Y \to (-\infty, \infty]$ *is (quasi-)convex.*

Proof. Suppose f is convex. Take $y_1, y_2 \in Y$ and $\alpha \in [0, 1]$. For each $j = 1, 2$, take any $u_j > g(y_j)$. By the definition of g, we can take x_j such that $g(y_j) \leq f(x_j, y_j) \leq u_j$. Define $x = (1 - \alpha)x_1 + \alpha x_2$ and similarly for y. Using the definition of g and the convexity of f, we obtain

$$g(y) \leq f(x, y) \leq (1 - \alpha)f(x_1, y_1) + \alpha f(x_2, y_2) \leq (1 - \alpha)u_1 + \alpha u_2.$$

Letting $u_j \downarrow g(y_j)$, we obtain

$$g(y) \leq (1 - \alpha)g(y_1) + \alpha g(y_2),$$

so g is convex. The proof of quasi-convexity is left as Problem 11.4. $\qquad\square$

11.3 DIFFERENTIAL CHARACTERIZATION

The inequalities (11.1) and (11.3) that define convexity and quasi-convexity involve three parameters x_1, x_2, α, which may not be easy to verify directly. In this section, we provide first-order and second-order characterization of convex and quasi-convex functions, which involve fewer parameters.

The following proposition provides a first-order characterization of convex functions.

Proposition 11.7 (First-order characterization of convexity). *Let $U \subset \mathbb{R}^N$ be an open convex set and $f : U \to \mathbb{R}$ be differentiable. Then f is (strictly) convex if and only if*

$$f(y) - f(x) \geq (>) \langle \nabla f(x), y - x \rangle \tag{11.7}$$

for all $x \neq y$.

Proof. Suppose that f is (strictly) convex. Let $x \neq y \in U$ and define $g : [0,1] \to \mathbb{R}$ by $g(t) = f(x + t(y - x))$. Then g is (strictly) convex, so for any $0 < s < t \leq 1$, if we let $\alpha := s/t \in (0,1)$, we obtain

$$g(s) = g((1-\alpha)0 + \alpha t) \leq (<)(1-\alpha)g(0) + \alpha g(t)$$

$$\iff \frac{g(s) - g(0)}{s} \leq (<) \frac{g(t) - g(0)}{t}.$$

Therefore the function $h(t) := (g(t) - g(0))/t$ is (strictly) increasing, so letting $s \downarrow 0$ and $t \uparrow 1$, we obtain

$$\langle \nabla f(x), y - x \rangle = g'(0) \leq (<)g(1) - g(0) = f(y) - f(x),$$

which is (11.7).

Conversely, suppose (11.7) holds for all $x \neq y$. Take any $x_1 \neq x_2$ and $\alpha \in (0,1)$. Setting $y = x_1, x_2$ and $x = (1-\alpha)x_1 + \alpha x_2$ in (11.7), we get

$$f(x_1) - f((1-\alpha)x_1 + \alpha x_2) \geq (>) \langle \nabla f(x), x_1 - x \rangle$$
$$f(x_2) - f((1-\alpha)x_1 + \alpha x_2) \geq (>) \langle \nabla f(x), x_2 - x \rangle .$$

Multiplying both sides by $1 - \alpha$ and α respectively and adding the two inequalities, we get

$$(1-\alpha)f(x_1) + \alpha f(x_2) - f((1-\alpha)x_1 + \alpha x_2) \geq (>)0,$$

so f is (strictly) convex by the convex inequality (11.1). $\qquad\square$

Figure 11.3 shows the geometric intuition of Proposition 11.7. Since QR $= f(y) - f(x)$ and SR $= \langle \nabla f(x), y - x \rangle$, we have $f(y) - f(x) \geq \langle \nabla f(x), y - x \rangle$.

In Chapter 2, we showed that the first-order necessary condition is actually sufficient for minimizing a one-variable convex function (Proposition 2.5). This remarkable property of convex minimization problems is true in general, as the following proposition shows.

Proposition 11.8 (Sufficiency of first-order condition for convex minimization). *Let $U \subset \mathbb{R}^N$ be an open convex set and $f : U \to \mathbb{R}$ be convex and differentiable. If $\nabla f(\bar{x}) = 0$, then $f(\bar{x}) = \min_{x \in U} f(x)$.*

Proof. Take any $x \in U$. Since f is convex and $\nabla f(\bar{x}) = 0$, by Proposition 11.7, we have

$$f(x) - f(\bar{x}) \geq \langle \nabla f(\bar{x}), x - \bar{x} \rangle = 0,$$

so $f(\bar{x}) \leq f(x)$. Hence $f(\bar{x}) = \min_{x \in U} f(x)$. $\qquad\square$

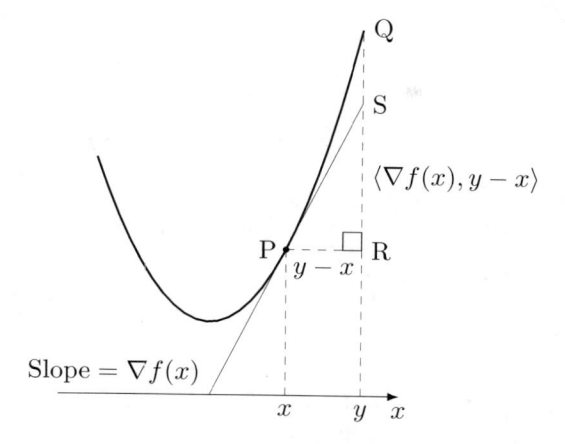

FIGURE 11.3: Characterization of a convex function.

Remark. Proposition 11.8 does not hold for quasi-convex functions. For example, $f : \mathbb{R} \to \mathbb{R}$ defined by $f(x) = x^3$ is quasi-convex (because it is increasing as $f'(x) = 3x^2 \geq 0$) and $f'(0) = 0$, but $\bar{x} = 0$ is not a minimum.

As we discussed in Chapter 2, a twice differentiable function $f : \mathbb{R} \to \mathbb{R}$ is convex if and only if $f''(x) \geq 0$ for all x. The following proposition generalizes this result and provides a second-order characterization of convex functions.

Proposition 11.9 (Second-order characterization of convexity). *Let $U \subset \mathbb{R}^N$ be an open convex set and $f : U \to \mathbb{R}$ be C^2. Then f is convex if and only if the Hessian*

$$\nabla^2 f(x) = \left[\frac{\partial^2 f(x)}{\partial x_m \partial x_n} \right]$$

is positive semidefinite for all x. Furthermore, if $\nabla^2 f$ is positive definite for all x, then f is strictly convex.

Proof. Take any $x \neq y \in U$ and let $v := y - x \neq 0$. Applying Taylor's theorem (Proposition 2.4) to $g(t) = f(x + tv)$ for $t \in [0, 1]$, there exists $s \in (0, 1)$ such that

$$f(y) - f(x) = g(1) - g(0) = g'(0) + \frac{1}{2} g''(s)$$

$$= \langle \nabla f(x), v \rangle + \frac{1}{2} \langle v, \nabla^2 f(x + sv)v \rangle.$$

If f is convex, by Proposition 11.7 we obtain

$$\frac{1}{2} \langle v, \nabla^2 f(x + sv)v \rangle = f(y) - f(x) - \langle \nabla f(x), y - x \rangle \geq 0. \tag{11.8}$$

Since U is open and $y \neq x$ is arbitrary, for any $0 \neq u \in \mathbb{R}^N$, we have $y = x + \epsilon u \in U$ if $\epsilon > 0$ is small enough. Hence letting $v = \epsilon u$ in (11.8), dividing both sides by $\epsilon^2/2 > 0$, and letting $\epsilon \to 0$, we obtain

$$0 \leq \langle u, \nabla^2 f(x + s\epsilon u)u \rangle \to \langle u, \nabla^2 f(x)u \rangle,$$

so $\nabla^2 f(x)$ is positive semidefinite.

Conversely, if $\nabla^2 f(x)$ is positive (semi)definite for all x, then

$$f(y) - f(x) - \langle \nabla f(x), y - x \rangle = \frac{1}{2} \langle v, \nabla^2 f(x + sv)v \rangle \geq (>)0,$$

so by Proposition 11.7, f is (strictly) convex. $\qquad\qquad\square$

Remark. Even if f is strictly convex, $\nabla^2 f$ need not be positive definite for all x. A counterexample is $f : \mathbb{R} \to \mathbb{R}$ defined by $f(x) = x^4$, which is strictly convex but $f''(0) = 0$.

The following proposition provides a first-order characterization of quasi-convex functions.

Proposition 11.10 (First-order characterization of quasi-convexity). *Let $U \subset \mathbb{R}^N$ be an open convex set and $f : U \to \mathbb{R}$ be differentiable. Then f is quasi-convex if and only if*

$$f(y) \leq f(x) \implies \langle \nabla f(x), y - x \rangle \leq 0 \qquad (11.9)$$

for all $x \neq y$.

Proof. Suppose that f is quasi-convex and $f(y) \leq f(x)$. Then for any $t \in (0, 1]$ we have

$$f((1 - t)x + ty) \leq \max\{f(x), f(y)\} = f(x)$$
$$\implies \frac{1}{t}(f(x + t(y - x)) - f(x)) \leq 0.$$

Letting $t \to 0$, we obtain $\langle \nabla f(x), y - x \rangle \leq 0$, so (11.9) holds.

If f is not quasi-convex, by the definition (11.3), there exist $x_1 \neq x_2$ and $\alpha \in (0, 1)$ such that

$$f((1 - \alpha)x_1 + \alpha x_2) > \max\{f(x_1), f(x_2)\}. \qquad (11.10)$$

Let $v := x_2 - x_1 \neq 0$ and $g(t) = f(x_1 + tv)$. Since f is differentiable, it is continuous, and so is g. By the extreme value theorem, the set of maximizers

$$T := \arg\max_{t \in [0, 1]} g(t)$$

is nonempty. Clearly T is closed and bounded, so T has a minimal element $t = \min T$ (Figure 11.4). Since $g(0) = f(x_1)$ and $g(1) = f(x_2)$, (11.10) implies

$$g(t) > \max\{g(0), g(1)\},$$

so $t \in (0,1)$. Furthermore, by the definition of t, we have $g(s) < g(t)$ for all $s \in [0,t)$. By the continuity of g, we can take $\epsilon > 0$ such that $g(1) < g(s) < g(t)$ for all $s \in [t - \epsilon, t)$. By the mean value theorem, we can take $s \in [t - \epsilon, t)$ such that

$$0 < \frac{g(t) - g(t - \epsilon)}{\epsilon} = g'(s)$$

$$= \langle \nabla f(x_1 + sv), v \rangle = \frac{1}{1-s} \langle \nabla f(x), y - x \rangle, \tag{11.11}$$

where we set $x = x_1 + sv$ and $y = x_2$. On the other hand, we also have

$$f(x) = f(x_1 + sv) = g(s) > g(1) = f(y). \tag{11.12}$$

Combining (11.11) and (11.12), the condition (11.9) does not hold. $\quad\square$

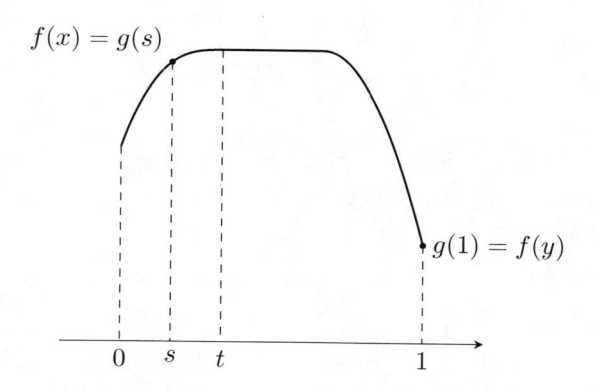

FIGURE 11.4: Proof of Proposition 11.10.

The following proposition provides a second-order characterization of quasi-convex functions.

Proposition 11.11 (Second-order characterization of quasi-convexity). *Let $U \subset \mathbb{R}^N$ be an open convex set and $f : U \to \mathbb{R}$ be C^2. Then the following statements are true.*

(i) If f is quasi-convex, then for all x and $v \neq 0$, we have

$$\langle \nabla f(x), v \rangle = 0 \implies \langle v, \nabla^2 f(x)v \rangle \geq 0. \tag{11.13}$$

(ii) If for all x and $v \neq 0$ we have

$$\langle \nabla f(x), v \rangle = 0 \implies \langle v, \nabla^2 f(x)v \rangle > 0, \tag{11.14}$$

then f is strictly quasi-convex.

Proof. (i) Let f be quasi-convex. To show (11.13), suppose $\langle \nabla f(x), v \rangle = 0$ but $\langle v, \nabla^2 f(x)v \rangle < 0$. Let $g(t) := f(x + tv)$. Then g is quasi-convex, $g'(0) = \langle \nabla f(x), v \rangle = 0$, and $g''(0) = \langle v, \nabla^2 f(x)v \rangle < 0$. By Proposition 2.6, $t = 0$ is a strict local maximum. Then for sufficiently small $\epsilon > 0$, we have $g(\pm \epsilon) < g(0)$, which contradicts (11.3).

(ii) We prove the contrapositive. Suppose that f is not strictly quasi-convex. Then we can take $x \neq y$ and $t \in (0,1)$ such that

$$f((1-t)x + ty) \geq \max \{f(x), f(y)\}. \tag{11.15}$$

Let $v = y - x \neq 0$ and $g(t) := f(x + tv)$. Then (11.15) implies $g(t) \geq \max \{g(0), g(1)\}$. In particular, we may assume that $t \in (0,1)$ achieves the maximum of g. Then by Proposition 2.6, we have

$$0 = g'(t) = \langle \nabla f(x + tv)v \rangle,$$
$$0 \geq g''(t) = \langle v, \nabla^2 f(x + tv)v \rangle.$$

Replacing $x + tv$ with x, the condition (11.14) fails. $\qquad \square$

11.4 CONTINUITY OF CONVEX FUNCTIONS

A nice property of convex functions is that they are continuous except at boundary points of the domain.

Theorem 11.12. *Let $U \subset \mathbb{R}^N$ be an open convex set and $f : U \to \mathbb{R}$ be convex. Then f is continuous.*

Proof. Equip $\mathbb{R}^N$ with the supremum norm $\|x\| = \max_n |x_n|$. For any $x \in \mathbb{R}^N$ and $r > 0$, define the closed ball with center x and radius r by

$$\bar{B}_r(x) := \{y \in \mathbb{R}^N : \|y - x\| \leq r\}.$$

By the definition of the supremum norm, $\bar{B}_r(x)$ is actually the hypercube

$$[x_1 - r, x_1 + r] \times \cdots \times [x_N - r, x_N + r]$$

with 2^N vertices $(x_1 \pm r, \dots, x_N \pm r)$.

Take any $x \in U$. Since U is open, we can take $r > 0$ such that $\bar{B}_r(x) \subset U$. Let the vertices of $\bar{B}_r(x)$ be denoted by $\{\bar{x}_k\}_{k=1}^K$, where $K = 2^N$. Define $M := \max_k f(\bar{x}_k) < \infty$. Since clearly any point of $\bar{B}_r(x)$ can be expressed as a convex combination of $\{\bar{x}_k\}_{k=1}^K$ (the proof is by induction on N), we have

$$f(z) \leq M \text{ for all } z \in \bar{B}_r(x). \tag{11.16}$$

Now take any $y \in \bar{B}_r(x) \setminus \{x\}$, let $0 \neq d = y - x$, $\epsilon = \|d\| / r \in (0,1]$, and define the points z_1, z_2 by $z_1 = x + d/\epsilon$ and $z_2 = x - d/\epsilon$ (Figure 11.5). Then clearly $\|z_j - x\| = \|d\| / \epsilon = r$ for $j = 1, 2$, so $z_j \in \bar{B}_r(x)$.

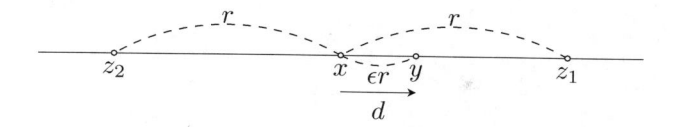

FIGURE 11.5: Proof of continuity of convex functions.

By the definition of z_j, we have

$$y - x = d = \epsilon(z_1 - x) \iff y = (1 - \epsilon)x + \epsilon z_1,$$
$$y - x = d = -\epsilon(z_2 - x) \iff x = \frac{1}{1+\epsilon}y + \frac{\epsilon}{1+\epsilon}z_2.$$

Hence by the convex inequality (11.1) and the upper bound (11.16), we obtain

$$f(y) \le (1 - \epsilon)f(x) + \epsilon f(z_1) \implies f(y) - f(x) \le \epsilon(M - f(x)),$$
$$f(x) \le \frac{1}{1+\epsilon}f(y) + \frac{\epsilon}{1+\epsilon}f(z_2) \implies f(x) - f(y) \le \epsilon(M - f(x)).$$

Combining these two inequalities, we obtain

$$|f(y) - f(x)| \le \epsilon(M - f(x)) = \frac{M - f(x)}{r}\,\|y - x\|. \tag{11.17}$$

Therefore $f(y) \to f(x)$ as $y \to x$, so f is continuous. $\qquad\square$

A convex function need not be continuous at boundary points of the domain. For example, define $f : [0, 1] \to \mathbb{R}$ by $f(x) = 0$ if $x < 1$ and $f(1) = 1$. Then clearly f is convex but not continuous at $x = 1$.

A corollary of the proof of Theorem 11.12 is that convex functions are actually locally Lipschitz continuous. Recall that $f : U \to \mathbb{R}$ is Lipschitz continuous with Lipschitz constant $L \ge 0$ if for all $x, y \in U$, we have

$$|f(x) - f(y)| \le L\,\|x - y\|.$$

We say that f is locally Lipschitz on U if f is Lipschitz on compact (closed and bounded) subsets of U.

Corollary 11.13. *Let $U \subset \mathbb{R}^N$ be a nonempty open convex set and $f : U \to \mathbb{R}$ be convex. Then f is locally Lipschitz.*

Proof. Take any $x \in U$ and $r > 0$ such that $\bar{B}_r(x) \subset U$, and define $V = \bar{B}_{r/3}(x)$. Let us show that f is Lipschitz on V. Since by Theorem 11.12 f is continuous on the compact set $\bar{B}_r(x)$, it attains a minimum m and a maximum M. Take any $x_1, x_2 \in V$. Then

$$\|x_1 - x_2\| \le \|x_1 - x\| + \|x - x_2\| \le \frac{2r}{3},$$

so $x_1 \in \bar{B}_{2r/3}(x_2)$. If $y \in \bar{B}_{2r/3}(x_2)$, then

$$\|y - x\| \leq \|y - x_2\| + \|x_2 - x\| \leq \frac{2r}{3} + \frac{r}{3} = r,$$

so $\bar{B}_{2r/3}(x_2) \subset \bar{B}_r(x)$. Applying (11.17) to $y = x_1$ and $x = x_2$, we obtain

$$|f(x_1) - f(x_2)| \leq \frac{M - m}{2r/3} \|x_1 - x_2\|,$$

which shows that f is Lipschitz on V with Lipschitz constant $L := \frac{3(M-m)}{2r}$.
□

Unlike convex functions, quasi-convex functions need not be continuous. For example, any strictly increasing function $f : \mathbb{R} \to \mathbb{R}$ is quasi-convex, but there are many of them that are discontinuous.

11.5 HOMOGENEOUS QUASI-CONVEX FUNCTIONS

We have seen that all convex functions are quasi-convex but not all quasi-convex functions are convex. The following theorem, which is slightly stronger than Berge (1963, p. 208, Theorem 3), shows that quasi-convex (concave) functions that are homogeneous and have constant signs are always convex (concave). This result is sometimes useful because checking quasi-convexity is easier than checking convexity.

We say that a function $f : \mathbb{R}^N \to [-\infty, \infty]$ is *homogeneous (of degree 1)* if $f(\lambda x) = \lambda f(x)$ for all x and $\lambda > 0$.

Theorem 11.14. *Let $C \subset \mathbb{R}^N$ be a nonempty convex cone. Let $f : C \to (-\infty, \infty]$ be (i) quasi-convex, (ii) homogeneous, and (iii) either $f(x) > 0$ for all $x \in C \backslash \{0\}$ or $f(x) < 0$ for all $x \in C \backslash \{0\}$. Then f is convex.*

Proof. Take any $x_1, x_2 \in C$ and $\alpha \in [0, 1]$. Let us show the convex inequality (11.1). The claim is trivial if $\alpha = 0$ or $\alpha = 1$, so assume $\alpha \in (0, 1)$. Similarly, (11.1) is trivial if $f(x_1) = \infty$ or $f(x_2) = \infty$, so assume $f(x_1) < \infty$ and $f(x_2) < \infty$.

If $x_1 = 0$, using homogeneity for $\lambda = 2$ and $f(x_1) < \infty$, we obtain $f(0) = f(2 \cdot 0) = 2f(0)$, implying $f(0) = 0$. Again using homogeneity for $\lambda = \alpha$ and noting that $x_1 = 0$ and $f(x_1) = f(0) = 0$, we obtain

$$f((1 - \alpha)x_1 + \alpha x_2) = f(\alpha x_2) = \alpha f(x_2) = (1 - \alpha)f(x_1) + \alpha f(x_2),$$

so (11.1) holds. The case for $x_2 = 0$ is similar.

Therefore we may assume $x_1, x_2 \neq 0$. Since by assumption f has constant sign on $C \backslash \{0\}$, it follows that $(1 - \alpha)f(x_1)$ and $\alpha f(x_2)$ are both nonzero real numbers with the same sign. Define $k = \frac{\alpha f(x_2)}{(1-\alpha)f(x_1)} > 0$ and $x = (1 - \alpha)x_1 +$

αx_2. Using the homogeneity and quasi-convexity of f, we obtain

$$\frac{k}{1+k}f(x) = f\left(\frac{k}{1+k}x\right) = f\left(\frac{1}{1+k}k(1-\alpha)x_1 + \frac{k}{1+k}\alpha x_2\right)$$
$$\leq \max\{f(k(1-\alpha)x_1), f(\alpha x_2)\} = \max\{k(1-\alpha)f(x_1), \alpha f(x_2)\}.$$

By construction, $k(1-\alpha)f(x_1) = \alpha f(x_2)$, so the last expression is also equal to

$$\frac{1}{1+k}k(1-\alpha)f(x_1) + \frac{k}{1+k}\alpha f(x_2) = \frac{k}{1+k}((1-\alpha)f(x_1) + \alpha f(x_2)).$$

Therefore

$$\frac{k}{1+k}f(x) \leq \frac{k}{1+k}((1-\alpha)f(x_1) + \alpha f(x_2)),$$

and dividing both sides by $\frac{k}{1+k} > 0$, we obtain (11.1). $\qquad\square$

Remark. By replacing f with $-f$ and "convex" by "concave", etc., the statement in Theorem 11.14 remains true.

Remark. In Theorem 11.14, the assumption that f has a constant sign on C is essential (Problem 11.12).

Example 11.2. Let $1 \leq p < \infty$ and define $f : \mathbb{R}^N \to \mathbb{R}$ by

$$f(x) = \|x\|_p := \left(\sum_{n=1}^{N} |x_n|^p\right)^{1/p}.$$

Then f is convex. To see this, note that f is nonnegative and homogeneous of degree 1, with $f(x) = 0$ if and only if $x = 0$. Let $\phi(y) = \frac{1}{p}y^p$ for $y \geq 0$. Then $\phi'(y) = y^{p-1} \geq 0$ and $\phi''(y) = (p-1)y^{p-2} \geq 0$, so ϕ is increasing and convex. Clearly the function $x \mapsto |x_n|$ is convex. Hence by Proposition 11.4,

$$g(x) := \phi(f(x)) = \frac{1}{p}\sum_{n=1}^{N}|x_n|^p$$

is convex (in particular, quasi-convex). By Corollary 11.5, $f = \phi^{-1} \circ g$ is quasi-convex. Hence by Theorem 11.14, f is convex.

Setting $\alpha = 1/2$ in (11.1) and recalling the definition of the ℓ^p norm in (1.7c), for all $x, y \in \mathbb{R}^N$ we obtain

$$\left\|\frac{x+y}{2}\right\|_p \leq \frac{1}{2}\|x\|_p + \frac{1}{2}\|y\|_p \iff \|x+y\|_p \leq \|x\|_p + \|y\|_p. \qquad (11.18)$$

The inequality (11.18) is called the *Minkowski inequality*, which is a generalization of the Cauchy-Schwarz inequality (corresponding to $p = 2$) and establishes that the ℓ^p norm $\|\cdot\|_p$ is indeed a norm.

Example 11.3. Define $f : \mathbb{R}_{++}^N \to \mathbb{R}$ by $f(x) = x_1^{\alpha_1} \cdots x_N^{\alpha_N}$, where $\alpha_n > 0$ and $\sum_{n=1}^N \alpha_n = 1$. Then f is concave. To see this, note that f is positive and homogeneous of degree 1. Furthermore,

$$\log f(x) = \sum_{n=1}^N \alpha_n \log x_n$$

is concave, so its monotonic transformation $f(x) = \exp(\log f(x))$ is quasi-concave by Corollary 11.5. Hence by Theorem 11.14, f is concave.

Example 11.4. Define $f : \mathbb{R}_{++}^N \to \mathbb{R}$ by

$$f(x) = \left(\sum_{n=1}^N \alpha_n x_n^{1-\gamma} \right)^{\frac{1}{1-\gamma}},$$

where $\alpha_n > 0$ for all n and $0 < \gamma \neq 1$. Then f is concave. To see this, note that f is positive and homogeneous of degree 1. Let $\phi(y) = \frac{y^{1-\gamma}}{1-\gamma}$ for $y > 0$. Then $\phi'(y) = y^{-\gamma} > 0$, so ϕ is increasing. Furthermore,

$$g(x) := \phi(f(x)) = \sum_{n=1}^N \alpha_n \frac{x_n^{1-\gamma}}{1-\gamma}$$

is concave (compute the Hessian and apply Proposition 11.9), so $f = \phi^{-1} \circ g$ is quasi-concave. Hence by Theorem 11.14, f is concave. For an economic application of this example, see Toda and Walsh (2020, Theorems 1, 2).

11.6   LOG-CONVEX FUNCTIONS

We say that a positive function $f : \mathbb{R}^N \to (0, \infty]$ is *log-convex* if $\log f$ is convex. If f is log-convex, since by definition $g(x) = \log f(x)$ is convex, $f(x) = \exp(g(x))$ is convex by setting $\phi(x) = e^x$ (a monotone convex function) in Proposition 11.4. Hence the set of log-convex functions is a subset of convex functions.

The following proposition shows that the set of log-convex functions is closed under addition, multiplication, and taking positive power. This proposition allows us to construct many convex functions.

Proposition 11.15. *Let $f, g : \mathbb{R}^N \to (0, \infty]$ be log-convex and $p > 0$. Then $f + g$, fg, $\max \{f, g\}$, and f^p are log-convex.*

Proof. Since f, g are log-convex, by definition $\log f, \log g$ are convex. Then $\log(fg) = \log f + \log g$ and $\log(\max \{f, g\}) = \max \{\log f, \log g\}$ are convex by Propositions 11.2 and 11.3, so fg and $\max \{f, g\}$ are log-convex. Similarly, $\log(f^p) = p \log f$ is convex, so f^p is log-convex.

To show that $f+g$ is log-convex, take any x_1, x_2 and $\alpha \in (0,1)$. To simplify notation, let $f_1 = f(x_1)$ and $f = f((1-\alpha)x_1 + \alpha x_2)$ etc. Since f is log-convex, $\log f$ is convex, so by definition

$$\log f \leq (1-\alpha)\log f_1 + \alpha \log f_2 \iff f \leq f_1^{1-\alpha} f_2^{\alpha}. \tag{11.19}$$

The same inequality holds for g. Define the vectors in $\mathbb{R}^2_{++}$ by

$$u = (f_1^{1-\alpha}, g_1^{1-\alpha}),$$
$$v = (f_2^{\alpha}, g_2^{\alpha}).$$

Define $p, q > 1$ by $1/p = 1 - \alpha$ and $1/q = \alpha$. Since $1/p + 1/q = 1$, it follows from the definition of the ℓ^p norm and Hölder's inequality (2.12) that

$$(f_1 + g_1)^{1-\alpha}(f_2 + g_2)^{\alpha} = \|u\|_p \|v\|_q \geq \langle u, v \rangle$$
$$= f_1^{1-\alpha} f_2^{\alpha} + g_1^{1-\alpha} g_2^{\alpha} \geq f + g,$$

where the last inequality follows from (11.19). Taking the logarithm of both sides, we obtain

$$\log(f + g) \leq (1-\alpha)\log(f_1 + g_1) + \alpha \log(f_2 + g_2),$$

so $\log(f + g)$ is convex. Hence $f + g$ is log-convex. □

Example 11.5. For each $i = 1, \ldots, I$, let $a_i > 0$ and $b_i \in \mathbb{R}^N$. Then the function

$$f(x) := \log\left(\sum_{i=1}^{I} a_i e^{\langle b_i, x \rangle}\right)$$

is convex. To see why, let $g_i(x) = a_i e^{\langle b_i, x \rangle}$. Then $\log g_i(x) = \langle b_i, x \rangle + \log a_i$ is an affine function and hence convex. Thus g_i is log-convex, and so is $g := \sum_{i=1}^{I} g_i(x)$ by Proposition 11.15. Hence $f = \log g$ is convex.

PROBLEMS

11.1. Prove that epi f is a convex set if and only if

$$f((1-\alpha)x_1 + \alpha x_2) \leq (1-\alpha)f(x_1) + \alpha f(x_2)$$

for all $x_1, x_2 \in \mathbb{R}^N$ and $\alpha \in [0, 1]$.

11.2. Prove that f is quasi-convex if and only if

$$f((1-\alpha)x_1 + \alpha x_2) \leq \max\{f(x_1), f(x_2)\}$$

for all $x_1, x_2 \in \mathbb{R}^N$ and $\alpha \in [0, 1]$.

11.3. Prove Proposition 11.4.

11.4. Prove Proposition 11.6 for the case of quasi-convexity.

11.5. Let X be a vector space, Y a set, $\Gamma : X \twoheadrightarrow Y$ a correspondence (so for each $x \in X$, $\Gamma(x)$ is a subset of Y), and $f : Y \to [-\infty, \infty]$. Suppose that Γ satisfies

$$\Gamma((1 - \alpha)x_1 + \alpha x_2) \subset \Gamma(x_1) \cup \Gamma(x_2)$$

for all $x_1, x_2 \in X$ and $\alpha \in [0, 1]$. Define

$$\bar{g}(x) = \sup_{y \in \Gamma(x)} f(y),$$

$$\underline{g}(x) = \inf_{y \in \Gamma(x)} f(y).$$

Prove that $\bar{g}$ is quasi-convex and $\underline{g}$ is quasi-concave.

11.6. For real symmetric matrices $A, B \in \mathbb{R}^{N \times N}$, define $A \geq B$ if $\langle x, Ax \rangle \geq \langle x, Bx \rangle$ for all $x \in \mathbb{R}^N$.

(i) Show that $\geq$ is a partial order, that is, it satisfies

    (a) (Reflexivity) $A \geq A$ for all A,

    (b) (Antisymmetry) if $A \geq B$ and $B \geq A$, then $A = B$,

    (c) (Transitivity) if $A \geq B$ and $B \geq C$, then $A \geq C$.

(ii) Let $A \in \mathbb{R}^{N \times N}$ be symmetric and positive definite, $\xi \in \mathbb{R}^N$, and define

$$f(x) = \langle \xi, x \rangle - \frac{1}{2} \langle x, Ax \rangle.$$

Prove that f is strictly concave and find the maximum of f as well as the maximum value.

(iii) Prove that if $A, B \in \mathbb{R}^{N \times N}$ are symmetric and positive definite, then $A \geq B$ if and only if $B^{-1} \geq A^{-1}$.

11.7. Let C be a convex set of a vector space X. We say that $x \in C$ is an *extreme point* if there exist no $x_1 \neq x_2 \in C$ and $\alpha \in (0, 1)$ such that $x = (1 - \alpha)x_1 + \alpha x_2$. If $f : C \to \mathbb{R}$ is strictly quasi-convex and $\bar{x} \in C$ achieves the maximum of f over C, prove that $\bar{x}$ is an extreme point of C.

11.8. Let $f : [a, b] \to \mathbb{R}$ be convex, continuous, and $f(a) < 0 < f(b)$. Show that there exists a unique $x \in (a, b)$ such that $f(x) = 0$.

11.9. Let $f : (a, b) \to \mathbb{R}$ be convex.

(i) Show that for each $x \in (a, b)$,

$$g^{\pm}(x) := \lim_{h \to \pm 0} \frac{f(x + h) - f(x)}{h}$$

    exist.

(ii) Show that $g^-(x) \le g^+(x)$ for each $x \in (a, b)$.

(iii) Show that f is differentiable on (a, b) except at most countably many points.

11.10. Let $\emptyset \ne X \subset \mathbb{R}^N$ and $u : X \to \mathbb{R}$. Define $e : \mathbb{R}^N \times \mathbb{R} \to [-\infty, \infty]$ by

$$e(p, u) = \inf \{p \cdot x : x \in X, u(x) \ge u\},$$

where by convention we define $\inf \emptyset = \infty$. (Economically, X is a consumption set, u is a utility function, p is a price vector, and e is the minimum expenditure to achieve utility level u given the price vector p, which is called the *expenditure function*.) Prove that $e(p, u)$ is concave in p.

11.11. Let $\emptyset \ne X \subset \mathbb{R}^N$ and $u : X \to \mathbb{R}$. Define $v : \mathbb{R}^N \times \mathbb{R} \to [-\infty, \infty]$ by

$$v(p, w) = \sup \{u(x) : x \in X, p \cdot x \le w\},$$

where by convention we define $\sup \emptyset = -\infty$. (Economically, X is a consumption set, u is a utility function, p is a price vector, w is wealth, and v is the maximum utility given the price vector p and wealth w, which is called the *indirect utility function*.)

(i) Take any $(p_j, w_j) \in \mathbb{R}^N \times \mathbb{R}$ and define $p = (1 - \alpha)p_1 + \alpha p_2$, $w = (1 - \alpha)w_1 + \alpha w_2$, where $\alpha \in [0, 1]$. Show that if $x \in X$ satisfies $p \cdot x \le w$, then $p_j \cdot x \le w_j$ for at least one j.

(ii) Prove that $v(p, w)$ is quasi-convex in (p, w).

11.12. Define the sets

$$C_1 := \{(x_1, x_2) \in \mathbb{R}^2 : x_1 > 0, x_2 > 0\},$$
$$C_2 := \{(x_1, x_2) \in \mathbb{R}^2 : x_1 \le 0, x_2 > 0\},$$
$$C := C_1 \cup C_2 = \{(x_1, x_2) \in \mathbb{R}^2 : x_2 > 0\}.$$

Define the function $f : C \to \mathbb{R}$ by

$$f(x) = \begin{cases} -\frac{x_1 x_2}{x_1 + x_2}, & (x \in C_1) \\ 0. & (x \in C_2) \end{cases}$$

(i) Show that C_1, C_2, C are cones.

(ii) Show that $f : C \to \mathbb{R}$ is homogeneous.

(iii) For each $y \in \mathbb{R}$, characterize the lower contour set of f defined by

$$L_f(y) := \{x \in C : f(x) \le y\}.$$

(iv) Prove that $f : C \to \mathbb{R}$ is quasi-convex.

(v) Setting $x_1 = (1, 1)$, $x_2 = (-1, 1)$, and $\alpha = 1/2$, show that the convex inequality (11.1) does not hold and hence f is not convex.

CHAPTER 12

Nonlinear Programming

12.1 INTRODUCTION

In Chapter 4, we studied constrained optimization problems with linear constraints. However, the discussion was largely based on geometric intuition and not necessarily mathematically rigorous. This chapter studies constrained optimization rigorously.

Consider the minimization problem

$$\begin{array}{ll} \text{minimize} & f(x) \\ \text{subject to} & x \in C. \end{array} \tag{12.1}$$

When the objective function f or the constraint set C do not have particular structure (such as linearity or convexity), the problem (12.1) is called a *nonlinear programming problem* or a *nonlinear program*. Recall that $\bar{x} \in C$ is called a *(global) solution* if $f(\bar{x}) \leq f(x)$ for all $x \in C$. We say that $\bar{x}$ is a *local solution* if there exists an open neighborhood U of $\bar{x}$ such that $f(\bar{x}) \leq f(x)$ for all $x \in C \cap U$. When the inequality is strict whenever $x \neq \bar{x}$, we say that $\bar{x}$ is a *strict local solution*.

12.2 NECESSARY CONDITION

In this section, we derive the first-order necessary condition for optimality using the tangent cone of the constraint set.

Let $C \subset \mathbb{R}^N$ be any nonempty set and $\bar{x} \in C$ be any point. The *tangent cone* of C at $\bar{x}$ is defined by

$$T_C(\bar{x}) :=$$
$$\left\{ y \in \mathbb{R}^N : (\exists) \{\alpha_k\} \geq 0, \{x_k\} \subset C, \lim_{k \to \infty} x_k = \bar{x}, y = \lim_{k \to \infty} \alpha_k(x_k - \bar{x}) \right\}.$$

That is, we have $y \in T_C(\bar{x})$ if y points to the same direction as the limiting direction of $\{x_k - \bar{x}\}$ as x_k approaches to $\bar{x}$. Intuitively, the tangent cone of

DOI: 10.1201/9781032698953-12

C at $\bar{x}$ consists of all directions from which we can approach the point $\bar{x} \in C$, starting from any point in C that is very close to $\bar{x}$. Figure 12.1 shows an example. Here C is the region in between the two curves, and the tangent cone is the shaded area.

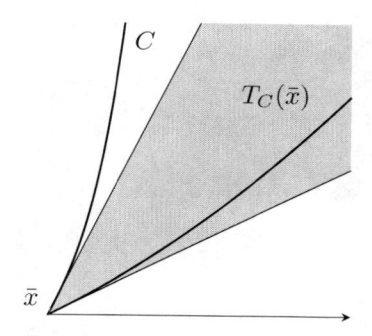

FIGURE 12.1: Tangent cone.

Lemma 12.1. $T_C(\bar{x})$ *is a nonempty closed cone.*

Proof. Setting $\alpha_k = 0$ for all k we get $0 \in T_C(\bar{x})$, so $T_C(\bar{x}) \neq \emptyset$. If $y \in T_C(\bar{x})$, then $y = \lim \alpha_k(x_k - \bar{x})$ for some $\{\alpha_k\} \geq 0$ and $\{x_k\} \subset C$ such that $\lim x_k = \bar{x}$. Then for $\beta \geq 0$ we have $\beta y = \lim \beta \alpha_k(x_k - \bar{x}) \in T_C(\bar{x})$, so $T_C(\bar{x})$ is a cone. To show that $T_C(\bar{x})$ is closed, let $\{y_l\} \subset T_C(\bar{x})$ and $y_l \to \bar{y}$. For each l we can take a sequence such that $\alpha_{k,l} \geq 0$, $\lim_{k \to \infty} x_{k,l} = \bar{x}$, and $y_l = \lim_{k \to \infty} \alpha_{k,l}(x_{k,l} - \bar{x})$. Hence we can take k_l such that $\|x_{k_l,l} - \bar{x}\| < 1/l$ and $\|y_l - \alpha_{k_l,l}(x_{k_l,l} - \bar{x})\| < 1/l$. Then $x_{k_l,l} \to \bar{x}$ and

$$\|\bar{y} - \alpha_{k_l,l}(x_{k_l,l} - \bar{x})\| \leq \|\bar{y} - y_l\| + \|y_l - \alpha_{k_l,l}(x_{k_l,l} - \bar{x})\| \to 0,$$

so $\bar{y} \in T_C(\bar{x})$. □

The dual cone of $T_C(\bar{x})$ is called the *normal cone* at $\bar{x}$ and is denoted by $N_C(\bar{x})$ (Figure 12.2). By the definition of the dual cone (see (10.9)), we have

$$N_C(\bar{x}) = (T_C(\bar{x}))^* = \left\{ z \in \mathbb{R}^N : (\forall y \in T_C(\bar{x})) \langle y, z \rangle \leq 0 \right\}. \tag{12.2}$$

The following theorem is fundamental for constrained optimization.

Theorem 12.2 (First-order necessary condition). *If f is differentiable and $\bar{x}$ is a local solution to (12.1), then $-\nabla f(\bar{x}) \in N_C(\bar{x})$.*

Proof. By the definition of the normal cone in (12.2), it suffices to show that for all $y \in T_C(\bar{x})$, we have

$$\langle -\nabla f(\bar{x}), y \rangle \leq 0 \iff \langle \nabla f(\bar{x}), y \rangle \geq 0.$$

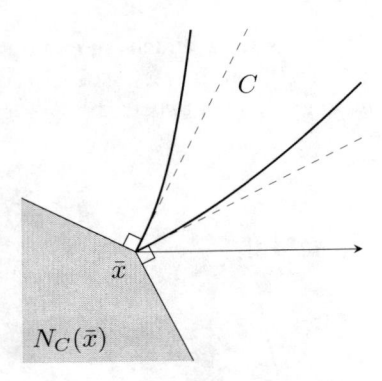

FIGURE 12.2: Normal cone.

Let $y \in T_C(\bar{x})$ and take a sequence such that $\alpha_k \geq 0$, $x_k \to \bar{x}$, and $\alpha_k(x_k - \bar{x}) \to y$. Since $\bar{x}$ is a local solution, for sufficiently large k we have $f(x_k) \geq f(\bar{x})$. Since f is differentiable, we have

$$0 \leq f(x_k) - f(\bar{x}) = \langle \nabla f(\bar{x}), x_k - \bar{x} \rangle + o(\|x_k - \bar{x}\|).^1$$

Multiplying both sides by $\alpha_k \geq 0$ and letting $k \to \infty$, we obtain

$$0 \leq \langle \nabla f(\bar{x}), \alpha_k(x_k - \bar{x}) \rangle + \|\alpha_k(x_k - \bar{x})\| \cdot \frac{o(\|x_k - \bar{x}\|)}{\|x_k - \bar{x}\|}$$

$$\to \langle \nabla f(\bar{x}), y \rangle + \|y\| \cdot 0 = \langle \nabla f(\bar{x}), y \rangle. \qquad \square$$

12.3 KARUSH-KUHN-TUCKER THEOREM

Theorem 12.2 is very general. Usually, we are interested in the case where the constraint set C is given parametrically. Consider the minimization problem

$$
\begin{array}{lll}
\text{minimize} & f(x) & \\
\text{subject to} & g_i(x) \leq 0 & (i = 1, \ldots, I), \\
& h_j(x) = 0 & (j = 1, \ldots, J).
\end{array} \tag{12.3}
$$

This problem is a special case of problem (12.1) by setting

$$C = \left\{ x \in \mathbb{R}^N : (\forall i) g_i(x) \leq 0, (\forall j) h_j(x) = 0 \right\}.$$

Let $\bar{x} \in C$ be a local solution. To study the shape of C around $\bar{x}$, we introduce some definitions. The set of indices for which the inequality constraints bind,

$$I(\bar{x}) := \left\{ i : g_i(\bar{x}) = 0 \right\},$$

is called the *active set*. Assume that g_i's and h_j's are differentiable. The set

$$L_C(\bar{x}) = \left\{ y \in \mathbb{R}^N : (\forall i \in I(\bar{x})) \langle \nabla g_i(\bar{x}), y \rangle \leq 0, (\forall j) \langle \nabla h_j(\bar{x}), y \rangle = 0 \right\} \tag{12.4}$$

---

[1] The notation $o(h)$ represents any quantity $q(h)$ such that $q(h)/h \to 0$ as $h \to 0$.

is called the *linearizing cone* of the constraints g_i's and h_j's. The reason why $L_C(\bar{x})$ is called the linearizing cone is the following. Since

$$g_i(\bar{x} + ty) - g_i(\bar{x}) = t \langle \nabla g_i(\bar{x}), y \rangle + o(t),$$

the point $x = \bar{x} + ty$ satisfies the constraint $g_i(x) \le 0$ to the first-order approximation if $g_i(\bar{x}) = 0$ (i is an active constraint) and $\langle \nabla g_i(\bar{x}), y \rangle \le 0$. The same holds for h_j's. Thus $y \in L_C(\bar{x})$ implies that from $\bar{x}$ we can move slightly toward the direction of y and still (approximately) satisfy the constraints. Thus we can expect that the linearizing cone is approximately equal to the tangent cone. The following proposition makes this intuition precise.

Proposition 12.3. *If $\bar{x} \in C$, then* $\operatorname{co} T_C(\bar{x}) \subset L_C(\bar{x})$.

Proof. Clearly the linearizing cone (12.4) is a closed convex cone, so it suffices to prove $T_C(\bar{x}) \subset L_C(\bar{x})$. Let $y \in T_C(\bar{x})$. Take $\{x_k\} \subset C$ and $\{\alpha_k\} \subset \mathbb{R}_+$ such that $x_k \to \bar{x}$ and $\alpha_k(x_k - \bar{x}) \to y$. Since $g_i(\bar{x}) = 0$ for $i \in I(\bar{x})$ and g_i is differentiable, we get

$$0 \ge g_i(x_k) = g_i(x_k) - g_i(\bar{x}) = \langle \nabla g_i(\bar{x}), x_k - \bar{x} \rangle + o(\|x_k - \bar{x}\|).$$

Multiplying both sides by $\alpha_k \ge 0$ and letting $k \to \infty$, we get

$$0 \ge \langle \nabla g_i(\bar{x}), \alpha_k(x_k - \bar{x}) \rangle + \|\alpha_k(x_k - \bar{x})\| \cdot \frac{o(\|x_k - \bar{x}\|)}{\|x_k - \bar{x}\|}$$
$$\to \langle \nabla g_i(\bar{x}), y \rangle + \|y\| \cdot 0 = \langle \nabla g_i(\bar{x}), y \rangle.$$

A similar argument applies to h_j. Hence $y \in L_C(\bar{x})$. $\qquad\square$

Remark. While the tangent cone is directly defined by the constraint set C, the linearizing cone is defined through the functions that define the set C. Therefore different parameterizations of the same set C may lead to different linearizing cones (Problem 12.3).

The main result of this chapter is the following.

Theorem 12.4 (Karush-Kuhn-Tucker theorem for nonlinear programming). *Consider the minimization problem* (12.3), *where f, g_i, h_j's are differentiable. If $\bar{x}$ is a local solution and $L_C(\bar{x}) \subset \operatorname{co} T_C(\bar{x})$, then there exist $\lambda \in \mathbb{R}_+^I$ and $\mu \in \mathbb{R}^J$ such that*

$$\nabla f(\bar{x}) + \sum_{i=1}^{I} \lambda_i \nabla g_i(\bar{x}) + \sum_{j=1}^{J} \mu_j \nabla h_j(\bar{x}) = 0, \tag{12.5a}$$

$$(\forall i) \ \lambda_i \ge 0, \ g_i(\bar{x}) \le 0, \ \lambda_i g_i(\bar{x}) = 0. \tag{12.5b}$$

Proof. By Theorem 12.2, we have $-\nabla f(\bar{x}) \in N_C(\bar{x}) = (T_C(\bar{x}))^*$. By Proposition 12.3 and the assumption $L_C(\bar{x}) \subset \operatorname{co} T_C(\bar{x})$, we have $L_C(\bar{x}) = \operatorname{co} T_C(\bar{x})$. Hence by Proposition 10.5, we obtain $(T_C(\bar{x}))^* = (\operatorname{co} T_C(\bar{x}))^* = (L_C(\bar{x}))^*$.

Now let K be the polyhedral cone generated by $\{\nabla g_i(\bar{x})\}_{i \in I(\bar{x})}$ and $\{\pm \nabla h_j(\bar{x})\}_{j=1}^J$. By Farkas' lemma (Proposition 10.7), it follows that

$$
\begin{aligned}
K^* &= \left\{ y \in \mathbb{R}^N : (\forall i \in I(\bar{x})) \langle \nabla g_i(\bar{x}), y \rangle \le 0, (\forall j) \langle \pm \nabla h_j(\bar{x}), y \rangle \le 0 \right\} \\
&= \left\{ y \in \mathbb{R}^N : (\forall i \in I(\bar{x})) \langle \nabla g_i(\bar{x}), y \rangle \le 0, (\forall j) \langle \nabla h_j(\bar{x}), y \rangle = 0 \right\},
\end{aligned}
$$

which is precisely the linearizing cone $L_C(\bar{x})$ in (12.4). Again by Farkas' lemma, we have $(L_C(\bar{x}))^* = K$. Therefore $-\nabla f(\bar{x}) \in K$, so there exist numbers $\lambda_i \ge 0$ ($i \in I(\bar{x})$) and $\alpha_j, \beta_j \ge 0$ such that

$$
-\nabla f(\bar{x}) = \sum_{i \in I(\bar{x})} \lambda_i \nabla g_i(\bar{x}) + \sum_{j=1}^J (\alpha_j - \beta_j) \nabla h_j(\bar{x}).
$$

Letting $\lambda_i = 0$ for $i \notin I(\bar{x})$ and $\mu_j = \alpha_j - \beta_j$, we get (12.5a). Finally, (12.5b) holds for $i \in I(\bar{x})$ since $g_i(\bar{x}) = 0$. It also holds for $i \notin I(\bar{x})$ since we defined $\lambda_i = 0$ for such i. $\qquad \square$

Here is an easy way to remember the conditions in (12.5). Define the *Lagrangian* of the minimization problem (12.3) by

$$
L(x, \lambda, \mu) = f(x) + \sum_{i=1}^I \lambda_i g_i(x) + \sum_{j=1}^J \mu_j h_j(x), \qquad (12.6)
$$

which is the sum of the objective function $f(x)$ and the constraint functions $g_i(x)$, $h_j(x)$ weighted by the Lagrange multipliers λ_i, μ_j. Then (12.5a) implies that the derivative of $L(\cdot, \lambda, \mu)$ at $\bar{x}$ is zero. (12.5a) is called the *first-order condition*. (12.5b) is called the *complementary slackness condition*. Together, (12.5a) and (12.5b) are called *Karush-Kuhn-Tucker (KKT) conditions*.

12.4 CONSTRAINT QUALIFICATIONS

Conditions of the form $L_C(\bar{x}) \subset \operatorname{co} T_C(\bar{x})$ in Theorem 12.4 are called *constraint qualifications* (CQ), which are prerequisites for applying the KKT theorem. In general, we cannot omit such conditions, as the following example shows.

Example 12.1. Consider the minimization problem

$$
\begin{array}{lc}
\text{minimize} & x \\
\text{subject to} & x^3 \ge 0.
\end{array}
$$

Because the constraint $x^3 \ge 0$ is equivalent to $x \ge 0$, the solution is clearly $\bar{x} = 0$. However, suppose we mechanically apply the KKT theorem. Let $f(x) = x$ be the objective function and $g(x) = -x^3$. Then the problem is

$$
\begin{array}{lc}
\text{minimize} & f(x) \\
\text{subject to} & g(x) \le 0.
\end{array}
$$

The Lagrangian is

$$L(x, \lambda) = f(x) + \lambda g(x) = x - \lambda x^3.$$

At $\bar{x} = 0$, we obtain

$$\nabla_x L(\bar{x}, \lambda) = 1 - 3\lambda \bar{x}^2 = 1 \neq 0,$$

so the first-order condition does not hold. The reason is that the tangent cone is $T_C(\bar{x}) = \{x \in \mathbb{R} : x \geq 0\}$ but the linearizing cone is

$$L_C(\bar{x}) = \{y \in \mathbb{R} : g'(\bar{x})y \leq 0\} = \{y \in \mathbb{R} : 0y \leq 0\} = \mathbb{R},$$

so $L_C(\bar{x}) \not\subset \operatorname{co} T_C(\bar{x})$.

There are many constraint qualifications in the literature.

Guignard (GCQ). $L_C(\bar{x}) \subset \operatorname{co} T_C(\bar{x})$.

Abadie (ACQ). $L_C(\bar{x}) \subset T_C(\bar{x})$.

Mangasarian-Fromovitz (MFCQ). $\{\nabla h_j(\bar{x})\}_{j=1}^{J}$ are linearly independent, and there exists $y \in \mathbb{R}^N$ such that $\langle \nabla g_i(\bar{x}), y \rangle < 0$ for all $i \in I(\bar{x})$ and $\langle \nabla h_j(\bar{x}), y \rangle = 0$ for all j.

Slater (SCQ). g_i's are convex, $h_j(x) = \langle a_j, x \rangle - c_j$ with $\{a_j\}_{j=1}^{J}$ linearly independent, and there exists $x_0 \in \mathbb{R}^N$ such that $g_i(x_0) < 0$ for all i and $h_j(x_0) = 0$ for all j.

Linear independence (LICQ). The set of vectors

$$\{\nabla g_i(\bar{x})\}_{i \in I(\bar{x})} \cup \{\nabla h_j(\bar{x})\}_{j=1}^{J}$$

is linearly independent.

The point of listing these constraint qualifications is that some of them are general but hard to verify (GCQ and ACQ), while others are special but easy to verify (SCQ and LICQ). Users of the KKT theorem need to select the appropriate constraint qualification for the problem under consideration. The following theorem shows the relation between these constraint qualifications.

Theorem 12.5. *The following implications hold for constraint qualifications:*

$$LICQ \text{ or } SCQ \implies MFCQ \implies ACQ \implies GCQ.$$

Proof. ACQ $\implies$ GCQ: Trivial because $T_C(\bar{x}) \subset \operatorname{co} T_C(\bar{x})$.

MFCQ $\implies$ ACQ: By dropping non-binding constraints if necessary, without loss of generality we may assume all constraints bind, so $I(\bar{x}) = \{1, \ldots, I\}$. Define $G : \mathbb{R}^N \to \mathbb{R}^I$ by $G(x) = (g_1(x), \ldots, g_I(x))'$ and $H : \mathbb{R}^N \to \mathbb{R}^J$ by

$H(x) = (h_1(x), \ldots, h_J(x))'$. Then MFCQ holds if and only if the $J \times N$ Jacobian $DH(\bar{x})$ has full row rank and there exists $y \in \mathbb{R}^N$ such that $[DG(\bar{x})]y \ll 0$ and $[DH(\bar{x})]y = 0$, where $v \ll 0$ means that all entries of v are strictly negative.

Define the set

$$\tilde{L}_C(\bar{x}) = \left\{ y \in \mathbb{R}^N : [DG(\bar{x})]y \ll 0, [DH(\bar{x})]y = 0 \right\}.$$

Since MFCQ holds, by definition we have $\tilde{L}_C(\bar{x}) \neq \emptyset$. Since $\mathrm{cl}\, \tilde{L}_C(\bar{x}) = L_C(\bar{x})$ by the definition of the linearizing cone (12.4), and since $T_C(\bar{x})$ is closed, it suffices to show $\tilde{L}_C(\bar{x}) \subset T_C(\bar{x})$.

Since $DH(\bar{x})$ has full row rank, by relabeling the variables if necessary, we may assume that we can split the variables as $x = (x_1, x_2) \in \mathbb{R}^{N-J} \times \mathbb{R}^J$ and write $DH(\bar{x}) = [D_{x_1}H, D_{x_2}H]$, where $D_{x_2}H = D_{x_2}H(\bar{x})$ is invertible. By the implicit function theorem (Theorem 8.3), for x close enough to $\bar{x}$, we can write

$$0 = H(x) = H(x_1, x_2) \iff x_2 = \phi(x_1), \tag{12.7}$$

where ϕ is C^1 and $D\phi = -[D_{x_2}H]^{-1}D_{x_1}H$.

Take any $y = (y_1, y_2) \in \tilde{L}_C(\bar{x})$, where $y_1 \in \mathbb{R}^{N-J}$ and $y_2 \in \mathbb{R}^J$. For small enough $t > 0$, define

$$x(t) = (x_1(t), x_2(t)) = (\bar{x}_1 + ty_1, \phi(\bar{x}_1 + ty_1)).$$

Let us show that $x(0) = \bar{x}$, $x(t) \in C$ for sufficiently small $t > 0$, and $x'(0) = y$, which imply that $y \in T_C(\bar{x})$.

Since $H(\bar{x}) = 0$, by the implicit function theorem we have $x(0) = (\bar{x}_1, \phi(\bar{x}_1)) = (\bar{x}_1, \bar{x}_2) = \bar{x}$.

Using the chain rule, we obtain $x'(0) = (y_1, [D\phi]y_1)$. Since $y \in \tilde{L}_C(\bar{x})$, it follows that

$$0 = [DH(\bar{x})]y = [DH_{x_1}]y_1 + [DH_{x_2}]y_2$$
$$\iff y_2 = -[DH_{x_2}]^{-1}[DH_{x_1}]y_1 = [D\phi]y_1$$

by the implicit function theorem. Therefore $x'(0) = (y_1, y_2) = y$.

Finally, by the chain rule and the definition of $\tilde{L}_C(\bar{x})$, at $t = 0$ we have

$$\frac{\mathrm{d}}{\mathrm{d}t}G(x(t))\bigg|_{t=0} = [DG(\bar{x})]x'(0) = [DG(\bar{x})]y \ll 0.$$

Therefore for small enough $t > 0$, we have

$$\frac{G(x(t))}{t} = \frac{G(x(t)) - G(\bar{x})}{t} \ll 0$$

because $G(\bar{x}) = 0$, so $G(x(t)) \ll 0$. Since $H(x(t)) = H(x_1(t), \phi(x_1(t))) = 0$, it follows that $x(t) \in C$ for small enough $t > 0$.

SCQ $\implies$ MFCQ: Suppose that g_i's are convex, $h_j(x) = \langle a_j, x \rangle - c_j$ where $\{a_j\}_{j=1}^J$ are linearly independent, and there exists $x_0 \in \mathbb{R}^N$ such that $g_i(x_0) < 0$ for all i and $h_j(x_0) = 0$ for all j.

Since $\nabla h_j = a_j$ and $\{a_j\}_{j=1}^J$ are linearly independent, $\{\nabla h_j(\bar{x})\}_{j=1}^J$ are linearly independent. If $i \in I(\bar{x})$, since g_i is convex, by Proposition 11.7 we have

$$0 > g_i(x_0) = g_i(x_0) - g_i(\bar{x}) \geq \langle \nabla g_i(\bar{x}), x_0 - \bar{x} \rangle.$$

Setting $y = x_0 - \bar{x}$, we have $\langle \nabla g_i(\bar{x}), y \rangle < 0$ for all $i \in I(\bar{x})$. Since $\bar{x}, x_0$ are feasible, we have $\langle a_j, \bar{x} \rangle - c_j = 0$ and $\langle a_j, x_0 \rangle - c_j = 0$, so taking the difference $\langle \nabla h_j(\bar{x}), y \rangle = \langle a_j, x_0 - \bar{x} \rangle = 0$. Therefore MFCQ holds.

LICQ $\implies$ MFCQ: As in the previous case we may assume $I(\bar{x}) = \{1, \ldots, I\}$. Suppose to the contrary that MFCQ does not hold. Then there exist no y such that $\langle \nabla g_i(\bar{x}), y \rangle < 0$ for all i and $\langle \nabla h_j(\bar{x}), y \rangle = 0$ for all j. Let $G(x) = (g_1(x), \ldots, g_I(x))'$, $H(x) = (h_1(x), \ldots, h_J(x))'$, and define the $(I + J) \times N$ matrix M by $M = \begin{bmatrix} DG(\bar{x}) \\ DH(\bar{x}) \end{bmatrix}$. Define the sets $A, B \subset \mathbb{R}^{I+J}$ by

$$A = -\mathbb{R}_{++}^I \times \{0\} \subset \mathbb{R}^I \times \mathbb{R}^J,$$
$$B = \{z \in \mathbb{R}^{I+J} : (\exists y \in \mathbb{R}^N) z = My\}.$$

Since MFCQ does not hold, we have $A \cap B = \emptyset$. Clearly A, B are nonempty and convex. By the separating hyperplane theorem (Theorem 10.2), there exists $0 \neq a \in \mathbb{R}^{I+J}$ such that

$$\sup_{z \in A} \langle a, z \rangle \leq \inf_{z \in B} \langle a, z \rangle = \inf_{y \in \mathbb{R}^N} a'My.$$

Since $y \mapsto a'My$ is linear and $\sup_{z \in A} \langle a, z \rangle > -\infty$ because $A \neq \emptyset$, in order for the above inequality to hold, it is necessary that $a'M = 0$. Letting $a = (\lambda, \mu) \in \mathbb{R}^I \times \mathbb{R}^J$, then

$$0 = M'a = \sum_{i=1}^I \lambda_i \nabla g_j(\bar{x}) + \sum_{j=1}^J \mu_j \nabla h_j(\bar{x}).$$

Since $a = (\lambda, \mu) \neq 0$, $\{\nabla g_i(\bar{x})\}_{i=1}^I$ and $\{\nabla h_j(\bar{x})\}_{j=1}^J$ are not linearly independent. Hence LICQ does not hold. $\qquad \square$

In many applications, constraints are linear. In that case, the following proposition shows that ACQ (hence GCQ) is automatically satisfied, so there is no need to check it.

Proposition 12.6. *Consider the minimization problem (12.3). If g_i, h_j's are all affine, then the Abadie constraint qualification holds.*

Proof. Consider the equality constraint $h(x) = 0$, where $h(x) = \langle a, x \rangle - b$ with $a \neq 0$. Clearly the equality constraint $h(x) = 0$ is equivalent to the two inequality constraints

$$\langle a, x \rangle - b \leq 0,$$
$$\langle -a, x \rangle + b \leq 0.$$

Therefore without loss of generality, we may assume that there are no equality constraints.

For each $i = 1, \ldots, I$, let $g_i(x) = \langle a_i, x \rangle - b_i$, where $0 \neq a_i \in \mathbb{R}^N$. Let $A := [a_1, \ldots, a_I]' \in \mathbb{R}^{I \times N}$ and $b := (b_1, \ldots, b_I)' \in \mathbb{R}^I$. Then the constraint set is

$$C = \left\{ x \in \mathbb{R}^N : Ax \leq b \right\}.$$

Let $\bar{x} \in C$. By relabeling the constraints if necessary, without loss of generality we may assume

$$g_i(\bar{x}) \begin{cases} = 0, & (i \leq I_1) \\ < 0, & (i > I_1) \end{cases}$$

where $I_1 \leq I$. By partitioning A, b as $A' = [A_1', A_2']$ and $b' = (b_1', b_2')$, we then have $A_1 \bar{x} = b_1$ and $A_2 \bar{x} \ll b_2$. By the definition of the linearizing cone (12.4), we have

$$L_C(\bar{x}) = \left\{ y \in \mathbb{R}^N : (\forall i \leq I_1) \langle a_i, y \rangle \leq 0 \right\} = \left\{ y \in \mathbb{R}^N : A_1 y \leq 0 \right\}.$$

Let $y \in L_C(\bar{x})$. For small enough $t > 0$, define $x(t) = \bar{x} + ty$. Then

$$A_1 x(t) = A_1(\bar{x} + ty) = b_1 + t A_1 y \leq b_1$$

for all $t > 0$, and

$$A_2 x(t) = A_2(\bar{x} + ty) \to A_2 \bar{x} \ll b_2$$

as $t \to 0$, so $x(t) \in C$ for small enough $t > 0$. Therefore

$$y = \lim_{t \to 0} \frac{x(t) - \bar{x}}{t} \in T_C(\bar{x}),$$

so $L_C(\bar{x}) \subset T_C(\bar{x})$. □

Remark. Proposition 12.6 justifies Theorem 4.3. It is known that GCQ is the weakest possible condition (Gould and Tolle, 1971).

Remark. The classical theorem of Lagrange states that if f, h_j's are differentiable, $\bar{x}$ is a local solution to

$$\text{minimize} \qquad f(x)$$
$$h_j(x) = 0, \qquad\qquad (j = 1, \ldots, J)$$

and the vectors $\{\nabla h_j(\bar{x})\}_{j=1}^{J}$ are linearly independent, then there exists $\mu \in \mathbb{R}^J$ such that

$$\nabla f(\bar{x}) + \sum_{j=1}^{J} \mu_j \nabla h_j(\bar{x}) = 0.$$

The Lagrange theorem is usually proved by applying the implicit function theorem. However, it is clear that the Lagrange theorem is a special case of the KKT theorem (Theorem 12.4) by dropping inequality constraints and applying the linear independence constraint qualification (LICQ).

12.5   SADDLE POINT THEOREM

The Karush-Kuhn-Tucker theorem (Theorem 12.4) provides a necessary condition for a local solution assuming the differentiability of functions. In this section we consider necessary and sufficient conditions for a global solution by focusing on *convex programming problems* (minimization problems in which the objective function and constraints are convex) but dropping differentiability.

Consider the minimization problem (12.3), where f, g_i's are convex and h_j's are affine. Let

$$\Omega := (\operatorname{dom} f) \cap \bigcap_{i=1}^{I} (\operatorname{dom} g_i) \tag{12.8}$$

be the intersection of the domains of the objective function and the constraint functions, which we assume to be nonempty. Since h_j is affine, we may write $h_j(x) = \langle a_j, x \rangle - b_j$ for $a_j \neq 0$. Without loss of generality, we may assume that $\{a_j\}$ is linearly independent, for otherwise either the constraint set is empty or some constraints are redundant (Problem 12.4). Letting $A = [a_1, \ldots, a_J]' \in \mathbb{R}^{J \times N}$ and $b = (b_1, \ldots, b_J)' \in \mathbb{R}^J$, the equality constraints can be compactly written as $Ax - b = 0$.

Define the Lagrangian by

$$L(x, \lambda, \mu) = \begin{cases} f(x) + \sum_{i=1}^{I} \lambda_i g_i(x) + \sum_{j=1}^{J} \mu_j h_j(x), & (\lambda \in \mathbb{R}_+^I) \\ -\infty, & (\lambda \notin \mathbb{R}_+^I) \end{cases} \tag{12.9}$$

where $\lambda = (\lambda_1, \ldots, \lambda_I) \in \mathbb{R}^I$ and $\mu = (\mu_1, \ldots, \mu_J) \in \mathbb{R}^J$ are Lagrange multipliers. (We simply define L to be $-\infty$ when $\lambda \notin \mathbb{R}_+^I$ to avoid mentioning this constraint.) A point $(\bar{x}, \bar{\lambda}, \bar{\mu}) \in \Omega \times \mathbb{R}^I \times \mathbb{R}^J$ is called a *saddle point* if it achieves the minimum with respect to x and maximum with respect to (λ, μ). Formally, $(\bar{x}, \bar{\lambda}, \bar{\mu})$ is a saddle point if

$$L(\bar{x}, \lambda, \mu) \leq L(\bar{x}, \bar{\lambda}, \bar{\mu}) \leq L(x, \bar{\lambda}, \bar{\mu}) \tag{12.10}$$

for all $(x, \lambda, \mu) \in \Omega \times \mathbb{R}^I \times \mathbb{R}^J$.

The following theorem provides necessary and sufficient conditions for optimality.

Theorem 12.7 (Saddle point theorem). *Consider the minimization problem (12.3), where f, g_i's are convex and h_j's are affine. Let Ω in (12.8) be the effective domain and*

$$(h_1(x), \ldots, h_J(x))' = Ax - b,$$

where $A \in \mathbb{R}^{J \times N}$ and $b \in \mathbb{R}^J$. Then the following statements are true.

(i) If (a) $\bar{x}$ is a solution to the minimization problem (12.3), (b) there exists $x_0 \in \mathbb{R}^N$ such that $g_i(x_0) < 0$ for all i and $Ax_0 - b = 0$, and (c) $0 \in \text{int}(A\Omega - b)$, then there exist Lagrange multipliers $\bar{\lambda} \in \mathbb{R}^I_+$ and $\bar{\mu} \in \mathbb{R}^J$ such that $(\bar{x}, \bar{\lambda}, \bar{\mu})$ is a saddle point of L.

(ii) If there exist Lagrange multipliers $\bar{\lambda} \in \mathbb{R}^I_+$ and $\bar{\mu} \in \mathbb{R}^J$ such that $(\bar{x}, \bar{\lambda}, \bar{\mu})$ is a saddle point of L, then $\bar{x}$ is a solution to the minimization problem (12.3).

Proof. We prove claim (i). Suppose $\bar{x} \in \Omega$ is a solution to (12.3). Define the sets $C, D \subset \mathbb{R}^{1+I+J}$ by

$$C = \left\{ (u, v, w) \in \mathbb{R}^{1+I+J} : (\exists x \in \Omega) u \geq f(x), (\forall i) v_i \geq g_i(x), w = Ax - b \right\},$$
$$D = \left\{ (u, v, w) \in \mathbb{R}^{1+I+J} : u < f(\bar{x}), (\forall i) v_i < 0, (\forall j) w_j = 0 \right\}.$$

(See Figure 12.3 for the case $J = 0$.)

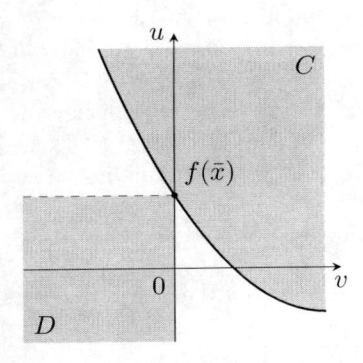

FIGURE 12.3: Saddle point theorem.

Clearly C, D are convex since f, g_i's are convex and Ω is convex. Since

$$(f(\bar{x}), \bar{v}, A\bar{x} - b) \in C$$

for $\bar{v}_i = g_i(\bar{x})$, C is nonempty. Letting $v_{0i} = g_i(x_0) < 0$, $v_0 = (v_{01}, \ldots, v_{0I})$, and $u_0 < f(\bar{x})$, we have $(u_0, v_0, 0) \in D$, so D is nonempty. If $(u, v, w) \in C \cap D$, since $(u, v, w) \in D$ we have $u < f(\bar{x})$, $v \ll 0$, and $w = 0$. Then since $(u, v, 0) \in C$ there exists $x \in \Omega$ such that $f(x) \leq u < f(\bar{x})$, $g_i(x) < 0$ for all i, and $Ax - b = 0$, contradicting the optimality of $\bar{x}$. Therefore $C \cap D = \emptyset$. By the separating hyperplane theorem (Theorem 10.2), there exists $0 \neq (\alpha, \beta, \gamma) \in \mathbb{R} \times \mathbb{R}^I \times \mathbb{R}^J$ such that

$$\sup_{(u,v,w) \in D} \alpha u + \langle \beta, v \rangle + \langle \gamma, w \rangle \leq \inf_{(u,v,w) \in C} \alpha u + \langle \beta, v \rangle + \langle \gamma, w \rangle . \qquad (12.11)$$

Taking $(u, v, w) \in D$ and letting $u \to -\infty$, it must be $\alpha \geq 0$. Similarly, letting $v_i \to -\infty$, it must be $\beta_i \geq 0$ for all i.

Let us show that $\alpha > 0$. Let $1 = (1, \ldots, 1)$ denote the vector of ones. For any $\epsilon > 0$, we have $(f(\bar{x}) - \epsilon, -\epsilon 1, 0) \in D$, so (12.11) implies

$$\alpha(f(\bar{x}) - \epsilon) - \epsilon \langle \beta, 1 \rangle \leq \alpha f(x) + \sum_{i=1}^{I} \beta_i g_i(x) + \sum_{j=1}^{J} \gamma_j h_j(x) \qquad (12.12)$$

for any x. Letting $x = x_0$ and $\epsilon \to 0$, we obtain

$$\alpha f(\bar{x}) \leq \alpha f(x_0) + \sum_{i=1}^{I} \beta_i g_i(x_0).$$

Suppose to the contrary that $\alpha = 0$. Then $\sum_{i=1}^{I} \beta_i g_i(x_0) \geq 0$. Since by assumption $g_i(x_0) < 0$, it must be $\beta_i = 0$ for all i. If $J = 0$ (no equality constraints), then $(\alpha, \beta) = 0$, a contradiction. If $J > 0$, then (12.11) implies

$$\sup_{(u,v,w) \in D} \langle \gamma, w \rangle \leq \inf_{(u,v,w) \in C} \langle \gamma, w \rangle \iff (\forall x \in \Omega) \langle \gamma, Ax - b \rangle \geq 0.$$

Since by assumption 0 is an interior point of $A\Omega - b$, for small enough $\delta > 0$ there exists $x \in \Omega$ with $-\delta \gamma = Ax - b$. Therefore $-\delta \|\gamma\|^2 \geq 0$ implies $\gamma = 0$. Then $(\alpha, \beta, \gamma) = 0$, a contradiction. Hence $\alpha > 0$.

Now that we know $\alpha > 0$, define $\bar{\lambda} = \beta/\alpha$ and $\bar{\mu} = \gamma/\alpha$. Then letting $\epsilon \to 0$ in (12.12), we obtain

$$f(\bar{x}) \leq f(x) + \sum_{i=1}^{I} \bar{\lambda}_i g_i(x) + \sum_{j=1}^{J} \bar{\mu}_j h_j(x) = L(x, \bar{\lambda}, \bar{\mu}) \qquad (12.13)$$

for all x. Since $\bar{\lambda}_i \geq 0$ and $g_i(\bar{x}) \leq 0$ for all i and $h_j(\bar{x}) = 0$ for all j, it follows from (12.13) that

$$L(\bar{x}, \bar{\lambda}, \bar{\mu}) = f(\bar{x}) + \sum_{i=1}^{I} \bar{\lambda}_i g_i(\bar{x}) + \sum_{j=1}^{J} \bar{\mu}_j h_j(\bar{x})$$

$$\leq f(\bar{x}) \leq f(x) + \sum_{i=1}^{I} \bar{\lambda}_i g_i(x) + \sum_{j=1}^{J} \bar{\mu}_j h_j(x) = L(x, \bar{\lambda}, \bar{\mu}),$$

which is the right inequality of (12.10). Furthermore, since $h_j(\bar{x}) = 0$ for all j, it must be $\bar{\lambda}_i g_i(\bar{x}) = 0$ for all i.

It remains to show the left inequality of (12.10). If $\lambda \notin \mathbb{R}_+^I$, by the definition of the Lagrangian in (12.9), we have $L(x, \lambda, \mu) = -\infty$, so it is trivial. If $\lambda \in \mathbb{R}_+^I$, then since $g_i(\bar{x}) \leq 0$ and $h_j(\bar{x}) = 0$, we obtain

$$L(\bar{x}, \lambda, \mu) = f(\bar{x}) + \sum_{i=1}^{I} \lambda_i g_i(\bar{x}) + \sum_{j=1}^{J} \mu_j h_j(\bar{x})$$

$$\leq f(\bar{x}) = L(\bar{x}, \bar{\lambda}, \bar{\mu}),$$

which is the left inequality of (12.10).

We next prove claim (ii). Assume that $(\bar{x}, \bar{\lambda}, \bar{\mu}) \in \Omega \times \mathbb{R}_+^I \times \mathbb{R}^J$ is a saddle point of L. By the left inequality of (12.10), for any $\lambda \in \mathbb{R}_+^I$ and $\mu \in \mathbb{R}^J$ we obtain

$$f(\bar{x}) + \sum_{i=1}^{I} \lambda_i g_i(\bar{x}) + \sum_{j=1}^{J} \mu_j h_j(\bar{x}) \leq f(\bar{x}) + \sum_{i=1}^{I} \bar{\lambda}_i g_i(\bar{x}) + \sum_{j=1}^{J} \bar{\mu}_j h_j(\bar{x})$$

$$\implies \sum_{i=1}^{I} \lambda_i g_i(\bar{x}) + \sum_{j=1}^{J} \mu_j h_j(\bar{x}) \leq \sum_{i=1}^{I} \bar{\lambda}_i g_i(\bar{x}) + \sum_{j=1}^{J} \bar{\mu}_j h_j(\bar{x}).$$

Letting $\mu_j \to \pm\infty$, it must be $h_j(\bar{x}) = 0$ for all j. Letting $\lambda_i \to \infty$, we get $g_i(\bar{x}) \leq 0$ for all i. Letting $\lambda = 0$, we get $0 \leq \sum_{i=1}^{I} \bar{\lambda}_i g_i(\bar{x})$, so it must be $\bar{\lambda}_i g_i(\bar{x}) = 0$ for all i. Then by the right inequality of (12.10), for any $x \in \Omega$ we obtain

$$f(\bar{x}) + \sum_{i=1}^{I} \bar{\lambda}_i g_i(\bar{x}) + \sum_{j=1}^{J} \bar{\mu}_j h_j(\bar{x}) \leq f(x) + \sum_{i=1}^{I} \bar{\lambda}_i g_i(x) + \sum_{j=1}^{J} \bar{\mu}_j h_j(x)$$

$$\implies f(\bar{x}) \leq f(x) + \sum_{i=1}^{I} \bar{\lambda}_i g_i(x) + \sum_{j=1}^{J} \bar{\mu}_j h_j(x).$$

Since $\bar{\lambda}_i \geq 0$, if $g_i(x) \leq 0$ and $h_j(x) = 0$ it follows that $f(\bar{x}) \leq f(x)$, so $\bar{x}$ is a solution to the constrained minimization problem (12.3). □

12.6 DUALITY

An application of the saddle point theorem (Theorem 12.7) is to convert a constrained optimization problem into another (potentially) simpler problem.

Consider the constrained minimization problem

$$\begin{aligned}
&\text{minimize} && f(x) \\
&\text{subject to} && g_i(x) \leq 0 && (i = 1, \ldots, I)
\end{aligned} \tag{12.14}$$

with Lagrangian

$$L(x, \lambda) = \begin{cases} f(x) + \sum_{i=1}^{I} \lambda_i g_i(x), & (\lambda \in \mathbb{R}_+^I) \\ -\infty. & (\lambda \notin \mathbb{R}_+^I) \end{cases} \tag{12.15}$$

The following discussion can easily accommodate equality constraints as well but we omit for simplicity. Suppose the assumptions of the saddle point theorem (Theorem 12.7) are satisfied, so there exists a saddle point $(\bar{x}, \bar{\lambda})$:

$$L(\bar{x}, \lambda \le L(\bar{x}, \bar{\lambda}) \le L(x, \bar{\lambda})$$

for all (x, λ). Taking the supremum over λ and infimum over x, we obtain

$$\sup_{\lambda} L(\bar{x}, \lambda) \le L(\bar{x}, \bar{\lambda}) \le \inf_{x} L(x, \bar{\lambda}).$$

Therefore viewing $\bar{x}$ in the left-hand side and $\bar{\lambda}$ as free variables, we obtain

$$\inf_{x} \sup_{\lambda} L(x, \lambda) \le L(\bar{x}, \bar{\lambda}) \le \sup_{\lambda} \inf_{x} L(x, \lambda). \tag{12.16}$$

On the other hand, $L(x, \lambda) \le \sup_{\lambda} L(x, \lambda)$ always, so taking the infimum with respect to x, we get

$$\inf_{x} L(x, \lambda) \le \inf_{x} \sup_{\lambda} L(x, \lambda).$$

Noting that the right-hand side is just a constant, taking the supremum of the left-hand side with respect to λ, we get

$$\sup_{\lambda} \inf_{x} L(x, \lambda) \le \inf_{x} \sup_{\lambda} L(x, \lambda). \tag{12.17}$$

Combining (12.16) and (12.17), it follows that

$$L(\bar{x}, \bar{\lambda}) = \inf_{x} \sup_{\lambda} L(x, \lambda) = \sup_{\lambda} \inf_{x} L(x, \lambda). \tag{12.18}$$

Define the functions

$$\theta(x) = \sup_{\lambda} L(x, \lambda),$$
$$\omega(\lambda) = \inf_{x} L(x, \lambda).$$

Then (12.18) is equivalent to

$$L(\bar{x}, \bar{\lambda}) = \inf_{x} \theta(x) = \sup_{\lambda} \omega(\lambda). \tag{12.19}$$

Note that by the definition of the Lagrangian (12.15), we have

$$\theta(x) = \sup_{\lambda} L(x, \lambda) = \begin{cases} f(x) & \text{if } g_i(x) \le 0 \text{ for all } i, \\ \infty & \text{if } g_i(x) > 0 \text{ for some } i. \end{cases}$$

Therefore the constrained minimization problem (12.14) is equivalent to the unconstrained minimization problem

$$\text{minimize } \theta(x). \tag{P}$$

For this reason the problem (P) is called the *primal problem*. In view of (12.19), define the *dual problem* by

$$\text{maximize } \omega(\lambda). \tag{D}$$

Then (12.19) implies that the primal and dual values coincide.

The above discussion suggests that to solve the constrained minimization problem (12.14) and hence the primal problem (P), it might be sufficient to solve the dual problem (D). Since $L(x, \lambda)$ is linear in λ, $\omega(\lambda) = \inf_x L(x, \lambda)$ is always a concave function of λ no matter what f or g_i's are. Therefore we can expect that solving the dual problem is much easier than solving the primal problem.

Example 12.2 (Linear programming). A typical linear programming problem is

$$\begin{aligned} &\text{minimize} && \langle c, x \rangle \\ &\text{subject to} && Ax \geq b, \end{aligned}$$

where $x \in \mathbb{R}^N$ is the vector of decision variables, $c \in \mathbb{R}^N$ is the vector of coefficients, A is an $M \times N$ matrix, and $b \in \mathbb{R}^M$ is a vector. The Lagrangian is

$$L(x, \lambda) = \langle c, x \rangle + \langle \lambda, b - Ax \rangle,$$

where $\lambda \in \mathbb{R}_+^M$ is the vector of Lagrange multipliers. Since

$$\begin{aligned} \omega(\lambda) = \inf_x L(x, \lambda) &= \inf_x [\langle c - A'\lambda, x \rangle + \langle b, \lambda \rangle] \\ &= \begin{cases} \langle b, \lambda \rangle, & (A'\lambda = c) \\ -\infty, & (A'\lambda \neq c) \end{cases} \end{aligned}$$

the dual problem is

$$\begin{aligned} &\text{maximize} && \langle b, \lambda \rangle \\ &\text{subject to} && A'\lambda = c, \ \lambda \geq 0. \end{aligned}$$

Example 12.3 (Entropy maximization). Let $p = (p_1, \dots, p_N)$ be a multinomial distribution, so $p_n \geq 0$ and $\sum_{n=1}^N p_n = 1$. The quantity

$$H(p) := - \sum_{n=1}^N p_n \log p_n$$

is called the *entropy* of p.

In many applications, we want to find the distribution p that has the maximum entropy satisfying some moment constraints. Suppose the constraints are given by

$$\sum_{n=1}^N a_{in} p_n = b_i,$$

where $i = 1, \ldots, I$. Since maximizing H is equivalent to minimizing $-H$, the problem is

$$\text{minimize} \qquad \sum_{n=1}^{N} p_n \log p_n$$

$$\text{subject to} \qquad \sum_{n=1}^{N} a_{in} p_n = b_i, \qquad (i = 0, \ldots, I) \qquad (12.20)$$

where a_{in}'s and b_i's are given and we define $a_{0n} = 1$ and $b_0 = 1$ to accommodate the constraint $\sum_n p_n = 1$ (accounting of probability).

If the number of unknown variables N is large (say $N \sim 10000$), then it would be difficult to solve the problem even using a computer since the objective function $p_n \log p_n$ is nonlinear. However, it turns out that the dual problem is very simple.

Although $p \log p$ is not well-defined when $p \leq 0$, define

$$p \log p = \begin{cases} 0, & (p = 0) \\ \infty. & (p < 0) \end{cases}$$

Then the constraint $p_n \geq 0$ is built into the problem. The Lagrangian is

$$L(p, \lambda) = \sum_{n=1}^{N} p_n \log p_n + \sum_{i=0}^{I} \lambda_i \left(b_i - \sum_{n=1}^{N} a_{in} p_n \right)$$

$$= \langle b, \lambda \rangle + \sum_{n=1}^{N} \left(p_n \log p_n - \langle a_n, \lambda \rangle p_n \right),$$

where $b = (b_0, \ldots, b_I)$ and $a_n = (a_{0n}, \ldots, a_{In})$. To derive the dual problem, we need to compute $\inf_p L(p, \lambda)$, which reduces to computing

$$\inf_p [p \log p - cp]$$

for $c = \langle a_n, \lambda \rangle$ above. However, this problem is a straightforward one-variable optimization problem. Since the objective function is convex, differentiating with respect to p, the first-order condition is

$$\log p + 1 - c = 0 \iff p = e^{c-1}, \qquad (12.21)$$

with minimum value

$$p \log p - cp = e^{c-1}(c - 1) - ce^{c-1} = -e^{c-1}.$$

Substituting $p_n = e^{\langle a_n, \lambda \rangle - 1}$ in the Lagrangian, after some algebra the objective function of the dual problem becomes

$$\omega(\lambda) = \inf_p L(p, \lambda) = \langle b, \lambda \rangle - \sum_{n=1}^{N} e^{\langle a_n, \lambda \rangle - 1}.$$

Hence the dual problem of (12.20) is

$$\text{maximize } \langle b, \lambda \rangle - \sum_{n=1}^{N} e^{\langle a_n, \lambda \rangle - 1}. \tag{12.22}$$

Numerically solving (12.22) is much easier than (12.20) because the dual problem (12.22) is unconstrained and the number of unknown variables $1 + I$ is typically much smaller than N. After solving (12.22), using (12.21), we may recover the optimal probability as $p_n = e^{\langle a_n, \lambda \rangle - 1}$. For more discussion of duality in entropy-like minimization problems, see Borwein and Lewis (1991).

Example 12.4 (General case). More generally, consider

$$\begin{aligned} \text{minimize} \qquad & f(x) \\ \text{subject to} \qquad & Ax = b. \end{aligned}$$

The Lagrangian is

$$\begin{aligned} L(x, \lambda) &= f(x) + \langle \lambda, b - Ax \rangle \\ &= \langle b, \lambda \rangle + f(x) - \langle A'\lambda, x \rangle. \end{aligned}$$

Therefore the dual objective function is

$$\omega(\lambda) = \inf_x L(x, \lambda) = \langle b, \lambda \rangle - f^*(A'\lambda),$$

where

$$f^*(\xi) := \sup_x [\langle \xi, x \rangle - f(x)]$$

is called the *convex conjugate function* of f. Noting that $\langle \xi, x \rangle - f(x)$ is affine in ξ, by Proposition 11.3, f^* is always convex. Therefore ω is concave. As long as the convex conjugate function f^* can be computed analytically, the primal problem can be solved by maximizing the dual objective function ω.

12.7 SUFFICIENT CONDITIONS

The Karush-Kuhn-Tucker theorem (Theorem 12.4) provides necessary conditions for optimality: if the constraint qualification holds, then a local solution must satisfy the KKT conditions (first-order and complementary slackness conditions). We next consider sufficient conditions.

The following theorem shows that for convex programming problems, the first-order condition is sufficient.

Theorem 12.8 (Sufficiency of KKT conditions for convex programming). *Consider the minimization problem (12.3), where f, g_i's are differentiable and convex and h_j's are affine. If $\bar{x}, \lambda, \mu$ satisfy the KKT conditions, then $\bar{x}$ is a solution.*

Proof. Let $L(x, \lambda, \mu)$ be the Lagrangian in (12.6). Since f, g_i's are convex, h_j's are affine, and $\lambda \geq 0$, by Proposition 11.2, L is convex in x. By assumption, the first-order condition (12.5a) holds at $\bar{x}$, so $\nabla_x L(\bar{x}, \lambda, \mu) = 0$. By Proposition 11.8, $\bar{x}$ achieves the minimum of L. Therefore, for any feasible x, it follows that

$$
\begin{aligned}
f(\bar{x}) &= f(\bar{x}) + \sum_{i=1}^{I} \lambda_i g_i(\bar{x}) + \sum_{j=1}^{J} \mu_j h_j(\bar{x}) && (\because (12.5b), \ h_j(\bar{x}) = 0) \\
&= L(\bar{x}, \lambda, \mu) \leq L(x, \lambda, \mu) && (\because \nabla_x L(\bar{x}, \lambda, \mu) = 0) \\
&= f(x) + \sum_{i=1}^{I} \lambda_i g_i(x) + \sum_{j=1}^{J} \mu_j h_j(x) \\
&\leq f(x). && (\because \lambda_i \geq 0, \ g_i(x) \leq 0, \ h_j(x) = 0)
\end{aligned}
$$

Therefore $\bar{x}$ is a solution. $\qquad\square$

Theorem 12.8 is very useful. The reason is that the KKT conditions are sufficient for optimality, and there is no need to verify the Slater condition (unlike for necessity in Theorem 12.4). A typical application is the utility maximization problem discussed in Chapter 4.

Recipe for solving convex minimization problems

(i) Verify that the functions f, g_i's are differentiable and convex and h_j's are affine.

(ii) Define the Lagrangian

$$
L(x, \lambda, \mu) = f(x) + \sum_{i=1}^{I} \lambda_i g_i(x) + \sum_{j=1}^{J} \mu_j h_j(x).
$$

Derive the first-order condition (12.5a) and complementary slackness condition (12.5b).

(iii) Solve these conditions. If there is a solution $\bar{x}$, it is a solution to the minimization problem.

When f, g_i are not convex but only quasi-convex, we can still give a sufficient condition for optimality. The following theorem is important for economic analysis because, in many situations, the objective function is quasi-convex but not necessarily convex.

Theorem 12.9 (Sufficiency of KKT conditions for quasi-convex programming). *Consider the minimization problem (12.3), where f, g_i's are differentiable and quasi-convex and h_j's are affine. If the Slater condition holds (so there exists x_0 such that $g_i(x_0) < 0$ for all i and $h_j(x_0) = 0$ for all j), $\bar{x}, \lambda, \mu$ satisfy the KKT conditions, and $\nabla f(\bar{x}) \neq 0$, then $\bar{x}$ is a solution.*

Proof. Since h_j is affine, we may write $h_j(x) = \langle a_j, x \rangle - b_j$. Then $\nabla h_j = a_j$. Let us show

$$\langle \nabla f(\bar{x}), x - \bar{x} \rangle \geq 0 \tag{12.23}$$

for all feasible x. Multiplying $x - \bar{x}$ as an inner product to the first-order condition (12.5a), we obtain

$$\langle \nabla f(\bar{x}), x - \bar{x} \rangle = - \sum_{i=1}^{I} \lambda_i \langle \nabla g_i(\bar{x}), x - \bar{x} \rangle - \sum_{j=1}^{J} \mu_j \langle a_j, x - \bar{x} \rangle. \tag{12.24}$$

Since $x, \bar{x}$ are both feasible, we have $\langle a_j, x \rangle = \langle a_j, \bar{x} \rangle = b_j$, so $\langle a_j, x - \bar{x} \rangle = 0$. Hence by (12.24), to show (12.23), it suffices to show $\lambda_i \langle \nabla g_i(\bar{x}), x - \bar{x} \rangle \leq 0$ for all i. If $g_i(\bar{x}) < 0$, by complementary slackness we have $\lambda_i = 0$, so the claim is trivial. If $g_i(\bar{x}) = 0$, since x is feasible, we have $g_i(x) \leq 0 = g_i(\bar{x})$. Hence by Proposition 11.10, we have $\langle \nabla g_i(\bar{x}), x - \bar{x} \rangle \leq 0$. Since $\lambda_i \geq 0$, we have $\lambda_i \langle \nabla g_i(\bar{x}), x - \bar{x} \rangle \leq 0$. Thus (12.23) holds.

Consider the point x_0 in the Slater condition. For sufficiently small $\epsilon > 0$, define $x_1 = x_0 + \epsilon \nabla f(\bar{x})$. Then

$$\langle \nabla f(\bar{x}), x_1 - \bar{x} \rangle = \langle \nabla f(\bar{x}), x_0 + \epsilon \nabla f(\bar{x}) - \bar{x} \rangle$$
$$= \langle \nabla f(\bar{x}), x_0 - \bar{x} \rangle + \epsilon \| \nabla f(\bar{x}) \|^2 > 0,$$

where the last inequality follows from (12.23) for $x = x_0$ and $\nabla f(\bar{x}) \neq 0$. Take any feasible x. Since (12.23) holds, for any $t \in (0, 1)$ we have

$$\langle \nabla f(\bar{x}), (1 - t)x + tx_1 - \bar{x} \rangle = \langle \nabla f(\bar{x}), (1 - t)(x - \bar{x}) + t(x_1 - \bar{x}) \rangle$$
$$= (1 - t) \langle \nabla f(\bar{x}), x - \bar{x} \rangle + t \langle \nabla f(\bar{x}), x_1 - \bar{x} \rangle > 0.$$

Since f is quasi-convex, by Proposition 11.10 this inequality implies that

$$f((1 - t)x + tx_1) > f(\bar{x}).$$

Letting $t \to 0$, we get $f(x) \geq f(\bar{x})$. Since x is arbitrary, $\bar{x}$ is a solution. $\qquad \square$

Example 12.5 (Utility maximization problem). Consider the utility maximization problem introduced in Chapter 0:

$$\begin{aligned} \text{maximize} \quad & u(x) \\ \text{subject to} \quad & \langle p, x \rangle \leq w, \\ & x \geq 0. \end{aligned}$$

Here $u : \mathbb{R}^N_{++} \to \mathbb{R}$ is the utility function, which we assume to be differentiable and quasi-concave, $p \gg 0$ is the price vector, and $w > 0$ is the wealth. Assume the agent prefers more consumption to less, so $\nabla u \gg 0$. Furthermore, to prevent zero consumption, suppose for each n the Inada condition $\partial u / \partial x_n \to \infty$ as $x_n \to 0$ holds. (See Proposition 4.4 for details.)

Since the utility maximization problem is a maximization problem, we convert the inequality constraint to $w - \langle p, x \rangle \geq 0$. Hence the Lagrangian is

$$L(x, \lambda) = u(x) + \lambda(w - \langle p, x \rangle).$$

The first-order condition is

$$0 = \nabla_x L(x, \lambda) = \nabla u(x) - \lambda p.$$

By assumption, we have $\nabla u(x) \neq 0$. Therefore if we can find $\bar{x}, \lambda \in \mathbb{R}^N$ such that the first-order condition and the complementary slackness condition $\lambda(w - \langle p, x \rangle) = 0$ hold, by Theorem 12.9, $\bar{x}$ is a solution. If in addition u is strictly quasi-concave, then the solution is unique by Proposition 11.1.

For general nonlinear programming problems, we can only hope to obtain sufficient conditions for local optimality. Consider the minimization problem (12.3). Assume that the KKT conditions (12.5) hold at $\bar{x}$ with corresponding Lagrange multipliers $\lambda \in \mathbb{R}^I_+$ and $\mu \in \mathbb{R}^J$. Recall that the active set of the inequality constraints is $I(\bar{x}) = \{i : g_i(\bar{x}) = 0\}$. Let $\tilde{I}(\bar{x}) = \{i : \lambda_i > 0\}$ be the set of constraints such that the Lagrange multiplier is positive. Since $\lambda_i g_i(\bar{x}) = 0$ by complementary slackness, $\lambda_i > 0$ implies $g_i(\bar{x}) = 0$, so necessarily $\tilde{I}(\bar{x}) \subset I(\bar{x})$. Define the cone

$$\tilde{L}_C(\bar{x}) = \big\{ y \in \mathbb{R}^N : (\forall i \in I(\bar{x}) \backslash \tilde{I}(\bar{x})) \, \langle \nabla g_i(\bar{x}), y \rangle \leq 0,$$
$$(\forall i \in \tilde{I}(\bar{x})) \, \langle \nabla g_i(\bar{x}), y \rangle = 0, (\forall j) \, \langle \nabla h_j(\bar{x}), y \rangle = 0 \big\}. \quad (12.25)$$

Clearly $\tilde{L}_C(\bar{x}) \subset L_C(\bar{x})$. The following theorem gives a second-order sufficient condition for local optimality.

Theorem 12.10 (Sufficient condition for local optimality). *Suppose that f, g_i, h_j's are C^2, the KKT conditions (12.5) hold at $x = \bar{x}$, and*

$$\langle y, \nabla^2_x L(\bar{x}, \lambda, \mu) y \rangle > 0 \quad (12.26)$$

for all $0 \neq y \in \tilde{L}_C(\bar{x})$. Then $\bar{x}$ is a strict local solution to the minimization problem (12.3).

Proof. Suppose that $\bar{x}$ is not a strict local solution. Then we can take a sequence $C \ni x^k \to \bar{x}$ such that $f(x^k) \leq f(\bar{x})$. Let $\alpha_k = 1 / \|x^k - \bar{x}\| > 0$. Then $\|\alpha_k(x^k - \bar{x})\| = 1$, so by taking a subsequence if necessary we may assume $\alpha_k(x^k - \bar{x}) \to y$ with $\|y\| = 1$. Let us show that $y \in \tilde{L}_C(\bar{x})$.

Multiplying both sides of

$$f(x^k) - f(\bar{x}) \leq 0, \ g_i(x^k) - g_i(\bar{x}) \leq 0 \ (i \in I(\bar{x})), \ h_j(x^k) - h_j(\bar{x}) = 0$$

by α_k and letting $k \to \infty$, we get

$$\langle \nabla f(\bar{x}), y \rangle \leq 0, \ \langle \nabla g_i(\bar{x}), y \rangle \leq 0 \ (i \in I(\bar{x})), \ \langle \nabla h_j(\bar{x}), y \rangle = 0. \qquad (12.27)$$

Multiplying both sides of the first-order condition (12.5a) by y as an inner product, noting that $\lambda_i = 0$ if $i \notin I(\bar{x})$ by complementary slackness, and using (12.27), we get

$$\langle \nabla f(\bar{x}), y \rangle + \sum_{i \in I(\bar{x})} \lambda_i \langle \nabla g_i(\bar{x}), y \rangle = 0.$$

Again by (12.27) it must be $\langle \nabla f(\bar{x}), y \rangle = 0$ and $\lambda_i \langle \nabla g_i(\bar{x}), y \rangle = 0$ for all $i \in I(\bar{x})$. Therefore if $i \in \tilde{I}(\bar{x})$, so $\lambda_i > 0$, it must be $\langle \nabla g_i(\bar{x}), y \rangle = 0$. Hence by definition we have $y \in \tilde{L}_C(\bar{x})$.

Since $f(x^k) \leq f(\bar{x})$, $\lambda_i \geq 0$, $g_i(x^k) \leq 0$, and $\lambda_i g_i(\bar{x}) = 0$, it follows that

$$L(x^k, \lambda, \mu) = f(x^k) + \sum_{i \in I(\bar{x})} \lambda_i g_i(x^k) \leq f(\bar{x}) = L(\bar{x}, \lambda, \mu).$$

By Taylor's theorem, we have

$$\begin{aligned} 0 \geq L(x^k, \lambda, \mu) - L(\bar{x}, \lambda, \mu) &= \langle \nabla_x L(\bar{x}, \lambda, \mu), x^k - \bar{x} \rangle \\ &+ \frac{1}{2} \langle x^k - \bar{x}, \nabla_x^2 L(\bar{x}, \lambda, \mu)(x^k - \bar{x}) \rangle + o(\|x^k - \bar{x}\|^2). \end{aligned}$$

By the KKT conditions, the first term in the right-hand side is zero. Multiplying both sides by α_k^2 and letting $k \to \infty$, we get

$$0 \geq \frac{1}{2} \langle y, \nabla_x^2 L(\bar{x}, \lambda, \mu) y \rangle,$$

which contradicts (12.26). Therefore $\bar{x}$ is a strict local solution. $\qquad \square$

12.8 PARAMETRIC DIFFERENTIABILITY

In many applications, the optimization problem contains some parameters. For example, in the utility maximization problem

$$\begin{aligned} &\text{maximize} &&u(x) \\ &\text{subject to} &&\langle p, x \rangle \leq w, \end{aligned}$$

where $u : \mathbb{R}_{++}^N \to \mathbb{R}$ is the utility function, $p \in \mathbb{R}_{++}^N$ is the price vector, and $w > 0$ is the wealth, the control variable is x while p, w are parameters. In such cases, we may view the solution $\bar{x}$ as a function $\bar{x}(p, w)$ of parameters, and we may be interested in knowing how the parameters p, w affect the solution as well as the optimal value.

More generally, consider the parametric minimization problem

$$\underset{x}{\text{minimize}} \qquad f(x, \theta)$$

$$\text{subject to} \qquad g_i(x, \theta) \le 0 \qquad\qquad (i = 1, \ldots, I). \qquad (12.28)$$

Here $x \in \mathbb{R}^N$ is the control variable, $\theta \in \Theta$ is a parameter (Θ is an open set in some Euclidean space), and for simplicity we consider only inequality constraints. (The case with equality constraints is similar and is left to Problem 12.5.) Let

$$\phi(\theta) = \underset{x}{\inf} \left\{ f(x, \theta) : (\forall i) g_i(x, \theta) \le 0 \right\}$$

be the minimum value function. We are interested in how $\phi(\theta)$ changes together with θ.

Recall the second-order sufficient condition for optimality (Theorem 12.10). The *active set* of the inequality constraints is $I(\bar{x}) = \{i : g_i(\bar{x}) = 0\}$, and let $\tilde{I}(\bar{x}) = \{i : \lambda_i > 0\}$ be the set of constraints such that the Lagrange multiplier is positive. Since $\lambda_i g_i(\bar{x}) = 0$ by complementary slackness, $\lambda_i > 0$ implies $g_i(\bar{x}) = 0$, so necessarily $\tilde{I}(\bar{x}) \subset I(\bar{x})$. Define the cone $\tilde{L}_C(\bar{x})$ by (12.25). The second-order sufficient condition for local optimality is (12.26).

The following theorem shows that, under the linear independence constraint qualification (LICQ) and strict complementary slackness, the solution and Lagrange multipliers of the parametric optimization problem (12.28) depend smoothly on the parameter θ.

Theorem 12.11 (Parametric differentiability). *Suppose that the parametric optimization problem* (12.28) *has a local solution* $\bar{x} \in \mathbb{R}^N$ *for parameter* $\bar{\theta} \in \Theta$. *Suppose that* f, g_i's *are* C^2 *in* x *and* C^1 *in* θ *around* $(\bar{x}, \bar{\theta})$. *Assume that*

(i) the vectors $\left\{ \nabla_x g_i(\bar{x}, \bar{\theta}) \right\}_{i \in I(\bar{x})}$ *are linearly independent, so the Karush-Kuhn-Tucker theorem holds with Lagrange multiplier* $\bar{\lambda} \in \mathbb{R}_+^I$,

(ii) strict complementary slackness holds, so $g_i(\bar{x}, \bar{\theta}) = 0$ *implies* $\bar{\lambda}_i > 0$ *and therefore* $I(\bar{x}) = \tilde{I}(\bar{x})$, *and*

(iii) the second-order condition (12.26) *holds.*

Then there exists a neighborhood U *of* $\bar{\theta}$ *and* C^1 *functions* $x(\theta), \lambda(\theta)$ *such that for any* $\theta \in U$, $x(\theta)$ *is the local solution to the parametric optimization problem* (12.28) *and* $\lambda(\theta)$ *is the corresponding Lagrange multiplier.*

In our case, since strict complementary slackness holds and there are no equality constraints, condition (12.26) reduces to

$$y \ne 0, \ (\forall i \in I(\bar{x})) \left\langle \nabla_x g_i(\bar{x}, \bar{\theta}), y \right\rangle = 0 \implies \left\langle y, \nabla_x^2 L(\bar{x}, \bar{\lambda}, \bar{\theta}) y \right\rangle > 0. \quad (12.29)$$

We need the following lemma in order to prove the theorem.

Lemma 12.12. *Let everything be as in Theorem 12.11. Define the* $(N+I) \times (N+I)$ *matrix* A *by*

$$A = \begin{bmatrix} \nabla_x^2 L & \nabla_x g_1 & \cdots & \nabla_x g_I \\ \bar{\lambda}_1 \nabla_x g_1' & g_1 & \cdots & 0 \\ \vdots & \vdots & \ddots & \vdots \\ \bar{\lambda}_I \nabla_x g_I' & 0 & \cdots & g_I \end{bmatrix},$$

where all functions are evaluated at $(\bar{x}, \bar{\lambda}, \bar{\theta})$. *Then* A *is invertible.*

Proof. Suppose that

$$A \begin{bmatrix} v \\ w \end{bmatrix} = 0,$$

where $v \in \mathbb{R}^N$ and $w \in \mathbb{R}^I$. By Theorem 5.9, it suffices to show $v = 0$ and $w = 0$. By the definition of A, we get

$$\nabla_x^2 L v + \sum_{i=1}^{I} w_i \nabla_x g_i = 0, \tag{12.30a}$$

$$(\forall i) \; \bar{\lambda}_i \langle \nabla_x g_i, v \rangle + w_i g_i = 0. \tag{12.30b}$$

For $i \in I(\bar{x})$ (hence $g_i(\bar{x}, \bar{\theta}) = 0$), by (12.30b) and strict complementary slackness we have $\bar{\lambda}_i > 0$ and therefore $\langle \nabla_x g_i, v \rangle = 0$. For $i \notin I(\bar{x})$ (hence $g_i(\bar{x}, \bar{\theta}) < 0$), again by (12.30b) and strict complementary slackness we have $\bar{\lambda}_i = 0$ and therefore $w_i = 0$. Therefore (12.30a) becomes

$$\nabla_x^2 L v + \sum_{i \in I(\bar{x})} w_i \nabla_x g_i = 0. \tag{12.31}$$

Multiplying (12.31) by v as an inner product and using $\langle \nabla_x g_i, v \rangle = 0$ for $i \in I(\bar{x})$, we obtain

$$\langle v, \nabla_x^2 L v \rangle = 0.$$

By condition (12.29), it must be $v = 0$. Then by (12.31) we obtain

$$\sum_{i \in I(\bar{x})} w_i \nabla_x g_i = 0.$$

Since $\{\nabla_x g_i\}_{i \in I(\bar{x})}$ are linearly independent, it must be $w_i = 0$ for all i. Therefore $v = 0$ and $w = 0$. □

Proof of Theorem 12.11. Define $f : \mathbb{R}^N \times \mathbb{R}^I \times \Theta \to \mathbb{R}^N \times \mathbb{R}^I$ by

$$f(x, \lambda, \theta) = \begin{bmatrix} \nabla_x L(x, \lambda, \theta) \\ \lambda_1 g_i(x, \theta) \\ \vdots \\ \lambda_I g_I(x, \theta) \end{bmatrix}.$$

Then the Jacobian of f with respect to (x, λ) evaluated at $(\bar{x}, \bar{\lambda}, \bar{\theta})$ is A, which is invertible by Lemma 12.12. Furthermore, since $\bar{x}$ is a local solution corresponding to $\theta = \bar{\theta}$, by the KKT Theorem we have $f(\bar{x}, \bar{\lambda}, \bar{\theta}) = 0$. Therefore by the implicit function theorem (Theorem 8.3), there exists a neighborhood U of $\bar{\theta}$ and C^1 functions $x(\theta), \lambda(\theta)$ such that

$$f(x(\theta), \lambda(\theta), \theta) = 0$$

for $\theta \in U$. By the second-order sufficient condition (Theorem 12.10), $x(\theta)$ is the strict local solution to the parametric optimization problem (12.28) and $\lambda(\theta)$ is the corresponding Lagrange multiplier. $\qquad\square$

If we further assume the quasi-convexity of objective and constraint functions, we can strengthen Theorem 12.11 as follows.

Corollary 12.13 (Parametric differentiability with quasi-convexity). *Consider the setting in Theorem 12.11. Suppose in addition that each g_i is quasi-convex and f is differentiably strictly quasi-convex in x in the sense that*

$$\langle \nabla_x f(x, \theta), v \rangle = 0 \implies \langle v, \nabla_x^2 f(x, \theta) v \rangle > 0 \qquad (12.32)$$

for all $v \neq 0$ (see Proposition 11.11). Then under conditions (i) and (ii), the conclusion of Theorem 12.11 is true.

Proof. By Theorem 12.11, it suffices to show the second-order condition, which reduces to (12.29). Under the maintained assumptions, note that the cone $\tilde{L}_C(\bar{x})$ in (12.25) is given by

$$\tilde{L}_C(\bar{x}) = \left\{ y \in \mathbb{R}^N : (\forall i \in I(\bar{x})) \, \langle \nabla_x g_i, y \rangle = 0 \right\},$$

where we write $\nabla_x g_i = \nabla_x g_i(\bar{x}, \bar{\theta})$. Since each g_i is quasi-convex, by Proposition 11.11, for any $0 \neq y \in \tilde{L}_C(\bar{x})$, we have $\langle y, \nabla_x^2 g_i y \rangle \geq 0$. By the first-order condition, we have

$$\nabla_x f = -\sum_{i=1}^{I} \lambda_i \nabla_x g_i = -\sum_{i \in I(\bar{x})} \lambda_i \nabla_x g_i.$$

Multiplying $0 \neq y \in \tilde{L}_C(\bar{x})$ as an inner product, we obtain

$$\langle \nabla_x f, y \rangle = -\sum_{i \in I(\bar{x})} \lambda_i \langle \nabla_x g_i, y \rangle = 0.$$

Therefore using (12.32), we obtain $\langle y, \nabla_x^2 f y \rangle > 0$. Therefore

$$\langle y, \nabla_x^2 L y \rangle = \langle y, \nabla_x^2 f y \rangle + \sum_{i \in I(\bar{x})} \lambda_i \langle y, \nabla_x^2 g_i y \rangle > 0,$$

so (12.29) holds. $\qquad\square$

Using parametric differentiability and applying the chain rule, we obtain the following envelope theorem.

Theorem 12.14 (Envelope theorem). *Let everything be as in Theorem 12.11. Let $\phi(\theta) = f(x(\theta), \theta)$ be the local minimum value function and*

$$L(x, \lambda, \theta) = f(x, \theta) + \sum_{i=1}^{I} \lambda_i g_i(x, \theta)$$

the Lagrangian. Then ϕ is differentiable and

$$\nabla \phi(\theta) = \nabla_\theta L(x(\theta), \lambda(\theta), \theta). \tag{12.33}$$

Proof. The existence and differentiability of ϕ follow from Theorem 12.11. By the definition of ϕ and complementary slackness, we obtain

$$\phi(\theta) = f(x(\theta), \theta) = L(x(\theta), \lambda(\theta), \theta).$$

Differentiating both sides with respect to θ and applying the chain rule, we get

$$\underbrace{D_\theta \phi(\theta)}_{1 \times H} = \underbrace{D_x L}_{1 \times N} \underbrace{D_\theta x(\theta)}_{N \times H} + \underbrace{D_\lambda L}_{1 \times I} \underbrace{D_\theta \lambda(\theta)}_{I \times H} + \underbrace{D_\theta L}_{1 \times H},$$

where H denotes the dimension of Θ. By the KKT theorem, we have $D_x L = 0$. By strict complementary slackness, we have $\lambda_i(\theta) = 0$ for $i \notin I(\bar{x})$ and

$$D_{\lambda_i} L(x(\theta), \lambda(\theta), \theta) = g_i(x(\theta), \theta) = 0$$

for $i \in I(\bar{x})$, so $D_\lambda L D_\theta \lambda(\theta) = 0$. Therefore $\nabla \phi(\theta) = \nabla_\theta L(x(\theta), \lambda(\theta), \theta)$. □

Remark. The result (12.33) implies that we can compute the derivative of ϕ by differentiating the Lagrangian with respect to the parameter θ alone, treating x and λ as constants.

Corollary 12.15. *Consider the special case*

$$\begin{array}{ll} \underset{x}{\text{minimize}} & f(x) \\ \text{subject to} & g_i(x) \leq \theta_i \qquad\qquad (i = 1, \dots, I). \end{array}$$

Then $\nabla \phi(\theta) = -\lambda(\theta)$.

Proof. The Lagrangian is

$$L(x, \lambda, \theta) = f(x) + \sum_{i=1}^{I} \lambda_i [g_i(x) - \theta_i].$$

By the envelope theorem, $\nabla \phi(\theta) = \nabla_\theta L(x(\theta), \lambda(\theta), \theta) = -\lambda(\theta)$. □

Remark. Corollary 12.15 implies that the Lagrange multiplier equals the rate of change in the optimal value when the corresponding constraint is relaxed or tightened. For this reason, sometimes we interpret the Lagrange multiplier as the *shadow price*.

12.9 PARAMETRIC CONTINUITY

For a parametric optimization problem such as (12.28), the sufficient conditions for parametric differentiability in Theorem 12.11 are rather strong. In many applications, we may not need differentiability but only continuity. Thus we seek to provide relatively weak sufficient conditions for parametric continuity.

To this end, we introduce some terminology. Let X, Y be nonempty sets. If for each $x \in X$ there corresponds a subset $\Gamma(x) \subset Y$, we say that Γ is a *correspondence* (or *multi-valued function*) from X to Y and denote it by $\Gamma : X \twoheadrightarrow Y$. Note that we use an arrow with two heads "$\twoheadrightarrow$" for a correspondence, while we use the usual arrow "$\rightarrow$" for a function. Another common notation for a correspondence is $\Gamma : X \rightrightarrows Y$. Clearly, a function f can be viewed as a correspondence Γ by considering the singleton $\Gamma(x) = \{f(x)\}$. For any property P (e.g., nonempty, compact, or convex, etc.), we say that Γ is P-valued if $\Gamma(x)$ satisfies property P for all $x \in X$.

We now define notions of continuity for correspondences. Recall from §1.6, 1.A that a function f from a topological space X to another Y is continuous at $x_0 \in X$ if for any open $V \ni f(x_0)$, there exists an open $U \ni x_0$ such that $x \in U$ implies $f(x) \in V$. There are two natural generalizations of continuity for correspondences.

Definition 12.1 (Upper and lower hemicontinuity). Let X, Y be topological spaces and $\Gamma : X \twoheadrightarrow Y$. Then

- Γ is *upper hemicontinuous (uhc)* at x_0 if for any open $V \supset \Gamma(x_0)$, there exists an open $U \ni x_0$ such that $x \in U$ implies $\Gamma(x) \subset V$,

- Γ is *lower hemicontinuous (lhc)* at x_0 if for any open V with $\Gamma(x_0) \cap V \neq \emptyset$, there exists an open $U \ni x_0$ such that $x \in U$ implies $\Gamma(x) \cap V \neq \emptyset$.

A correspondence that is both upper and lower hemicontinuous is called *continuous*. When $\Gamma(x) = \{f(x)\}$, clearly upper and lower hemicontinuity of Γ are both equivalent to the continuity of f.

The intuition for the upper and lower hemicontinuity is the following. If Γ is uhc at x_0, then $\Gamma(x)$ is included in V whenever V includes $\Gamma(x_0)$ and x is close to x_0. This means that uhc correspondences can suddenly "expand" but not "shrink" (Figure 12.4). If Γ is lhc at x_0, then $\Gamma(x)$ intersects V whenever V intersects $\Gamma(x_0)$ and x is close to x_0. This means that lhc correspondences can suddenly "shrink" but not "expand".

In most applications, we work with metric spaces such as the Euclidean space. In this case a function $f : X \rightarrow Y$ is continuous at $x \in X$ if and only if for all sequences $\{x_k\}_{k=1}^{\infty} \subset X$ such that $x_k \rightarrow x$, we have $f(x_k) \rightarrow f(x)$ (Proposition 1.8). Similar sequential characterizations of upper and lower hemicontinuity are possible. Below, let X, Y be some metric spaces. Recall the notion of the open ball

$$B_\epsilon(x_0) := \{x \in X : d(x, x_0) < \epsilon\}.$$

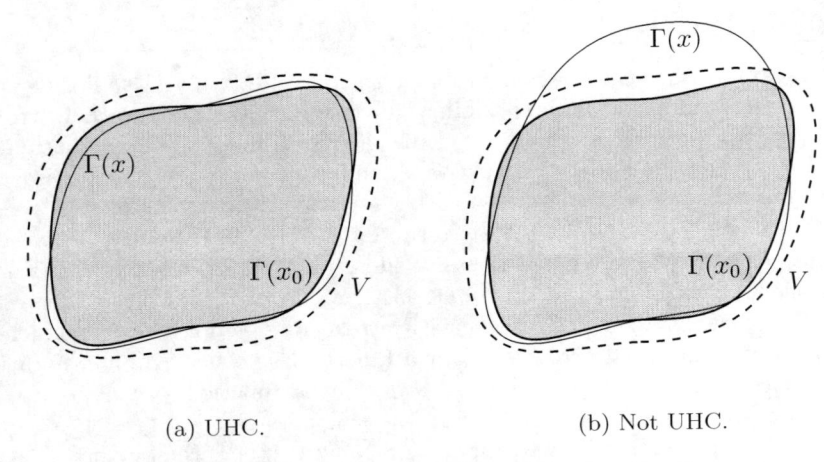

(a) UHC.   (b) Not UHC.

FIGURE 12.4: Upper hemicontinuous correspondence.

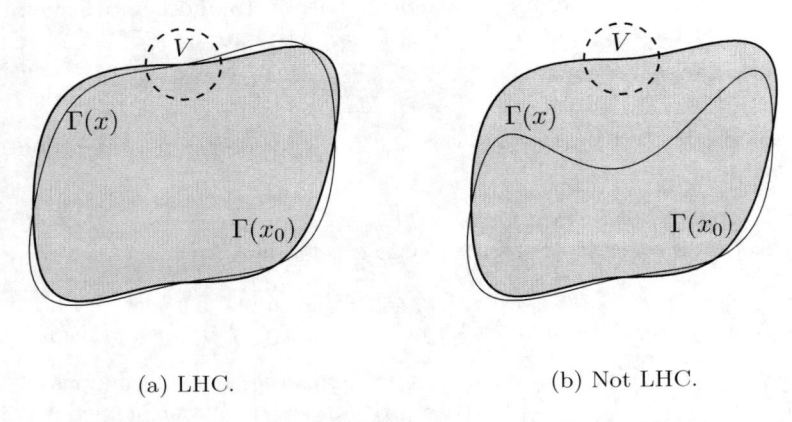

(a) LHC.   (b) Not LHC.

FIGURE 12.5: Lower hemicontinuous correspondence.

Proposition 12.16 (Sequential characterization of upper hemicontinuity). *Let $\Gamma : X \twoheadrightarrow Y$ be nonempty. Then the following conditions are equivalent.*

(i) Γ is upper hemicontinuous at x and $\Gamma(x)$ is compact.

(ii) For any sequence $\{(x_k, y_k)\} \subset X \times Y$ with $x_k \to x$ and $y_k \in \Gamma(x_k)$, there exists a convergent subsequence $\{y_{k_l}\}$ such that $y_{k_l} \to y \in \Gamma(x)$.

Proof. $(i) \implies (ii)$: Suppose Γ is uhc at x and $\Gamma(x)$ is compact. Take any sequence $\{(x_k, y_k)\} \subset X \times Y$ with $x_k \to x$ and $y_k \in \Gamma(x_k)$. For each k, let y_k' be the point in $\Gamma(x)$ that is closest to y_k, so

$$y_k' \in \arg\min_{y \in \Gamma(x)} d(y, y_k),$$

which exists by the extreme value theorem because $\Gamma(x)$ is compact. Since $y'_k \in \Gamma(x)$ and $\Gamma(x)$ is compact, we may take a subsequence such that $y'_{k_l} \to y_0 \in \Gamma(x)$. Therefore to show that $\{y_k\}$ has a subsequence converging to $y_0 \in \Gamma(x)$, it suffices to show that $\liminf_{k \to \infty} d(y'_k, y_k) = 0$. Suppose to the contrary that $\liminf_{k \to \infty} d(y'_k, y_k) > \epsilon > 0$. Then $d(y'_k, y_k) > \epsilon$ for large enough k, so for any $y \in \Gamma(x)$, we have

$$d(y, y_k) \geq d(y'_k, y_k) > \epsilon. \tag{12.34}$$

If we take $V = \bigcup_{y \in \Gamma(x)} B_{\epsilon/2}(y)$, then clearly V is open and $\Gamma(x) \subset V$. Since Γ is uhc, for large enough k we have $\Gamma(x_k) \subset V$, so in particular $d(y, y_k) < \epsilon/2$ for some $y \in \Gamma(x)$, which contradicts (12.34).

$(ii) \implies (i)$: If we set $x_k = x$ for all k, we immediately see that $\Gamma(x)$ is compact. Suppose to the contrary that Γ is not uhc at x. By the definition of upper hemicontinuity, there exists an open $V \supset \Gamma(x)$ and a sequence $\{x_k\}$ such that $x_k \to x$ but $\Gamma(x_k) \not\subset V$. Take any $y_k \in \Gamma(x_k) \backslash V$. Then $y_k \in V^c$, which is a closed set, so for any convergent subsequence $\{y_{k_l}\}$ with $y_{k_l} \to y$, we have $y \in V^c \subset \Gamma(x)^c$. Therefore $y \notin \Gamma(x)$, so $\{y_k\}$ does not have a subsequence converging to a point in $\Gamma(x)$, which is a contradiction. □

Regarding lower hemicontinuity, we have the following sequential characterization.

Proposition 12.17 (Sequential characterization of lower hemicontinuity). *Let $\Gamma : X \twoheadrightarrow Y$ be nonempty. Then the following conditions are equivalent.*

(i) Γ is lower hemicontinuous at x.

(ii) For any sequence $\{x_k\}$ with $x_k \to x$ and any $y \in \Gamma(x)$, there exists a subsequence $\{x_{k_l}\} \subset X$ and a sequence $\{y_l\} \subset Y$ such that $y_l \in \Gamma(x_{k_l})$ for all l and $y_l \to y$.

Proof. $(i) \implies (ii)$: Suppose Γ is lhc at x. Take any sequence $\{x_k\}$ with $x_k \to x$ and any $y \in \Gamma(x)$. Let $V_l := B_{1/l}(y)$ be the open ball in Y with center y and radius $1/l > 0$. Clearly $\Gamma(x) \cap V_l \neq \emptyset$. By the definition of lower hemicontinuity, there exists an open $U_l \ni x$ such that $x' \in U_l$ implies $\Gamma(x') \cap V_l \neq \emptyset$. Since $x_k \to x \in U_l$, we can take x_{k_l} such that $x_{k_l} \in U_l$. Then $\Gamma(x_{k_l}) \cap V_l \neq \emptyset$, so we can take $y_l \in \Gamma(x_{k_l}) \cap V_l$. This implies $y_l \in \Gamma(x_{k_l})$ and $d(y_l, y) < 1/l$, so $y_l \to y$.

$(ii) \implies (i)$: Suppose Γ is not lhc at x. By the definition of lower hemicontinuity, there exists an open V with $\Gamma(x) \cap V \neq \emptyset$ such that for any open $U \ni x$, there exists $x' \in U$ such that $\Gamma(x') \cap V = \emptyset$. Take any $y \in \Gamma(x) \cap V$. For each k, let $U_k := B_{1/k}(x)$ be the open ball in X with center x and radius $1/k$ and take $x_k \in U_k$ such that $\Gamma(x_k) \cap V = \emptyset$. Then for any subsequence $\{x_{k_l}\}$ and any $y_l \in \Gamma(x_{k_l})$, we have $y_l \notin V$. Since V is open and $y \in V$, it cannot be $y_l \to y$. □

The next maximum theorem guarantees that the maximum value of a parametric maximization problem is continuous and the solution set is upper hemicontinuous.

Theorem 12.18 (Maximum theorem). *Let X, Y be nonempty metric spaces, $f : X \times Y \to \mathbb{R}$ be a continuous function, and $\Gamma : X \twoheadrightarrow Y$ be a nonempty, compact, continuous correspondence. Let*

$$f^*(x) = \max_{y \in \Gamma(x)} f(x, y),$$

$$\Gamma^*(x) = \arg\max_{y \in \Gamma(x)} f(x, y) \neq \emptyset,$$

which exist by the extreme value theorem. Then $f^* : X \to \mathbb{R}$ is continuous and $\Gamma^* : X \twoheadrightarrow Y$ is upper hemicontinuous.

Although the proof of the maximum theorem is not so difficult, it is clearer to weaken the assumptions and prove two weaker statements. For that purpose, recall the definition of semicontinuity of functions in §1.6.

Lemma 12.19. *Let $f : X \times Y \to \mathbb{R}$ be upper semicontinuous and $\Gamma : X \twoheadrightarrow Y$ be nonempty, compact, and upper hemicontinuous. Then $f^*(x) = \max_{y \in \Gamma(x)} f(x, y)$ is upper semicontinuous.*

Proof. Take any sequence $\{x_k\}$ with $x_k \to x$. Take a subsequence $\{x_{k_l}\}$ such that $f^*(x_{k_l}) \to \limsup_{k \to \infty} f^*(x_k)$. For each l, take $y_{k_l} \in \Gamma(x_{k_l})$ such that $f(x_{k_l}, y_{k_l}) = f^*(x_{k_l})$. Since Γ is uhc and compact, by Proposition 12.16, by taking a subsequence if necessary, we may assume $y_{k_l} \to y \in \Gamma(x)$. Since f is usc, we have

$$f^*(x) \geq f(x, y) \geq \limsup_{l \to \infty} f(x_{k_l}, y_{k_l}) = \lim_{l \to \infty} f^*(x_{k_l}) = \limsup_{k \to \infty} f^*(x_k).$$

Therefore f^* is upper semicontinuous. □

Lemma 12.20. *Let $f : X \times Y \to \mathbb{R}$ be lower semicontinuous and $\Gamma : X \twoheadrightarrow Y$ be nonempty and lower hemicontinuous. Then $f^*(x) = \sup_{y \in \Gamma(x)} f(x, y)$ is lower semicontinuous.*

Proof. Take any sequence $\{x_k\}$ with $x_k \to x$ and any $u < f^*(x)$. By the definition of f^*, we can take $y \in \Gamma(x)$ such that $f(x, y) > u$. By taking a subsequence if necessary, assume $f^*(x_k) \to \liminf_{k \to \infty} f^*(x_k)$. Since Γ is lhc, by Proposition 12.17 we may take a subsequence $\{x_{k_l}\}$ and a sequence $\{y_l\}$ such that $y_l \in \Gamma(x_{k_l})$ for all l and $y_l \to y$. Then $f^*(x_{k_l}) \geq f(x_{k_l}, y_l)$. Since f is lower semicontinuous, we have

$$\liminf_{k \to \infty} f^*(x_k) = \liminf_{l \to \infty} f^*(x_{k_l}) \geq \liminf_{l \to \infty} f(x_{k_l}, y_l) \geq f(x, y) > u.$$

Letting $u \uparrow f^*(x)$, it follows that f^* is lower semicontinuous. □

Proof of Theorem 12.18. By Lemmas 12.19 and 12.20, f^* is continuous. Since $\Gamma^*(x) \subset \Gamma(x)$ and Γ is compact, so is Γ^*. Take any $x_k \to x$, $y_k \in \Gamma^*(x_k)$, and assume $y_{k_l} \to y$. Since f and f^* are continuous, we have

$$f(x, y) = \lim_{l \to \infty} f(x_{k_l}, y_{k_l}) = \lim_{l \to \infty} f^*(x_{k_l}) = f^*(x),$$

so $y \in \Gamma^*(x)$. Hence by Proposition 12.16, Γ^* is uhc. $\qquad\square$

Remark. The general form of the maximum theorem (Theorem 12.18) first appeared in print in Berge (1963), though special cases have been used before such as Arrow and Debreu (1954). For a more complete treatment of correspondences, see Aliprantis and Border (2006, Ch. 17).

PROBLEMS

12.1. Let C be any set and suppose $\bar{x} \in \text{int}\, C$ (interior point of C).

  (i) Compute the tangent cone $T_C(\bar{x})$ and the normal cone $N_C(\bar{x})$.

  (ii) Interpret Theorem 12.2.

12.2. Let $p > 1$, and define the function $f : \mathbb{R}^N_+ \to \mathbb{R}$ by

$$f(x) = \frac{1}{p} \sum_{n=1}^N x_n^p.$$

  (i) Prove that f is strictly convex.

  (ii) Solve the constrained minimization problem

$$\text{minimize} \qquad\qquad f(x)$$
$$\text{subject to} \qquad\qquad \sum_{n=1}^N x_n = 1,$$
$$(\forall n) x_n \geq 0.$$

  (iii) Solve the constrained maximization problem

$$\text{maximize} \qquad\qquad f(x)$$
$$\text{subject to} \qquad\qquad \sum_{n=1}^N x_n = 1,$$
$$(\forall n) x_n \geq 0.$$

  (Hint: since f is strictly convex, if $x_1 \neq x_2$ satisfy the constraints and $\alpha \in (0, 1)$, then $f((1-\alpha)x_1 + \alpha x_2) < (1-\alpha)f(x_1) + \alpha f(x_2)$ so $(1-\alpha)x_1 + \alpha x_2$ cannot be a solution.)

(iv) Find the best constants $0 \leq c \leq C$ to satisfy the inequality

$$c\|x\|_1 \leq \|x\|_p \leq C\|x\|_1,$$

where $\|x\|_p$ denotes the ℓ^p norm of $x \in \mathbb{R}^N$. (The best constants mean the largest c and smallest C satisfying the above inequality for all x.)

12.3. Let $x \in \mathbb{R}$ and consider the constraints (i) $x \leq 0$ and (ii) $x^3 \leq 0$.

(i) Show that the two constraints are equivalent, and compute the tangent cone at $x = 0$.

(ii) Compute the linearizing cones corresponding to each constraint at $\bar{x} = 0$. Are they the same?

(iii) Construct an example such that the Slater condition $g_i(x_0) < 0$ holds and g_i is quasi-convex (but not convex) but the KKT conditions do not hold.

12.4. Let $\{a_j\}_{j=1}^J$ be vectors in $\mathbb{R}^N$ and $\{b_j\}_{j=1}^J$ be scalars. Define the set

$$C = \left\{x \in \mathbb{R}^N : (\forall j)\, \langle a_j, x \rangle = b_j\right\}.$$

Show that if $\{a_j\}_{j=1}^J$ are linearly dependent, then either $C = \emptyset$ or some constraints are redundant (i.e., we may drop some j without affecting the set C).

12.5. Extend Theorem 12.11 to the case with equality constraints.

12.6. Compute the convex conjugate functions of the following functions.

(i) $f(x) = \frac{1}{p}|x|^p$, where $p > 1$. (Express the solution using $q > 1$ such that $1/p + 1/q = 1$.)

(ii) $f(x) = \begin{cases} \infty, & (x < 0) \\ 0, & (x = 0) \\ x \log \frac{x}{a}, & (x > 0) \end{cases}$ where $a > 0$.

(iii) $f(x) = \begin{cases} \infty, & (x \leq 0) \\ -\log x. & (x > 0) \end{cases}$

(iv) $f(x) = \langle a, x \rangle$, where $a \in \mathbb{R}^N$.

(v) $f(x) = \delta_a(x) := \begin{cases} 0, & (x = a) \\ \infty, & (x \neq a) \end{cases}$ where $a \in \mathbb{R}^N$.

(vi) $f(x) = \frac{1}{2}\langle x, Ax \rangle$, where A is an $N \times N$ symmetric positive definite matrix.

12.7. Derive the dual problem of

$$\text{minimize} \qquad \langle c, x \rangle$$
$$\text{subject to} \qquad Ax \geq b,$$
$$x \geq 0.$$

12.8. Derive the dual problem of

$$\text{minimize} \qquad \langle c, x \rangle + \frac{1}{2} \langle x, Qx \rangle$$
$$\text{subject to} \qquad Ax \geq b,$$

where Q is a symmetric positive definite matrix.

12.9. Consider the utility maximization problem (UMP)

$$\text{maximize} \qquad \alpha \log x_1 + (1 - \alpha) \log x_2$$
$$\text{subject to} \qquad p_1 x_1 + p_2 x_2 \leq w,$$

where $0 < \alpha < 1$ is a parameter, $p_1, p_2 > 0$ are prices, and $w > 0$ is wealth.

(i) Solve the UMP.

(ii) Let $v(p_1, p_2, w)$ be the value function. Compute the partial derivatives of v with respect to each of p_1, p_2, and w.

(iii) Verify *Roy's identity* $x_n = -\frac{\partial v}{\partial p_n} / \frac{\partial v}{\partial w}$ for $n = 1, 2$, where x_n is the optimal demand of good n.

12.10. Consider the UMP

$$\text{maximize} \qquad u(x)$$
$$\text{subject to} \qquad x \in \mathbb{R}_+^L, \ \ \langle p, x \rangle \leq w,$$

where $w > 0$ is the wealth of the consumer, $p \in \mathbb{R}_{++}^L$ is the price vector, $x \in \mathbb{R}_+^L$ is the demand, and $u : \mathbb{R}_+^L \to \mathbb{R}$ is differentiable and strictly quasiconcave. Let $x(p, w)$ be the solution to UMP (called *Marshallian demand*) and $v(p, w)$ the value function. If $x(p, w) \gg 0$, prove *Roy's identity*

$$x(p, w) = -\frac{\nabla_p v(p, w)}{\nabla_w v(p, w)}.$$

(Hint: envelope theorem.)

12.11. Consider the *expenditure minimization problem* (EMP)

$$\text{minimize} \qquad p_1 x_1 + p_2 x_2$$
$$\text{subject to} \qquad \alpha \log x_1 + (1 - \alpha) \log x_2 \geq u$$

where $0 < \alpha < 1$ is a parameter, $p_1, p_2 > 0$ are prices, and $u \in \mathbb{R}$ is the desired utility level.

(i) Solve the EMP.

(ii) Let $e(p_1, p_2, u)$ be the value function. Compute the partial derivatives of e with respect to p_1 and p_2.

(iii) Verify *Shephard's lemma* $x_n = \frac{\partial e}{\partial p_n}$ for $n = 1, 2$, where x_n is the optimal demand of good n.

12.12. Consider the EMP

$$
\begin{aligned}
&\text{minimize} && \langle p, x \rangle \\
&\text{subject to} && u(x) \geq u,
\end{aligned}
$$

where $p \in \mathbb{R}^L_{++}$ is the price vector, $x \in \mathbb{R}^L$ is the demand, $u(x)$ is a strictly quasi-concave differentiable utility function, and $u \in \mathbb{R}$ is the desired utility level. Let $h(p, u)$ be the solution to EMP (called *Hicksian demand*) and $e(p, u)$ be the minimum expenditure (called *expenditure function*). Prove *Shephard's lemma*

$$
h(p, u) = \nabla_p e(p, u).
$$

12.13. Prove the following *Slutsky equation*:

$$
\underbrace{D_p x(p, w)}_{L \times L} = \underbrace{D_p^2 e(p, u)}_{L \times L} - \underbrace{[D_w x(p, w)]}_{L \times 1} \underbrace{[x(p, w)]'}_{1 \times L},
$$

where $x(p, w)$ is the Marshallian demand, $u = u(x(p, w))$ is the utility level evaluated at the demand, and $e(p, u)$ is the expenditure function.

IV

Dynamic Optimization

CHAPTER 13

Introduction to Dynamic Programming

13.1 INTRODUCTION

So far, we have only considered the maximization or minimization of a given function subject to some constraints. Such a problem is sometimes called a *static* optimization problem because there is only one decision to make, namely choosing the variables that optimize the objective function. In some cases, writing down or evaluating the objective function itself may be complicated. Furthermore, in many problems, the decision maker makes multiple decisions over time instead of a single decision.

Dynamic programming (DP) is a mathematical programming (optimization) technique that exploits the sequential structure of the problem. It is easier to understand the logic through examples instead of the abstract formulation. Suppose that we want to minimize the function

$$f(x_1, x_2) = 2x_1^2 - 2x_1 x_2 + x_2^2 - 2x_1 - 4x_2.$$

One way to solve this is to compute the gradient and set it equal to zero, so

$$\nabla f(x_1, x_2) = \begin{bmatrix} 4x_1 - 2x_2 - 2 \\ -2x_1 + 2x_2 - 4 \end{bmatrix} = \begin{bmatrix} 0 \\ 0 \end{bmatrix} \iff \begin{bmatrix} x_1 \\ x_2 \end{bmatrix} = \begin{bmatrix} 3 \\ 5 \end{bmatrix}.$$

(This is only a necessary condition for optimality, but we can easily show sufficiency since the Hessian $\nabla^2 f$ is positive definite.)

Another way to solve this problem is in two steps. First, suppose that we have already determined the value of x_1, so treat x_1 as a constant. Then the objective function is a (convex) quadratic function in x_2. Taking the partial derivative with respect to x_2 and setting it equal to zero, we get

$$\frac{\partial f}{\partial x_2} = -2x_1 + 2x_2 - 4 = 0 \iff x_2 = x_1 + 2.$$

DOI: 10.1201/9781032698953-13

Then the function value becomes

$$
\begin{aligned}
g(x_1) &:= f(x_1, x_1 + 2) \\
&= 2x_1^2 - 2x_1(x_1 + 2) + (x_1 + 2)^2 - 2x_1 - 4(x_1 + 2) \\
&= x_1^2 - 6x_1 - 4.
\end{aligned}
$$

Here $g(x)$ is the minimum value that we can attain if we choose x_2 optimally, given $x_1 = x$. Clearly we can solve the original problem by choosing x_1 so as to minimize g. Since g is a convex quadratic function, setting the derivative equal to zero, we get

$$
g'(x_1) = 2x_1 - 6 = 0 \iff x_1 = 3.
$$

Therefore the solution is $(x_1, x_2) = (x_1, x_1 + 2) = (3, 5)$, as it should be.

Essentially, dynamic programming amounts to dividing a single optimization problem with many variables into multiple optimization problems with fewer variables. By doing so, the problem sometimes becomes easier to handle, especially when the problem is stochastic (probabilistic). In the above example, we have solved the single problem with two variables

$$
\min_{x_1, x_2} f(x_1, x_2)
$$

by dividing it into two problems with one variable each,

$$
g(x_1) := \min_{x_2} f(x_1, x_2) \text{ and } \min_{x_1} g(x_1).
$$

In the next few sections, we present more examples.

13.2   KNAPSACK PROBLEM

Suppose you are a thief who has broken into a jewelry shop. You have a knapsack of size $S \geq 0$ (an integer) to pack what you have stolen. There are I types of jewelry indexed by $i = 1, 2, \ldots, I$, and a type i jewelry has integer size $s_i > 0$ and is worth $w_i \geq 0$. You want to pack your knapsack so as to maximize the total worth of jewelry that you have stolen.

Formulating this problem as a constrained optimization problem is not particularly difficult. Letting n_i be the number of type i jewelry that you pack, the total value is $\sum_{i=1}^{I} w_i n_i$ and the total size is $\sum_{i=1}^{I} s_i n_i$. Therefore the problem is equivalent to

$$
\text{maximize} \qquad \sum_{i=1}^{I} w_i n_i
$$

$$
\text{subject to} \qquad \sum_{i=1}^{I} s_i n_i \leq S,
$$

$$
(\forall i) n_i \in \mathbb{Z}_+.
$$

Although writing down the problem is simple enough, solving it is not because the choice variable is discrete and hence we cannot take derivatives.

We solve the knapsack problem by dynamic programming. Let $V(S)$ be the maximum total value of jewelry that can be packed in a size S knapsack, which we call the *value function*. Clearly $V(S) = 0$ if $S < \min_i s_i$ since you cannot pack anything in this case. If you put anything at all in your knapsack (so $S \geq \min_i s_i$), clearly you start packing with some type of jewelry. If you put object i first (with $s_i \leq S$), then you get value w_i and you are left with remaining size $S - s_i$. By the definition of the value function, if you continue packing optimally, you get total value $V(S - s_i)$ from the remaining space. Therefore the maximum value that you can get (if you first pack object i) is

$$w_i + V(S - s_i).$$

Since you want to pick the first object optimally, you want to maximize this value with respect to i, which will give you the total maximum value $V(S)$ of the original problem. Therefore

$$V(S) = \max_{i:s_i \leq S}[w_i + V(S - s_i)] \tag{13.1}$$

holds, which is called the *Bellman equation*. We can iterate the Bellman equation (13.1) backwards starting from $V(S) = 0$ for $S < \min_i s_i$ to find the maximum value. This process is called *backward induction* or *value function iteration*.

For example, let $I = 3$ (three types), $(s_1, s_2, s_3) = (1, 2, 5)$, and $(w_1, w_2, w_3) = (1, 3, 8)$. Then

$V(0) = 0,$

$V(1) = w_1 + V(0) = 1,$

$V(2) = \max_i[w_i + V(2 - s_i)] = \max\{1 + V(1), 3 + V(0)\} = \max\{2, 3\} = 3,$

$V(3) = \max_i[w_i + V(3 - s_i)] = \max\{1 + V(2), 3 + V(1)\} = \max\{4, 4\} = 4,$

$V(4) = \max\{1 + V(3), 3 + V(2)\} = \max\{5, 6\} = 6,$

$V(5) = \max\{1 + V(4), 3 + V(3), 8 + V(0)\} = \max\{7, 7, 8\} = 8,$

etc. Although this problem does not admit a closed-form solution, it is straightforward to write a computer program to solve the problem for any S.

13.3 SHORTEST PATH PROBLEM

Suppose that there are finitely many locations indexed by $i = 1, \ldots, I$. Traveling directly from i to $j \neq i$ costs $c_{ij} \geq 0$. (If there is no direct route from i to j, simply define $c_{ij} = \infty$.) You want to find the cheapest way to travel from any point i to any other point j.

To solve this problem, let $V_N(i,j)$ be the minimum cost to travel from i to j in at most N steps. For convenience, allow the possibility $i = j$ (staying at the same location) and set $c_{ii} = 0$. Let k be the first connection (including possibly $k = i$). Traveling from i to k costs c_{ik}, and now you need to travel from k to j in at most $N - 1$ steps. If you continue optimally, the cost from k to j is (by the definition of the value function) $V_{N-1}(k,j)$. Therefore the Bellman equation is

$$V_N(i,j) = \min_k \left\{ c_{ik} + V_{N-1}(k,j) \right\}. \tag{13.2}$$

Since $0 \leq V_N(i,j) \leq V_{N-1}(i,j)$ (because $c_{ii} = 0$), the limit $\lim_{N\to\infty} V_N(i,j)$ exists.[1] Therefore the cheapest path can be found by iterating backwards from $V_1(i,j) = c_{ij}$.

13.4   OPTIMAL SAVINGS PROBLEM

Suppose that time is indexed by $t = 0, 1, \ldots, T$. You have initial wealth $w_0 > 0$. At each point in time, you can either consume some of your wealth or save it at a gross interest rate $R > 0$, meaning that if you save 1 dollar, it will grow to R dollars next period.[2] You cannot go into debt. What is the optimal consumption-saving plan?

To solve this problem, let w_t be the wealth at the beginning of time t. If you consume c_t at time t, the next period's wealth will be

$$w_{t+1} = R(w_t - c_t) \geq 0. \tag{13.3}$$

For concreteness, assume that the utility function is

$$U_T(c_0, \ldots, c_T) = \sum_{t=0}^{T} \beta^t \log c_t.$$

(The subscript T in U_T means that the planning horizon is T.) Clearly we have

$$U_T(c_0, \ldots, c_T) = \log c_0 + \beta U_{T-1}(c_1, \ldots, c_T).$$

Let $V_T(w)$ be the maximum utility you get when you start with initial wealth w and the planning horizon is T. If $T = 0$, you have no choice but to consume everything, so $V_0(w) = \log w$. If $T > 0$ and you consume c this period, by the budget constraint (13.3) you will have wealth $w' = R(w - c)$ next period and the planning horizon will be $T - 1$. Therefore the Bellman equation is

$$V_T(w) = \max_{0 \leq c \leq w} \left[\log c + \beta V_{T-1}(R(w - c)) \right]. \tag{13.4}$$

---

[1] In fact, it converges in finite steps. This is because since you visit each point at most once, the number of connections is at most $I - 1$, so $V_N = V_{N-1}$ for $N \geq I$.

[2] For instance, if the interest rate is 5% per period, then the net interest rate is $r = 0.05$ and the gross interest rate is $R = 1 + r = 1.05$.

In principle, we can compute $V_T(w)$ by iterating backwards from $T = 0$ using $V_0(w) = \log w$. Let us compute $V_1(w)$, for example. Combining (13.4) for $T = 1$ and $V_0(w) = \log w$, we have

$$
\begin{aligned}
V_1(w) &= \max_{0 \leq c \leq w} \left[\log c + \beta V_0(R(w - c)) \right] \\
&= \max_{0 \leq c \leq w} \left[\log c + \beta \log(R(w - c)) \right].
\end{aligned}
$$

The right-hand side inside the brackets is concave in c, so we can maximize it by setting the derivative equal to zero (Proposition 11.8). The first-order condition is

$$
\frac{1}{c} - \beta \frac{1}{w - c} = 0 \iff w - c = \beta c \iff c = \frac{w}{1 + \beta}.
$$

Therefore the value function for $T = 1$ is

$$
V_1(w) = \log \frac{w}{1 + \beta} + \beta \log \left(R \frac{\beta w}{1 + \beta} \right) = (1 + \beta) \log w + \text{constant},
$$

where "constant" is some constant that depends only on the given parameters β and R.

For general T, we may guess that the functional form of V_T is

$$
V_T(w) = (1 + \beta + \cdots + \beta^T) \log w + \text{constant}
$$

and then apply mathematical induction to confirm it. For instance, conjecture that the value function takes the form

$$
V_T(w) = a_T + b_T \log w, \tag{13.5}
$$

where $a_T \in \mathbb{R}$ and $b_T > 0$ are some constants. For $T = 0$, we know $(a_0, b_0) = (0, 1)$. For $T = 1$, we know from the above derivation that $b_1 = 1 + \beta$, and we did not bother computing a_1. Suppose that (13.5) holds up to some $T - 1$ and consider T. Then the Bellman equation (13.4) becomes

$$
V_T(w) = \max_{0 \leq c \leq w} \left[\log c + \beta(a_{T-1} + b_{T-1} \log(R(w - c))) \right].
$$

Since $b_{T-1} > 0$ by the induction hypothesis, the expression inside the bracket is a strictly concave function of c. Since a_{T-1} is a constant, the first-order condition is

$$
\frac{1}{c} - \beta b_{T-1} \frac{1}{w - c} = 0 \iff c = \frac{w}{1 + \beta b_{T-1}}.
$$

Substituting this c into the Bellman equation, after some algebra we obtain the functional form (13.5), where

$$
b_T = 1 + \beta b_{T-1}. \tag{13.6}
$$

Therefore by induction, the functional form (13.5) holds for all T, and solving the difference equation (13.6), we obtain

$$b_T = 1 + \beta + \cdots + \beta^T.$$

Therefore the optimal consumption when the horizon is T is

$$c = \frac{w}{1 + \beta b_{T-1}} = \frac{w}{b_T} = \frac{w}{1 + \beta + \cdots + \beta^T}.$$

This trick of guessing the functional form of the value function and confirming it by mathematical induction is called *guess-and-verify*. Although guess-and-verify is rarely applicable in practice, when it is, we can easily solve a dynamic programming problem. See Problems 13.3–13.5 for other examples.

13.5 OPTIMAL STOPPING PROBLEM

Suppose there are equal numbers of black and red cards (say N each), and you draw one card at a time. You have the option to stop at any time. The score you get when you stop is

"number of black cards drawn" − "number of red cards drawn".

You want to maximize the expected score. What is the optimal strategy?

Let b, r be the number of black and red cards that remain. Then you have already drawn $N - b$ black cards and $N - r$ red cards, so your current score is $(N - b) - (N - r) = r - b$. If you stop, you get $r - b$. If you continue, on the next draw you draw a black card with probability $\frac{b}{b+r}$ (and b decreases by 1) and a red card with probability $\frac{r}{b+r}$ (and r decreases by 1). Let $V(b, r)$ be the expected score when b black cards and r red cards remain. Then the Bellman equation is

$$V(b, r) = \max \left\{ \underbrace{r - b}_{\text{stop}}, \underbrace{\frac{b}{b+r} V(b-1, r) + \frac{r}{b+r} V(b, r-1)}_{\text{continue}} \right\}.$$

We can find the optimal strategy by iterating backwards from $V(0, 0) = 0$.

13.6 SECRETARY PROBLEM

The classical secretary problem can be described as follows. A known number N of job applicants are to be interviewed one by one in random order, all $N!$ possible orders being equally likely. The administrator is able at any time to rank the applicants that have so far been interviewed from the best to worst. As each applicant is interviewed, the administrator must either accept, in which case the search is terminated, or reject, in which case the next applicant is interviewed and the administrator faces the same choice as before. The administrator's objective is to maximize the probability of accepting the very best among all N applicants.

Formulating the secretary problem as a dynamic programming problem requires some ingenuity. When the n-th applicant shows up for an interview and is (is not) the best among those already interviewed, call the state "1" ("0"). For $x \in \{0, 1\}$, let $V_n(x)$ be the value function (probability of accepting the very best by following the optimal strategy from that point on). Let us derive the Bellman equation. First, consider the case $x = 0$. Then the administrator will surely reject applicant n and will interview applicant $n + 1$. Since the ranking is random, the rank orders of the applicants $\{1, \ldots, n + 1\}$ are equally likely. Hence conditional on $x = 0$ after seeing n applicants, the probability of $x = 1$ after seeing $n + 1$ applicants is $\frac{1}{n+1}$. Therefore the Bellman equation is

$$V_n(0) = \underbrace{\frac{1}{n + 1}}_{=\Pr(x=1)} V_{n+1}(1) + \underbrace{\frac{n}{n + 1}}_{=\Pr(x=0)} V_{n+1}(0). \tag{13.7}$$

Next, consider the case $x = 1$. Then the administrator needs to decide whether to accept or reject applicant n. If accept, the continuation value is

$$\Pr(n \text{ is best among all} \mid n \text{ is best among first } n)$$
$$= \Pr(n \text{ is best among all and first } n) / \Pr(n \text{ is best among first } n)$$
$$= \Pr(n \text{ is best among all}) / \Pr(n \text{ is best among first } n)$$
$$= (1/N)/(1/n) = \frac{n}{N}.$$

If reject, the continuation value is the same as the right-hand side of (13.7). Therefore the Bellman equation is

$$V_n(1) = \max \left\{ \frac{n}{N}, \frac{1}{n + 1} V_{n+1}(1) + \frac{n}{n + 1} V_{n+1}(0) \right\}$$
$$= \max \left\{ n/N, V_n(0) \right\}, \tag{13.8}$$

where we have used (13.7). Changing n to $n + 1$ in (13.8) and combining with (13.7), we obtain

$$V_n(0) = \frac{1}{n + 1} \max \left\{ \frac{n + 1}{N}, V_{n+1}(0) \right\} + \frac{n}{n + 1} V_{n+1}(0).$$

If we define $v_n = V_n(0)/n$, then we can simplify to

$$v_n = \frac{1}{n} \max \left\{ \frac{1}{N}, v_{n+1} \right\} + v_{n+1}. \tag{13.9}$$

If $n = N$, the administrator has interviewed all applicants, so $V_N(0) = 0$ and $V_N(1) = 1$. Thus $v_N = 0$, and we may solve (13.9) by backward induction.

For the secretary problem, we may obtain a closed-form solution as follows. Since $v_n - v_{n+1} > 0$ by (13.9), the sequence $\{v_n\}$ is strictly decreasing. The following proposition characterizes the solution to the difference equation (13.9).

Proposition 13.1. *Let $N \geq 2$ and define $1 \leq n^* \leq N - 1$ by*

$$n^* = \min \left\{ n : \sum_{k=n}^{N-1} \frac{1}{k} \leq 1 \right\}. \tag{13.10}$$

Then for $n = n^* - 1, \ldots, N - 1$, we have

$$v_n = \frac{1}{N} \sum_{k=n}^{N-1} \frac{1}{k}. \tag{13.11}$$

Furthermore, $v_1 = 2v_2 = \cdots = (n^* - 1)v_{n^*-1}$.

Proof. We prove by mathematical induction. For $n = N - 1$, it follows from (13.9) and $v_N = 0$ that $v_{N-1} = \frac{1}{N(N-1)}$, which satisfies (13.11). Suppose the claim holds for some $n, \ldots, N - 1$ with $n \geq n^* - 1$. Using (13.10) and (13.11), we obtain $v_n \leq 1/N$. Therefore (13.9) implies

$$v_{n-1} = \frac{1}{N(n-1)} + v_n = \frac{1}{N} \sum_{k=n-1}^{N-1} \frac{1}{k},$$

so (13.11) holds. By the definition of n^* and (13.11), we have $v_{n^*-1} > 1/N$. Since v_n is decreasing $v_n > 1/N$ for $n \leq n^* - 1$. Therefore (13.9) implies

$$v_{n-1} = \frac{1}{n-1} v_n + v_n = \frac{n}{n-1} v_n \iff (n-1)v_{n-1} = nv_n. \qquad \square$$

By Proposition 13.1, the optimal strategy in the secretary problem is to reject the first $n^* - 1$ applicants and then accept the next candidate who is the best among those already interviewed. The probability of accepting the best candidate under the optimal strategy is

$$V_1(1) = \max\{1/N, V_1(0)\} = \max\{1/N, v_1\}$$

$$= v_1 = (n^* - 1)v_{n^*-1} = \frac{n^* - 1}{N} \sum_{k=n^*-1}^{N-1} \frac{1}{k},$$

which converges to $1/e \approx 0.37$ as $N \to \infty$.

13.7   ABSTRACT FORMULATION

Having seen many examples of dynamic programming problems, we generalize to an abstract setting. At an abstract level, a dynamic programming problem or a dynamic program can be defined as follows.

Definition 13.1. A *dynamic program* is a tuple $\mathcal{D} = \{X, A, \Gamma, V, H\}$, where

- X is a nonempty set called the *state space*,

- A is a nonempty set called the *action space*,

- $\Gamma : X \twoheadrightarrow A$ is a nonempty correspondence called the *feasible correspondence*, with its graph denoted by

$$G := \{(x, a) \in X \times A : a \in \Gamma(x)\},$$

- V is a nonempty space of functions $v : X \to [-\infty, \infty]$ called the *value space*,

- $H : G \times V \to [-\infty, \infty]$ is a function called the *aggregator*, which is increasing in the last argument:

$$v_1 \le v_2 \implies H(x, a, v_1) \le H(x, a, v_2).$$

The idea of this definition is as follows. Given the state $x \in X$, the decision maker can take some actions $a \in A$; let $\Gamma(x) \subset A$ denote all possible actions. (An action is also called a *control variable*.) Let $v(x')$ be the continuation value that a decision maker expects when the next state is $x' \in X$. This is a function on X, and write $v \in V$. Now given the current state x, the action $a \in \Gamma(x)$, and the continuation value v, the decision maker should be able to evaluate the reward (utility); write it $H(x, a, v) \in [-\infty, \infty]$.

Let $\mathcal{D} = \{X, A, \Gamma, V, H\}$ be a dynamic program. Without loss of generality, we consider maximization problems, so the decision maker wishes to maximize the reward. Hence given $v \in V$, define the function $Tv : X \to [-\infty, \infty]$ by

$$(Tv)(x) := \sup_{a \in \Gamma(x)} H(x, a, v). \tag{13.12}$$

The operator T in (13.12) defined on the value space V is called the *Bellman operator*. Obviously, if the problem is a minimization problem, the supremum in (13.12) becomes an infimum.

We now define the solution concept of a dynamic program.

Definition 13.2. Let $\mathcal{D} = \{X, A, \Gamma, V, H\}$ be a dynamic program with Bellman operator T. We say that $v \in V$ is a *value function* of $\mathcal{D}$ if v is a fixed point of T, that is, $v = Tv$. The equation $v = Tv$ is called the *Bellman equation*.

The interpretation of Definition 13.2 is straightforward. Let $v(x')$ be the continuation value that the decision maker expects if the next state is $x' \in X$ and the decision maker continues to choose the optimal actions. Currently the state is $x \in X$, and the decision maker can choose $a \in \Gamma(x)$. The optimal choice is to maximize the utility $H(x, a, v)$, which (by the definition of the Bellman operator) is $(Tv)(x)$. But if v were the optimal value, by definition it must be $v(x) = (Tv)(x)$. Thus $v = Tv$. The condition $v = Tv$ is also called the *principle of optimality*: an optimal policy has the property that whatever the initial state and actions are, the remaining actions must constitute an optimal policy with regard to the state resulting from the first action.

We verify that all previous examples fit into this abstract formulation.

Example 13.1 (Knapsack problem). The state space is $\mathsf{X} = \{0, 1, \ldots\} = \mathbb{Z}_+$, with state denoted by $S \in \mathsf{X}$. The action space is $\mathsf{A} = \{0, 1, \ldots, I\}$, with action denoted by $i \in \mathsf{A}$ (where "0" corresponds to packing nothing). The feasible correspondence is $\Gamma(S) = \{i = 1, \ldots, I : s_i \leq S\}$ if this is nonempty and $\Gamma(S) = \{0\}$ otherwise. The value space V is the set of all functions $v : \mathsf{X} \to \mathbb{R}$ with $v(S) = 0$ for $S < \min_i s_i$. The aggregator is

$$H(S, i, v) = \begin{cases} w_i + v(S - s_i) & \text{if } i \geq 1, \\ v(S) & \text{if } i = 0. \end{cases}$$

Example 13.2 (Shortest path problem). The state space is $\mathsf{X} = \mathbb{N} \times \{1, \ldots, I\}^2$, with state denoted by $(n, i, j) \in \mathsf{X}$ (where n is the number of trips allowed and i, j denote the origin and destination). The action space is $\mathsf{A} = \{1, \ldots, I\}$, with action denoted by the transit point $k \in \mathsf{A}$. The feasible correspondence is $\Gamma(n, i, j) = \mathsf{A}$, the entire space. The value space V is the set of all functions $v : \mathsf{X} \to [0, \infty]$. The aggregator is

$$H(n, i, j, k, v) = \begin{cases} c_{ik} + v(n - 1, k, j) & \text{if } n > 1, \\ c_{ij} & \text{if } n = 1 \text{ and } k = j, \\ \infty & \text{if } n = 1 \text{ and } k \neq j. \end{cases}$$

Note that for the shortest path problem, the Bellman equation is expressed using minimization (compare (13.2) and (13.12)).

Example 13.3 (Optimal savings problem). The state space is $\mathsf{X} = \mathbb{Z}_+ \times \mathbb{R}_+$, with state denoted by $(T, w) \in \mathsf{X}$ (where T is the horizon and $w \geq 0$ is the wealth). The action space is $\mathsf{A} = \mathbb{R}_+$, with action denoted by consumption $c \in \mathsf{A}$. The feasible correspondence is $\Gamma(T, w) = [0, w]$. The value space V is the set of all functions $v : \mathsf{X} \to [-\infty, \infty)$. The aggregator is

$$H(T, w, c, v) = \begin{cases} \log c + \beta v(T - 1, R(w - c)) & \text{if } T \geq 1, \\ \log c & \text{if } T = 0. \end{cases}$$

Example 13.4 (Optimal stopping problem). The state space is $\mathsf{X} = \{0, 1, \ldots, N\}^2 \times \{0, 1\}$, with state denoted by $(b, r, x) \in \mathsf{X}$ (where b, r are the number of black and red cards remaining and $x = 0, 1$ stands for "stop" and "continue"). The action space is $\mathsf{A} = \{0, 1\}$, with action denoted by $a \in \mathsf{A}$ (where $0, 1$ correspond to "stop" and "continue"). The feasible correspondence is $\Gamma(b, r, x) = \{0, 1\}$ if $b + r > 0$ and $x = 1$ and $\Gamma(b, r, x) = \{0\}$ otherwise. The value space V is the set of all functions $v : \mathsf{X} \to \mathbb{R}$. The aggregator is

$$H(b, r, x, a, v)$$
$$= \begin{cases} \frac{b}{b+r} v(b-1, r, 1) + \frac{r}{b+r} v(b, r-1, 1) & \text{if } b + r > 0, \ x = 1, \ a = 1, \\ r - b & \text{if } (x, a) = (1, 0) \text{ or } x = 0. \end{cases}$$

We omit the secretary problem because it is cumbersome.

In practice, optimization problems are not necessarily formulated as a dynamic program. For instance, the shortest path problem does not have an apparent sequential structure. Being able to formulate a given optimization problem as a dynamic program by identifying each object (the state space X, the action space A, the feasible correspondence Γ, the value space V, the aggregator H) is a valuable skill that requires practice. Once a problem is formulated as a dynamic program, we may apply specific techniques that are applicable in each context.

Here we present a class of dynamic programs that always admit unique solutions, namely finite-horizon dynamic programs.

Proposition 13.2. *Let* $\mathcal{D} = \{\mathsf{X}, \mathsf{A}, \Gamma, \mathsf{V}, H\}$ *be a dynamic program with Bellman operator* $T : \mathsf{V} \to \mathsf{V}$. *Suppose that*

  (i) *there exists a sequence of subsets* $\emptyset = \mathsf{X}_0 \subset \mathsf{X}_1 \subset \cdots \subset \mathsf{X}_n \subset \cdots \subset \mathsf{X}$ *with* $\bigcup_{n=1}^{\infty} \mathsf{X}_n = \mathsf{X}$,

  (ii) *for any* n, $x \in \mathsf{X}_n$, $a \in \Gamma(x)$, *and* $v_1, v_2 \in \mathsf{V}$ *with* $v_1 = v_2$ *on* X_{n-1}, *we have* $H(x, a, v_1) = H(x, a, v_2)$.

Then $\mathcal{D}$ *has a unique value function.*

Proof. We first construct a fixed point of T. Take any $v_0 \in \mathsf{V}$ and define $v_n = T^n v_0$. By condition (ii), for $x \in \mathsf{X}_1$, the value of $H(x, a, v)$ does not depend on v_0. Therefore for $x \in \mathsf{X}_1$, the value of

$$v_1(x) = (Tv_0)(x) = \sup_{a \in \Gamma(x)} H(x, a, v_0)$$

also does not depend on v_0. In particular, setting $v_0 = v_1$, we obtain $v_1 = Tv_1$ on X_1. Let us show by induction that $v_n = Tv_n$ on X_n. The claim is true for $n = 1$. Suppose the claim is true up to some n, and let $u_n = Tv_n$. By the induction hypothesis, we have $v_n = u_n$ on X_n. Therefore by condition (ii), for $x \in \mathsf{X}_{n+1}$, we have $H(x, a, v_n) = H(x, a, u_n)$, and therefore

$$v_{n+1}(x) = (Tv_n)(x) = \sup_{a \in \Gamma(x)} H(x, a, v_n) = \sup_{a \in \Gamma(x)} H(x, a, u_n)$$
$$= (Tu_n)(x) = (T^2 v_n)(x) = (Tv_{n+1})(x).$$

Hence the claim also holds for $n + 1$.

Next, define $v \in \mathsf{V}$ by $v(x) = v_n(x)$ if $x \in \mathsf{X}_n$. To see that v is well defined, suppose $x \in \mathsf{X}_m \cap \mathsf{X}_n$ for some $m < n$. Then by condition (i) $\mathsf{X}_m \subset \mathsf{X}_n$, and by what we have just proved $v_n = T^{n-m}v_m = v_m$ on X_m, so the value of v is unambiguous. Furthermore, by condition (i), we have $x \in \mathsf{X}_n$ for some n, so v is defined on the entire X. Thus $v \in \mathsf{V}$ is well defined.

To show that v is a fixed point of T, take any $x \in \mathsf{X}$. Then by condition (i), we have $x \in \mathsf{X}_n$ for some n, so $v(x) = v_n(x) = (Tv_n)(x) = (Tv)(x)$. Since x is arbitrary, $v = Tv$.

Finally, we show the uniqueness of the fixed point. Suppose u, v are fixed points of T. Then on X_1, we have $H(x, a, u) = H(x, a, v)$, so $u = Tu = Tv = v$. Using condition (ii) and applying induction, we have $u = v$ on X_n for all n. Hence by condition (i), $u = v$ on X. $\qquad\square$

When the dynamic program $\mathcal{D}$ satisfies the assumptions of Proposition 13.2, we say that $\mathcal{D}$ is a *finite-horizon dynamic program*. A finite horizon dynamic program has the following features: (i) the state space X is covered by an increasing sequence of subsets $\{\mathsf{X}_n\}$, (ii) to evaluate the right-hand side of the Bellman equation (13.12) on X_n, we only need to know the value of v on the smaller set X_{n-1}, (iii) $\mathsf{X}_0 = \emptyset$, implying that the right-hand side of (13.12) on X_1 is unambiguous. When a dynamic program has this feature, for any initial state $x \in \mathsf{X}$, we may obtain the value $v(x)$ by iterating the Bellman operator T finitely many times. All examples discussed in this chapter are finite-horizon dynamic programs.

NOTES

For historical background on the secretary problem discussed in §13.6, see Ferguson (1989). The abstract approach to dynamic programming in §13.7 can already be seen in Denardo (1967), but it was popularized by Bertsekas (2018). For a modern treatment of dynamic programming, see Sargent and Stachurski (2024).

PROBLEMS

13.1. There are N types of coins. A coin of type n has an integer value w_n. You want to find the minimum number of coins needed for the value of the coins to sum to S, where $S \geq 0$ is an integer.

  (i) Write down the Bellman equation.

  (ii) Solve the problem for $S = 10$ when $N = 3$ and $(w_1, w_2, w_3) = (1, 2, 4)$.

13.2. Using your favorite programming language (Matlab, Python, etc.), write computer programs that numerically solve the knapsack problem, the shortest path problem, and the optimal stopping problem (drawing cards) given the model inputs.

13.3. You are a potato farmer. You start with some stock of potatoes. At each time, you can eat some of them and plant the rest. If you plant x potatoes, you will harvest $A x^\alpha$ potatoes at the beginning of the next period, where $A > 0$ and $\alpha \in (0, 1)$. You want to maximize your utility from consuming potatoes

$$\sum_{t=0}^{T} \beta^t \log c_t,$$

where $0 < \beta < 1$ is the discount factor, $c_t > 0$ is consumption of potatoes at time t, and T is the number of periods you live.

(i) If you have k potatoes now and consume c out of it, how many potatoes can you harvest next period?

(ii) Let $V_T(k)$ be the maximum utility you get when you start with k potatoes. Write down the Bellman equation.

(iii) Solve for the optimal consumption when $T = 1$.

(iv) Guess that $V_T(k) = a_T + b_T \log k$ for some constants a_T, b_T. Assuming that this guess is correct, derive a relation between b_T and b_{T-1}.

13.4. Consider the optimal savings problem with the utility function

$$\sum_{t=0}^{T} \beta^t \frac{c_t^{1-\gamma}}{1 - \gamma},$$

where $0 < \gamma \neq 1$.

(i) Write down the Bellman equation.

(ii) Show that the value function must be of the form $V_T(w) = a_T \frac{w^{1-\gamma}}{1-\gamma}$ for some $a_T > 0$ with $a_0 = 1$.

(iii) Take the first-order condition and express the optimal consumption as a function of a_{T-1}.

(iv) Substitute the optimal consumption into the Bellman equation and derive a relation between a_T and a_{T-1}.

(v) Solve for a_T and the optimal consumption rule.

13.5. Consider the optimal savings problem with stochastic interest rates. Let R_z be the gross interest rate in state $z \in \{1, \dots, Z\}$, and let $p_{zz'}$ be the transition probability from state z to z'.

(i) Write down the Bellman equation.

(ii) Show that the value function must be of the form $V_T(w, z) = a_{z,T} \frac{w^{1-\gamma}}{1-\gamma}$ for some $a_{z,T} > 0$ with $a_{z,0} = 1$.

(iii) By solving for the optimal consumption rule, derive a relation between $a_{z,T}$ and $\{a_{z',T-1}\}_{z'=1}^{S}$.

13.6. Confirm the details of the secretary problem.

CHAPTER 14

Contraction Methods

14.1 INTRODUCTION

In Chapter 13, we introduced several dynamic programming problems and provided an abstract formulation. The main theoretical result is that under weak assumptions, a finite-horizon dynamic program admits a unique value function, which can be obtained by value function iteration in finitely many steps. However, many interesting dynamic programs are not finite-horizon (they are *infinite-horizon!dynamic programs*).

As an example, consider the following optimal savings problem:

$$\text{maximize} \quad \mathrm{E}_0 \sum_{t=0}^{\infty} \beta^t u(c_t) \tag{14.1a}$$

$$\text{subject to} \quad (\forall t) w_{t+1} = R(z_t, z_{t+1})(w_t - c_t) + y(z_{t+1}), \tag{14.1b}$$

$$(\forall t) 0 \leq c_t \leq w_t, \tag{14.1c}$$

$$w_0 > 0, \; z_0 \text{ given.} \tag{14.1d}$$

Here $u : \mathbb{R}_+ \to [-\infty, \infty)$ is the flow utility function from consumption $c_t \geq 0$ at time t; the parameter $\beta \in [0, 1)$ is the discount factor; E_t denotes the expectation conditional on time t information; $w_t \geq 0$ is the financial wealth at the beginning of time t; $\{z_t\}_{t=0}^{\infty}$ is a Markov chain taking values in the finite set $\mathsf{Z} = \{1, \ldots, Z\}$ with transition probability matrix $P = (P(z, z'))$; $y : \mathsf{Z} \to \mathbb{R}_+$ specifies the non-financial income of the agent in each state $z \in \mathsf{Z}$; and $R : \mathsf{Z}^2 \to \mathbb{R}_+$ specifies the gross return on savings conditional on transitioning from state z to z'. The expression (14.1a) is the objective function; the condition (14.1b) is the budget constraint; the condition (14.1c) implies that consumption is nonnegative and the agent cannot borrow; and (14.1d) is the initial condition. To understand the budget constraint (14.1b), note that the next period's financial wealth w' is the sum of the next period's non-financial income y' and the return from savings, which is R times $w - c$.

The problem (14.1) is a generalization of the optimal savings problem studied in §13.4. There the horizon was finite (T) instead of infinite; the

DOI: 10.1201/9781032698953-14

utility function was $u(c) = \log c$; there was no uncertainty ($Z = 1$); and there was no non-financial income ($y = 0$).

Studying a constrained optimization problem like (14.1) could be challenging because the number of control variables is infinite and the finite-dimensional methods in Part III are not directly applicable. For infinite-horizon dynamic programs, different techniques become necessary for establishing the existence of solutions and studying their properties. This chapter discusses methods based on the contraction principle introduced in Chapter 7.

14.2 MARKOV DYNAMIC PROGRAM

We say that the dynamic program $\mathcal{D} = \{X, A, \Gamma, V, H\}$ is an additive *Markov dynamic program* or *Markov decision problem* (MDP) if the following conditions hold.

- The state space can be written as $X \times Z$, where $Z = \{1, \ldots, Z\}$ is a finite set associated with a stochastic matrix $P = (P(z, z'))_{z,z' \in Z}$.

- The aggregator takes the additive (expected utility) form

$$H(x, z, a, v) = r(x, z, a) + \beta \sum_{z'=1}^{Z} P(z, z')v(g(x, z, z', a), z'), \quad (14.2)$$

  where $r : X \times Z \times A \to [-\infty, \infty)$ is the *reward function*, $g : X \times Z^2 \times A \to X$ is the *law of motion* or *transition function*, and $\beta \in [0, 1)$ is the *discount factor*.

Note that in the definition of the aggregator (14.2), the summation can be interpreted as the conditional expectation $\mathrm{E}[v(x_{t+1}, z_{t+1}) \mid z_t = z]$, where the next state is

$$x_{t+1} = g(x_t, z_t, z_{t+1}, a_t).$$

Thus we may write the Bellman operator T as

$$(Tv)(x, z) := \sup_{a \in \Gamma(x,z)} H(x, z, a, v)$$

$$= \sup_{a \in \Gamma(x,z)} \{r(x, z, a) + \beta \, \mathrm{E}_z[v(x', z')]\}, \quad (14.3)$$

where $\mathrm{E}_z = \mathrm{E}[\cdot \mid z]$ denotes the conditional expectation and it is understood that $x' = g(x, z, z', a)$. We write an additive Markov dynamic program as

$$\mathcal{D} = \{X, Z, P, A, \Gamma, V, r, g, \beta\}. \quad (14.4)$$

Example 14.1 (Optimal savings problem). Consider the optimal savings problem (14.1). Then we may identify each object of the additive Markov dynamic program as follows.

- The state space is $X = [0, \infty)$, where the state is wealth $w \in X$.

- The action space is $A = [0, \infty)$, where the action is consumption $c \in A$.

- The feasible correspondence is $\Gamma(w, z) = [0, w]$.

- The reward is the utility $r(w, z, c) = u(c)$.

- The transition function is

$$g(w, z, z', c) = R(z, z')(w - c) + y(z'). \tag{14.5}$$

The following theorem is fundamental. Recall that we denote by bX or $b(X)$ the space of all bounded functions defined on X, which by Proposition 7.1 is a Banach space endowed with the sup norm $\|\cdot\|$.

Theorem 14.1. *Let $\mathcal{D} = \{X, Z, P, A, \Gamma, V, r, g, \beta\}$ be an additive Markov dynamic program, where $V = b(X \times Z)$. Suppose that $r \in b(X \times Z \times A)$, so r is bounded. Then the Bellman operator T defined by (14.3) is a contraction with modulus $\beta \in [0, 1)$. Consequently, the following statements are true.*

(i) $\mathcal{D}$ has a unique value function $v \in V$, which is the unique fixed point of T.

(ii) For any $v_0 \in V$, we have $v = \lim_{k \to \infty} T^k v_0$.

(iii) The approximation error $\left\| T^k v_0 - v \right\|$ has order of magnitude β^k.

Proof. By the contraction mapping theorem (Theorem 7.3), it suffices to show that T is a contraction on V with modulus β. To this end, we verify Blackwell's sufficient conditions (Proposition 7.5).

If $v \in V = b(X \times Z)$, then v is bounded, so for any scalar $c \geq 0$, we have $v + c \in V$. Therefore V satisfies the upward shift property. If $v_1, v_2 \in V$, then the triangle inequality implies $\|v_1 - v_2\| \leq \|v_1\| + \|v_2\| < \infty$, so V satisfies the bounded difference property. If $v \in V$, noting that $|r(x, z, a)| \leq \|r\|$ and $|v(x', z')| \leq \|v\|$, we obtain

$$
\begin{aligned}
|(Tv)(x, z)| &= \left| \sup_{a \in \Gamma(x,z)} \{r(x, z, a) + \beta \, \mathrm{E}_z[v(x', z')]\} \right| \\
&\leq \sup_{a \in \Gamma(x,z)} \{|r(x, z, a)| + \beta \, \mathrm{E}_z[|v(x', z')|]\} \\
&\leq \sup_{a \in \Gamma(x,z)} \{\|r\| + \beta \, \mathrm{E}_z \|v\|\} = \|r\| + \beta \|v\| < \infty,
\end{aligned}
$$

so $T : V \to V$.

If $v_1, v_2 \in V$ and $v_1 \leq v_2$ pointwise, then for any $(x, z) \in X \times Z$, we have

$$
\begin{aligned}
(Tv_1)(x, z) &= \sup_{a \in \Gamma(x,z)} \{r(x, z, a) + \beta \, \mathrm{E}_z[v_1(x', z')]\} \\
&\leq \sup_{a \in \Gamma(x,z)} \{r(x, z, a) + \beta \, \mathrm{E}_z[v_2(x', z')]\} = (Tv_2)(x, z),
\end{aligned}
$$

so $Tv_1 \leq Tv_2$ and T is monotone. If $v \in V$ and $c \geq 0$, then

$$
\begin{aligned}
(T(v+c))(x,z) &= \sup_{a \in \Gamma(x,z)} \{r(x,z,a) + \beta\, \mathrm{E}_z[v(x',z') + c]\} \\
&= \sup_{a \in \Gamma(x,z)} \{r(x,z,a) + \beta\, \mathrm{E}_z[v(x',z')]\} + \beta c \\
&= (Tv)(x,z) + \beta c,
\end{aligned}
$$

so $T(v+c) = Tv + \beta c$ (in particular, $\leq$) and T satisfies the discounting property. Therefore by Proposition 7.5, T is a contraction with modulus β. $\quad\square$

We say that an additive Markov dynamic program $\mathcal{D}$ in (14.4) is a *bounded dynamic program* if the reward function r is bounded. In that case, we always take the value space V to be the space of bounded functions (or its subset), so $V = b(X \times Z)$. For bounded dynamic programs, Theorem 14.1 not only establishes the existence and uniqueness of the value function but also a computational algorithm: value function iteration is guaranteed to converge. For instance, if the utility function u in Example 14.1 is bounded, we can easily verify that all assumptions of Theorem 14.1 are satisfied (Problem 14.1).

14.3 SEQUENTIAL AND RECURSIVE FORMULATIONS

Consider the additive Markov dynamic program $\mathcal{D}$ studied in §14.2. By Theorem 14.1, there exists a unique value function v, which satisfies $v = Tv$. Therefore (14.3) reduces to the *Bellman equation*

$$
v(x,z) = \sup_{a \in \Gamma(x,z)} \{r(x,z,a) + \beta\, \mathrm{E}_z[v(x',z')]\}. \tag{14.6}
$$

When we study a dynamic optimization problem, we may formulate it *recursively* by writing down the Bellman equation as in (14.6). In contrast, we may also formulate it *sequentially* as in the optimal savings problem (14.1). For instance, by iterating the aggregator, the additive Markov dynamic program $\mathcal{D}$ can be formulated sequentially as

$$
\text{maximize} \qquad \mathrm{E}_{z_0} \sum_{t=0}^{\infty} \beta^t r(x_t, z_t, a_t) \tag{14.7a}
$$

$$
\text{subject to} \qquad (\forall t)x_{t+1} = g(x_t, z_t, z_{t+1}, a_t), \tag{14.7b}
$$

$$
(\forall t)a_t \in \Gamma(x_t, z_t), \tag{14.7c}
$$

$$
(x_0, z_0) \in X \times Z \text{ given}. \tag{14.7d}
$$

A natural question is whether the value function v in (14.6) is related to the solution to the optimization problem (14.7).

To answer this question, we introduce some terminology. We say that the stochastic process of the state-action pair $\{(x_t, a_t)\}_{t=0}^{\infty}$ is *feasible* if $a_t \in \Gamma(x_t, z_t)$ for all t given the initial state x_0 and the Markov chain $\{z_t\}_{t=0}^{\infty}$.

A function $\sigma : \mathsf{X} \times \mathsf{Z} \to \mathsf{A}$ satisfying $\sigma(x, z) \in \Gamma(x, z)$ is called a (feasible) *policy function*. Given $v \in \mathsf{V}$, if $a = \sigma(x, z)$ achieves the maximum of the right-hand side of (14.3) for all $(x, z) \in \mathsf{X} \times \mathsf{Z}$, we say that the policy function σ is *v-greedy*.

The following theorem shows that, for bounded additive Markov dynamic programs, solving the recursive dynamic program is necessary and sufficient for solving the sequential dynamic program (14.7).

Theorem 14.2 (Equivalence of recursive and sequential dynamic programs). *Let everything be as in Theorem 14.1 and $v \in \mathsf{V}$ be the unique fixed point of the Bellman operator T. Then the following statements are true.*

   (i) The supremum value $\bar{v}(x_0, z_0)$ of the sequential dynamic program (14.7) is well-defined and finite.

  (ii) We have $v(x, z) = \bar{v}(x, z)$ for all $(x, z) \in \mathsf{X} \times \mathsf{Z}$.

 (iii) If a v-greedy policy σ exists and we define the state-action process $\{(x_t, a_t)\}_{t=0}^{\infty}$ by $a_t = \sigma(x_t, z_t)$ for all t, then $\{(x_t, a_t)\}_{t=0}^{\infty}$ solves the sequential dynamic program (14.7).

Proof. (i) By assumption, r is bounded, so the value of the objective function in (14.7a) is bounded as

$$\left| \mathrm{E}_{z_0} \sum_{t=0}^{\infty} \beta^t r(x_t, z_t, a_t) \right| \leq \sum_{t=0}^{\infty} \beta^t \|r\| = \frac{\|r\|}{1 - \beta} < \infty.$$

Therefore the objective function is well defined and the supremum value $\bar{v}(x_0, z_0)$ of the sequential dynamic program (14.7) exists and is finite.

(ii) To prove $v = \bar{v}$, we show $v \leq \bar{v}$ and $v \geq \bar{v}$. Take any $(x, z) \in \mathsf{X} \times \mathsf{Z}$ and set $(x_0, z_0) = (x, z)$. Take any feasible $\{(x_t, a_t)\}$. Then the Bellman equation (14.6) implies

$$v(x_t, z_t) \geq r(x_t, z_t, a_t) + \beta \, \mathrm{E}_{z_t}[v(x_{t+1}, z_{t+1})].$$

Iterating this inequality, for any $T > 0$, we obtain

$$v(x_0, z_0) \geq \mathrm{E}_{z_0} \sum_{t=0}^{T-1} \beta^t r(x_t, z_t, a_t) + \mathrm{E}_{z_0} \beta^T v(x_T, z_T). \tag{14.8}$$

Noting that $\|v\| < \infty$ and $\beta \in [0, 1)$, we have

$$\left| \mathrm{E}_{z_0} \beta^T v(x_T, z_T) \right| \leq \beta^T \|v\| \to 0$$

as $T \to \infty$. Therefore letting $T \to \infty$ in (14.8),[1] we obtain

$$v(x_0, z_0) \geq \mathrm{E}_{z_0} \sum_{t=0}^{\infty} \beta^t r(x_t, z_t, a_t).$$

---

[1]Here we are interchanging the order of infinite summation and expectation. Its justification requires the dominated convergence theorem in measure theory. See, for instance, Folland (1999).

Taking the supremum over all feasible state-action processes, we obtain $v(x_0, z_0) \geq \bar{v}(x_0, z_0)$. Therefore $v \geq \bar{v}$.

To show the reverse inequality, take any $\epsilon > 0$. For any (x_t, z_t), by the Bellman equation (14.6), we can take $a_t \in \Gamma(x_t, z_t)$ such that

$$v(x_t, z_t) \leq r(x_t, z_t, x_t) + \beta \, \mathrm{E}_{z_t}[v(x_{t+1}, z_{t+1})] + (1 - \beta)\epsilon.$$

Iterating this inequality, for any $T > 0$, we obtain

$$v(x_0, z_0) \leq \mathrm{E}_{z_0} \sum_{t=0}^{T-1} \beta^t r(x_t, z_t, a_t) + \mathrm{E}_{z_0} \beta^T v(x_T, z_T) + (1 - \beta^T)\epsilon. \qquad (14.9)$$

Letting $T \to \infty$ in (14.9), we obtain

$$v(x_0, z_0) \leq \mathrm{E}_{z_0} \sum_{t=0}^{\infty} \beta^t r(x_t, z_t, a_t) + \epsilon$$

$$\leq \sup \mathrm{E}_{z_0} \sum_{t=0}^{\infty} \beta^t r(x_t, z_t, a_t) + \epsilon = \bar{v}(x_0, z_0) + \epsilon,$$

where sup means the supremum over all feasible state-action processes. Letting $\epsilon \downarrow 0$, we obtain $v(x_0, z_0) \leq \bar{v}(x_0, z_0)$, so $v \leq \bar{v}$.

(iii) If σ is v-greedy and $a_t = \sigma(x_t, z_t)$ for all t, then the Bellman equation (14.6) implies

$$v(x_t, z_t) = r(x_t, z_t, a_t) + \beta \, \mathrm{E}_{z_t}[v(x_{t+1}, z_{t+1})].$$

Iterating this equation yields

$$v(x_0, z_0) = \mathrm{E}_{z_0} \sum_{t=0}^{T-1} \beta^t r(x_t, z_t, a_t) + \mathrm{E}_{z_0} \beta^T v(x_T, z_T).$$

Letting $T \to \infty$, we obtain

$$\bar{v}(x_0, z_0) = v(x_0, z_0) = \mathrm{E}_{z_0} \sum_{t=0}^{\infty} \beta^t r(x_t, z_t, a_t). \qquad \square$$

By Theorem 14.2, in any bounded dynamic program in which a greedy policy exists, we may generate a solution to the sequential dynamic program (14.7) by iterating $a_t = \sigma(x_t, z_t)$ and $x_{t+1} = g(x_t, z_t, z_{t+1}, a_t)$. Given this equivalence, from now on we will use only the recursive formulation because it is more tractable.

14.4 PROPERTIES OF VALUE FUNCTION

In many applications, we are not only interested in proving the existence (and uniqueness) of a value function but also establishing its properties such as continuity, monotonicity, and convexity/concavity.

For this purpose, we note the following very simple lemma (which was Problem 7.2).

Lemma 14.3 (Closed subset lemma). *Let* (V, d) *be a complete metric space and* $T : \mathsf{V} \to \mathsf{V}$ *a contraction with a unique fixed point* $v \in \mathsf{V}$. *If* $\emptyset \neq \mathsf{V}_1 \subset \mathsf{V}$ *is closed and* $T\mathsf{V}_1 \subset \mathsf{V}_1$, *then* $v \in \mathsf{V}_1$.

Proof. Since V_1 is closed, (V_1, d) is a complete metric space. Since $T : \mathsf{V}_1 \to \mathsf{V}_1$ is a contraction, it has a unique fixed point $v_1 \in \mathsf{V}_1$, which is also a fixed point of $T : \mathsf{V} \to \mathsf{V}$. Since v is unique, we must have $v = v_1 \in \mathsf{V}_1$. $\qquad\square$

We present several applications of Lemma 14.3. Below, let $\mathcal{D}$ in (14.4) be a bounded additive Markov dynamic program with Bellman operator T and value function v. The set of maximizers in (14.6) (which could be empty),

$$\sigma(x, z) := \arg\max_{a \in \Gamma(x,z)} \{r(x, z, a) + \beta \, \mathrm{E}_z[v(x', z')]\}, \qquad (14.10)$$

is called the *policy correspondence*. When σ is a singleton or we specify some rule to select one action, we call it a *policy function*.

Proposition 14.4 (Continuity of value function). *Let* $\mathcal{D}$ *in* (14.4) *be a bounded additive Markov dynamic program. Let* X, A *be topological spaces, r, g continuous, and Γ nonempty, compact, and continuous. Then the value function v is continuous and the policy correspondence σ is nonempty and upper hemicontinuous.*

Proof. Let $\mathsf{V}_1 \subset \mathsf{V}$ be the space of bounded continuous functions equipped with the sup norm $\|\cdot\|$. By Corollary 7.2, V_1 is a nonempty closed subset of V and hence Banach. Under the maintained assumptions, for $v \in \mathsf{V}_1$, an application of the maximum theorem (Theorem 12.18) implies $Tv \in \mathsf{V}_1$. Therefore $T\mathsf{V}_1 \subset \mathsf{V}_1$, so the value function satisfies $v \in \mathsf{V}_1$ by Lemma 14.3. Since v is continuous and Γ is nonempty and compact, by the extreme value theorem the policy correspondence σ is nonempty, and it is upper hemicontinuous by the maximum theorem. $\qquad\square$

We next consider monotonicity. Before we do so, we need to introduce the notion of a partial order. Let X be a set. We say that a binary relation $\leq$ on X is a *partial order* if

(i) (Reflexivity) $x \leq x$ for all $x \in X$,

(ii) (Antisymmetry) if $x \leq y$ and $y \leq x$, then $x = y$,

(iii) (Transitivity) if $x \leq y$ and $y \leq z$, then $x \leq z$.

A set with a partial order is called a *partially ordered set*, or *poset* for short. The Euclidean space $X = \mathbb{R}^N$ is a partially ordered Banach space by declaring $x \leq y$ whenever $x_n \leq y_n$ for all n. Similarly, a function space (such as V in Example 7.1) is partially ordered by declaring $v_1 \leq v_2$ whenever $v_1(x) \leq v_2(x)$ for all x. When dealing with spaces of functions taking real values, we always endow the partial order defined by pointwise order.

Proposition 14.5 (Monotonicity of value function). *Let $\mathcal{D}$ in (14.4) be a bounded additive Markov dynamic program. Suppose that X is partially ordered and Γ, r, g are monotone in the sense that, for all $x_1 \leq x_2$, $z, z' \in \mathsf{Z}$, and $a \in \Gamma(x_1, z)$, we have*

$$\Gamma(x_1, z) \subset \Gamma(x_2, z),$$
$$r(x_1, z, a) \leq r(x_2, z, a),$$
$$g(x_1, z, z', a) \leq g(x_2, z, z', a).$$

Then the value function is monotone: $x_1 \leq x_2 \implies v(x_1, z) \leq v(x_2, z)$.

Proof. Let $\mathsf{V}_1 \subset \mathsf{V}$ be the set of bounded monotone functions. Suppose $\{v_k\} \subset \mathsf{V}_1$ and $v_k \to v$ in V. Then for any $x_1 \leq x_2$ and $z \in \mathsf{Z}$, we have $v_k(x_1, z) \leq v_k(x_2, z)$. Letting $k \to \infty$, we have $v(x_1, z) \leq v(x_2, z)$, so v is monotone and $v \in \mathsf{V}_1$. Thus V_1 is closed. If $v \in \mathsf{V}_1$, then for any $x_1 \leq x_2$, we have

$$
\begin{aligned}
(Tv)(x_1, z) &= \sup_{a \in \Gamma(x_1, z)} \{r(x_1, z, a) + \beta \, \mathrm{E}_z[v(g(x_1, z, z', a), z')]\} \\
&\leq \sup_{a \in \Gamma(x_1, z)} \{r(x_2, z, a) + \beta \, \mathrm{E}_z[v(g(x_2, z, z', a), z')]\} \\
&\leq \sup_{a \in \Gamma(x_2, z)} \{r(x_2, z, a) + \beta \, \mathrm{E}_z[v(g(x_2, z, z', a), z')]\} \\
&= (Tv)(x_2, z),
\end{aligned}
$$

where the first inequality uses the monotonicity of r, g, v and the second inequality uses the monotonicity of Γ. Therefore Tv is monotone and $T\mathsf{V}_1 \subset \mathsf{V}_1$, so the claim follows from Lemma 14.3. □

We next establish the concavity of the value function. If X is a vector space and $(Y, \leq)$ is a partially ordered vector space, we say that the map $f : X \to Y$ is *convex* if

$$f((1 - \alpha)x_1 + \alpha x_2) \leq (1 - \alpha)f(x_1) + \alpha f(x_2).$$

A concave map is defined by flipping the inequality.

Proposition 14.6 (Concavity of value function). *Let everything be as in Proposition 14.5 and suppose that the state space X and the action space A are vector spaces. If r, g are concave in (x, a), then the value function is monotone and concave in x.*

Proof. Let $\mathsf{V}_1 \subset \mathsf{V}$ be the set of bounded monotone functions and $\mathsf{V}_2 \subset \mathsf{V}_1$ be the set of bounded monotone concave functions. By the same argument as in the proof of Proposition 14.5, V_2 is closed. Let $v \in \mathsf{V}_2$. Since g is a monotone concave map, by Proposition 11.4, $v(g(x, z, z', a), z')$ is concave in (x, a). Since r is concave, by Proposition 11.2,

$$r(x, z, a) + \beta \, \mathrm{E}_z[v(g(x, z, z', a), z')]$$

is concave in (x, a). Therefore by Proposition 11.6,

$$(Tv)(x, z) = \sup_{a \in \Gamma(x,z)} \{r(x, z, a) + \beta \, \mathrm{E}_z[v(g(x, z, z', a), z')]\}$$

is concave in x. By Proposition 14.5, Tv is also monotone in x, so $T\mathsf{V}_2 \subset \mathsf{V}_2$ and the claim follows from Lemma 14.3. $\qquad\qquad\square$

Example 14.2 (Optimal savings problem with concave utility). Consider the optimal savings problem in Example 14.1. If the utility function u is bounded and concave, then the value function is increasing and concave. To see this, we verify the assumptions of Propositions 14.5 and 14.6. If $w_1 \leq w_2$, the feasible correspondence satisfies

$$\Gamma(w_1, z) = [0, w_1] \subset [0, w_2] = \Gamma(w_2, z).$$

The reward function satisfies

$$r(w_1, z, c) = u(c) = r(w_2, z, c).$$

The transition function satisfies

$$\begin{aligned} g(w_1, z, z', c) &= R(z, z')(w_1 - c) + y(z') \\ &\leq R(z, z')(w_2 - c) + y(z') = g(w_2, z, z'c). \end{aligned}$$

Therefore the assumptions of Proposition 14.5 are satisfied. Furthermore, clearly $r(w, z, c) = u(c)$ is concave in (w, c) and $g(w, z, z', c)$ is affine (hence concave) in (w, c), so the assumptions of Proposition 14.6 are satisfied.

14.5 RESTRICTING SPACES

Although solving additive Markov dynamic programs based on the contraction principle (Theorem 14.1) is elegant, to directly apply these results, the reward function needs to be bounded. However, some reward functions that are commonly used in applications are unbounded. For instance, consider the optimal savings problem (14.1). The most common utility function is the constant relative risk aversion (CRRA) specification

$$u(c) = \begin{cases} \frac{c^{1-\gamma}}{1-\gamma} & \text{if } 0 < \gamma \neq 1, \\ \log c & \text{if } \gamma = 1, \end{cases} \tag{14.11}$$

where the parameter $\gamma > 0$ governs risk aversion. Note that u in (14.11) is unbounded above if $0 < \gamma < 1$, unbounded below if $\gamma > 1$, and unbounded both from above and below if $\gamma = 1$.

In some cases, we may apply the contraction principle by restricting the spaces.

Example 14.3 (Optimal savings with utility unbounded below). Consider the optimal savings problem (14.1). Suppose that the utility function u is bounded above, strictly increasing on $[0, \infty)$, and finite-valued on $(0, \infty)$, for example the CRRA specification (14.11) with $\gamma > 1$. Suppose that income is always positive, so $\underline{y} := \min_{z \in \mathsf{Z}} y(z) > 0$. By assumption, we have

$$\underline{u} := u(\underline{y}) > -\infty \quad \text{and} \quad \bar{u} := u(\infty) < \infty.$$

Note that due to the budget constraint (14.1b) and the borrowing constraint (14.1c), for any $t \geq 0$, the agent is guaranteed to have wealth $w_t \geq \underline{y} > 0$. Once we solve the problem starting at $t = 1$, solving the problem at $t = 0$ is straightforward because it reduces to a finite-horizon (one period) problem. Therefore without loss of generality, we may restrict the state space to $\mathsf{X} = [\underline{y}, \infty)$. Furthermore, for any feasible state-action process $\{(w_t, c_t)\}$, using (14.1a), the value the agent gets is restricted to the range

$$\frac{\underline{u}}{1 - \beta} \leq \mathrm{E}_0 \sum_{t=0}^{\infty} \beta^t u(c_t) \leq \frac{\bar{u}}{1 - \beta}.$$

Therefore, without loss of generality we may restrict the value space to functions v such that

$$\frac{\underline{u}}{1 - \beta} \leq v(x, z) \leq \frac{\bar{u}}{1 - \beta} \tag{14.12}$$

for all $(x, z) \in \mathsf{X} \times \mathsf{Z}$. This bound on the value space allows us to obtain a bound on the action space as well. To see why, suppose the agent consumes $c \geq 0$ today. Using the bound (14.12), the continuation value can be bounded from above as

$$u(c) + \beta \, \mathrm{E}_z[v(w', z')] \leq u(c) + \frac{\beta}{1 - \beta}\bar{u}.$$

If c is optimal, in order for the Bellman operator to be a self-map on the value space defined by (14.12), we must have

$$\frac{\underline{u}}{1 - \beta} \leq u(c) + \frac{\beta}{1 - \beta}\bar{u} \iff u(c) \geq \frac{\beta\bar{u} - \underline{u}}{1 - \beta}.$$

Thus without loss of generality, we may restrict consumption to this range and assume that u is bounded below. Then we can apply the same proof as Theorem 14.1 and the conclusion remains valid.

We consider another example.

Example 14.4 (Stochastic growth model). Consider the following *stochastic growth model*:

$$\begin{array}{lll} \text{maximize} & \mathrm{E}_0 \displaystyle\sum_{t=0}^{\infty} \beta^t u(c_t) & (14.13\text{a}) \\[2ex] \text{subject to} & (\forall t)w_{t+1} = g(w_t, z_t, z_{t+1}, c_t), & (14.13\text{b}) \\[1ex] & (\forall t)0 \leq c_t \leq w_t, & (14.13\text{c}) \\[1ex] & w_0 > 0, \; z_0 \text{ given.} & (14.13\text{d}) \end{array}$$

The optimal savings problem (14.1) is mathematically a special case of the stochastic growth model (14.13) by setting the transition function to (14.5). However, the economic interpretation is different. While the optimal savings problem describes the behavior of a single agent, the stochastic growth model describes the behavior of the aggregate economy, where w is available resources and g is the production function. A common example is to set

$$g(w, z, z', c) = A(z, z')k^\alpha + (1 - \delta)k, \tag{14.14}$$

where $k := w - c$ is capital, $A(z, z') > 0$ is productivity, $\alpha \in (0, 1)$ governs decreasing returns to scale, and $\delta \in (0, 1)$ is capital depreciation rate. If the utility function u is bounded, we may apply Theorem 14.1.

For the stochastic growth model with transition function (14.14), utility functions that are unbounded above (such as the CRRA specification (14.11) with $0 < \gamma < 1$) can be easily handled by restricting the state space. To see this, solve

$$w = Aw^\alpha + (1 - \delta)w \iff w = \bar{w} := (A/\delta)^{\frac{1}{1-\alpha}}, \tag{14.15}$$

where $A := \max_{z, z' \in \mathsf{Z}} A(z, z')$. Then (14.14) implies that

$$0 \leq w \leq \bar{w} \implies 0 \leq g(w, z, z', c) \leq \bar{w},$$
$$w \geq \bar{w} \implies 0 \leq g(w, z, z', c) \leq w$$

for all $z, z' \in \mathsf{Z}$ and $c \in [0, w]$. Thus we may restrict the state space X to any bounded interval including $[0, \bar{w}]$. Then u is bounded, and we may apply Theorem 14.1.

14.6 STATE-DEPENDENT DISCOUNTING

The discount factor $\beta \in [0, 1)$ in the Markov dynamic program (14.4) governs the patience of the decision maker. When β is large (small), the decision maker puts relatively more (less) weight on future rewards and thus can be considered more (less) patient. For some applications, we may want to consider situations where patience changes over time. For instance, if the decision maker is considered to be the head of a dynasty, even if a parent is patient and lives frugally, the child may be impatient and spend extravagantly. Furthermore, for modeling purposes, there is no need to restrict the discount factor to be less than 1. We thus consider a more general setting where the discount factor could be state dependent.[2]

For this purpose, all we need to do is to change the definition of the aggregator from (14.2) to

$$H(x, z, a, v) = r(x, z, a) + \sum_{z'=1}^{Z} P(z, z')\beta(z, z')v(g(x, z, z', a), z'), \tag{14.16}$$

---

[2]Krusell and Smith (1998) numerically found that introducing state-dependent discounting in an optimal savings problem helps to explain large wealth inequality. Toda (2019) proved this claim in a particular model.

where $\beta : \mathsf{Z}^2 \to \mathbb{R}_+$. Here $\beta(z, z') \geq 0$ is the discount factor conditional on transitioning from state z to z'. When the aggregator takes the form (14.16), we say that the additive Markov dynamic program exhibits *state-dependent discounting*.

The following theorem generalizes Theorems 14.1 and 14.2 by using the properties of Perov contractions introduced in §7.5.

Theorem 14.7. *Let $\mathcal{D}$ in (14.4) be a bounded additive Markov dynamic program with state-dependent discounting. If the matrix $B := (P(z, z')\beta(z, z'))$ has spectral radius $\rho(B) < 1$, the following statements are true.*

   (i) The Bellman operator T is a Perov contraction with coefficient matrix B.

  (ii) $\mathcal{D}$ has a unique value function v, which is the unique fixed point of T.

 (iii) For any $v_0 \in \mathsf{V}$, we have $v = \lim_{k \to \infty} T^k v_0$.

 (iv) For any $\gamma \in (\rho(B), 1)$, the approximation error $\left\| T^k v_0 - v \right\|$ has order of magnitude γ^k.

  (v) If the policy correspondence σ is nonempty, the state-action process generated by σ achieves the maximum of the sequential problem.

Proof. We only provide a sketch. The first four statements follow by checking that the assumptions of Proposition 7.7 are satisfied. The last statement follows from the same argument as the proof of Theorem 14.2 and applying the Gelfand spectral radius formula (Theorem 6.15). $\qquad\square$

14.7 WEIGHTED SUPREMUM NORM

As we have seen in the discussion of the optimal savings problem (Example 14.3) and the stochastic growth model (Example 14.4), some common applications violate the boundedness assumption of Theorem 14.1. While we may get around this issue in some cases by restricting the state space or the value space, such approaches are ad hoc and lack generality. We thus seek to extend Theorem 14.1 to allow certain kinds of unboundedness.

To this end, let $\kappa : \mathsf{X} \times \mathsf{Z} \to (0, \infty)$ be some positive function and suppose that we normalize the value function as $\tilde{v} = v/\kappa$. Then the Bellman equation (14.6) becomes

$$\kappa(x, z)\tilde{v}(x, z) = \sup_{a \in \Gamma(x,z)} \{r(x, z, a) + \mathrm{E}_z[\beta(z, z')\kappa(x', z')\tilde{v}(x', z')]\},$$

where we allow state-dependent discounting as in §14.6. Dividing both sides by $\kappa(x, z) > 0$, we may define a scaled Bellman operator $\tilde{T}$ by

$$(\tilde{T}\tilde{v})(x, z) = \sup_{a \in \Gamma(x,z)} \left\{ \tilde{r}(x, z, a) + \mathrm{E}_z \left[\beta(z, z') \frac{\kappa(x', z')}{\kappa(x, z)} \tilde{v}(x', z') \right] \right\}, \quad (14.17)$$

where $\tilde{r} := r/\kappa$. To make $\tilde{T}$ a (Perov) contraction, all we need is to control the ratio $\kappa(x', z')/\kappa(x, z)$. We thus define

$$\tilde{\beta}(z, z') := \beta(z, z') \sup_{x \in \mathsf{X}} \sup_{a \in \Gamma(x,z)} \frac{\kappa(g(x, z, z', a), z')}{\kappa(x, z)} < \infty. \tag{14.18}$$

To come up with the appropriate function space, let V be the space of functions $v : \mathsf{X} \times \mathsf{Z} \to \mathbb{R}$ with

$$\|v\|_{\kappa} := \sup_{z \in \mathsf{Z}} \sup_{x \in \mathsf{X}} \frac{|v(x, z)|}{\kappa(x, z)} < \infty. \tag{14.19}$$

Because $\kappa > 0$, it is straightforward to show by imitating the proof of Proposition 7.1 that $(\mathsf{V}, \|\cdot\|_{\kappa})$ is a Banach space. The norm (14.19) is called the *weighted supremum norm* with weight function κ. For $v_1, v_2 \in \mathsf{V}$, if we define $d : \mathsf{V} \times \mathsf{V} \to \mathbb{R}_+^Z$ by

$$d_z(v_1, v_2) = \sup_{x \in \mathsf{X}} \frac{|v_1(x, z) - v_2(x, z)|}{\kappa(x, z)},$$

then (V, d) becomes a complete vector-valued metric space by the discussion in §7.5.

With this preparation, we obtain the following theorem, which generalizes both Theorems 14.1 and 14.7.

Theorem 14.8. *Let $\mathcal{D} = \{\mathsf{X}, \mathsf{Z}, P, \mathsf{A}, \Gamma, \mathsf{V}, r, g, \beta\}$ be an additive Markov dynamic program associated with a function $\kappa : \mathsf{X} \times \mathsf{Z} \to (0, \infty)$. Let (V, d) be the complete vector-valued metric space just described. Suppose that*

$$\sup_{x \in \mathsf{X}} \sup_{a \in \Gamma(x,z)} \frac{|r(x, z, a)|}{\kappa(x, z)} < \infty \tag{14.20}$$

and $\rho(B) < 1$, where $B := (P(z, z')\tilde{\beta}(z, z'))$ is defined using (14.18). Then the following statements are true.

(i) The (scaled) Bellman operator T $(\tilde{T})$ is a Perov contraction on V $(b(\mathsf{X} \times \mathsf{Z}))$ with coefficient matrix B.

(ii) $\mathcal{D}$ has a unique value function $v = \kappa \tilde{v}$, where $\tilde{v}$ is the unique fixed point of $\tilde{T}$ in $b(\mathsf{X} \times \mathsf{Z})$.

Proof. (i) It suffices to show the claim for $\tilde{T}$. Below, we view $\tilde{v} \in b(\mathsf{X} \times \mathsf{Z})$ as a bounded function from X to $\mathbb{R}^Z$, so we identify $b(\mathsf{X} \times \mathsf{Z})$ as $(b\mathsf{X})^Z$. We verify the assumptions of Proposition 7.7. It is clear that $(b\mathsf{X})^Z$ satisfies the upward shift and bounded difference properties. The monotonicity of $\tilde{T}$ immediately follows from the definition (14.17). To show discounting, take any $c \in \mathbb{R}_+^Z$.

Using (14.17), we obtain

$$(\tilde{T}(\tilde{v} + c))(x, z)$$

$$= \sup_{a \in \Gamma(x,z)} \left\{ \tilde{r}(x, z, a) + \mathrm{E}_z \left[\beta(z, z') \frac{\kappa(x', z')}{\kappa(x, z)} (\tilde{v}(x', z') + c(z')) \right] \right\}$$

$$\leq (\tilde{T}\tilde{v})(x, z) + \sup_{a \in \Gamma(x,z)} \mathrm{E}_z \left[\beta(z, z') \frac{\kappa(x', z')}{\kappa(x, z)} c(z') \right]$$

$$\leq (\tilde{T}\tilde{v})(x, z) + \mathrm{E}_z [\tilde{\beta}(z, z') c(z')]$$

$$= (\tilde{T}\tilde{v})(x, z) + (Bc)_z.$$

Therefore $\tilde{T}(\tilde{v} + c) \leq \tilde{T}\tilde{v} + Bc$, so discounting holds.

(ii) Obvious by (14.6) and (14.17). □

Remark. Theorem 14.7 is a special case of Theorem 14.8 by setting $\kappa \equiv 1$.

Example 14.5 (Optimal savings with unbounded utility). Consider the optimal savings problem (14.1) with transition function (14.5), where u could be unbounded both from above and below. We have already seen in Example 14.3 that unboundedness from below can be handled by restricting the state and value spaces. Consider the weight function $\kappa(w, z) = w + b$, where $b > 0$. Then

$$\frac{\kappa(g(w, z, z', c), z')}{\kappa(w, z)} = \frac{R(z, z')(w - c) + y(z') + b}{w + b}$$

$$\leq \frac{R(z, z')w + y(z') + b}{w + b}. \tag{14.21}$$

Noting that

$$\frac{Rw + y + b}{w + b} \leq \frac{\max\{1, R\}(w + b) + y}{w + b} \leq \max\{1, R\} + \frac{y}{b},$$

it follows from (14.21) that

$$\frac{\kappa(g(w, z, z', c), z')}{\kappa(w, z)} \leq \max\{1, R(z, z')\} + \frac{y(z')}{b} \to \max\{1, R(z, z')\}$$

as $b \to \infty$. Therefore by taking b large enough, a sufficient condition for the existence of a solution is that $u(w)/(w + b)$ is bounded above (concavity of u suffices) and that

$$\tilde{\beta}(z, z') := \beta \max\{1, R(z, z')\}$$

satisfies the assumption of Theorem 14.8.

Example 14.6 (Optimal savings with CRRA utility). In Example 14.5, suppose that the utility function is given by (14.11) with $0 < \gamma < 1$. If we consider the weight function $\kappa(w, z) = (w + b)^{1-\gamma}$, by a similar argument we may set

$$\tilde{\beta}(z, z') := \beta \max\{1, R(z, z')^{1-\gamma}\},$$

and satisfying the assumptions of Theorem 14.8 becomes even easier (because $R^{1-\gamma} < R$ whenever $R > 1$).

14.8   NUMERICAL DYNAMIC PROGRAMMING

Almost all dynamic programming problems do not admit closed-form solutions and must be solved numerically on a computer. This section provides an introduction to numerical dynamic programming and some theoretical background.

Suppose we would like to solve the Markov dynamic program (14.4) with Bellman operator (14.6). For simplicity, suppose both the state x and action a are real-valued, and the feasible correspondence $\Gamma(x, z)$ is an interval. Because a computer can accept only finitely many objects, the first step to solve the problem is to discretize the state space X. Take some N, and let $\mathsf{X}_N = \{x_1, \ldots, x_N\}$ be a finite grid, where $x_1 < \cdots < x_N$. We parameterize the value function by finitely many numbers $\{v(x_n, z)\}_{n=1}^{N} {}_{z=1}^{Z} \in \mathbb{R}^{NZ}$. Then the value space is $\mathsf{V}_N := \mathbb{R}^{NZ}$, which is a Banach space. Suppose we use some interpolation/extrapolation method to evaluate v on the entire state space X, for instance, linear interpolation on the interval $[x_1, x_N]$ and extrapolation by constants outside. With a slight abuse of notation, we use the same symbol V_N to denote the space of functions defined on the entire X by interpolation/extrapolation.

Recall that the Bellman operator T is defined by

$$(Tv)(x, z) := \max_{a \in \Gamma(x,z)} \{r(x, z, a) + \beta \, \mathrm{E}_z[v(x', z')]\}$$

$$= \max_{a \in \Gamma(x,z)} \left\{ r(x, z, a) + \beta \sum_{z'=1}^{Z} P(z, z')v(g(x, z, z,' a), z') \right\}. \quad (14.22)$$

If $v \in \mathsf{V}_N$ and we use a particular interpolation/extrapolation method to evaluate $v(g(x, z, z,' a), z')$, then computing the right-hand side of (14.22) for each (w_n, z) pair, we obtain new numbers $\{(Tv)(x_n, z)\}_{n=1}^{N} {}_{z=1}^{Z}$. Thus we may view T as a self-map from V_N to V_N. An application of Blackwell's sufficient condition shows that T is a contraction with modulus β. Therefore T has a unique fixed point in V_N, which could be thought of as an approximation to the true value function $v \in \mathsf{V}$.

As an illustration, we consider a simple specification for the stochastic growth model in Example 14.4. The Bellman operator (14.22) can be explicitly written as

$$(Tv)(w, z) =$$

$$\max_{0 \leq k \leq w} \left\{ u(w - k) + \beta \sum_{z'=1}^{Z} P(z, z')v(A(z, z')k^{\alpha} + (1 - \delta)k, z') \right\}, \quad (14.23)$$

where $k = w - c$ is capital. We consider a two-state Markov chain with $\mathsf{Z} = \{1, 2\}$ and transition probability $P(z, z') = 0.8$ if $z = z'$ and $P(z, z') = 0.2$ if

$z \neq z'$. The productivity is

$$A(z, z') = \begin{cases} 1.1 & \text{if } z' = 1, \\ 0.9 & \text{if } z' = 2, \end{cases}$$

so state 1 is the high-productivity state. We set $\alpha = 0.36$ and $\delta = 0.08$, which are standard values. The discount factor is $\beta = 0.95$ and the relative risk aversion in (14.11) is $\gamma = 0.5$. We use an N-point exponential grid $\{w_n\}_{n=1}^N$ on $[0, 120]$ with $N = 100$ to evaluate the value function. (See Gouin-Bonenfant and Toda (2023) for the details on the grid.) Starting from some v_0, we iterate the Bellman operator (14.23) by numerically maximizing the objective function (14.23) for each (w_n, z) pair. Matlab codes are available at the book website https://github.com/alexisakira/EME.

Figure 14.1 plots the sequence of value functions $\{v_k\}$ obtained by value function iteration. In the left panel, we start with $v_0 \equiv 0$, in which case convergence is monotonic (because the utility function is positive). In the right panel, we start with an unnatural function, namely the sine curve flipped upside down. Although convergence is not monotonic, the conclusions of Theorem 14.1 remain valid.

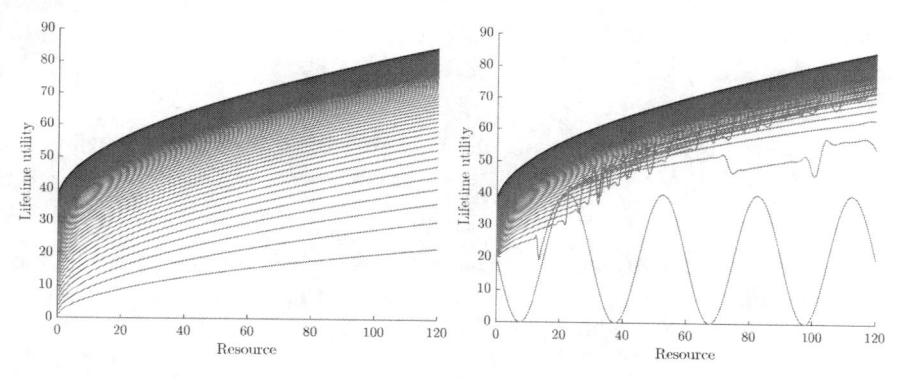

FIGURE 14.1: Value function iteration in stochastic growth model.

For a bounded additive Markov dynamic program, Theorem 14.1 guarantees that value function iteration (VFI) converges. However, this does not imply that we need to use VFI to solve dynamic programs. In fact, it is well known that VFI is a slow algorithm, for two reasons. First, by Theorem 14.1, the theoretical error is $O(\beta^k)$ after k iterations, which decays only exponentially. Second, at each iteration one needs to solve an optimization problem (maximize or minimize over $a \in \Gamma(x, z)$), which is computationally intensive.

One way to get around the second issue is to perform the optimization step only occasionally. For instance, take a natural number m and suppose we update the k-th value function v_k using the Bellman operator (14.3)

$$v_{k+1} := (Tv_k)(x, z) = \sup_{a \in \Gamma(x,z)} \{r(x, z, a) + \beta \, \mathrm{E}_z[v_k(x', z')]\}$$

only when $k = ml$ for $l = 0, 1, \ldots$, and otherwise we skip the optimization step as

$$v_{k+1} := r(x, z, a) + \beta \, \mathrm{E}_z[v_k(x', z')],$$

where for action a, we use the optimal action for the last optimization step. Following Sargent and Stachurski (2024), we refer to this algorithm as *optimistic policy iteration* (OPI). The following theorem shows that, with a suitable choice of initial value, OPI converges.

Theorem 14.9. *Let everything be as in Proposition 14.4. If $v_0 \in \mathsf{V}$ satisfies $v_0 \leq Tv_0$, then the sequence $\{v_k\}_{k=0}^\infty$ obtained by optimistic policy iteration converges to the value function v.*

To prove Theorem 14.9, we establish a series of lemmas following the approach of Sargent and Stachurski (2024, §9.1.4). Let V be the space of bounded continuous functions. For $v \in \mathsf{V}$, by the extreme value theorem, there exists a v-greedy policy

$$\sigma(x, z) \in \arg\max_{a \in \Gamma(x,z)} \{r(x, z, a) + \beta \, \mathrm{E}_z[v(x', z')]\}. \tag{14.24}$$

For this σ, define the policy iteration operator T_σ by skipping the optimization step, so for any $w \in \mathsf{V}$, let

$$(T_\sigma w)(x, z) := r(x, z, a) + \beta \, \mathrm{E}_z[w(x', z')]$$

for $a = \sigma(x, z)$. Finally, define the OPI operator W by $Wv = T_\sigma^{m-1} Tv$ for $v \in \mathsf{V}$, where σ implicitly depends on v because σ is v-greedy. Define the subset $\mathsf{V}_u := \{v \in \mathsf{V} : v \leq Tv\}$. By assumption, we have $v_0 \in \mathsf{V}_u$.

Lemma 14.10. *The set V_u is W-invariant: $W\mathsf{V}_u \subset \mathsf{V}_u$.*

Proof. Take any $v \in \mathsf{V}_u$ and let σ be v-greedy. Since $a = \sigma(x, z)$ is the maximizer of the right-hand side of (14.24), which defines the Bellman operator T, we have $T_\sigma v = Tv$. Therefore

$$
\begin{aligned}
Wv = T_\sigma^{m-1} Tv = T_\sigma^m v &\leq T_\sigma^m Tv && (\because v \leq Tv, \, T_\sigma \text{ monotone}) \\
&= T_\sigma T_\sigma^{m-1} Tv = T_\sigma Wv \leq TWv. && (\because T_\sigma \leq T)
\end{aligned}
$$

Therefore $Wv \in \mathsf{V}_u$. □

Lemma 14.11. *If $v \in \mathsf{V}_u$, then $Tv \leq Wv \leq T^m v$.*

Proof. Since T, T_σ are monotone and $T_\sigma \leq T$, we have

$$Wv = T_\sigma^{m-1} Tv \leq T^{m-1} Tv = T^m v.$$

To show the left inequality, let us show by induction that $T_\sigma^j Tv \geq Tv$ for all $j = 0, 1, \ldots$. If $j = 0$, the claim is trivial. If the claim holds for some j, then

$$
\begin{aligned}
T_\sigma^{j+1} Tv = T_\sigma T_\sigma^j Tv &\geq T_\sigma Tv && (\because T_\sigma^j Tv \geq Tv, \, T_\sigma \text{ monotone}) \\
&\geq T_\sigma v && (\because Tv \geq v, \, T_\sigma \text{ monotone}) \\
&= Tv, && (\because \sigma \text{ is } v\text{-greedy})
\end{aligned}
$$

so the claim holds for $j+1$ as well. In particular, setting $j = m-1$, we obtain $Wv = T_\sigma^{m-1}Tv \geq Tv$. □

Proof of Theorem 14.9. By Lemma 14.10, W is a self-map on V_u. Hence by iterating the inequality in Lemma 14.11 k times, for any $v_0 \in \mathsf{V}_u$, we obtain $T^k v_0 \leq W^k v_0 \leq T^{km} v_0$. Letting $k \to \infty$, by Theorem 14.1 we have $W^k v_0 \to v$. □

Remark. To apply Theorem 14.9, we need to select an initial value v_0 satisfying $v_0 \leq T v_0$. For bounded dynamic programs, this is simple. To see why, if the reward function r is bounded, by adding a positive constant if necessary, without loss of generality we may assume that $r \geq 0$. If we start from $v_0 \equiv 0$, then clearly

$$(Tv_0)(x,z) = (T0)(x,z) = \max_{a \in \Gamma(x,z)} r(x,z,a) \geq 0 = v_0(x,z),$$

so $v_0 \leq T v_0$ holds.

In general, OPI converges much faster than VFI because it avoids optimization most of the time. As an example, Figure 14.2 plots the process of optimistic policy iteration with $m = 10$. For the same convergence criterion (which was set to maximum value error 10^{-4}), VFI took $k = 196$ iterations in about 18 seconds until convergence on a standard laptop computer, whereas OPI took $k = 205$ iterations in 3 seconds. Note that for OPI, convergence is less smooth (and hence requires more iterations) because maximization is skipped most of the time.

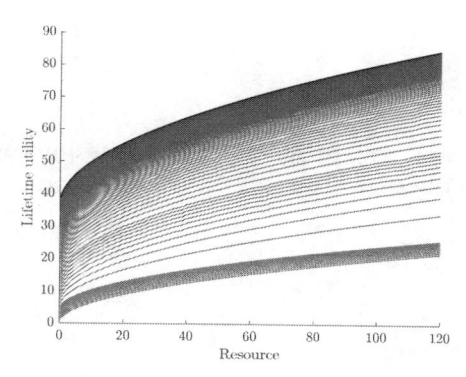

FIGURE 14.2: Optimistic policy iteration in stochastic growth model.

NOTES

The first application of the contraction mapping theorem to study dynamic programming problems seems to be Shapley (1953). The contraction approach to dynamic programming is standard, for instance, Blackwell (1965) and

Denardo (1967). For a modern treatment of dynamic programming, see Sargent and Stachurski (2024). Stachurski and Zhang (2021) and Toda (2021b) study the theory of dynamic programming with state-dependent discounting, and the latter pointed out the usefulness of Perov contractions. The idea of using weighted supremum norms for solving unbounded dynamic programming problems dates back to Lippman (1975) and Wessels (1977) and was applied to economics by Boyd (1990) and Durán (2000, 2003). Theorem 14.8 significantly simplifies the analysis because it applies the Perov contraction theorem instead of the Banach contraction theorem. §14.7 is largely based on Toda (2024). The optimistic policy iteration algorithm was proposed by Howard (1960) (with $m = \infty$) and is called by various names such as Howard's policy improvement or policy iteration. For more results related to §14.8, see Rauch and Toda (2024).

PROBLEMS

14.1. In Example 14.1, verify that all assumptions of Theorem 14.1 are satisfied.

14.2. Fill in the details of the proof of Theorem 14.7.

14.3. Verify the details of Example 14.6.

14.4. Consider the optimal savings problem (14.1). Suppose that the utility function u is continuous, bounded below, and satisfies

$$\lim_{c \to \infty} \frac{u(c)}{c^\alpha} = 0$$

for all $\alpha > 0$.

(i) Show that $u(c) = \log(c + \gamma)$, where $\gamma > 0$ is any constant, satisfies the above assumption.

(ii) Fix $\alpha > 0$ and $b > 0$, and consider the weight function

$$\kappa(w, z) = (w + b)^\alpha.$$

Explicitly compute

$$\sup_{0 \le c \le w} \frac{\kappa(w', z')}{\kappa(w, z)},$$

where $w' = g(w, z, z', c) = R(z, z')(w - c) + y(z')$.

(iii) Show that for any $\epsilon > 0$, we can take a large enough $b > 0$ such that

$$\sup_{w \ge 0} \sup_{0 \le c \le w} \frac{\kappa(w', z')}{\kappa(w, z)} \le \max\left\{1, R(z, z')^\alpha\right\} + \epsilon.$$

(iv) Show that if $\alpha > 0$ is sufficiently close to 0 and $b > 0$ is large enough, then the optimal savings problem has a unique value function within the space of functions $v(w, z)$ satisfying

$$\sup_{z} \sup_{w \geq 0} \frac{|v(w, z)|}{(w + b)^\alpha} < \infty.$$

CHAPTER 15

Variational Methods

15.1 INTRODUCTION

In Chapter 14, we studied infinite-horizon dynamic programming problems by applying the contraction mapping theorem. One drawback of this approach is that in addition to the control variables, the (unknown) value function always enters the Bellman equation, so there are many objects to pin down. This chapter presents an alternative (and much more classical) approach based on variational principles (first-order conditions), which is sometimes called the calculus of variations. Although this approach lacks generality because it requires additional structure such as differentiability and restrictions on the law of motion, when it is applicable, we may gain additional insights.

To illustrate the variational approach, consider the optimal savings problem introduced in §14.1:

$$\text{maximize} \qquad \mathrm{E}_0 \sum_{t=0}^{\infty} \beta^t u(c_t) \qquad\qquad (15.1\text{a})$$

$$\text{subject to} \qquad (\forall t) w_{t+1} = R_{t+1}(w_t - c_t) + y_{t+1}, \qquad (15.1\text{b})$$

$$(\forall t) 0 \le c_t \le w_t, \qquad\qquad (15.1\text{c})$$

where the initial wealth $w_0 > 0$ is given and the stochastic process for gross returns and non-financial income $\{(R_t, y_t)\}_{t=1}^{\infty}$ is exogenous. Consider an agent seeking to make a decision at time t. Given w_t, the continuation utility is

$$\mathrm{E}_t \sum_{s=0}^{\infty} \beta^{t+s} u(c_{t+s}) = \beta^t u(c_t) + \mathrm{E}_t[\beta^{t+1} u(c_{t+1})] + \bullet,$$

where E_t denotes the expectation conditional on time t information and $\bullet$ denotes a quantity whose exact expression we omit but which can be inferred from the context. Let $\{(w_t, c_t)\}_{t=0}^{\infty}$ be a feasible state-action process with $w_t, c_t > 0$ for all t, and consider the following feasible deviation. At time t, the agent increases savings by ϵ; using the budget constraint (15.1b), the next period's wealth increases by $R_{t+1}\epsilon$; at $t+1$, the agent consumes this extra

DOI: 10.1201/9781032698953-15

wealth so that the plan after $t + 1$ remains unchanged. Under this deviation, the continuation utility becomes

$$\beta^t u(c_t - \epsilon) + \mathrm{E}_t[\beta^{t+1} u(c_{t+1} + R_{t+1}\epsilon)] + \bullet, \tag{15.2}$$

where the terms expressed by $\bullet$ do not dependent on ϵ. Obviously, an optimal plan needs to remain optimal under any deviation. The derivative of (15.2) with respect to ϵ is

$$-\beta^t u'(c_t - \epsilon) + \mathrm{E}_t[\beta^{t+1} R_{t+1} u'(c_{t+1} + R_{t+1}\epsilon)]. \tag{15.3}$$

Setting (15.3) equal to 0 at $\epsilon = 0$ and dividing by β^t, a necessary condition for optimality is

$$u'(c_t) = \mathrm{E}_t[\beta R_{t+1} u'(c_{t+1})]. \tag{15.4}$$

The equation (15.4) is known as the *Euler equation*. It is the discrete-time analogue of the Euler-Lagrange equation that appears in the classical calculus of variations developed by Euler and Lagrange in the 18th century.

15.2 EULER EQUATION

To simplify the discussion and to help develop intuition, we start with the analysis of the deterministic, finite-horizon optimal control problems. Consider the optimization problem

$$\text{maximize} \qquad \sum_{t=0}^{T} r_t(x_t, a_t) \tag{15.5a}$$

$$\text{subject to} \qquad (\forall t) x_{t+1} = g_{t+1}(x_t, a_t), \tag{15.5b}$$

$$(\forall t) a_t \in \Gamma_t(x_t), \tag{15.5c}$$

$$x_0 \text{ given.} \tag{15.5d}$$

The problem (15.5) is similar to the additive Markov dynamic program in the sequential form introduced in §14.3 except that (i) the problem is deterministic and has a finite horizon and (ii) the reward function r_t, transition function g_t, and feasible correspondence Γ_t may depend on time. Note that in (15.5a) there is no discount factor because it can always be included in the reward r_t.

To derive necessary conditions for optimality, we introduce the following assumption.

Assumption 15.1. *The following conditions hold.*

(i) *The state and action spaces are* $\mathsf{X} = \mathbb{R}^{N_x}$ *and* $\mathsf{A} = \mathbb{R}_+^{N_a}$.

(ii) *For all t, $r_t : \mathsf{X} \times \mathsf{A} \to [-\infty, \infty)$ is continuous, and it is differentiable on the domain* $\operatorname{dom} r_t := \{(x, a) \in \mathsf{X} \times \mathsf{A} : r(x, a) > -\infty\}$.

(iii) *For all t, g_{t+1} depends only on $a \in \mathsf{A}$, and is continuous on $\mathbb{R}_+^{N_a}$ and differentiable on $\mathbb{R}_{++}^{N_a}$.*

(iv) *Nonnegativity constraint:* $\Gamma_t(x_t) = \mathsf{A} = \mathbb{R}_+^{N_a}$.

The condition (i) that the state and action spaces X, A consist of the entire $\mathbb{R}^{N_x}, \mathbb{R}_+^{N_a}$ seems strong, but this is not a restriction because we may always define the reward $r_t(x, a) = -\infty$ if (x, a) is outside the domain. (See §11.1 for more discussion.) The condition (iii) that the law of motion depends only on the action and not on the state is obviously strong, but it is crucial for considering one-shot deviations as discussed in the introduction. In condition (iv), we can obviously accommodate other lower bounds such as $a_t \geq \underline{a}_t$ by redefining the action variable as $\tilde{a}_t := a_t - \underline{a}_t$, etc. Below, we denote the Jacobian with respect to variables x, a by D_x, D_a. The following proposition provides necessary conditions for optimality.

Proposition 15.1 (Necessity). *Consider the dynamic optimization problem (15.5) and suppose Assumption 15.1 holds. If $\{(x_t, a_t)\}_{t=0}^{T}$ is optimal with a finite value, then the following conditions hold:*

$$\underbrace{D_a r_t(x_t, a_t)}_{1 \times N_a} + \underbrace{D_x r_{t+1}(x_{t+1}, a_{t+1})}_{1 \times N_x} \underbrace{D_a g_{t+1}(a_t)}_{N_x \times N_a} \leq 0, \tag{15.6a}$$

$$[D_a r_t(x_t, a_t) + D_x r_{t+1}(x_{t+1}, a_{t+1}) D_a g_{t+1}(a_t)] a_t = 0, \tag{15.6b}$$

and

$$(D_a r_T(x_T, a_T)) a_T = 0. \tag{15.7}$$

Proof. Suppose that $\{(x_t, a_t)\}_{t=0}^{T}$ is optimal. Then fixing t and changing a_t only will not result in any gain. Consider the restricted optimization problem where we optimize only over a_t. If $t < T$, the problem reduces to

$$\begin{aligned} \text{maximize} \quad & r_t(x_t, a_t) + r_{t+1}(g_{t+1}(a_t), a_{t+1}) \\ \text{subject to} \quad & a_t \geq 0. \end{aligned}$$

Letting $\lambda_t \in \mathbb{R}_+^{N_a}$ be the Lagrange multiplier on the nonnegativity constraint, the Lagrangian is

$$L = r_t(x_t, a_t) + r_{t+1}(g_{t+1}(a_t), a_{t+1}) + \lambda_t' a_t.$$

Since by assumption r_t is differentiable whenever its value is finite, we may apply the Karush-Kuhn-Tucker theorem (Theorem 12.4). Using the chain rule, the first-order condition is

$$D_a r_t(x_t, a_t) + D_x r_{t+1}(x_{t+1}, a_{t+1}) D_a g_{t+1}(a_t) + \lambda_t' = 0. \tag{15.8}$$

Since $\lambda_t \geq 0$, we obtain the inequality (15.6a). Multiplying a_t from right to (15.8) and using the complementary slackness condition $\lambda_t' a_t = 0$, we obtain (15.6b).

If $t = T$, the problem reduces to

$$\begin{aligned} \text{maximize} \quad & r_T(x_T, a_T) \\ \text{subject to} \quad & a_T \geq 0. \end{aligned}$$

The Lagrangian is

$$L = r_T(x_T, a_T) + \lambda'_T a_T.$$

The first-order condition is $D_a r_T(x_T, a_T) + \lambda'_T = 0$. Multiplying a_T from the right and using the complementary slackness condition, we obtain (15.7). □

The necessary condition (15.6) is called the *Euler inequality*. When the nonnegativity constraint for the n-th entry $a_{nt} \geq 0$ does not bind and the inequality holds with equality, it is called an *Euler equation*.

We next consider sufficient conditions. To this end, we introduce the following monotonicity and concavity assumption.

Assumption 15.2. *The following conditions hold.*

(i) *For all t, $r_t : \mathsf{X} \times \mathsf{A} \to [-\infty, \infty)$ is concave, $D_x r_t \geq 0$, and $D_a r_t \leq 0$.*

(ii) *For all t, $g_{t+1} : \mathsf{A} \to \mathsf{X}$ is a concave map.*

If we interpret the state variable x as "resource" and the control variable as "savings", because increasing savings reduces current consumption (and hence, utility), the conditions $D_x r_t \geq 0$ and $D_a r_t \leq 0$ become natural. The following proposition shows that, under monotonicity and concavity, the Euler equation (15.6) and the terminal condition (15.7) are sufficient for optimality.

Proposition 15.2 (Sufficiency)**.** *Consider the dynamic optimization problem (15.5) and suppose Assumptions 15.1, 15.2 hold. Let $\{(x_t, a_t)\}_{t=0}^T$ be a feasible plan. If for all t (15.6), (15.7) hold, then $\{(x_t, a_t)\}_{t=0}^T$ is optimal.*

Proof. Take any feasible $\{(\hat{r}_t, \hat{a}_t)\}_{t=0}^\infty$, so $\hat{x}_0 = x_0$ and $\hat{x}_{t+1} = g_{t+1}(\hat{a}_t)$ for all t. Since r_t is differentiable and concave, by Proposition 11.7 we have

$$r_t(\hat{x}_t, \hat{a}_t) - r_t(x_t, a_t) \leq (D_x r_t)(\hat{x}_t - x_t) + (D_a r_t)(\hat{a}_t - a_t), \tag{15.9}$$

where for simplicity we suppress the arguments of $D_x r_t, D_a r_t$. Similarly, since g_{t+1} is a concave map, we have

$$g_{t+1}(\hat{a}_t) - g_{t+1}(a_t) \leq (D_a g_{t+1})(\hat{a}_t - a_t). \tag{15.10}$$

Therefore the difference in the value can be bounded from above as

$$\Delta := \sum_{t=0}^T [r_t(\hat{x}_t, \hat{a}_t) - r_t(x_t, a_t)]$$

$$\leq \sum_{t=0}^T [(D_x r_t)(\hat{x}_t - x_t) + (D_a r_t)(\hat{a}_t - a_t)] \qquad (\because (15.9))$$

$$= \sum_{t=1}^T (D_x r_t)(\hat{x}_t - x_t) + \sum_{t=0}^T (D_a r_t)(\hat{a}_t - a_t) \qquad (\because \hat{x}_0 = x_0)$$

$$= \sum_{t=0}^{T-1} (D_x r_{t+1})(g_{t+1}(\hat{a}_t) - g_{t+1}(a_t)) + \sum_{t=0}^T (D_a r_t)(\hat{a}_t - a_t),$$

where the last equation shifts the index by 1 and uses the feasibility $x_{t+1} = g_{t+1}(a_t)$ etc. Multiplying $D_x r_{t+1} \geq 0$ from the left to (15.10), we obtain

$$\Delta \leq \sum_{t=0}^{T-1} [D_x r_{t+1} D_a g_{t+1} + D_a r_t](\hat{a}_t - a_t) + (D_a r_T)(\hat{a}_T - a_T)$$

$$= -\sum_{t=0}^{T-1} \lambda'_t(\hat{a}_t - a_t) + (D_a r_T)(\hat{a}_T - a_T), \qquad (15.11)$$

where we define $\lambda_t \in \mathbb{R}^{N_a}$ using the first-order condition (15.8). By assumption, (15.6a) implies $\lambda_t \geq 0$ and (15.6b) implies $\lambda'_t a_t = 0$. Therefore (15.11) becomes

$$\Delta \leq -\underbrace{\sum_{t=0}^{T-1} \lambda'_t \hat{a}_t}_{\geq 0} + \underbrace{\sum_{t=0}^{T-1} \lambda'_t a_t}_{=0} + (D_a r_T)(\hat{a}_T - a_T)$$

$$\leq (D_a r_T)(\hat{a}_T - a_T) \leq -(D_a r_T)a_T, \qquad (15.12)$$

where the last inequality follows from $D_a r_T \leq 0$ and $\hat{a}_T \geq 0$. By (15.7), the right-hand side of (15.12) equals 0. Therefore $\Delta \leq 0$, so $\{(x_t, a_t)\}_{t=0}^T$ is optimal. $\qquad \square$

15.3   TRANSVERSALITY CONDITION

We next study infinite-horizon optimal control problems, while still maintaining a deterministic environment. For infinite-horizon problems, the objective function $\sum_{t=0}^{\infty} r_t(x_t, a_t)$ may not even be defined unless some structure is imposed such as $r_t(x_t, a_t) = \beta^t u(x_t, a_t)$ with $0 \leq \beta < 1$ and u is bounded. To avoid imposing strong conditions that guarantee convergence, we define optimality by the following *overtaking criterion*: we say that a feasible plan $\{(x_t, a_t)\}_{t=0}^{\infty}$ is *optimal* if for any other feasible plan $\{(\hat{x}_t, \hat{a}_t)\}_{t=0}^{\infty}$, we have

$$\limsup_{T \to \infty} \sum_{t=0}^{T} [r_t(\hat{x}_t, \hat{a}_t) - r_t(x_t, a_t)] \leq 0. \qquad (15.13)$$

When (15.13) holds, the partial sum $\sum_{t=0}^{T} r_t(\hat{x}_t, \hat{a}_t)$ cannot overtake $\sum_{t=0}^{T} r_t(x_t, a_t)$ by a finite positive amount infinitely often, which motivates the definition. Obviously, if $\sum_{t=0}^{\infty} r_t(x_t, a_t)$ is always well defined and finite, then (15.13) is equivalent to

$$\sum_{t=0}^{\infty} r_t(\hat{x}_t, \hat{a}_t) \leq \sum_{t=0}^{\infty} r_t(x_t, a_t),$$

so we recover optimality in the usual sense.

Motivated by the terminal condition (15.7) in the finite-horizon problem, we introduce the following definition: for a feasible plan $\{(x_t, a_t)\}_{t=0}^{\infty}$, we say that the *transversality condition* holds if

$$\lim_{t \to \infty} (D_a r_t(x_t, a_t)) a_t = 0. \tag{15.14}$$

We may now extend the sufficiency result in Proposition 15.2 to the infinite-horizon case.

Theorem 15.3 (Sufficiency). *Consider the infinite-horizon dynamic optimization problem* (15.5) *with $T = \infty$ and suppose Assumptions 15.1, 15.2 hold. Let $\{(x_t, a_t)\}_{t=0}^{\infty}$ be a feasible plan. If for all t the Euler inequality* (15.6) *and the transversality condition* (15.14) *hold, then $\{(x_t, a_t)\}_{t=0}^{\infty}$ is optimal in the sense of* (15.13).

Proof. Take any feasible plan $\{(\hat{x}_t, \hat{a}_t)\}_{t=0}^{\infty}$ and let

$$\Delta_T := \sum_{t=0}^{T} [r_t(\hat{x}_t, \hat{a}_t) - r_t(x_t, a_t)].$$

All derivations in the proof of Proposition 15.2 hold up to (15.12). Therefore (15.14) implies $\limsup_{T \to \infty} \Delta_T \leq 0$, so $\{(x_t, a_t)\}_{t=0}^{\infty}$ is optimal. □

Example 15.1 (Optimal savings). Consider the optimal savings problem discussed in the introduction but without uncertainty. Let the state space be $\mathsf{X} = \mathbb{R}$, where the state is wealth $w \in \mathsf{X}$. Let the action space be $\mathsf{A} = \mathbb{R}_+$, where the action is savings $s \in \mathsf{A}$. By accounting, consumption is $c := w - s$. Let the reward be discounted utility $r_t(w, s) = \beta^t u(w - s)$, where u is increasing, concave, and $u(c) = -\infty$ for $c \leq 0$. Let the transition function be

$$g_{t+1}(s_t) = R_{t+1} s_t + y_{t+1}.$$

Clearly Assumptions 15.1, 15.2 hold. Letting $c_t = w_t - s_t$ be consumption, the Euler inequality (15.6a) is

$$-\beta^t u'(c_t) + \beta^{t+1} u'(c_{t+1}) R_{t+1} \leq 0 \iff u'(c_t) \geq \beta R_{t+1} u'(c_{t+1}),$$

with equality if $s_t > 0 \iff c_t < w_t$. The transversality condition (15.14) is

$$\lim_{t \to \infty} \beta^t u'(c_t) s_t = 0.$$

Example 15.2 (Optimal savings with log utility). In Example 15.1, suppose $u(c) = \log c$ and $y_{t+1} = 0$, so utility is logarithmic and there is no non-financial income. We studied such a special case in §13.4 in finite horizon with constant returns. There, the optimal consumption was given by

$$c = \frac{w}{1 + \beta + \cdots + \beta^T} = \frac{1 - \beta}{1 - \beta^{T+1}} w.$$

Letting $T \to \infty$, we may conjecture that the optimal consumption in infinite horizon is $c = (1 - \beta)w$. Let us verify that this is indeed true by applying Theorem 15.3. If we set $c_t = (1 - \beta)w_t$, the budget constraint (15.1b) (with $y_{t+1} = 0$) implies $w_{t+1} = \beta R_{t+1} w_t$. Then

$$u'(c_t) - \beta R_{t+1} u'(c_{t+1}) = \frac{1}{(1 - \beta)w_t} - \frac{\beta R_{t+1}}{(1 - \beta)\beta R_{t+1} w_t} = 0,$$

so the Euler equation holds. Furthermore,

$$\beta^t u'(c_t)s_t = \beta^t \frac{s_t}{c_t} = \beta^t \frac{\beta}{1 - \beta} \to 0$$

as $t \to \infty$, so the transversality condition holds. Therefore by Theorem 15.3, $c_t = (1 - \beta)w_t$ is indeed optimal.

Example 15.3 (Optimal growth). Consider the following deterministic version of the stochastic growth model discussed in Example 14.4:

$$\text{maximize} \qquad \sum_{t=0}^{\infty} \beta^t u(c_t)$$

$$\text{subject to} \qquad (\forall t)c_t + k_{t+1} = f(k_t),$$

$$(\forall t)c_t, k_{t+1} \geq 0,$$

$$k_0 > 0 \text{ given.}$$

This problem can be interpreted as the optimization problem of Robinson Crusoe marooned on a desert island: c_t is the consumption of potatoes at time t, k_{t+1} is the stock of potatoes to be planted for time $t + 1$, and $f(k_t)$ is the harvest of potatoes at time t. It is convenient to define $x_t = f(k_t)$, which can be interpreted as resources available at time t. Let the state space be $X = \mathbb{R}$, where the state is $x \in X$. Let the action space be $A = \mathbb{R}_+$, where the action is savings $a_t = k_{t+1} = x_t - c_t$. Let the reward be $r_t(x_t, a_t) = \beta^t u(x_t - a_t)$. Let the transition function be $g_{t+1}(a_t) = f(a_t)$. The Euler equation (15.6a) is

$$u'(c_t) = \beta u'(c_{t+1})f'(a_t).$$

The transversality condition (15.14) is

$$\lim_{t \to \infty} \beta^t u'(c_t)a_t = 0.$$

Example 15.4 (Optimal growth with log utility). In Example 15.3, suppose $u(c) = \log c$ and $f(k) = Ak^{\alpha}$, where $A > 0$ is productivity and $\alpha \in (0, 1)$. We solve this problem in closed-form by guess-and-verify. Letting $V(x)$ be the value function, the Bellman equation is

$$V(x) = \max_{0 \leq k \leq x} \left\{ \log(x - k) + \beta V(Ak^{\alpha}) \right\}.$$

Conjecture that $V(x) = a + b \log x$ for some $a \in \mathbb{R}$ and $b > 0$. Then

$$a + b \log x = \max_{0 \le k \le x} \{\log(x - k) + \beta(a + b \log(Ak^\alpha))\}.$$

Taking the first-order condition with respect to k yields

$$-\frac{1}{x - k} + \beta b\alpha \frac{1}{k} = 0 \iff k = \frac{b\alpha\beta}{1 + b\alpha\beta} x.$$

Substituting this into the Bellman equation and comparing the coefficients of $\log x$, we obtain

$$b = 1 + \beta b\alpha \iff b = \frac{1}{1 - \alpha\beta}.$$

Therefore the optimal savings is $k = \alpha\beta x$ and optimal consumption is $c = (1 - \alpha\beta)x$. Since $x_{t+1} = Ak_{t+1}^\alpha$, we obtain

$$u'(c_t) - \beta u'(c_{t+1})f'(k_{t+1}) = \frac{1}{c_t} - \beta \frac{A\alpha k_{t+1}^{\alpha-1}}{c_{t+1}} = \frac{1}{c_t} - \beta \frac{\alpha x_{t+1}}{c_{t+1} k_{t+1}}$$

$$= \frac{1}{(1 - \alpha\beta)x_t} - \frac{\alpha\beta x_{t+1}}{(1 - \alpha\beta)x_{t+1}\alpha\beta x_t} = 0,$$

so the Euler equation holds. Furthermore,

$$\beta^t u'(c_t)k_{t+1} = \beta^t \frac{k_{t+1}}{c_t} = \beta^t \frac{\alpha\beta}{1 - \alpha\beta} \to 0$$

as $t \to \infty$, so the transversality condition holds. Therefore by Theorem 15.3, $c_t = (1 - \alpha\beta)x_t$ is indeed optimal.

We next consider necessary conditions. By considering one-shot deviations, the necessity of the Euler inequality (15.6) is obvious by the same argument as in the proof of Proposition 15.1. Therefore we focus on the transversality condition (15.14).

Theorem 15.4 (Necessity). *Consider the infinite-horizon dynamic optimization problem (15.5) with $T = \infty$ and suppose Assumptions 15.1, 15.2 hold. Let $\{(x_t, a_t)\}_{t=0}^\infty$ be an optimal plan. For $t \ge 1$ and $\theta \in [0, 1]$, define $f_t : [0, 1] \to [-\infty, \infty)$ by $f_t(\theta) = r_t(g_t(\theta a_{t-1}), \theta a_t)$. If there exists $\theta_0 \in (0, 1)$ such that $\sum_{t=1}^\infty f_t(\theta)$ converges to a finite value for all $\theta \in [\theta_0, 1]$, then the transversality condition (15.14) holds.*

Proof. Let us first show that f_t is concave. The proof is similar to Proposition 11.4 but we repeat it for completeness. Take $\theta_1, \theta_2 \in [0, 1]$ and $\alpha \in [0, 1]$. Let $\theta := (1 - \alpha)\theta_1 + \alpha\theta_2$. Since g_t is a concave map, we have

$$x := g_t(\theta a_{t-1}) \ge (1 - \alpha)g_t(\theta_1 a_{t-1}) + \alpha g(\theta_2 a_{t-1}) =: (1 - \alpha)x_1 + \alpha x_2.$$

Furthermore, by definition

$$b := \theta a_t = (1 - \alpha)\theta_1 a_t + \alpha\theta_2 a_t =: (1 - \alpha)b_1 + \alpha b_2.$$

By considering the value $r_t(x, b)$, we obtain

$$
\begin{aligned}
f_t(\theta) &= r_t(g_t(\theta a_{t-1}), \theta a_t) \\
&= r_t(x, b) && (\because \text{definition of } x, b) \\
&\geq r_t((1-\alpha)x_1 + \alpha x_2, (1-\alpha)b_1 + \alpha b_2) && (\because r_t \text{ increasing in } x) \\
&\geq (1-\alpha)r_t(x_1, b_1) + \alpha r_t(x_2, b_2) && (\because r_t \text{ concave}) \\
&= (1-\alpha)f_t(\theta_1) + \alpha f_t(\theta_2),
\end{aligned}
$$

so f is concave.

Next, take any $\theta \in [\theta_0, 1]$. Write

$$
\theta = (1-\alpha)\theta_0 + \alpha \iff \alpha = \frac{\theta - \theta_0}{1 - \theta_0} \in [0, 1].
$$

Since f_t is concave, we obtain

$$
f_t(\theta) \geq (1-\alpha)f_t(\theta_0) + \alpha f_t(1) \iff \frac{f_t(1) - f_t(\theta)}{1 - \theta} \leq \frac{f_t(1) - f_t(\theta_0)}{1 - \theta_0}. \quad (15.15)
$$

Finally, we prove the transversality condition. Let $\{(x_t, a_t)\}_{t=0}^{\infty}$ be optimal. For any $\theta \in [\theta_0, 1]$ and $T > 0$, define $\{(\hat{x}_t(\theta), \hat{a}_t(\theta))\}_{t=0}^{\infty}$ by

$$
\hat{a}_t(\theta) = \begin{cases} a_t & \text{if } t \leq T, \\ \theta a_t & \text{if } t \geq T+1, \end{cases}
$$

$$
\hat{x}_t(\theta) = \begin{cases} x_0 & \text{if } t = 0, \\ g_t(\hat{a}_{t-1}) & \text{if } t \geq 1. \end{cases}
$$

Since $A = \mathbb{R}_+^{N_a}$ is convex and contains zero, clearly $\{(\hat{x}_t(\theta), \hat{a}_t(\theta))\}_{t=0}^{\infty}$ is feasible. Furthermore, by the definition of f_t, we have $r_t(\hat{x}_t(\theta), \hat{a}_t(\theta)) = f_t(\theta)$ for $t > T$, which is summable by assumption. Since $\{(x_t, a_t)\}_{t=0}^{\infty}$ is optimal, we obtain

$$
0 \geq \sum_{t=0}^{\infty} [r_t(\hat{x}_t(\theta), \hat{a}_t(\theta)) - r_t(x_t, a_t)]
$$

$$
= r_T(x_T, \theta a_T) - r_T(x_T, a_T) + \sum_{t=T+1}^{\infty} [f_t(\theta) - f_t(1)]
$$

$$
\iff r_T(x_T, \theta a_T) - r_T(x_T, a_T) \leq \sum_{t=T+1}^{\infty} [f_t(1) - f_t(\theta)].
$$

Dividing both sides by $1 - \theta > 0$ and using (15.15), we obtain

$$
\frac{r_T(x_T, \theta a_T) - r_T(x_T, a_T)}{1 - \theta} \leq \sum_{t=T+1}^{\infty} \frac{f_t(1) - f_t(\theta)}{1 - \theta} \leq \sum_{t=T+1}^{\infty} \frac{f_t(1) - f_t(\theta_0)}{1 - \theta_0}.
$$

Since the right-hand side does not depend on θ, letting $\theta \uparrow 1$ in the left-hand side, we obtain

$$0 \le -(D_a r_T(x_T, a_T))a_T \le \sum_{t=T+1}^{\infty} \frac{f_t(1) - f_t(\theta_0)}{1 - \theta_0},$$

where the left inequality follows from $D_a r_T \le 0$ and $a_T \ge 0$. Letting $T \to \infty$ and noting that $\{f_t(\theta)\}$ is summable, the right-hand side converges to 0, and hence the transversality condition (15.14) holds. □

15.4 STOCHASTIC CASE

The generalization of the Euler equation and the transversality condition to stochastic optimization problems is straightforward. The only technical complications are that (i) we may allow the reward function r_t and the transition function g_t to be random (more precisely, letting $\{\mathcal{F}_t\}_{t=0}^{\infty}$ be a filtration on a probability space $(\Omega, \mathcal{F}, P)$, fixing x_t, a_t, the functions $r_t(x_t, a_t, \omega)$ and $g_t(a_t, \omega)$ are $\mathcal{F}_t$-measurable), and (ii) we need to be careful about exchanging the order of differentiation, integration (taking expectations), and taking infinite sums. These technicalities are beyond the scope of this book and we refer the reader to textbooks on measure theory such as Folland (1999).

Let E_t denote the time t conditional expectation operator. Generalizing the overtaking criterion (15.13), we say that a feasible state-action process $\{(x_t, a_t)\}_{t=0}^{\infty}$ is *optimal* if for any other feasible plan $\{(\hat{x}_t, \hat{a}_t)\}_{t=0}^{\infty}$, we have

$$\limsup_{T \to \infty} E_0 \sum_{t=0}^{T} [r_t(\hat{x}_t, \hat{a}_t) - r_t(x_t, a_t)] \le 0.$$

The Euler inequality (15.6a) can be generalized as

$$D_a r_t(x_t, a_t) + E_t[D_x r_{t+1}(x_{t+1}, a_{t+1})D_a g_{t+1}(a_t)] \le 0.$$

The transversality condition (15.14) can be generalized as

$$\lim_{t \to \infty} E_0[(D_a r_t(x_t, a_t))a_t] = 0.$$

With these changes in notation, all results in Propositions 15.1–Theorem 15.4 hold (subject to the technicalities mentioned above).

15.5 OPTIMAL SAVINGS PROBLEM

As an application of optimal control theory, we solve the optimal savings problem without assuming the boundedness of the utility function following the Euler equation iteration approach of Li and Stachurski (2014) and Ma, Stachurski, and Toda (2020).

Because we have already seen the optimal savings problem many times, the model description is brief. Let $Z = \{1, \ldots, Z\}$ be a finite set and $\{z_t\}_{t=0}^{\infty}$ be a Markov chain with transition probability matrix $P = (P(z, z'))$, where $P(z, z') = \Pr(z_{t+1} = z' \mid z_t = z)$. We assume that the discount factor and gross return on savings between time $t - 1$ and t as well as the non-financial income at time t satisfy

$$\beta_t = \beta(z_{t-1}, z_t), \quad R_t = R(z_{t-1}, z_t), \quad y_t = y(z_{t-1}, z_t), \tag{15.16}$$

where $\beta, R, y : Z^2 \to \mathbb{R}_+$. Letting $w \geq 0$ be wealth and $c \geq 0$ be consumption, given (w, z), the objective of the agent is to maximize

$$u(c) + \mathrm{E}_z[\beta(z, z')u(c')] + \bullet$$

subject to the budget constraint

$$w' = R(z, z')(w - c) + y(z, z') \tag{15.17}$$

and the nonnegativity and borrowing constraints $0 \leq c \leq w$.

Suppose the utility function u is continuously differentiable on $(0, \infty)$ and that the marginal utility u' is positive, continuous, and strictly decreasing, so u is strictly increasing and strictly concave. Furthermore, assume the Inada condition $u'(0) = \infty$ so that the nonnegativity constraint $c \geq 0$ never binds. Suppose an optimal consumption function $c(w, z)$ exists. Then by Example 15.1, we obtain the Euler inequality

$$u'(c(w, z)) \geq \mathrm{E}_z[\beta(z, z')R(z, z')u'(c(w', z'))], \tag{15.18}$$

where the next period's wealth w' satisfies the budget constraint (15.17) and the Euler inequality (15.18) holds with equality if $c(w, z) < w$. Let us convert the Euler inequality to a single equation. If $c(w, z) < w$, (15.18) holds with equality. Furthermore, since u is concave (hence u' is decreasing), we have $u'(c(w, z)) \geq u'(w)$. If $c(w, z) = w$, then (15.18) is an inequality, and we obviously have $u'(c(w, z)) = u'(w)$. Therefore by combining the two cases, we obtain a single equation

$$u'(c(w, z)) = \max\{\mathrm{E}_z[\beta(z, z')R(z, z')u'(c(w', z'))], u'(w)\}. \tag{15.19}$$

To simplify notation, let us suppress the arguments of β, R, y. To solve the Euler equation (15.19), we apply the ideas of Coleman (1990) and Li and Stachurski (2014). Let c be a guess of the consumption function and consider updating it. To this end, set $\xi = c(w, z)$, and using the budget constraint (15.17) to eliminate w', rewrite (15.19) as

$$u'(\xi) - \max\{\mathrm{E}_z[\beta R u'(c(R(w - \xi) + y, z'))], u'(w)\} = 0. \tag{15.20}$$

The idea of Euler equation iteration (EEI) is that, given a candidate policy function c, we update it at the point (w, z) by the value ξ solving the Euler equation (15.20). If we can show that this updating rule is a (Perov) contraction, then we obtain a unique fixed point, which satisfies the Euler equation.

To carry out this idea, we need to define an appropriate functional space. It is reasonable to assume that the consumption function $c(w, z)$ is continuous and increasing in w. Then the marginal utility function $f_z(w) := u'(c(w, z))$ becomes continuous and decreasing in w. We thus define the space $\mathcal{F}$ of candidate marginal utility functions by the set of all functions $f : (0, \infty) \to \mathbb{R}^Z_{++}$ such that f is continuous, decreasing, and its difference from u' is bounded:

$$(\forall z \in \mathsf{Z}) \sup_{w \in (0, \infty)} |f_z(w) - u'(w)| < \infty. \tag{15.21}$$

Define $d : \mathcal{F}^2 \to \mathbb{R}^Z_+$ by $d(f, g) = (d_1(f, g), \ldots, d_Z(f, g))$ with

$$d_z(f, g) = \sup_{w \in (0, \infty)} |f_z(w) - g_z(w)|.$$

It is straightforward to show that $(\mathcal{F}, d)$ is a complete vector-value metric space (see §7.5 and Problem 15.4). The following lemma shows that, for any $f \in \mathcal{F}$, by setting $c(w, z) = (u')^{-1}(f(w, z))$, we can uniquely solve (15.20).

Lemma 15.5. *Let $f \in \mathcal{F}$ and define $c = (u')^{-1} \circ f$. Then for all $(w, z) \in (0, \infty) \times \mathsf{Z}$, there exists a unique $\xi = \xi(w, z) \in (0, w]$ solving the Euler equation (15.20). Furthermore, ξ is continuous and increasing in w.*

Proof. We first show the existence and uniqueness of ξ. By the definition of c, we have $u' \circ c = f$. Define $\phi : (0, w] \to \mathbb{R}$ by

$$\phi(\xi, w) = u'(\xi) - \max \left\{ \mathrm{E}_z[\beta R f_{z'}(R(w - \xi) + y)], u'(w) \right\}.$$

By assumption, $\xi \mapsto u'(\xi)$ is continuous and strictly decreasing. Since f is continuous and decreasing, $\xi \mapsto \mathrm{E}_z[\beta R f_{z'}(R(w - \xi) + y)]$ is continuous and increasing. Therefore ϕ is continuous and strictly decreasing in ξ. Since

$$\phi(0, w) = u'(0) - \max \left\{ \mathrm{E}_z[\beta R f_{z'}(Rw + y)], u'(w) \right\} = \infty,$$
$$\phi(w, w) = u'(w) - \max \left\{ \mathrm{E}_z[\beta R f_{z'}(y)], u'(w) \right\} \le 0,$$

by the intermediate value theorem, there exists a unique $\xi \in (0, w]$ satisfying $\phi(\xi, w) = 0$.

We next show the continuity and monotonicity of ξ. Since f, u' are continuous, so is ξ. To show monotonicity, let $w_1 < w_2$ and take the corresponding ξ_1, ξ_2. To show $\xi_1 \le \xi_2$, suppose to the contrary that $\xi_1 > \xi_2$. Since f, u' are decreasing, ϕ is increasing in w. Noting that ϕ is strictly decreasing in ξ, we obtain

$$0 = \phi(\xi_1, w_1) \le \phi(\xi_1, w_2) < \phi(\xi_2, w_2) = 0,$$

which is a contradiction. □

The following lemma shows that we may define a self-map $T : \mathcal{F} \to \mathcal{F}$ by using the updating rule in Lemma 15.5.

Lemma 15.6. *Suppose $y(z, z') > 0$ for all $(z, z') \in Z^2$. For $f \in \mathcal{F}$, define $(Tf)_z(w) = u'(\xi(w, z))$ using Lemma 15.5. Then $T : \mathcal{F} \to \mathcal{F}$.*

Proof. Let $\xi(w, z)$ be as in Lemma 15.5. Since u' is continuous and strictly decreasing, and $\xi(w, z)$ is continuous and increasing in w, it follows that $(Tf)_z(w) = u'(\xi(w, z))$ is continuous and decreasing in w. Therefore to show that T is a self-map on $\mathcal{F}$, it suffices to show (15.21). Letting $\xi = \xi(w, z)$ and using (15.20), we obtain

$$(Tf)_z(w) = u'(\xi) = \max \{ \mathrm{E}_z[\beta R f_{z'}(R(w - \xi) + y)], u'(w) \} \geq u'(w). \quad (15.22)$$

Since $f \in \mathcal{F}$ and (15.21) holds, we can take a constant $M > 0$ such that $\sup_{w,z} |f_z(w) - u'(w)| \leq M$. Therefore

$$
\begin{aligned}
(Tf)_z(w) - u'(w) &= \max \{ \mathrm{E}_z[\beta R f_{z'}(R(w - \xi) + y))] - u'(w), 0 \} \\
&\leq \mathrm{E}_z[\beta R f_{z'}(R(w - \xi) + y)] \\
&\leq \mathrm{E}_z[\beta R (u'(R(w - \xi) + y) + M)] \\
&\leq \mathrm{E}_z[\beta R (u'(y) + M)] < \infty, \quad (15.23)
\end{aligned}
$$

where the last line follows from the fact that u' is decreasing and $y(z, z') > 0$. Combining (15.22) and (15.23), we obtain

$$0 \leq (Tf)_z(w) - u'(w) \leq \mathrm{E}_z[\beta R (u'(y) + M)] < \infty,$$

so (15.21) holds for Tf. □

In what follows, we refer to $T : \mathcal{F} \to \mathcal{F}$ in Lemma 15.6 as the *Coleman operator*. The following lemma shows that under suitable conditions, the Coleman operator T is a Perov contraction and hence admit a unique fixed point.

Lemma 15.7. *Suppose $y(z, z') > 0$ for all $(z, z') \in Z^2$. Define the nonnegative matrix B by $B(z, z') = P(z, z')\beta(z, z')R(z, z')$ with spectral radius $\rho(B)$. If $\rho(B) < 1$, then $T : \mathcal{F} \to \mathcal{F}$ is a Perov contraction with coefficient matrix B.*

Proof. We verify the sufficient conditions in Proposition 7.7. The functional space $\mathcal{F}$ clearly satisfies the upward shift and bounded difference properties. To prove monotonicity, Let $f, g \in \mathcal{F}$ and suppose $f \leq g$. To show $Tf \leq Tg$, it suffices to show

$$\xi := (u')^{-1}((Tf)_z(w)) \geq (u')^{-1}((Tg)_z(w)) =: \eta$$

for all (w, z). Take any (w, z). If $\xi \geq \eta$, there is nothing to prove, so assume $\xi < \eta$. Then using (15.20), we obtain

$$
\begin{aligned}
u'(\xi) &= \max \{ \mathrm{E}_z[\beta R f_{z'}(R(w - \xi) + y)], u'(w) \} \\
&\leq \max \{ \mathrm{E}_z[\beta R g_{z'}(R(w - \xi) + y)], u'(w) \} \quad (\because f \leq g) \\
&\leq \max \{ \mathrm{E}_z[\beta R g_{z'}(R(w - \eta) + y)], u'(w) \} \quad (\because \xi < \eta, \ g \text{ decreasing}) \\
&= u'(\eta).
\end{aligned}
$$

Since u' is strictly decreasing, we obtain $\xi \geq \eta$. Therefore T is monotone.

To prove discounting, take any nonnegative vector $a \in \mathbb{R}_+^Z$. Fixing (w, z), define $\xi(a) := (u')^{-1}((T(f + a)_z(w))$. Using the already established monotonicity, it follows that $\xi(a)$ is decreasing in a. Therefore

$$
\begin{aligned}
(T(f + a)_z)(w) &= u'(\xi(a)) \\
&= \max\left\{ \mathrm{E}_z[\beta R(f + a)_{z'}(R(w - \xi(a)) + y)], u'(w) \right\} \\
&= \max\left\{ \mathrm{E}_z[\beta R f_{z'}(R(w - \xi(a)) + y) + \beta R a_{z'}], u'(w) \right\} \\
&\leq \max\left\{ \mathrm{E}_z[\beta R f_{z'}(R(w - \xi(a)) + y)], u'(w) \right\} + (Ba)_z \\
&\leq \max\left\{ \mathrm{E}_z[\beta R f_{z'}(R(w - \xi(0)) + y)], u'(w) \right\} + (Ba)_z \\
&= u'(\xi(0)) + (Ba)_z = (Tf)_z(w) + (Ba)_z,
\end{aligned}
$$

where the last inequality follows from $\xi(a) \leq \xi(0)$ and the fact that f is decreasing. Therefore discounting holds. Proposition 7.7 implies that $T : \mathcal{F} \to \mathcal{F}$ is a Perov contraction with coefficient matrix B. □

By combining Lemmas 15.5–15.7, we obtain the following theorem.

Theorem 15.8. *Consider the optimal savings problem. Suppose that*

(i) *the utility function u is continuously differentiable on $(0, \infty)$, u' is positive, continuous, strictly decreasing, and satisfies the Inada condition $u'(0) = \infty$,*

(ii) *the non-financial income satisfies $y(z, z') > 0$ for all (z, z'), and*

(iii) *the nonnegative matrix B defined by $B(z, z') = P(z, z')\beta(z, z')R(z, z')$ has spectral radius less than 1.*

Define the space of candidate consumption functions $\mathcal{C}$ by the set of all functions $c : (0, \infty) \times Z \to (0, \infty)$ such that c is continuous, increasing, and satisfies

$$
\sup_{(w,z) \in (0,\infty) \times Z} |u'(c(w, z)) - u'(w)| < \infty. \tag{15.24}
$$

Then there exists a unique $c \in \mathcal{C}$ satisfying the Euler equation (15.19). Furthermore, Euler equation iteration converges from any initial $c_0 \in \mathcal{C}$.

We discuss a few generalizations and limitations of Theorem 15.8.

Remark. Theorem 15.8 only establishes the existence and uniqueness of a consumption function satisfying the Euler equation. For optimality, we need to verify the transversality condition, which requires a separate argument. See Proposition 2.2 of Ma, Stachurski, and Toda (2020), which proves the transversality condition under the additional assumption that the matrix A defined by $A(z, z') = P(z, z')\beta(z, z')$ has a spectral radius less than 1.

Remark. In Theorem 15.8, we assumed that the discount factor, gross return, and non-financial income all depend on the pair of Markov variables (z_{t-1}, z_t) as in (15.16). However, we may let them also depend on an additional variable

ζ_t that is independent and identically distributed over time. By inspecting the proofs of the lemmas, all we need is to assume $y(z, z', \zeta') > 0$, $E_z[\beta R] < \infty$, $E_z[\beta R u'(y)] < \infty$, and modify the matrix B to

$$B(z, z') = P(z, z') \, E_{z,z'}[\beta(z, z', \zeta')R(z, z', \zeta')].$$

Remark. In Theorem 15.8, to simplify the argument we assumed the Inada condition $u'(0) = \infty$, but this can be easily dispensed with. If $u'(0)$ need not equal ∞, then the nonnegativity constraint $c \geq 0$ may bind. Thus in addition to the Euler inequality (15.18), we also need to include the reverse inequality, with equality if $c(w, z) = 0$. Then the Euler equation (15.19) needs to be modified to

$$u'(c(w, z)) = \min\left\{u'(0), \max\left\{E_z[\beta(z, z')R(z, z')u'(c(w', z'))], u'(w)\right\}\right\}.$$

The remaining argument is identical; see Ma and Toda (2021) for details.

Remark. Probably the most severe restriction of Theorem 15.8 is that it requires $y(z, z') > 0$. If $y(z, z') = 0$, the argument breaks down. To see why, consider the special case of $u(c) = \log c$, $\beta(z, z') = \beta \in (0, 1)$, and $y(z, z') = 0$ for all (z, z'). We know from Example 15.2 that the optimal consumption function is $c(w, z) = (1 - \beta)w$. But then

$$u'(c(w, z)) - u'(w) = \frac{1}{(1 - \beta)w} - \frac{1}{w} = \frac{\beta}{(1 - \beta)w} \to \infty$$

as $w \to 0$, so (15.24) does not hold.

As the last remark shows, we need a separate argument to treat the case $y(z, z') = 0$. Here we briefly present the results of Ma and Toda (2021) when the period utility function is the constant relative risk aversion (CRRA) specification

$$u(c) = \begin{cases} \frac{c^{1-\gamma}}{1-\gamma} & \text{if } 0 < \gamma \neq 1, \\ \log c & \text{if } \gamma = 1. \end{cases} \tag{15.25}$$

Because the problem is homogeneous, if an optimal consumption function exists, it must be of the form $c(w, z) = \bar{c}_z w$ for some vector $\bar{c} \in \mathbb{R}_+^Z$ with $\bar{c}_z \in (0, 1)$ for all z. Substituting this into the Euler equation (15.19) and noting that the borrowing constraint does not bind, we must have

$$\bar{c}_z^{-\gamma} = E_z[\beta R^{1-\gamma}\bar{c}_{z'}^{-\gamma}(1 - \bar{c}_z)^{-\gamma}].$$

Multiplying both sides by $(1 - \bar{c}_z)^\gamma$ and setting $x_z = \bar{c}_z^{-\gamma}$, after some algebra we obtain

$$(\forall z)x_z = \left(1 + \left(E_z[\beta R^{1-\gamma}x_{z'}]\right)^{1/\gamma}\right)^\gamma. \tag{15.26}$$

Define the nonnegative matrix $K(\theta)$ by $K(\theta)(z, z') = E_{z,z'}[\beta(z, z')R(z, z')^\theta]$. Then we may interpret (15.26) as

$$x = (1 + (K(1-\gamma)x)^{1/\gamma})^\gamma,$$

where $x \in \mathbb{R}^Z_{++}$ and powers are applied entry-wise. Letting the right-hand side be Tx, it follows that $T : \mathbb{R}^Z_+ \to \mathbb{R}^Z_+$ is a monotone self-map. Ma and Toda (2021, Proposition 14) shows that T has a unique fixed point if and only if $\rho(K(1 - \gamma)) < 1$. For instance, if $Z = 1$ so (β, R) are independent and identically distributed over time through a variable ζ, then (15.26) becomes

$$x = \left(1 + \left(\mathrm{E}[\beta R^{1-\gamma} x]\right)^{1/\gamma}\right)^{\gamma} \iff \bar{c} = x^{-1/\gamma} = 1 - \mathrm{E}[\beta R^{1-\gamma}]^{1/\gamma}.$$

Note that $\bar{c} > 0$ if and only if $\mathrm{E}[\beta R^{1-\gamma}] < 1$, which is a well-known condition (Ma and Toda, 2021, Footnote 11).

As we see from all these discussions, it is frustrating that the necessary or sufficient conditions for the existence of a solution as well as the approaches to solve optimal savings problems are different depending on the model specification. When non-financial income is positive ($y(z, z') > 0$ for all (z, z')), then Theorem 15.8 states that $\rho(K(1)) < 1$ is sufficient for the existence and uniqueness of a consumption function satisfying the Euler equation, and the proof is based on Euler equation iteration and the Perov contraction theorem. When the utility function exhibits constant relative risk aversion γ and non-financial income is zero ($y(z, z') = 0$ for all (z, z')), then the result of Ma and Toda (2021) shows that $\rho(K(1 - \gamma)) < 1$ is necessary and sufficient, and the proof is based on some properties of monotone convex/concave maps. There is still room for more research.

NOTES

The sufficiency of the Euler equation and the transversality condition for optimal control has been known for a long time. The necessity of the transversality condition used to be considered difficult, but Kamihigashi (2002) provided a simple proof under the assumption $x_{t+1} = a_t$ (so the transition function g_t is the identity map). Theorem 15.4 is an adaptation to the more general case $x_{t+1} = g_t(a_t)$. The Euler equation iteration as a solution algorithm was proposed by Coleman (1990) for solving stochastic growth models. Li and Stachurski (2014) adapted this approach to establish the existence of a solution to the optimal savings problem under constant discount factor and return on savings. Ma, Stachurski, and Toda (2020) extended to the case with stochastic discounting and returns. The Euler equation iteration approach has many applications. Stachurski and Toda (2019, 2020) proved that under constant discounting and returns, the tail behavior of the wealth distribution inherits that of the income distribution. Ma and Toda (2021, 2022) proved the asymptotic linearity of consumption functions when the marginal utility $u'(c)$ behaves like a power function and discuss computational efficiency.

PROBLEMS

15.1. Introduce appropriate assumptions on u, f in Example 15.3 so that Assumptions 15.1, 15.2 are satisfied.

15.2. Prove that the optimal consumption rule $c = (1 - \beta)w$ in Example 15.2 remains valid for arbitrary stochastic returns $\{R_t\}_{t=1}^{\infty}$.

15.3. Prove that the optimal consumption rule $c = (1 - \alpha\beta)w$ in Example 15.4 remains valid for arbitrary stochastic productivities $\{A_t\}_{t=0}^{\infty}$.

15.4. Consider the space $(\mathcal{F}, d)$ in §15.5.

(i) For each $z \in \mathsf{Z}$, show that $d_z : \mathcal{F}^2 \to \mathbb{R}_+$ satisfies the triangle inequality.

(ii) Prove that $(\mathcal{F}, d)$ is a complete vector-valued metric space.

15.5 (Ma et al., 2020, Proposition 2.3). Consider the optimal savings problem in §15.5. This problem asks you to prove that the optimal savings function $s(w, z) := w - c(w, z)$ is increasing in wealth w. Let $\mathcal{C}$ be the space of candidate consumption functions defined in Theorem 15.8 and let

$$\mathcal{C}_1 = \{c \in \mathcal{C} : (\forall z \in \mathsf{Z})w \mapsto w - c(w, z) \text{ is increasing in } w.\}$$

Let $\mathcal{F}, \mathcal{F}_1$ be the corresponding spaces of marginal utility functions and $T : \mathcal{C} \to \mathcal{C}$ be Coleman operator in Lemma 15.6.

(i) Show that $\mathcal{F}_1$ is a nonempty closed set.

(ii) Show that $T : \mathcal{F}_1 \to \mathcal{F}_1$.

(iii) Show that the optimal savings function $s(w, z) := w - c(w, z)$ is increasing in w. (Hint: use the Closed Subset Lemma 14.3.)

15.6 (Ma et al., 2020, Proposition 2.4). Consider the optimal savings problem in §15.5. This problem asks you to prove that the optimal consumption function is increasing in income. Use the same notation as Problem 15.5.

(i) Let $y_1, y_2 : \mathsf{Z}^2 \to \mathbb{R}_{++}$ be two income profiles and $T_1, T_2 : \mathcal{F} \to \mathcal{F}$ be the corresponding Coleman operators. If $y_1(z, z') \leq y_2(z, z')$ for all (z, z'), show that $T_1 f \geq T_2 f$ for all $f \in \mathcal{F}$.

(ii) Show by induction that $T_1^k f \geq T_2^k f$ for all $f \in \mathcal{F}$ and $k \in \mathbb{N}$.

(iii) Let $f_1, f_2 \in \mathcal{F}$ be the unique fixed points of T_1, T_2. Show that $f_1 \geq f_2$.

(iv) Letting c_1, c_2 be the corresponding consumption functions, show that $c_1 \leq c_2$.

Introduction to Numerical Analysis

A.1 INTRODUCTION

In the main text, we have studied optimization problems from a theoretical perspective. If the objective function happens to be convex or concave, to minimize or maximize it, all we need to do is to find a point at which the derivative is zero (Proposition 11.8). This is easier said than done. In practice, almost all problems have no closed-form solutions and hence we need to use numerical methods to find the approximate solution. This chapter provides an introduction to commonly used numerical methods. Some useful references include Davis and Rabinowitz (1984) and Trefethen (2019).

A.2 SOLVING NONLINEAR EQUATIONS

If a one-variable function f is differentiable, the first-order condition for optimality is $f'(x) = 0$. Letting $g(x) = f'(x)$, it thus suffices to solve the nonlinear equation $g(x) = 0$. Suppose that $g : \mathbb{R} \to \mathbb{R}$ is continuous and

$$g(x) \begin{cases} < 0, & (x < \bar{x}) \\ = 0, & (x = \bar{x}) \\ > 0. & (x > \bar{x}) \end{cases}$$

These inequalities show that we know exactly whether the current approximate solution x is greater or less than the true solution $\bar{x}$ according to $g(x) \gtrless 0$.

Bisection method

The idea of the *bisection method* is to decrease x if $g(x) > 0$ and increase x if $g(x) < 0$.

DOI: 10.1201/9781032698953-A

To describe the bisection algorithm, let

$$x = \text{current approximate solution,}$$
$$a = \text{current lower bound of } \bar{x},$$
$$b = \text{current upper bound of } \bar{x},$$
$$\varepsilon = \text{error tolerance for } \bar{x}.$$

The bisection algorithm is defined as follows (Figure A.1).

Algorithm A.1 (Bisection method).

(i) Pick initial values $a_0 < b_0$ and error tolerance $\varepsilon > 0$.

(ii) For each $k = 1, 2, \ldots$, let $x_k = (a_k + b_k)/2$ and

$$(a_{k+1}, b_{k+1}) = \begin{cases} (a_k, x_k) & \text{if } g(x_k) > 0, \\ (x_k, b_k) & \text{if } g(x_k) < 0. \end{cases}$$

(iii) Stop if $|x_{k+1} - x_k| < \varepsilon$. The approximate solution is x_{k+1}.

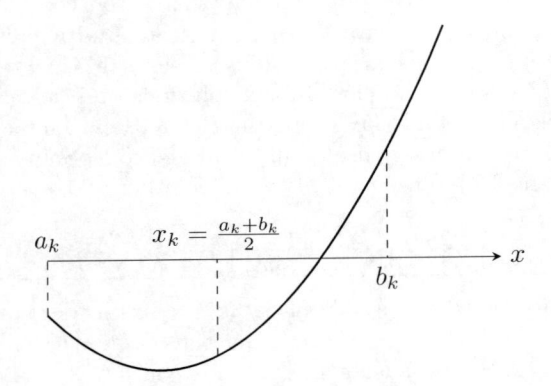

FIGURE A.1: Bisection method.

The bisection method also works when g crosses 0 from above, but the updating rule of the lower and upper bounds must be modified in an obvious way. The bisection method is a sure way to obtain a solution but is slow. Since the interval gets halved at each iteration, after k iterations the length of the interval is of the order 2^{-k}. Therefore convergence is (only) exponentially fast.

Order of convergence

At this point it is useful to define how fast an algorithm converges. Let $\{x_k\}_{k=0}^{\infty}$ be the sequence of approximate solutions generated by some algorithm. Let $\bar{x}$

be the true solution. We say that the *order of convergence* of the algorithm is α if there exist constants $\alpha \geq 1$ and $\beta > 0$ such that

$$|x_{k+1} - \bar{x}| \leq \beta \, |x_k - \bar{x}|^\alpha \tag{A.1}$$

for sufficiently large k. The cases $\alpha = 1, 2, 3$ are sometimes called *linear*, *quadratic*, and *cubic* convergence. If $\alpha = 1$ (linear convergence), we also require $\beta < 1$ to guarantee convergence. In that case, assuming (A.1) holds for all k and iterating, we get

$$|x_k - \bar{x}| \leq \beta^k \, |x_0 - \bar{x}| \,,$$

so $\{x_k\}$ converges to $\bar{x}$ exponentially fast. Therefore the bisection method has order of convergence 1 by setting $\beta = 1/2$.

If $\alpha > 1$, then $\{x_k\}$ converges to $\bar{x}$ *double exponentially*. To see this, let us find a constant $C > 0$ such that

$$C \, |x_{k+1} - \bar{x}| \leq (C \, |x_k - \bar{x}|)^\alpha.$$

Comparing with the definition of the order of convergence (A.1), it suffices to choose C such that $\beta = C^{\alpha-1} \iff C = \beta^{\frac{1}{\alpha-1}}$. Iterating (A.1) over n, we obtain

$$C \, |x_k - \bar{x}| \leq (C \, |x_0 - \bar{x}|)^{\alpha^k},$$

so provided that $|x_0 - \bar{x}| < 1/C$, we get

$$|x_k - \bar{x}| \leq C^{-1} (C \, |x_0 - \bar{x}|)^{\alpha^k} \to 0,$$

and the speed of convergence is double exponentially fast.

Newton method

Although the bisection method is simple, it is inefficient in the sense that the only information of $g(x)$ the algorithm uses is its sign. Unsurprisingly, the order of convergence is 1, which is slow. The *Newton method*, which is based on Taylor's theorem, achieves a much faster convergence by using both the function value and the derivative.

The idea of the Newton method is as follows. Let g be continuously differentiable. Suppose that we have an approximate solution at $x = a$. By Taylor's theorem (Proposition 2.4), we have

$$g(x) \approx g(a) + g'(a)(x - a).$$

Since the right-hand side is linear in x, we may solve it to obtain

$$0 = g(a) + g'(a)(x - a) \iff x = a - \frac{g(a)}{g'(a)}.$$

The formal algorithm of the Newton method is as follows (Figure A.2).

Algorithm A.2 (Newton method)**.**

(i) Pick an initial value x_0 and error tolerance $\varepsilon > 0$.

(ii) For $n = 1, 2, \ldots$, compute

$$x_{k+1} = x_k - \frac{g(x_k)}{g'(x_k)}. \tag{A.2}$$

(iii) Stop if $|x_{k+1} - x_k| < \varepsilon$. The approximate solution is x_{k+1}.

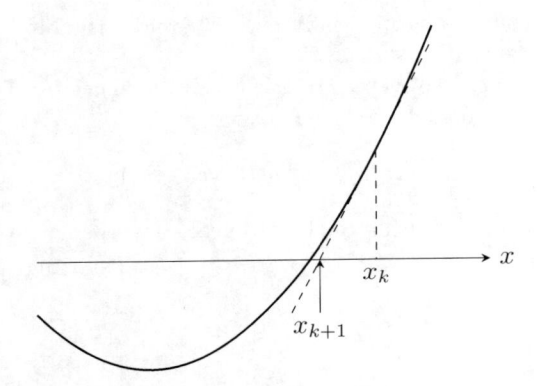

FIGURE A.2: Newton method.

The following theorem shows that the Newton method has order of convergence 2.

Theorem A.1. *Let* $g : \mathbb{R} \to \mathbb{R}$ *be* C^2. *Suppose that* $\bar{x} \in \mathbb{R}$ *satisfies* $g(\bar{x}) = 0$ *and* $g'(\bar{x}) \neq 0$. *Then there exists a constant* $\beta > 0$ *and a neighborhood* U *of* $\bar{x}$ *such that* $x_k \in U$ *implies* $|x_{k+1} - \bar{x}| \leq \beta |x_k - \bar{x}|^2$.

Proof. Let x_k be the current approximate solution. Subtracting $\bar{x}$ from both sides of (A.2), we get

$$x_{k+1} - \bar{x} = x_k - \bar{x} - \frac{g(x_k)}{g'(x_k)} = -\frac{g(x_k) + g'(x_k)(\bar{x} - x_k)}{g'(x_k)}. \tag{A.3}$$

Since g is C^2, applying Taylor's theorem to $g(\bar{x})$ around x_k, there exists $t \in [0,1]$ such that $\xi := (1-t)\bar{x} + t x_k$ satisfies

$$0 = g(\bar{x}) = g(x_k) + g'(x_k)(\bar{x} - x_k) + \frac{1}{2}g''(\xi)(\bar{x} - x_k)^2.$$

Substituting into (A.3) and assuming $g'(x_k) \neq 0$, we get

$$x_{k+1} - \bar{x} = \frac{g''(\xi)}{2g'(x_k)}(x_k - \bar{x})^2.$$

Since by assumption g is C^2 and $g'(\bar{x}) \neq 0$, we can take a neighborhood U of $\bar{x}$ such that $g'(x) \neq 0$ for $x \in U$ and

$$\beta := \sup_{t \in [0,1]} \sup_{x \in U} \left| \frac{g''((1-t)x + t\bar{x})}{2g'(x)} \right| < \infty.$$

Then $|x_{k+1} - \bar{x}| \leq \beta |x_k - \bar{x}|^2$ whenever $x_k \in U$, so by the definition (A.1), the order of convergence of the Newton method is (at least) 2. ☐

Remark. For $g(x) = x^2 - 2$, the right-hand side of (A.2) is

$$x_k - \frac{g(x_k)}{g'(x_k)} = x_k - \frac{x_k^2 - 2}{2x_k} = \frac{1}{2}x_k + \frac{1}{x_k},$$

which was the motivation behind Problem 1.4.

The Newton method can also be applied to solve a system of nonlinear equations. For example, let $g : \mathbb{R}^N \to \mathbb{R}^N$ and we would like to solve $g(x) = 0$. By Taylor's theorem, we have

$$g(x) \approx g(a) + Dg(a)(x - a) \iff x \approx a - [Dg(a)]^{-1}g(a),$$

where Dg denotes the $N \times N$ Jacobian of g. Thus if x_0 is close to the true solution $\bar{x}$ and $Dg(\bar{x})$ is invertible iterating

$$x_{k+1} = x_k - [Dg(x_k)]^{-1}g(x_k)$$

yields a fast convergence to $\bar{x}$ (Problem A.2).

Linear interpolation

The Newton method requires both the function value $g(x)$ and its derivative $g'(x)$ to implement it. Oftentimes, the derivative $g'(x)$ has a complicated form. In some cases (e.g., the objective function is defined only numerically, not analytically), it is impossible to compute the derivative. In such cases, we can use linear interpolation to solve for the solution.

Let x_k and x_{k-1} be the two most recent approximate solutions to $g(x) = 0$. Approximating g by the linear function that agrees with g at these two points, we obtain

$$g(x) \approx \frac{g(x_k) - g(x_{k-1})}{x_k - x_{k-1}}(x - x_k) + g(x_k).$$

Setting the right-hand side equal to 0, we obtain

$$\frac{g(x_k) - g(x_{k-1})}{x_k - x_{k-1}}(x - x_k) + g(x_k) = 0$$

$$\iff x_{k+1} = x_k - g(x_k)\frac{x_k - x_{k-1}}{g(x_k) - g(x_{k-1})}. \tag{A.4}$$

Problem A.4 shows that the order of convergence of the linear interpolation method is the golden ratio $\alpha = \frac{1+\sqrt{5}}{2} = 1.618\ldots$.

Quadratic interpolation

The linear interpolation method approximates a nonlinear function by a linear one by interpolating between two points. This way, we can solve for the new approximate solution explicitly by solving a linear equation. However, we can also solve quadratic equations explicitly. The quadratic interpolation method fits a quadratic function to three points.

Suppose that we have three approximate solutions $a < b < c$ to the nonlinear equation $g(x) = 0$, with $g(a)g(c) < 0$. The quadratic interpolation method constructs a quadratic function that agrees with g at these three points and then finds its root. By direct substitution, we can show that the quadratic function

$$q(x) = g(a)\frac{(x-b)(x-c)}{(a-b)(a-c)} + g(b)\frac{(x-c)(x-a)}{(b-c)(b-a)} + g(c)\frac{(x-a)(x-b)}{(c-a)(c-b)}$$
$$= Ax^2 + Bx + C$$

satisfies $q(x) = g(x)$ for $x = a, b, c$. Comparing the coefficients, we obtain

$$A = \frac{g(a)}{(a-b)(a-c)} + \frac{g(b)}{(b-c)(b-a)} + \frac{g(c)}{(c-a)(c-b)},$$
$$B = -\frac{g(a)(b+c)}{(a-b)(a-c)} - \frac{g(b)(c+a)}{(b-c)(b-a)} - \frac{g(c)(a+b)}{(c-a)(c-b)},$$
$$C = \frac{g(a)bc}{(a-b)(a-c)} + \frac{g(b)ca}{(b-c)(b-a)} + \frac{g(c)ab}{(c-a)(c-b)}.$$

Using the formula for the solution to a quadratic equation, we obtain

$$x = \frac{-B \pm \sqrt{B^2 - 4AC}}{2A},$$

where we should pick the sign $\pm$ such that $a < x < c$.

The quadratic interpolation method is defined as follows.

Algorithm A.3 (Quadratic interpolation method).

(i) Pick initial values $a_0 < b_0 < c_0$ and error tolerance $\varepsilon > 0$.

(ii) For each n, compute $d = x_{k+1}$ given current a_k, b_k, c_k. Stop if $|x_{k+1} - x_k| < \varepsilon$. Otherwise, set

$$(a_{k+1}, b_{k+1}, c_{k+1}) = \begin{cases} (a_k, d, b_k) & \text{if } a_k < d < b_k, \\ (b_k, d, c_k) & \text{if } b_k < d < c_k. \end{cases}$$

The order of convergence of the quadratic interpolation method is the root $\alpha > 1$ of the equation
$$x^3 - x^2 - x - 1 = 0,$$
which is $\alpha = 1.8393\dots.$

A.3 POLYNOMIAL APPROXIMATION

Polynomials are useful for approximating smooth functions because they can be differentiated and integrated analytically. Since a degree $n - 1$ polynomial is determined by n coefficients, once we specify n points on the xy plane, there exists (at most) one polynomial that passes through these points.

Lagrange interpolation

Lagrange interpolation gives an explicit formula for the interpolating polynomial.

Proposition A.2. *Let $x_1 < \cdots < x_n$ and define the k-th Lagrange polynomial*

$$L_k(x) := \frac{\prod_{l \neq k}(x - x_l)}{\prod_{l \neq k}(x_k - x_l)}$$

for $k = 1, \ldots, n$. Then $p(x) = \sum_{k=1}^{n} y_k L_k(x)$ is the unique polynomial of degree up to $n - 1$ satisfying $p(x_k) = y_k$ for $k = 1, \ldots, n$.

Proof. By the definition of $L_k(x)$, we have $L_k(x_l) = \delta_{kl}$ (Kronecker's delta). Therefore for all l, we have

$$p(x_l) = \sum_{k=1}^{n} y_k L_k(x_l) = \sum_{k=1}^{n} y_k \delta_{kl} = y_l.$$

Clearly $L_k(x)$ is a polynomial of degree $n - 1$, so $p(x)$ is a polynomial of degree up to $n - 1$. □

If we interpolate a function $f(x)$ at the points $x_1 < \cdots < x_n$ by a degree $n - 1$ polynomial, what is the approximation error? The following proposition gives an error bound if f is sufficiently smooth.

Proposition A.3. *Let $f : \mathbb{R} \to \mathbb{R}$ be C^n and p_{n-1} be the interpolating polynomial of f at $x_1 < \cdots < x_n$. Then for any x, there exists ξ in the convex hull of $\{x, x_1, \ldots, x_n\}$ such that*

$$f(x) - p_{n-1}(x) = \frac{f^{(n)}(\xi)}{n!} \prod_{k=1}^{n}(x - x_k). \tag{A.5}$$

Proof. If $x = x_k$ for some k, then $f(x_k) - p_{n-1}(x_k) = 0$, so (A.5) is trivial. Suppose $x \neq x_k$ for all k and let $I = \mathrm{co}\,\{x, x_1, \ldots, x_n\}$, which is an interval. For any $t \in I$, let $R(t) = f(t) - p_{n-1}(t)$ be the error term and define

$$g(t) = R(t)S(x) - R(x)S(t),$$

where $S(t) = \prod_{k=1}^{n}(t - x_k)$. Clearly $g(x) = 0$. Furthermore, since $R(x_k) = S(x_k) = 0$, we have $g(x_k) = 0$ for $k = 1, \ldots, n$. In general, if g is differentiable and $g(a) = g(b) = 0$, by the mean value theorem (Proposition 2.3) there exists $c \in (a, b)$ such that $g'(c) = 0$. Applying this to the n non-overlapping intervals with endpoints $x, x_1, \ldots, x_n$, there exist n distinct points $y_1, \ldots, y_n$ between $x, x_1, \ldots, x_n$ such that $g'(y_k) = 0$ for $k = 1, \ldots, n$. Continuing this argument, there exists $\xi \in I$ such that $g^{(n)}(\xi) = 0$. But since S is a degree n polynomial with leading coefficient 1, we have $S^{(n)} = n!$, so

$$0 = g^{(n)}(\xi) = R^{(n)}(\xi)S(x) - R(x)n!.$$

Since $R(t) = f(t) - p_{n-1}(t)$ and $\deg p_{n-1} \leq n-1$, we obtain $R^{(n)}(\xi) = f^{(n)}(\xi)$. Therefore

$$f(x) - p_{n-1}(x) = R(x) = \frac{1}{n!}f^{(n)}(\xi)S(x) = \frac{f^{(n)}(\xi)}{n!}\prod_{k=1}^{n}(x - x_k). \qquad \square$$

Chebyshev polynomial

If we want to interpolate a function on an interval by a polynomial but we are free to choose the interpolation nodes $x_1, \ldots, x_n$, how should we choose them? By mapping the interval with an affine function, without loss of generality we may assume that the interval is $[-1, 1]$. Since $f^{(n)}(\xi)$ in (A.5) depends on the particular function f but $\prod_{k=1}^{n}(x - x_k)$ does not, it is natural to choose $x_1, \ldots, x_n$ so as to minimize

$$\max_{x \in [-1,1]} \left| \prod_{k=1}^{n}(x - x_k) \right|.$$

Chebyshev solved this problem a long time ago.

The degree n *Chebyshev polynomial* $T_n(x)$ is obtained by expanding $\cos n\theta$ as a degree n polynomial of $\cos \theta$ and setting $x = \cos \theta$. For instance,

$$\begin{aligned} \cos 0\theta &= 1 & &\Longrightarrow\ T_0(x) = 1, \\ \cos \theta &= \cos \theta & &\Longrightarrow\ T_1(x) = x, \\ \cos 2\theta &= 2\cos^2 \theta - 1 & &\Longrightarrow\ T_2(x) = 2x^2 - 1, \end{aligned}$$

and so on. In general, adding

$$\begin{aligned} \cos(n+1)\theta &= \cos n\theta \cos \theta - \sin n\theta \sin \theta, \\ \cos(n-1)\theta &= \cos n\theta \cos \theta + \sin n\theta \sin \theta, \end{aligned}$$

and setting $x = \cos n\theta$, we obtain

$$T_{n+1}(x) = 2xT_n(x) - T_{n-1}(x). \tag{A.6}$$

The coefficients of Chebyshev polynomials can be easily computed by iterating (A.6). The following theorem provides the optimal nodes for polynomial interpolation.

Theorem A.4. *The solution to*

$$\min_{x_1 \geq \cdots \geq x_n} \max_{x \in [-1,1]} \left| \prod_{k=1}^{n} (x - x_k) \right|$$

is given by $x_k = \cos \frac{2k-1}{2n}\pi$, *in which case* $\prod_{k=1}^{n}(x - x_k) = 2^{1-n}T_n(x)$.

Proof. Let $p(x) = 2^{1-n}T_n(x)$. By the recursive formula (A.6), the leading coefficient of $T_n(x)$ is 2^{n-1}. Therefore the leading coefficient of $p(x)$ is 1. Since $p(\cos\theta) = 2^{1-n}\cos n\theta$, clearly

$$\sup_{x \in [-1,1]} |p(x)| = \sup_{\theta \in [-\pi,\pi]} 2^{1-n} |\cos n\theta| = 2^{1-n}.$$

Suppose that there exists a degree n polynomial $q(x)$ with leading coefficient 1 such that $\sup_{x \in [-1,1]} |q(x)| < 2^{1-n}$. Again since $p(\cos\theta) = 2^{1-n}\cos n\theta$, we have $p(x) = (-1)^k 2^{1-n}$ at $x = y_k = \cos k\pi/n$, where $k = 0, 1, \ldots, n$. Since $|q(x)| < 2^{1-n}$ for all $x \in [-1, 1]$, by the intermediate value theorem there exist $z_1, \ldots, z_n$ between $y_0, \ldots, y_n$ such that $p(z_k) - q(z_k) = 0$. But since p, q are polynomials of degree n with leading coefficient 1, $r(x) := p(x) - q(x)$ is a polynomial of degree up to $n - 1$. Since $r(z_k) = 0$ for $k = 1, \ldots, n$, it must be $r(x) \equiv 0$ or $p \equiv q$, which is a contradiction. Therefore $\prod_{k=1}^{n}(x - x_k) = 2^{1-n}T_n(x)$, so $x_k = \cos \frac{2k-1}{2n}\pi$ for $k = 1, \ldots, n$. □

A.4 QUADRATURE

Many economic problems involve maximizing expected value. Unless the distribution is discrete, expectations become integrals, which cannot be computed explicitly except for special cases. Therefore we need numerical methods to evaluate integrals, which are called *quadrature* (or numerical integration).

A typical quadrature formula takes the form

$$\int_a^b f(x)\, dx \approx \sum_{n=1}^{N} w_n f(x_n), \tag{A.7}$$

where f is a general integrand, $\{x_n\}_{n=1}^{N}$ are nodes, and $\{w_n\}_{n=1}^{N}$ are weights of the quadrature rule. This section covers the most basic theory of quadrature. See Davis and Rabinowitz (1984) for a more complete textbook treatment.

The simplest quadrature rule is to divide the interval $[a, b]$ into $N-1$ evenly spaced subintervals (so $x_n = a + \frac{n-1}{N-1}(b - a)$ for $n = 1, \ldots, N$) and choose the weights $\{w_n\}_{n=1}^{N}$ so that one can integrate all polynomials of degree $N - 1$ or less exactly. This quadrature rule is known as the N-point *Newton-Cotes rule*. Since we can map the interval $[0, 1]$ to $[a, b]$ through the affine transformation $x \mapsto a + (b - a)x$, without loss of generality, let us assume $(a, b) = (0, 1)$.

Trapezoidal rule

The 2-point Newton-Cotes rule is known as the *trapezoidal rule*. In this case we have $x_n = 0, 1$, and we choose w_1, w_2 to integrate an affine function exactly. Therefore requiring that (A.7) holds exactly for $f(x) = 1, x$, we obtain

$$1 = \int_0^1 1 \, \mathrm{d}x = w_1 + w_2,$$

$$\frac{1}{2} = \int_0^1 x \, \mathrm{d}x = w_2.$$

Solving these equations, we obtain $w_1 = w_2 = 1/2$. Changing the interval from $[0, 1]$ to $[a, b]$, the trapezoidal rule becomes

$$\int_a^b f(x) \, \mathrm{d}x \approx \frac{b-a}{2}(f(a) + f(b)). \tag{A.8}$$

Let us estimate the error of this approximation. Let $p(x)$ be the degree 1 interpolating polynomial of f at $x = a, b$. Since p agrees with f at a, b, clearly

$$\int_a^b p(x) \, \mathrm{d}x = \frac{b-a}{2}(f(a) + f(b)).$$

Therefore by Proposition A.3, we obtain

$$\int_a^b f(x) \, \mathrm{d}x - \frac{b-a}{2}(f(a) + f(b)) = \int_a^b (f(x) - p(x)) \, \mathrm{d}x$$
$$= \int_a^b \frac{f''(\xi(x))}{2}(x - a)(x - b) \, \mathrm{d}x,$$

where $\xi(x) \in (a, b)$. Since $(x - a)(x - b) < 0$ on (a, b), by the mean value theorem for Riemann-Stieltjes integrals, there exists $c \in (a, b)$ such that

$$\int_a^b \frac{f''(\xi(x))}{2}(x - a)(x - b) \, \mathrm{d}x = \frac{f''(c)}{2} \int_a^b (x - a)(x - b) \, \mathrm{d}x = -\frac{f''(c)}{12}(b - a)^3.$$

Therefore we can estimate the error in (A.8) as

$$\left| \int_a^b f(x) \, \mathrm{d}x - \frac{b-a}{2}(f(a) + f(b)) \right| \leq \frac{\|f''\|}{12}(b - a)^3, \tag{A.9}$$

where $\|\cdot\|$ denotes the supremum norm on $[a, b]$.

Simpson's rule

The 3-point Newton-Cotes rule is known as *Simpson's rule*. In this case the quadrature nodes are $x_n = 0, 1/2, 1$, and we choose the weights w_1, w_2, w_3 so as to integrate a quadratic function exactly. Therefore requiring that (A.7) holds exactly for $f(x) = 1, x, x^2$, we obtain

$$1 = \int_0^1 1 \, dx = w_1 + w_2 + w_3,$$

$$\frac{1}{2} = \int_0^1 x \, dx = \frac{1}{2} w_2 + w_3,$$

$$\frac{1}{3} = \int_0^1 x^2 \, dx = \frac{1}{4} w_2 + w_3.$$

Solving these equations, we obtain $w_1 = w_3 = 1/6$ and $w_2 = 2/3$. Changing the interval from $[0, 1]$ to $[a, b]$, Simpson's rule becomes

$$\int_a^b f(x) \, dx \approx \frac{b-a}{6} \left(f(a) + 4f \left(\frac{a+b}{2} \right) + f(b) \right). \tag{A.10}$$

Interestingly, since

$$\frac{1}{4} = \int_0^1 x^3 \, dx = \frac{1}{8} w_2 + w_3,$$

Simpson's rule actually integrates polynomials of degree 3 exactly, even though it is not designed to do so.

To estimate the error of Simpson's rule (A.10), take any point $d \in (a, b)$ and let $p(x)$ be a degree 3 interpolating polynomial of f at $x = a, \frac{a+b}{2}, b, d$. Since Simpson's rule integrates degree 3 polynomials exactly, by Proposition A.3 we have

$$\int_a^b f(x) \, dx - \frac{b-a}{6} \left(f(a) + 4f \left(\frac{a+b}{2} \right) + f(b) \right)$$

$$= \int_a^b (f(x) - p(x)) \, dx$$

$$= \int_a^b \frac{f^{(4)}(\xi(x))}{4!} (x-a) \left(x - \frac{a+b}{2} \right) (x-b)(x-d) \, dx.$$

Since $d \in (a, b)$ is arbitrary, we can take $d = \frac{a+b}{2}$. Since

$$(x-a) \left(x - \frac{a+b}{2} \right)^2 (x-b) \leq 0$$

on (a, b), as before we can apply the mean value theorem for integrals. Using the change of variable $x = \frac{a+b}{2} + \frac{b-a}{2} t$, we can compute

$$\int_a^b (x-a) \left(x - \frac{a+b}{2} \right)^2 (x-b) \, dx$$

$$= \left(\frac{b-a}{2} \right)^5 \int_{-1}^1 (t+1)t^2(t-1) \, dt = -\frac{1}{120} (b-a)^5.$$

Since $4! = 24$ and $24 \times 120 = 2880$, the integration error of (A.10) is

$$\left| \int_a^b f(x)\,\mathrm{d}x - \frac{b-a}{6}\left(f(a) + 4f\left(\frac{a+b}{2}\right) + f(b) \right) \right| \leq \frac{\|f^{(4)}\|}{2880}(b-a)^5. \quad \text{(A.11)}$$

Compound rule

Newton-Cotes rules with $N \geq 4$ are almost never used because beyond some degree N, some of the weights $\{w_n\}_{n=1}^N$ become negative, which causes rounding errors. One way to avoid this issue is to divide the interval $[a, b]$ into N evenly spaced subintervals and apply the trapezoidal rule or Simpson's rule to each subinterval. This method is known as the *compound* (or composite) rule.

If we apply the trapezoidal rule to N subintervals, then there are $N + 1$ endpoints. Letting $x_n = n/N$ for $n = 0, 1, \ldots, N$, the formula for $[0, 1]$ is

$$\int_0^1 f(x)\,\mathrm{d}x \approx \sum_{n=1}^N \frac{1}{2N}(f(x_{n-1}) + f(x_n))$$

$$= \frac{1}{2N}\left(f(x_0) + 2f(x_1) + \cdots + 2f(x_{N-1}) + f(x_N) \right).$$

(Just remember that the relative weights are 1 at endpoints and 2 in between.) Since $b - a = 1/N$ and there are N subintervals, using (A.9), the error of the $(N + 1)$-point trapezoidal rule is of order $\frac{\|f''\|}{12}N^{-2}$.

If we apply Simpson's rule, then there are 3 points on each subinterval, of which there are N, and $N - 1$ endpoints are counted twice. Therefore the total number of points is $3N - (N - 1) = 2N + 1$. Letting $x_n = n/(2N)$ for $n = 0, 1, \ldots, 2N$, the formula for $[0, 1]$ is

$$\int_0^1 f(x)\,\mathrm{d}x \approx \sum_{n=1}^N \frac{1}{6N}(f(x_{2n-2}) + 4f(x_{2n-1}) + f(x_{2n}))$$

$$= \frac{1}{6N}\left(f(x_0) + 4f(x_1) + 2f(x_2) + \cdots + 4f(x_{2N-1}) + f(x_{2N}) \right).$$

(Just remember that the relative weights are 1 at endpoints, and they alternate like $4, 2, \ldots, 4, 2, 4$ in between.) Since $b - a = 1/N$ and there are N subintervals, using (A.11), the error of the $(2N + 1)$-point Simpson's rule is of order $\frac{\|f^{(4)}\|}{2880}N^{-4}$.

Since the quadrature weights are given explicitly for trapezoidal and Simpson's rules, it is straightforward to write codes for computing numerical integrals. Tables A.1 and A.2 show the $\log_{10}$ relative errors of integrals over the interval $[0, 1]$ for several functions defined by

$$\log_{10}\left| \hat{I}/I - 1 \right|,$$

where I is the true integral and $\widehat{I}$ is the numerical one. As the above error analysis suggests, errors tend to be smaller when the integrand is smoother (has higher order derivatives). Furthermore, Simpson's rule is more accurate than the trapezoidal rule.

TABLE A.1: $\log_{10}$ relative errors of compound trapezoidal rule.

# points	$x^{1/2}$	$x^{3/2}$	$x^{5/2}$	$x^{7/2}$	$x^{9/2}$	e^x
3	-1.0238	-1.1743	-0.7343	-0.4896	-0.3041	-1.6830
5	-1.4550	-1.7558	-1.3394	-1.0875	-0.8937	-2.2838
9	-1.8926	-2.3438	-1.9427	-1.6885	-1.4928	-2.8855
17	-2.3346	-2.9361	-2.5452	-2.2902	-2.0941	-3.4874
33	-2.7795	-3.5314	-3.1474	-2.8922	-2.6960	-4.0895
65	-3.2264	-4.1287	-3.7495	-3.4943	-3.2980	-4.6915

TABLE A.2: $\log_{10}$ relative errors of compound Simpson's rule.

# points	$x^{1/2}$	$x^{3/2}$	$x^{5/2}$	$x^{7/2}$	$x^{9/2}$	e^x
3	-1.3676	-2.2275	-2.3780	-1.8192	-1.1040	-3.4722
5	-1.8179	-2.9667	-3.3705	-2.9823	-2.3199	-4.6667
9	-2.2691	-3.7142	-4.3841	-4.1584	-3.5289	-5.8684
17	-2.7206	-4.4649	-5.4112	-5.3435	-4.7350	-7.0720
33	-3.1722	-5.2168	-6.4470	-6.5346	-5.9399	-8.2759
65	-3.6237	-5.9692	-7.4884	-7.7297	-7.1443	-9.4800

Gaussian quadrature

In the Newton-Cotes quadrature, we assume that the nodes are evenly spaced, but of course there is no particular reason to do so. Can we do better by choosing the quadrature nodes optimally? In general, consider the integral

$$\int_a^b w(x)f(x)\,\mathrm{d}x, \tag{A.12}$$

where $-\infty \le a < b \le \infty$ are endpoints of integration, $w(x) > 0$ is some (fixed) weighting function, and f is a general integrand. A typical example is $a = -\infty$, $b = \infty$, and $w(x) = \frac{1}{\sqrt{2\pi\sigma^2}}e^{-(x-\mu)^2/2\sigma^2}$, in which case we want to compute the expectation $\mathrm{E}[f(X)]$ when the random variable X is normally distributed with mean μ and standard deviation σ.

It turns out that for any N, we can choose nodes $\{x_n\}_{n=1}^N$ and weights $\{w_n\}_{n=1}^N$ such that we can integrate all polynomials of degree up to $2N-1$ exactly using a quadrature formula of the form (A.7), which is known as the

Gaussian quadrature. In the discussion below, assume that $\int_a^b w(x)x^n\,\mathrm{d}x$ exists for all $n \geq 0$, where $-\infty \leq a < b \leq \infty$ are fixed. For functions f, g, define the inner product $\langle f, g \rangle$ by

$$\langle f, g \rangle = \int_a^b w(x)f(x)g(x)\,\mathrm{d}x. \tag{A.13}$$

As usual, define the norm of f by $\|f\| = \sqrt{\langle f, f \rangle}$. To simplify notation, let us omit a, b, so $\int$ means $\int_a^b$.

The first step is to construct orthogonal polynomials $\{p_n(x)\}_{n=0}^N$ corresponding to the inner product (A.13). We say that polynomials $\{p_n(x)\}_{n=0}^N$ are *orthogonal* if (i) $\deg p_n = n$ and the leading coefficient of p_n is 1, and (ii) for all $m \neq n$, we have $\langle p_m, p_n \rangle = 0$. Some authors require that the polynomials are orthonormal, so $\langle p_n, p_n \rangle = 1$. Here we normalize the polynomials by requiring that the leading coefficient is 1, which is useful for computation. The following three-term recurrence relation shows the existence of orthogonal polynomials and provides an explicit algorithm for computing them.

Proposition A.5 (Three-term recurrence relation). *Let $p_0(x) = 1$, $p_1(x) = x - \frac{\langle xp_0, p_0 \rangle}{\|p_0\|^2}$, and for $n \geq 1$ define*

$$p_{n+1}(x) = \left(x - \frac{\langle xp_n, p_n \rangle}{\|p_n\|^2} \right) p_n(x) - \frac{\|p_n\|^2}{\|p_{n-1}\|^2} p_{n-1}(x). \tag{A.14}$$

Then $p_n(x)$ is the degree n orthogonal polynomial.

Proof. Let us show by induction on n that (i) p_n is an degree n polynomial with leading coefficient 1, and (ii) $\langle p_n, p_m \rangle = 0$ for all $m < n$. The claim is trivial for $n = 0$. For $n = 1$, by construction p_1 is a degree 1 polynomial with leading coefficient 1, and since $p_0(x) = 1$, we obtain

$$\langle p_1, p_0 \rangle = \left\langle \left(x - \frac{\langle xp_0, p_0 \rangle}{\|p_0\|^2} \right) p_0, p_0 \right\rangle = \langle xp_0, p_0 \rangle - \langle xp_0, p_0 \rangle = 0.$$

Suppose the claim holds up to n. Then for $n + 1$, by (A.14) the leading coefficient of p_{n+1} is the same as that of xp_n, which is 1. If $m = n$, then

$$\langle p_{n+1}, p_n \rangle = \left\langle \left(x - \frac{\langle xp_n, p_n \rangle}{\|p_n\|^2} \right) p_n - \frac{\|p_n\|^2}{\|p_{n-1}\|^2} p_{n-1}, p_n \right\rangle$$

$$= \langle xp_n, p_n \rangle - \langle xp_n, p_n \rangle - \frac{\|p_n\|^2}{\|p_{n-1}\|^2} \langle p_{n-1}, p_n \rangle = 0.$$

If $m = n - 1$, then

$$
\begin{aligned}
\langle p_{n+1}, p_{n-1} \rangle &= \left\langle \left(x - \frac{\langle xp_n, p_n \rangle}{\|p_n\|^2} \right) p_n - \frac{\|p_n\|^2}{\|p_{n-1}\|^2} p_{n-1}, p_{n-1} \right\rangle \\
&= \langle xp_n, p_{n-1} \rangle - \frac{\langle xp_n, p_n \rangle}{\|p_n\|^2} \langle p_n, p_{n-1} \rangle - \|p_n\|^2 \\
&= \langle p_n, xp_{n-1} \rangle - \|p_n\|^2 .
\end{aligned}
$$

Since the leading coefficients of p_n, p_{n-1} are 1, we can write $xp_{n-1}(x) = p_n(x) + q(x)$, where $q(x)$ is a polynomial of degree at most $n - 1$. Clearly q can be expressed as a linear combination of $p_0, p_1, \ldots, p_{n-1}$, so $\langle p_n, q \rangle = 0$. Therefore

$$
\langle p_{n+1}, p_{n-1} \rangle = \langle p_n, p_n + q \rangle - \|p_n\|^2 = \|p_n\|^2 + \langle p_n, q \rangle - \|p_n\|^2 = 0.
$$

Finally, if $m < n - 1$, then

$$
\begin{aligned}
\langle p_{n+1}, p_m \rangle &= \left\langle \left(x - \frac{\langle xp_n, p_n \rangle}{\|p_n\|^2} \right) p_n - \frac{\|p_n\|^2}{\|p_{n-1}\|^2} p_{n-1}, p_m \right\rangle \\
&= \langle xp_n, p_m \rangle - \frac{\langle xp_n, p_n \rangle}{\|p_n\|^2} \langle p_n, p_m \rangle - \frac{\|p_n\|^2}{\|p_{n-1}\|^2} \langle p_{n-1}, p_m \rangle \\
&= \langle p_n, xp_m \rangle = 0
\end{aligned}
$$

because xp_m is a polynomial of degree $1 + m < n$. □

The following lemma shows that a degree n orthogonal polynomial has exactly n real roots (so they are all simple).

Lemma A.6. $p_n(x)$ has exactly n real roots on (a, b).

Proof. By the fundamental theorem of algebra, $p_n(x)$ has exactly n roots in $\mathbb{C}$. Suppose to the contrary that $p_n(x)$ has fewer than n real roots on (a, b). Let $x_1, \ldots, x_k$ $(k < n)$ be the roots at which $p_n(x)$ changes its sign and $q(x) = (x - x_1) \cdots (x - x_k)$. Since $p_n(x)q(x)$ has a constant sign but is not identically equal to zero, we have

$$
\langle p_n, q \rangle = \int w(x) p_n(x) q(x) \, \mathrm{d}x \neq 0
$$

because $w(x) > 0$. On the other hand, since $\deg q = k < n$, we have $\langle p_n, q \rangle = 0$, which is a contradiction. □

The following theorem shows that using the N roots of the degree N orthogonal polynomial $p_N(x)$ as quadrature nodes and choosing specific weights, we can integrate all polynomials of degree up to $2N - 1$ exactly. Thus Gaussian quadrature always exists.

Theorem A.7 (Gaussian quadrature). *Let $a < x_1 < \cdots < x_N < b$ be the N roots of the degree N orthogonal polynomial p_N established in Lemma A.6 and*

$$w_n := \int w(x) L_n(x) \, dx \tag{A.15}$$

for $n = 1, \ldots, N$, where

$$L_n(x) := \prod_{m \neq n} \frac{x - x_m}{x_n - x_m}$$

is the degree $N - 1$ polynomial that takes value δ_{mn} at x_m. Then

$$\int w(x) p(x) \, dx = \sum_{n=1}^{N} w_n p(x_n) \tag{A.16}$$

for all polynomials $p(x)$ of degree up to $2N - 1$.

Proof. Since $\deg p \leq 2N - 1$ and $\deg p_N = N$, we can write

$$p(x) = p_N(x) q(x) + r(x),$$

where $\deg q, \deg r \leq N - 1$. Since q can be expressed as a linear combination of orthogonal polynomials of degree up to $N - 1$, we have $\langle p_n, q \rangle = 0$. Hence

$$\int w(x) p(x) \, dx = \langle p_n, q \rangle + \int w(x) r(x) \, dx = \int w(x) r(x) \, dx.$$

On the other hand, since $\{x_n\}_{n=1}^{N}$ are roots of p_N, we have

$$p(x_n) = p_N(x_n) q(x_n) + r(x_n) = r(x_n)$$

for all n, so in particular

$$\sum_{n=1}^{N} w_n p(x_n) = \sum_{n=1}^{N} w_n r(x_n).$$

Therefore it suffices to show (A.16) for polynomials r of degree up to $N - 1$. Since $\deg r \leq N - 1$ and $\deg L_n = N - 1$, by Proposition A.2 we have

$$r(x) = \sum_{n=1}^{N} r(x_n) L_n(x)$$

identically. Since r can be represented as a linear combination of L_n's, it suffices to show (A.16) for all L_n's. But since by (A.15) we have

$$\int w(x) L_n(x) \, dx = w_n = \sum_{m=1}^{N} w_m \delta_{mn} = \sum_{m=1}^{N} w_m L_n(x_m),$$

the claim is true. $\square$

In practice, how can we compute the nodes $\{x_n\}_{n=1}^N$ and weights $\{w_n\}_{n=1}^N$ of the N-point Gaussian quadrature established in Theorem A.7? The solution is given by the following Golub-Welsch algorithm.

Theorem A.8 (Golub and Welsch, 1969). *For each $n \geq 1$, define α_n, β_n by*

$$\alpha_n = \frac{\langle xp_{n-1}, p_{n-1}\rangle}{\|p_{n-1}\|^2}, \quad \beta_n = \frac{\|p_n\|}{\|p_{n-1}\|} > 0.$$

Define the $N \times N$ symmetric tridiagonal matrix

$$T_N = \begin{bmatrix} \alpha_1 & \beta_1 & 0 & \cdots & & 0 \\ \beta_1 & \alpha_2 & \beta_2 & \ddots & & \vdots \\ 0 & \beta_2 & \alpha_3 & \ddots & & 0 \\ \vdots & \ddots & \ddots & \ddots & & \beta_{N-1} \\ 0 & \cdots & 0 & \beta_{N-1} & & \alpha_N \end{bmatrix}. \tag{A.17}$$

Then the Gaussian quadrature nodes $\{x_n\}_{n=1}^N$ are eigenvalues of T_N. Letting $v_n = (v_{n1}, \ldots, v_{nn})'$ be an eigenvector of T_N corresponding to the eigenvalue x_n, the weights $\{w_n\}_{n=1}^N$ in (A.15) are equal to

$$w_n = \frac{v_{n1}^2}{\|v_n\|^2} \int w(x)\, \mathrm{d}x > 0. \tag{A.18}$$

Proof. By (A.14) and the definition of α_n, β_n, for all $n \geq 0$ we have

$$p_{n+1}(x) = (x - \alpha_{n+1})p_n(x) - \beta_n^2 p_{n-1}(x). \tag{A.19}$$

Note that this is true for $n = 0$ by defining $p_{-1}(x) = 0$ and $\beta_0 = 0$. For each n, let $p_n^*(x) = p_n(x)/\|p_n\|$ be the normalized orthogonal polynomial. Then (A.19) becomes

$$\|p_{n+1}\| p_{n+1}^*(x) = \|p_n\| (x - \alpha_{n+1})p_n^*(x) - \|p_{n-1}\| \beta_n^2 p_{n-1}^*(x).$$

Dividing both sides by $\|p_n\| > 0$, using the definition of β_n, β_{n+1}, and rearranging terms, we obtain

$$\beta_n p_{n-1}^*(x) + \alpha_{n+1} p_n^*(x) + \beta_{n+1} p_{n+1}^*(x) = x p_n^*(x).$$

In particular, setting $x = x_k$ (where x_k is a root of p_N), we obtain

$$\beta_n p_{n-1}^*(x_k) + \alpha_{n+1} p_n^*(x_k) + \beta_{n+1} p_{n+1}^*(x_k) = x_k p_n^*(x_k). \tag{A.20}$$

for all n and $k = 1, \ldots, N$. Since $\beta_0 = 0$ by definition and $p_N^*(x_k) = 0$ (since x_k is a root of p_N and hence of $p_N^* = p_N/\|p_N\|$), letting $P(x) = (p_0^*(x), \ldots, p_{N-1}^*(x))'$ and collecting (A.20) into a vector, we obtain

$$T_N P(x_k) = x_k P(x_k)$$

for $k = 1, \ldots, N$. Define the $N \times N$ matrix P by $P = (P(x_1), \ldots, P(x_N))$. Then $T_N P = \mathrm{diag}(x_1, \ldots, x_N)P$, so $x_1, \ldots, x_N$ are eigenvalues of T_N provided that P is invertible. Now since $\{p_n^*\}_{n=0}^{N-1}$ are normalized and Gaussian quadrature integrates all polynomials of degree up to $2N - 1$ exactly, we have

$$\delta_{mn} = \langle p_m^*, p_n^* \rangle = \int w(x)p_m^*(x)p_n^*(x)\,\mathrm{d}x = \sum_{k=1}^{N} w_k p_m^*(x_k)p_n^*(x_k) \qquad \text{(A.21)}$$

for $m, n \leq N - 1$. Letting $W = \mathrm{diag}(w_1, \ldots, w_N)$ and collecting (A.21) into a matrix, we obtain $PWP' = I$. Therefore P, W are invertible and $x_1, \ldots, x_N$ are eigenvalues of T_N. Solving for W and taking the inverse, we obtain

$$W^{-1} = P'P \iff \frac{1}{w_n} = \sum_{k=0}^{N-1} p_k^*(x_n)^2 > 0$$

for all n. To show (A.18), let v_n be an eigenvector of T_N corresponding to the eigenvalue x_n. Then $v_n = cP(x_n)$ for some constant $c \neq 0$. Taking the norm, we obtain

$$\|v_n\|^2 = c^2 \|P(x_n)\|^2 = c^2 \sum_{k=0}^{N-1} p_k^*(x_n)^2 = \frac{c^2}{w_n} \iff w_n = \frac{c^2}{\|v_n\|^2}.$$

Comparing the first entry of $v_n = cP(x_n)$, noting that $p_0(x) = 1$ and hence $p_0^* = p_0/\|p_0\| = 1/\|p_0\|$, we obtain

$$c^2 = v_{n1}^2 \|p_0\|^2 = v_{n1}^2 \int w(x)p_0(x)^2\,\mathrm{d}x = v_{n1}^2 \int w(x)\,\mathrm{d}x,$$

which implies (A.18). $\qquad\qquad\qquad\qquad\qquad\qquad\qquad\qquad\square$

We list a few examples of the Gaussian quadrature.

Example A.1 (Gauss-Legendre quadrature). The case $(a, b) = (-1, 1)$, $w(x) = 1$ is useful for computing integrals without weighting.

Example A.2 (Gauss-Chebyshev quadrature). The case $(a, b) = (-1, 1)$, $w(x) = 1/\sqrt{1 - x^2}$ is useful for computing Fourier coefficients through the change of variable $x = \cos\theta$.

Example A.3 (Gauss-Hermite quadrature). The case $(a, b) = (-\infty, \infty)$, $w(x) = \mathrm{e}^{-x^2}$ is useful for computing the expectation with respect to the normal distribution.

Example A.4 (Gauss-Laguerre quadrature). The case $(a, b) = (0, \infty)$, $w(x) = \mathrm{e}^{-x}$ is useful for computing the expectation with respect to the exponential distribution.

TABLE A.3: $\log_{10}$ relative errors of Gauss-Legendre quadrature.

# points	$x^{1/2}$	$x^{3/2}$	$x^{5/2}$	$x^{7/2}$	$x^{9/2}$	e^x
3	-2.4237	-3.3289	-3.8570	-4.0525	-3.8824	-6.3191
5	-3.0245	-4.3578	-5.3560	-6.0948	-6.6082	-12.4194
9	-3.7418	-5.5649	-7.0688	-8.3362	-9.4106	-15.9546
17	-4.5396	-6.8986	-8.9436	-10.7592	-12.3913	-15.9546
33	-5.3862	-8.3108	-10.9229	-13.3092	-15.3525	$-\infty$

Table A.3 shows the $\log_{10}$ relative errors when using the N-point Gauss-Legendre quadrature. Comparing to Tables A.1 and A.2, we can see that Gaussian quadrature is overwhelmingly more accurate than Newton-Cotes.

If $(a, b) = (-\infty, \infty)$ and $\int_{-\infty}^{\infty} w(x)\,dx = 1$ in (A.12), then $w(x)$ can be viewed as a probability density and (A.12) becomes an expectation. After a suitable transformation, the Gauss-Legendre, Gauss-Hermite, and Gauss-Laguerre quadratures can then be viewed as approximations to the uniform, normal, and exponential distributions. The same idea can be applied to a wider class of distributions. Since by Theorem A.8, all we need for implementing the Gaussian quadrature are the polynomial moments $\int w(x)x^n\,dx$ of the weighting functions w, Gaussian quadrature can be used for approximating any distribution that has explicit moments. Toda (2021a) uses this idea to discretize nonparametric distributions from data.

A.5   DISCRETIZATION

If the goal is to solve a single optimization problem that involves expectations (e.g., static optimal portfolio problem as in §8.5), a highly accurate Gaussian quadrature is a natural choice. However, many economic problems are dynamic, in which case one needs to compute conditional expectations. Furthermore, to reduce the computational complexity of the problem, it is desirable that the quadrature nodes are preassigned instead of being dependent on the particular state of the model. Discretization is a useful tool for solving such problems. This section explains the Farmer and Toda (2017) method of discretizing Markov processes, which is based on the maximum entropy discretization method of distributions introduced by Tanaka and Toda (2013, 2015).

Example

For concreteness, consider the Gaussian AR(1) process

$$x_t = \rho x_{t-1} + u_t, \quad u_t \sim N(0, \sigma^2).$$

Then the conditional distribution of x_t given x_{t-1} is $N(\rho x_{t-1}, \sigma^2)$. How can we discretize (find a finite-state Markov chain approximation) of this stochastic process? One of the classic methods, the Tauchen and Hussey (1991) method, is based on the Gauss-Hermite quadrature (Example A.3). First consider discretizing $N(0, \sigma^2)$. Letting $\{x_n\}_{n=1}^{N}$ and $\{w_n\}_{n=1}^{N}$ be the nodes and weights of the N-point Gauss-Hermite quadrature, since for any integrand g we have

$$\mathrm{E}[g(X)] = \int_{-\infty}^{\infty} g(x) \frac{1}{\sqrt{2\pi\sigma^2}} e^{-\frac{x^2}{2\sigma^2}} \, \mathrm{d}x = \int_{-\infty}^{\infty} g(\sqrt{2}\sigma y) \frac{1}{\sqrt{\pi}} e^{-y^2} \, \mathrm{d}y$$

$$\approx \sum_{n=1}^{N} \frac{w_n}{\sqrt{\pi}} g(\sqrt{2}\sigma x_n),$$

we can use the nodes $x_n' = \sqrt{2}\sigma x_n$ and weights $w_n' = w_n/\sqrt{\pi}$ to discretize $N(0, \sigma^2)$.

The same idea can be used to discretize the Gaussian AR(1) process. Let us fix the nodes $\{x_n'\}_{n=1}^{N}$ as constructed above. For any integrand g, letting $\mu = \rho x_m'$ we have

$$\mathrm{E}[g(x_t) \mid x_{t-1} = x_m'] = \int_{-\infty}^{\infty} g(x) \frac{1}{\sqrt{2\pi\sigma^2}} e^{-\frac{(x-\mu)^2}{2\sigma^2}} \, \mathrm{d}x$$

$$= \int_{-\infty}^{\infty} g(x) e^{-\frac{\mu^2 - 2x\mu}{2\sigma^2}} \frac{1}{\sqrt{2\pi\sigma^2}} e^{-\frac{x^2}{2\sigma^2}} \, \mathrm{d}x$$

$$\approx \sum_{n=1}^{N} w_n' e^{-\frac{\mu^2 - 2x_n'\mu}{2\sigma^2}} g(x_n').$$

Therefore we can construct the transition probability matrix $P = (p_{mn})$ by

$$p_{mn} \propto w_n' e^{-\frac{\mu^2 - 2x_n'\mu}{2\sigma^2}},$$

where $\mu = \rho x_m'$ and the constant of proportionality is determined such that $\sum_{n=1}^{N} p_{mn} = 1$. The Tauchen-Hussey method is relatively accurate if $\rho \leq 0.5$, although a drawback is that it assumes Gaussian shocks. Furthermore, the performance deteriorates quickly when ρ becomes larger.

Maximum entropy discretization of probability distributions

The maximum entropy discretization method of Farmer and Toda (2017) is generally applicable and accurate. Thus it should be the first choice for discretizing general Markov processes. We start the discussion from discretizing a single probability distribution. Suppose that we are given a continuous probability density function $f : \mathbb{R}^K \to \mathbb{R}$, which we would like to discretize. Let X be a random vector with density f, and $g : \mathbb{R}^K \to \mathbb{R}$ be any bounded continuous function. The first step is to choose a quadrature formula

$$\mathrm{E}[g(X)] = \int_{\mathbb{R}^K} g(x) f(x) \, \mathrm{d}x \approx \sum_{n=1}^{N} w_n g(x_n), \tag{A.22}$$

where N is the number of quadrature nodes $\{x_n\}_{n=1}^{N}$ and $\{w_n\}_{n=1}^{N}$ are weights such that $w_n > 0$.

For now, we do not take a stance on the choice of the initial quadrature formula but take it as given. Given the quadrature formula (A.22), a coarse but valid discrete approximation of the density f would be to assign probability q_n to the point x_n proportional to w_n, so

$$q_n = \frac{w_n}{\sum_{n=1}^{N} w_n}. \qquad (A.23)$$

However, this is not necessarily a good approximation because the moments of the discrete distribution $\{q_n\}$ do not generally match those of f.

Tanaka and Toda (2015) propose to match a finite set of moments exactly by updating the probabilities $\{q_n\}$ in a particular way. Let $T : \mathbb{R}^K \to \mathbb{R}^L$ be a function that defines the moments that we wish to match and let $\bar{T} = \int_{\mathbb{R}^K} T(x)f(x)\,dx$ be the vector of exact moments. For example, if we want to match the first and second moments in the one-dimensional case ($K = 1$), then $T(x) = (x, x^2)'$. Tanaka and Toda (2015) update the probabilities $\{q_n\}$ by solving the optimization problem

$$\underset{\{p_n\}}{\text{minimize}} \qquad \sum_{n=1}^{N} p_n \log \frac{p_n}{q_n}$$

$$\text{subject to} \qquad \sum_{n=1}^{N} p_n T(x_n) = \bar{T}, \ \sum_{n=1}^{N} p_n = 1, \ p_n \geq 0. \qquad (P)$$

The objective function in the primal problem (P) is known as the *Kullback-Leibler information* or the *relative entropy* of $\{p_n\}$ relative to $\{q_n\}$. This method matches the given moments exactly while keeping the probabilities $\{p_n\}$ as close to the initial approximation $\{q_n\}$ in (A.23) as possible in the sense of the Kullback-Leibler information. Note that since (P) is a convex minimization problem, the solution (if it exists) is unique.

The optimization problem (P) is a constrained minimization problem with a large number (N) of unknowns ($\{p_n\}$) with $L+1$ equality constraints and N inequality constraints, which is in general computationally intensive to solve. However, we may efficiently solve it by applying the duality theory introduced in §12.6 to convert the primal problem (P) to the dual problem

$$\max_{\lambda \in \mathbb{R}^L} \left[\lambda' \bar{T} - \log \left(\sum_{n=1}^{N} q_n e^{\lambda' T(x_n)} \right) \right], \qquad (D)$$

which is a *low dimensional* (L unknowns) *unconstrained* concave maximization problem and hence computationally tractable. The following theorem shows how the solutions to the two problems (P) and (D) are related.

Theorem A.9. *Let* $X_N = \{x_n\}_{n=1}^{N}$ *be the set of initial quadrature nodes. Then the following statements are true.*

(i) *The primal problem* (P) *has a solution if and only if* $\bar{T} \in \operatorname{co} T(X_N)$. *If a solution exists, it is unique.*

(ii) *The dual problem* (D) *has a solution if and only if* $\bar{T} \in \operatorname{int} \operatorname{co} T(X_N)$. *If a solution exists, it is unique.*

(iii) *If the dual problem* (D) *has a (unique) solution* λ_N, *then the (unique) solution to the primal problem* (P) *is given by*

$$p_n = \frac{q_n e^{\lambda_N' T(x_n)}}{\sum_{n=1}^N q_n e^{\lambda_N' T(x_n)}} = \frac{q_n e^{\lambda_N'(T(x_n)-\bar{T})}}{\sum_{n=1}^N q_n e^{\lambda_N'(T(x_n)-\bar{T})}}. \tag{A.24}$$

Proof. See Farmer and Toda (2017, Theorem 2.1). $\qquad\square$

Theorem A.9 provides a practical way to implement the Tanaka-Toda method. After choosing the initial discretization $Q = \{q_n\}$ and the moment defining function T, one can numerically solve the unconstrained optimization problem (D). To this end, we can instead solve

$$\min_{\lambda \in \mathbb{R}^L} \sum_{n=1}^N q_n e^{\lambda'(T(x_n)-\bar{T})} \tag{D$'$}$$

because the objective function in (D$'$) is a monotonic transformation (-1 times the exponential) of that in (D). Since (D$'$) is an unconstrained convex minimization problem with a (relatively) small number (L) of unknowns (λ), solving it is computationally simple. Letting $J_N(\lambda)$ be the objective function in (D$'$), its gradient and Hessian can be analytically computed as

$$\nabla J_N(\lambda) = \sum_{n=1}^N q_n e^{\lambda'(T(x_n)-\bar{T})}(T(x_n) - \bar{T}), \tag{A.25a}$$

$$\nabla^2 J_N(\lambda) = \sum_{n=1}^N q_n e^{\lambda'(T(x_n)-\bar{T})}(T(x_n) - \bar{T})(T(x_n) - \bar{T})', \tag{A.25b}$$

respectively. In practice, we can quickly solve (D$'$) numerically using optimization routines by supplying the analytical gradient and Hessian.

If a solution to (D$'$) exists, it is unique, and we can compute the updated discretization $P = \{p_n\}$ by (A.24). If a solution does not exist, it means that the regularity condition $\bar{T} \in \operatorname{int} \operatorname{co} T(X_N)$ does not hold and we cannot match moments. Then one needs to select a smaller set of moments. Numerically checking whether moments are matched is straightforward: by (A.24), (D$'$), and (A.25a), the error is

$$\sum_{n=1}^N p_n T(x_n) - \bar{T} = \frac{\sum_{n=1}^N q_n e^{\lambda_N'(T(x_n)-\bar{T})}(T(x_n) - \bar{T})}{\sum_{n=1}^N q_n e^{\lambda_N'(T(x_n)-\bar{T})}} = \frac{\nabla J_N(\lambda_N)}{J_N(\lambda_N)}. \tag{A.26}$$

Maximum entropy discretization of Markov processes

Next we show how to extend the Tanaka-Toda method to the case of time-homogeneous Markov processes. Consider the time-homogeneous first-order Markov process

$$P(x_t \le x' \mid x_{t-1} = x) = F(x'; x),$$

where x_t is the vector of state variables and $F(\cdot; x)$ is the conditional cumulative distribution function (CDF) that determines the distribution of $x_t = x'$ given $x_{t-1} = x$. We can discretize the continuous process x by applying the Tanaka-Toda method to each conditional distribution separately.

More concretely, suppose that we have a set of grid points $X_N = \{x_n\}_{n=1}^N$ and an initial coarse approximation $Q = (q_{nn'})$, which is an $N \times N$ probability transition matrix. Suppose we want to match some conditional moments of x, represented by the moment-defining function $T(x)$. The exact conditional moments when the current state is $x_{t-1} = x_n$ are

$$\bar{T}_n = \mathrm{E}\left[T(x_t) \mid x_n\right] = \int T(x) \, \mathrm{d}F(x; x_n),$$

where the integral is over x, fixing x_n. By Theorem A.9, we can match these moments exactly by solving the optimization problem

$$
\begin{aligned}
\underset{\{p_{nn'}\}_{n'=1}^N}{\text{minimize}} \quad & \sum_{n'=1}^N p_{nn'} \log \frac{p_{nn'}}{q_{nn'}} \\
\text{subject to} \quad & \sum_{n'=1}^N p_{nn'} T(x_{n'}) = \bar{T}_n, \ \sum_{n'=1}^N p_{nn'} = 1, \ p_{nn'} \ge 0 \qquad (\mathrm{P}_n)
\end{aligned}
$$

for each $n = 1, 2, \ldots, N$, or equivalently the dual problem

$$\min_{\lambda \in \mathbb{R}^L} \sum_{n'=1}^N q_{nn'} e^{\lambda'(T(x_{n'}) - \bar{T}_n)}. \qquad (\mathrm{D}'_n)$$

By Theorem A.9, (D'_n) has a unique solution if and only if the regularity condition

$$\bar{T}_n \in \mathrm{int} \, \mathrm{co} \, T(X_N) \qquad (\mathrm{A.27})$$

holds. This discretization method can be summarized as follows.

Algorithm A.4 (Maximum entropy discretization of Markov processes).

(i) Select a finite set of points $X_N = \{x_n\}_{n=1}^N$ and an initial approximation $Q = (q_{nn'})$.

(ii) Select a moment defining function $T(x)$ and corresponding exact conditional moments $\{\bar{T}_n\}_{n=1}^N$. If necessary, approximate the exact conditional moments with a highly accurate numerical integral.

(iii) For each $n = 1, \dots, N$, solve minimization problem (D'_n) for λ_n. Check whether moments are matched using formula (A.26), and if not, select a smaller set of moments. Compute the conditional probabilities corresponding to row n of $P = (p_{nn'})$ using (A.24).

The resulting discretization of the process is given by the transition probability matrix $P = (p_{nn'})$. Since the dual problem (D'_n) is an unconstrained convex minimization problem with a typically small number of variables, standard Newton-type algorithms (Algorithm A.2) can be applied. Furthermore, since the probabilities (A.24) are strictly positive by construction, the transition probability matrix $P = (p_{nn'})$ is a strictly positive matrix, so the resulting Markov chain is stationary and ergodic (Theorem 9.1).

Remark. Farmer and Toda (2017) contain several applications to solving asset pricing models as well as performance evaluation against other methods. The Matlab package at

$$\texttt{https://github.com/alexisakira/discretization}$$

provides codes for discretizing various stochastic processes. Farmer (2021) applies discretization methods to efficiently estimate state-space models.

PROBLEMS

A.1. Let $f(x) = \sqrt{x^2 + 1}$.

(i) Compute $f'(x)$, $f''(x)$, and show that f is convex.

(ii) Find the minimum of f.

(iii) Using your favorite programming language, implement the Newton method for finding the minimum (solving $f'(x) = 0$). Experiment what happens when the initial values are $x_0 = 0.9, 1, 1.1$.

A.2. Let $g : \mathbb{R}^N \to \mathbb{R}^N$ be C^2. Suppose that $g(\bar{x}) = 0$ and the Jacobian $Dg(\bar{x})$ is invertible. Show that the Newton algorithm converges to $\bar{x}$ double exponentially fast if the initial value is close enough to $\bar{x}$. (Hint: use the mean value inequality (Proposition 8.2.)

A.3. Consider the nonlinear equation

$$g(x) = x^3 - 2 = 0,$$

where $x > 0$. Clearly the solution is $x = 2^{1/3} \in (1, 2)$. Using your favorite programming language, implement the bisection, linear interpolation, quadratic interpolation, and Newton methods and compare the speed of convergence. What if $g(x) = x^{100} - 2$?

A.4. This problem asks you to derive the order of convergence of the linear interpolation method. Let g be a twice continuously differentiable function with $g(\bar{x}) = 0$ and $g'(\bar{x}) \neq 0$. Consider the linear interpolation algorithm (A.4).

(i) Let $\phi(x; a) = \frac{g(x) - g(a)}{x - a}$ for $x \neq a$. Show that

$$x_{k+1} - \bar{x} = (x_k - \bar{x}) \frac{\phi(x_{k-1}; x_k) - \phi(\bar{x}; x_k)}{\phi(x_{k-1}; x_k)}.$$

(ii) Using the mean value theorem, show that there exists ξ_k between x_k and x_{k-1} such that $\phi(x_{k-1}; x_k) = g'(\xi_k)$.

(iii) Regard $\phi(x; a)$ as a function of x. Using the mean value theorem, show that there exists a number η_k between x_{k-1} and $\bar{x}$ such that

$$\phi(x_{k-1}; x_k) - \phi(\bar{x}; x_k) = \phi'(\eta_k; x_k)(x_{k-1} - \bar{x}).$$

(iv) Compute $\phi'(x; a)$ explicitly.

(v) Using Taylor's theorem, show that there exists a number ζ_k such that

$$\phi'(\eta_k; x_k) = \frac{1}{2} g''(\zeta_k).$$

(vi) Show that if x_k, x_{k-1} are sufficiently close to $\bar{x}$, there exists a constant $C > 0$ such that

$$|x_{k+1} - \bar{x}| \leq C |x_k - \bar{x}| |x_{k-1} - \bar{x}|.$$

(vii) Show that the order of convergence of the linear interpolation method is at least $\alpha = \frac{1 + \sqrt{5}}{2} = 1.618\ldots$.

A.5. Using your favorite programming language, write a code that computes the coefficients of a Chebyshev polynomial of a given degree.

A.6. Using your favorite programming language, write codes that implement various Gaussian quadratures.

Bibliography

Aliprantis, C. D. and K. C. Border (2006). *Infinite Dimensional Analysis*. 3rd ed. Springer.

Arrow, K. J. and G. Debreu (1954). "Existence of an Equilibrium for a Competitive Economy". *Econometrica* 22.3, 265–290. DOI: 10.2307/1907353.

Axler, S. (2024). *Linear Algebra Done Right*. Springer. DOI: 10.1007/978-3-031-41026-0.

Bapat, R. B. and T. E. S. Raghavan (1997). *Nonnegative Matrices and Applications*. Encyclopedia of Mathematics and Its Applications 64. Cambridge University Press.

Beare, B. K. and A. A. Toda (2022). "Determination of Pareto Exponents in Economic Models Driven by Markov Multiplicative Processes". *Econometrica* 90.4, 1811–1833. DOI: 10.3982/ECTA17984.

Berge, C. (1963). *Topological Spaces*. Edinburgh: Oliver & Boyd.

Berman, A. and R. J. Plemmons (1994). *Nonnegative Matrices in the Mathematical Sciences*. Classics in Applied Mathematics 9. Society for Industrial and Applied Mathematics. DOI: 10.1137/1.9781611971262.

Bertsekas, D. P. (2018). *Abstract Dynamic Programming*. 2nd ed. Belmont, MA: Athena Scientific.

Blackwell, D. (1965). "Discounted Dynamic Programming". *Annals of Mathematical Statistics* 36.1, 226–235. DOI: 10.1214/aoms/1177700285.

Borwein, J. M. and A. S. Lewis (1991). "Duality Relationships for Entropy-like Minimization Problems". *SIAM Journal on Control and Optimization* 29.2, 325–338. DOI: 10.1137/0329017.

Boyd III, J. H. (1990). "Recursive Utility and the Ramsey Problem". *Journal of Economic Theory* 50.2, 326–345. DOI: 10.1016/0022-0531(90)90006-6.

Chicone, C. (2006). *Ordinary Differential Equations with Applications*. 2nd ed. Texts in Applied Mathematics 34. Springer. DOI: 10.1007/0-387-35794-7.

Coleman II, W. J. (1990). "Solving the Stochastic Growth Model by Policy-Function Iteration". *Journal of Business & Economic Statistics* 8.1, 27–29. DOI: 10.1080/07350015.1990.10509769.

Davis, P. J. and P. Rabinowitz (1984). *Methods of Numerical Integration*. 2nd ed. Orlando, FL: Academic Press.

Denardo, E. V. (1967). "Contraction Mappings in the Theory Underlying Dynamic Programming". *SIAM Review* 9.2, 165–177. DOI: 10.1137/1009030.

Durán, J. (2000). "On Dynamic Programming with Unbounded Returns". *Economic Theory* 15.2, 339–352. DOI: 10.1007/s001990050016.

Durán, J. (2003). "Discounting Long Run Average Growth in Stochastic Dynamic Programs". *Economic Theory* 22.2, 395–413. DOI: 10.1007/s00199-002-0316-5.

Farmer, L. E. (2021). "The Discretization Filter: A Simple Way to Estimate Nonlinear State Space Models". *Quantitative Economics* 12.1, 41–76. DOI: 10.3982/QE1353.

Farmer, L. E. and A. A. Toda (2017). "Discretizing Nonlinear, Non-Gaussian Markov Processes with Exact Conditional Moments". *Quantitative Economics* 8.2, 651–683. DOI: 10.3982/QE737.

Ferguson, T. S. (1989). "Who Solved the Secretary Problem?" *Statistical Science* 4.3, 282–289. DOI: 10.1214/ss/1177012493.

Folland, G. B. (1999). *Real Analysis: Modern Techniques and Their Applications.* 2nd ed. Hoboken, NJ: John Wiley & Sons.

Golub, G. H. and J. H. Welsch (1969). "Calculation of Gauss Quadrature Rules". *Mathematics of Computation* 23.106, 221–230. DOI: 10.1090/S0025-5718-69-99647-1.

Gouin-Bonenfant, É. and A. A. Toda (2023). "Pareto Extrapolation: An Analytical Framework for Studying Tail Inequality". *Quantitative Economics* 14.1, 201–233. DOI: 10.3982/QE1817.

Gould, F. J. and J. W. Tolle (1971). "A Necessary and Sufficient Qualification for Constrained Optimization". *SIAM Journal of Applied Mathematics* 20.2, 164–172. DOI: 10.1137/0120021.

Harrison, J. M. and D. M. Kreps (1979). "Martingales and Arbitrage in Multiperiod Securities Market". *Journal of Economic Theory* 20.3, 381–408. DOI: 10.1016/0022-0531(79)90043-7.

Horn, R. A. and C. R. Johnson (2013). *Matrix Analysis.* 2nd ed. New York: Cambridge University Press.

Howard, R. A. (1960). *Dynamic Programming and Markov Processes.* Cambridge, MA: MIT Press.

Inada, K.-I. (1963). "On a Two-Sector Model of Economic Growth: Comments and a Generalization". *Review of Economic Studies* 30.2, 119–127. DOI: 10.2307/2295809.

Jänich, K. (1994). *Linear Algebra.* Undergraduate Texts in Mathematics. New York: Springer. DOI: 10.1007/978-1-4612-4298-7.

Kamihigashi, T. (2002). "A Simple Proof of the Necessity of the Transversality Condition". *Economic Theory* 20.2, 427–433. DOI: 10.1007/s001990100198.

Kjeldsen, T. H. (2000). "A Contextualized Historical Analysis of the Kuhn-Tucker Theorem in Nonlinear Programming: The Impact of World War II". *Historia Mathematica* 27.4, 331–361. DOI: 10.1006/hmat.2000.2289.

Krusell, P. and A. A. Smith Jr. (1998). "Income and Wealth Heterogeneity in the Macroeconomy". *Journal of Political Economy* 106.5, 867–896. DOI: 10.1086/250034.

Lax, P. D. (2007). *Linear Algebra and Its Applications*. 2nd ed. Hoboken, NJ: John Wiley & Sons.

Li, H. and J. Stachurski (2014). "Solving the Income Fluctuation Problem with Unbounded Rewards". *Journal of Economic Dynamics and Control* 45, 353–365. DOI: 10.1016/j.jedc.2014.06.003.

Lippman, S. A. (1975). "On Dynamic Programming with Unbounded Rewards". *Management Science* 21.11, 1225–1233. DOI: 10.1287/mnsc.21.11.1225.

Luenberger, D. G. (1969). *Optimization by Vector Space Methods*. New York: John Wiley & Sons.

Ma, Q., J. Stachurski, and A. A. Toda (2020). "The Income Fluctuation Problem and the Evolution of Wealth". *Journal of Economic Theory* 187, 105003. DOI: 10.1016/j.jet.2020.105003.

Ma, Q. and A. A. Toda (2021). "A Theory of the Saving Rate of the Rich". *Journal of Economic Theory* 192, 105193. DOI: 10.1016/j.jet.2021.105193.

Ma, Q. and A. A. Toda (2022). "Asymptotic Linearity of Consumption Functions and Computational Efficiency". *Journal of Mathematical Economics* 98, 102562. DOI: 10.1016/j.jmateco.2021.102562.

Page, L., S. Brin, R. Motwani, and T. Winograd (1998). *The PageRank Citation Ranking: Bringing Order to the Web*. Tech. rep. Stanford University.

Perov, A. I. (1964). "On the Cauchy Problem for a System of Ordinary Differential Equations". *Pviblizhen. Met. Reshen. Differ. Uvavn.* 2. (In Russian), 115–134.

Phelan, G. and A. A. Toda (2019). "Securitized Markets, International Capital Flows, and Global Welfare". *Journal of Financial Economics* 131.3, 571–592. DOI: 10.1016/j.jfineco.2018.08.011.

Rauch, J. E. and A. A. Toda (2024). "Visualizing the Contraction Mapping Theorem". *Qeios*. DOI: 10.32388/JS01M3.

Rockafellar, R. T. (1970). *Convex Analysis*. Princeton, NJ: Princeton University Press.

Rudin, W. (1976). *Principles of Mathematical Analysis*. 3rd ed. McGraw-Hill.

Sargent, T. J. and J. Stachurski (2024). *Dynamic Programming*. URL: https://dp.quantecon.org/.

Shapley, L. S. (1953). "Stochastic Games". *Proceedings of the National Academy of Sciences* 39.10, 1095–1100. DOI: 10.1073/pnas.39.10.1095.

Simon, C. P. and L. E. Blume (1994). *Mathematics for Economists*. New York: W. W. Norton & Company.

Stachurski, J. and A. A. Toda (2019). "An Impossibility Theorem for Wealth in Heterogeneous-agent Models with Limited Heterogeneity". *Journal of Economic Theory* 182, 1–24. DOI: 10.1016/j.jet.2019.04.001.

Stachurski, J. and A. A. Toda (2020). "Corrigendum to "An Impossibility Theorem for Wealth in Heterogeneous-agent Models with Limited Heterogeneity" [Journal of Economic Theory 182 (2019) 1–24]". *Journal of Economic Theory* 188, 105066. DOI: `10.1016/j.jet.2020.105066`.

Stachurski, J. and J. Zhang (2021). "Dynamic Programming with State-Dependent Discounting". *Journal of Economic Theory* 192, 105190. DOI: `10.1016/j.jet.2021.105190`.

Sundaram, R. K. (1996). *A First Course in Optimization Theory*. NY: Cambridge University Press.

Tanaka, K. and A. A. Toda (2013). "Discrete Approximations of Continuous Distributions by Maximum Entropy". *Economics Letters* 118.3, 445–450. DOI: `10.1016/j.econlet.2012.12.020`.

Tanaka, K. and A. A. Toda (2015). "Discretizing Distributions with Exact Moments: Error Estimate and Convergence Analysis". *SIAM Journal on Numerical Analysis* 53.5, 2158–2177. DOI: `10.1137/140971269`.

Tauchen, G. and R. Hussey (1991). "Quadrature-Based Methods for Obtaining Approximate Solutions to Nonlinear Asset Pricing Models". *Econometrica* 59.2, 371–396. DOI: `10.2307/2938261`.

Toda, A. A. (2019). "Wealth Distribution with Random Discount Factors". *Journal of Monetary Economics* 104, 101–113. DOI: `10.1016/j.jmoneco.2018.09.006`.

Toda, A. A. (2021a). "Data-based Automatic Discretization of Nonparametric Distributions". *Computational Economics* 57, 1217–1235. DOI: `10.1007/s10614-020-10012-6`.

Toda, A. A. (2021b). "Perov's Contraction Principle and Dynamic Programming with Stochastic Discounting". *Operations Research Letters* 49.5, 815–819. DOI: `10.1016/j.orl.2021.09.001`.

Toda, A. A. (2024). "Unbounded Markov Dynamic Programming with Weighted Supremum Norm Perov Contractions". *Economic Theory Bulletin*. DOI: `10.1007/s40505-024-00267-9`.

Toda, A. A. and K. J. Walsh (2020). "The Equity Premium and the One Percent". *Review of Financial Studies* 33.8, 3583–3623. DOI: `10.1093/rfs/hhz121`.

Trefethen, L. N. (2019). *Approximation Theory and Approximation Practice*. Philadelphia, PA: Society for Industrial and Applied Mathematics. DOI: `10.1137/1.9781611975949`.

Vohra, R. V. (2005). *Advanced Mathematical Economics*. NY: Routledge.

Wessels, J. (1977). "Markov Programming by Successive Approximations with Respect to Weighted Supremum Norms". *Journal of Mathematical Analysis and Applications* 58.2, 326–335. DOI: `10.1016/0022-247X(77)90210-4`.

Index

Printed in the United States
by Baker & Taylor Publisher Services